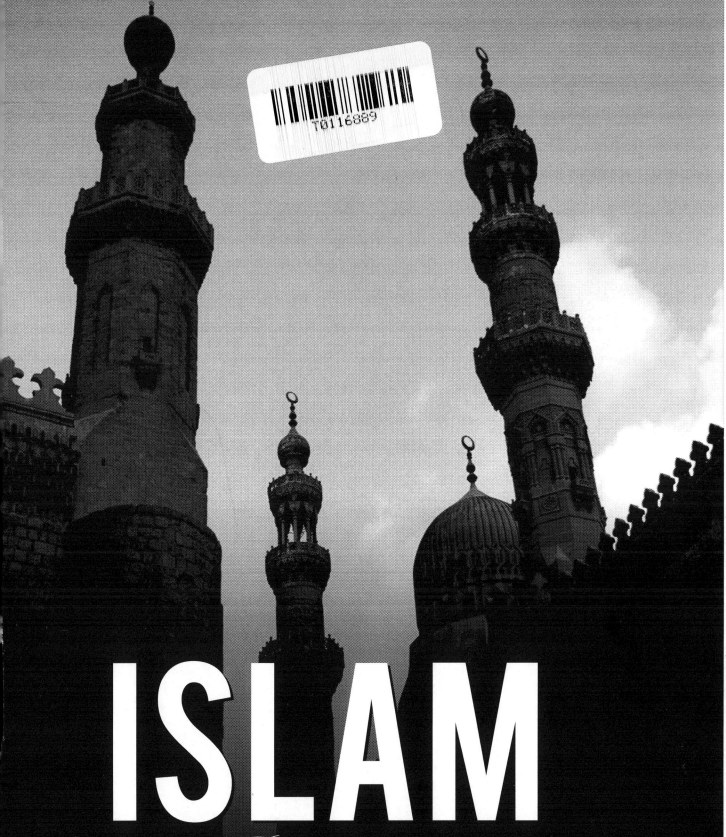

ISLAM

In Perspective

DR. SULTAN AHMAD

بِسْمِ اللهِ الرَّحْمنِ الرَّحِيم

In the Name of Allah
The Most Beneficent, the Most Merciful

Islam

In

Perspective

[Revised Edition]

Dr. Sultan Ahmad

AuthorHouse™
1663 Liberty Drive
Bloomington, IN 47403
www.authorhouse.com
Phone: 1-800-839-8640

First published by AuthorHouse 11/30/2012

ISBN: 978-1-4490-3992-9 (sc)
ISBN: 978-1-4490-3993-6 (e)

Library of Congress Control Number: 2011903416

Printed in the United States of America

Acknowledgement

I gratefully acknowledge the mercy and favor of Allah [the Exalted] for sending me in this world in a Muslim family and for His guidance for becoming a Muslim. Peace be upon the messenger and servant, Muhammad, upon his family and companions and whoever follows his guidance until the Day of Resurrection.

I acknowledge with sincere appreciation those who scarified their lives and wealth for the sake and benefit of this great religion since its inception more than fourteen hundred years ago and [will sacrifice] until the Day of Resurrection.

In this book, I have quoted texts from the various chapters of the Holy Quran - the constitution revealed by Allah to regulate and govern human life. Texts are recorded by the name of the chapter preceded by chapter and verse numbers in ().

وَمَا يَسْتَوِى الأَعْمَى وَالْبَصِيرُ

-وَلاَ الظُّلُمَاتُ وَلاَ النُّورُ

-وَلاَ الظِّلُّ وَلاَ الْحَرُورُ

-وَمَا يَسْتَوِى الأَحْيَاءُ وَلاَ الأَمْوَاتُ إِنَّ اللَّهَ يُسْمِعُ مَن يَشَاءُ وَمَا أَنتَ بِمُسْمِعٍ مَّن فِى الْقُبُورِ

The blind and the sighted are not equal,
Nor are the darkness and the light,
Nor are the shade and the heat,
The living and the dead are not alike,
Indeed, Allah causes to hear whom He wills,
But you cannot make hear those in the graves.
Surah Fatir (35:19-22)

PREFACE to the First Edition

After my arrival in USA in August 2004, most of the time I was living with my younger daughter in Jefferson City, Missouri. I used to offer my Jummah prayer with the Muslim community in the Jefferson Mosque. After a few days, the management of the Mosque requested me to give Jummah Khutba occasionally. I started looking for materials for the preparation of the Friday Khutba. I felt inspired [Subhan Allahu Taala] to write down articles on Islamic topics of interest to the Muslim community at large by the grace of Allah [swt]. This book is the collection of 52 articles arranged in alphabetic order. Each article can be used as a Friday khutba Ins Allah.

My wife Hosneara, for long, has been perusing me continuously to write a book that will benefit the mankind even after my death. I am glad that her persuasion has finally showed the light of the day.

My son Ahmad, daughters: Sakera and Abida, all the time was a source of my inspiration. Abida's husband Tanvir gave me the full technical support. Sakera's husband Omar gave me inspiration, encouragement, and provided the editorial support.

The Arabic text of the Qur'an and the relevant translations are taken from Tafsir [Abu Al-Fida, 'Imad Ad-Din Isma'il bin 'Umar bin Kathir Al-Quash Al-Busrawi-popularly known as Ibn Kathir] Ibn Kathir most of the time. May Allah [swt] give Ibn Kathir the proper reward? The Hadiths are mainly added from Internet search on Hadiths [www.searchtruth.com; www.sacred-texts.com.] Much of the information used in the writings of the articles is collected from books, articles posted primarily in web sites [www.alminbar.com; www.quranicstudies.com; www.khutbahbank.org.uk; www.islamcity.com;] are gratefully acknowledged.

I am extremely grateful to Dr. Mohammad Omar Farooq, professor of economics and finance at Upper Iowa University, USA, who took the painstaking task of reviewing an earlier draft of the book. His comments were extremely valuable and helped me a lot in improving the quality of the articles.

There is a possibility of some unintentional errors in the articles. I hope the readers will forgive me for the unintentional mistakes, if any. I will also request the readers to inform me the mistakes that will come to their knowledge so that necessary corrections may be made and the quality of the articles improved in the future.

May Allah [swt] accept this small effort and forgive me for any unintentional wrong interpretation anywhere in this book and I ask Allah [swt] for His mercy and forgiveness. I will feel myself fortunate if at least one of the readers is benefited from any of the articles included in the collection. Amin!

30 October, 2007   **Sultan Ahmad**
118 Arden Dr., Jefferson City, MO 65109
E-mail: dr.sultan_ahmad@yahoo.com

PREFACE to the Revised Edition

Since its first publication in 2007 with 52 articles, I revised many of the articles. 11 new articles are added to the revised edition. My grandchildren Ariana, Amani, Shafaat, Arya, Aleena, and Zariya will be extremely happy to see the revised edtion in the market.

In the revised edition, the English translations of the Arabic verses of the Holy Quran are taken from Tafsir-Ibn-Kathir and The Quran [Arabic Text with corresponding English Meanings – English; Revised and Edited by Saheeh International, Abul-Qasim Publishing House, and P.O. Box 6156, Jeddah 21442, Saudi Arabia]. I hope readers, Muslims and also of other faiths, will have better understanding of the basic principles, fundamentals, and teachings of the great religion Islam. I request readers of the revised edition to bring to my notice any inconsistency and/or error that might have been overlooked. Please keep me in your dua.

May this edition fufil its purpose and assist readers to grasp the message of Islam and apply it in worldly life. I Pray to Allah [the Most Praiseworthy] to accept my humble effort and forgive its shortcomings. I ask Allah [the Most Merciful] for His mercy and forgiveness. May Allah [swt] guide us all in the right and true path that will lead us to Heaven, Insallah?

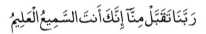

Our Lord, Accept [this service] from us. Indeed, You are the Hearing, the Knowing (2:127).

Amin!

15 November, 2010   *Sultan Ahmad*
118 Arden Dr.
Jefferson City, Mo 65109, USA.
Email: dr.sultan_ahmad@yahoo.com

CONTENT

Allah [swt] is omnipotent and omniscient: Some Proofs

Who is Allah (swt)? Is there any proof of the existence of Allah [swt]? These are the questions that come to our mind very often. How can we satisfy our mind with the answers to these questions? We can do that by using our power of thinking, knowledge, and our senses of hearing and seeing. As Allah [swt] says in **Surah al-Isra (17:36):**

وَلَا تَقْفُ مَا لَيْسَ لَكَ بِهِ عِلْمٌ إِنَّ السَّمْعَ وَالْبَصَرَ وَالْفُؤَادَ كُلُّ أُولَٰئِكَ كَانَ عَنْهُ مَسْؤُولًا

And do not pursue [do not assume and do not say] that of which you have no knowledge, unless you verify it for yourself. I have given you the hearing, the eyesight, and the brain, and you are responsible for using them.

In **Surah al-Baqarah (2:164)** Allah [swt] provides us with the proof of His existence through the description of His power in creating things as:

إِنَّ فِي خَلْقِ السَّمَوَاتِ وَالْأَرْضِ وَاخْتِلَافِ اللَّيْلِ وَالنَّهَارِ وَالْفُلْكِ الَّتِي تَجْرِي فِي الْبَحْرِ بِمَا يَنْفَعُ النَّاسَ وَمَا أَنْزَلَ اللَّهُ مِنَ السَّمَاءِ مِن

مَّاءٍ فَأَحْيَا بِهِ الْأَرْضَ بَعْدَ مَوْتِهَا وَبَثَّ فِيهَا مِن كُلِّ دَآبَّةٍ وَتَصْرِيفِ الرِّيَاحِ وَالسَّحَابِ الْمُسَخَّرِ بَيْنَ السَّمَاءِ وَالْأَرْضِ لَآيَاتٍ لِّقَوْمٍ

يَعْقِلُونَ-

Indeed, in the creation of the heavens and the earth, and in the alternation of night and day, and the ships which sail through the sea with that which is of use to mankind, and the water [rain] which Allah sends down from the sky and makes the earth alive therewith after its lifelessness, and the moving [living] creatures of all kinds [shapes, colors, and sizes] that He has scattered therein, and directing of the winds and clouds controlled between the heaven and the earth, are indeed Ayahs [proofs, evidences, signs, etc.] for people of understanding.

Therefore, the sky, with its height, intricate design, vastness, the heavenly objects in orbit, and this earth, with its density, its lowlands, mountains, seas, deserts, valleys, and other structures, and beneficial things that it has are the proofs of the power of Allah [swt]. The night comes and then goes followed by the other [the day] which does not delay for even an instant. Sometimes, the day grows shorter and the night longer, and sometimes vice versa, one takes from the length of the other. He extends the length of one from the other and vice versa. Shaping the sea in this manner, so that it is able to carry ships from one shore to another, so people benefit from what the other region has, and export what they have to them and vice versa

Allah [swt] says in **Surah an-Nazi 'at (79: 27-28)** that creation of heaven and earth is more challenging and difficult than the creation of mankind as.

أَءَنتُمْ أَشَدُّ خَلْقًا أَمِ السَّمَاءُ بَنَهَا - رَفَعَ سَمْكَهَا فَسَوَّاهَا - وَأَغْطَشَ لَيْلَهَا وَأَخْرَجَ ضُحَهَا

Are you more difficult to create or is the heaven that He constructed? He raised its height, and has perfected it.

Among Allah's signs are the countless huge celestial bodies, some of which are rotating, others are stationary, some are combined in groups, while others are separate. They move by Allah's command as adornments of the lower heaven and as missiles to drive away the [Shayateen] evil ones, as well as markers and signposts with which people can guide them.

In **Surah Fussilat (41:9-12)** Allah [swt] says:

قُلْ أَءِنَّكُمْ لَتَكْفُرُونَ بِالَّذِي خَلَقَ الْأَرْضَ فِي يَوْمَيْنِ وَتَجْعَلُونَ لَهُ أَندَادًا ذَلِكَ رَبُّ الْعَالَمِينَ - وَجَعَلَ فِيهَا رَوَاسِيَ مِن فَوْقِهَا وَبَارَكَ

فِيهَا وَقَدَّرَ فِيهَا أَقْوَاتَهَا فِي أَرْبَعَةِ أَيَّامٍ سَوَاءً لِّلسَّائِلِينَ - ثُمَّ اسْتَوَى إِلَى السَّمَاءِ وَهِيَ دُخَانٌ فَقَالَ لَهَا وَلِلْأَرْضِ ائْتِيَا طَوْعًا أَوْ كَرْهًا قَالَتَا

أَتَيْنَا طَائِعِينَ - فَقَضَاهُنَّ سَبْعَ سَمَوَاتٍ فِي يَوْمَيْنِ وَأَوْحَى فِي كُلِّ سَمَاءٍ أَمْرَهَا وَزَيَّنَّا السَّمَاءَ الدُّنْيَا بِمَصَابِيحَ وَحِفْظًا ذَلِكَ تَقْدِيرُ

الْعَزِيزِ الْعَلِيمِ -

Say: "Do you verily disbelieve in Him Who created the earth in two days and attribute to Him equals? That is the Lord of all that exists. And He placed therein firm mountains from above it, and He blessed it, and determined therein its sustenance in four days without distinction [for the information of] those who ask." Then He directed Himself to the heaven when it was smoke, and said to it and to the earth: "Come [into being] both of you willingly or unwillingly." They both said: "We have come willingly." And then He completed them as seven heavens in two days and He made in each heaven its affair. And We adorned the nearest [lowest] heaven with lamps [stars for beauty] and as protection. That is the determination of the Exalted in Might, the knowing.

O people! Everything in the universe carries an evidence of Allah's Oneness, perfect Lordship, Omnipotence, Greatness, Wisdom and Mercy, which also indicate that He is able to do all things and that He creates what He wills and chooses. Be sure that Allah did not set anyone to be the witness of the creation. He created the heavens and the earth and no one has any knowledge as to its reality except what came through revelation. Almighty Allah says **Surah al-Kahf (18:51):**

مَّا أَشْهَدتُّهُمْ خَلْقَ السَّمَوَاتِ وَالْأَرْضِ وَلَا خَلْقَ أَنفُسِهِمْ وَمَا كُنتُ مُتَّخِذَ الْمُضِلِّينَ عَضُدًا -

They did not witness the creation of the heavens and the earth or their own creation, and I would not have taken the misguides as 'Adudan' "Assistants".

Although the existence of Allah [swt] requires no proof simply because the existence of everything else is proved in reference to Him, The Most High, to make matters easy for the human intellect to comprehend, man is asked to contemplate his own creation and all that is in the Universe. Indeed the Ayah from **Surah Qaf (50:6-7)** is just one example:

أَفَلَمْ يَنظُرُوا إِلَى السَّمَاءِ فَوْقَهُمْ كَيْفَ بَنَيْنَاهَا وَزَيَّنَّاهَا وَمَا لَهَا مِن فُرُوجٍ - وَالْأَرْضَ مَدَدْنَاهَا وَأَلْقَيْنَا فِيهَا رَوَاسِيَ وَأَنبَتْنَا فِيهَا

Have they not looked at the heaven above them, - how We have structured it and adorned it, and there are no flaws in it. And the earth - We spread it out, and cast therein firmly set mountains, and made grow therein of beautiful growth in pairs.

Let us look at how the heaven was created by Allah [swt]. O Muslims! Almighty Allah created the heavens and the earth in six days and made the heavens seven layers one above the other. Allah [swt] says in **Surah Nuh (71:15-16):**

أَلَمْ تَرَوْا كَيْفَ خَلَقَ اللَّهُ سَبْعَ سَمَوَاتٍ طِبَاقًا - وَجَعَلَ الْقَمَرَ فِيهِنَّ نُورًا وَجَعَلَ الشَّمْسَ سِرَاجًا

See you not how Allah has created the seven heavens in layers. And made the moon therein a [reflected] light, and made the sun a burning lamp?

In **Surah adh-Dhariyat (51:47-8),** Allah (swt) explains about His ingenuity in creating the Heavens and Earth once again:

وَالسَّمَاءَ بَنَيْنَاهَا بِأَيْدٍ وَإِنَّا لَمُوسِعُونَ - وَالْأَرْضَ فَرَشْنَاهَا فَنِعْمَ الْمَاهِدُونَ

With Hands We constructed the heaven. Verily, We are able to expand the vastness of space thereof. And We have spread out the (spacious) earth; how excellent spreader [thereof] are We!

And in **Surah an-Naba (78: 6-7):**

أَلَمْ نَجْعَلِ الْأَرْضَ مِهَادًا - وَالْجِبَالَ أَوْتَادًا

Have We not made the earth as a resting place, and the mountains as pegs?

And also in ayah (12):

وَبَنَيْنَا فَوْقَكُمْ سَبْعًا شِدَادًا

And [have We not] built over you the seven Firmaments,

And also in **Surah al- Hijr (15:16-18):**

وَلَقَدْ جَعَلْنَا فِى السَّمَاءِ بُرُوجًا وَزَيَّنَّهَا لِلنَّظِرِينَ - وَحَفِظْنَهَا مِن كُلِّ شَيْطَنٍ رَّجِيمٍ -

It is We Who have set out the Zodiacal Signs in the heavens, and have beautified it for the observers. And [moreover] We have protected it from every evil spirit expelled, except one who steals a hearing by a clear burning flame.

In **Surah al-Mulk (67: 3-4),** Allah [swt] challenges the disbelievers to look at His Creation again and again, but they will never be able to find any fault or discrepancy:

الَّذِى خَلَقَ سَبْعَ سَمَوَتٍ طِبَاقًا مَّا تَرَى فِى خَلْقِ الرَّحْمَنِ مِن تَفَوُتٍ فَارْجِعِ الْبَصَرَ هَلْ تَرَى مِن فُطُورٍ - ثُمَّ ارْجِعِ الْبَصَرَ كَرَّتَيْنِ يَنقَلِبْ
إِلَيْكَ الْبَصَرُ خَاسِئًا وَهُوَ حَسِيرٌ -

Who has created the seven heavens one above the other; you can see no inconsistency. So return [your] vision [to the sky]; do you see any breaks? Then look again and yet again, your vision will return to you humbled while it is fatigued.

A confirmation and reminder to the believers and a challenge, a big and impossible challenge to the disbelievers, and those who associate partners with Alláh (swt) is described in the closing ayahs of **Surah al-Waqiah (56:63-74):**

أَفَرَءَيْتُم مَّا تَحْرُثُونَ - أَءَنتُمْ تَزْرَعُونَهُ أَمْ نَحْنُ الزَّرِعُونَ - لَوْ نَشَآءُ لَجَعَلْنَهُ حُطَمًا فَظَلْتُمْ تَفَكَّهُونَ - إِنَّا لَمُغْرَمُونَ - بَلْ نَحْنُ مَحْرُومُونَ -
أَفَرَءَيْتُمُ الْمَآءَ الَّذِى تَشْرَبُونَ - أَءَنتُمْ أَنزَلْتُمُوهُ مِنَ الْمُزْنِ أَمْ نَحْنُ الْمُنزِلُونَ - لَوْ نَشَآءُ جَعَلْنَهُ أُجَاجًا فَلَوْلَا تَشْكُرُونَ - أَفَرَءَيْتُمُ النَّارَ
الَّتِى تُورُونَ - أَءَنتُمْ أَنشَأْتُمْ شَجَرَتَهَا أَمْ نَحْنُ الْمُنشِئُونَ - نَحْنُ جَعَلْنَهَا تَذْكِرَةً وَمَتَعًا لِّلْمُقْوِينَ - فَسَبِّحْ بِاسْمِ رَبِّكَ الْعَظِيمِ -

And have you seen that [seed] which you sow? Is it you that makes it grow, or are We the Grower? If We willed, We could make it [dry debris], and you would remain in wonder, [Saying] Indeed, We are [now] in debt; rather we have been deprived! And have you seen the water that you drink? Is it you who brought it down [as rain] from the cloud or do We? If We willed, We verily could make it bitter; so why are you not grateful? And have you not seen the fire that you ignite? Is it you who produced its trees, or are We the producer? We have made it a reminder [of the great fire of Hell] and provision for travelers, so glorify the name of your Lord, the Most Great.

Indeed man may sow the seeds; whether that seed grows into a plant and bears fruit is not in the hands of man. Only Allah (swt) decides which seed will develop into a plant and which shall not germinate.

It is also Allah (swt) who controls the coming of rain from the cloud as described in **Surah al-Hajj (22:65)**:

أَلَمْ تَرَ أَنَّ اللَّهَ سَخَّرَ لَكُم مَّا فِي الْأَرْضِ وَالْفُلْكَ تَجْرِي فِي الْبَحْرِ بِأَمْرِهِ وَيُمْسِكُ السَّمَاءَ أَن تَقَعَ عَلَى الْأَرْضِ إِلَّا بِإِذْنِهِ إِنَّ اللَّهَ بِالنَّاسِ لَرَءُوفٌ رَّحِيمٌ

Do you not see that Allah has subjected to you all that is on the earth, and the ships which sail through the sea by His command? And He restraints the sky from falling upon the earth unless by permission. Indeed Allah, to the mankind, is Kind and Merciful.

Among Allah's signs are the night and the day. The night is made as a means of seeking rest and tranquility for Allah's servants. The day, on the other hand, is made a means of seeking sustenance and quest for livelihood out of Allah's Bounty. Allah said in **Surah al-Qasas (28:71-73)**:

قُلْ أَرَأَيْتُمْ إِن جَعَلَ اللَّهُ عَلَيْكُمُ اللَّيْلَ سَرْمَدًا إِلَى يَوْمِ الْقِيَامَةِ مَنْ إِلَٰهٌ غَيْرُ اللَّهِ يَأْتِيكُم بِضِيَاءٍ أَفَلَا تَسْمَعُونَ ۝ قُلْ أَرَأَيْتُمْ إِن جَعَلَ اللَّهُ عَلَيْكُمُ النَّهَارَ سَرْمَدًا إِلَى يَوْمِ الْقِيَامَةِ مَنْ إِلَٰهٌ غَيْرُ اللَّهِ يَأْتِيكُم بِلَيْلٍ تَسْكُنُونَ فِيهِ أَفَلَا تُبْصِرُونَ ۝ وَمِن رَّحْمَتِهِ جَعَلَ لَكُمُ اللَّيْلَ وَالنَّهَارَ لِتَسْكُنُوا فِيهِ وَلِتَبْتَغُوا مِن فَضْلِهِ وَلَعَلَّكُمْ تَشْكُرُونَ

Say: "Have you considered [inform me if you know]: If Allah should make for you the night continuous until the Day of Resurrection, who else besides Allah could bring you light? Will you not then hear?" Say: "Have you considered: If Allah should make for you the day continuous until the Day of Resurrection, who else besides Allah could bring you a night wherein you may rest? Then will you not see?" And out of His mercy He made for you the night and the day that you may rest therein and that you may seek of His bounty -- and in order that you may be grateful.

Among the signs of Allah are the sun and the moon. They go around their orbits since the time they were first created by Allah, until the destruction of the world. They move on an organized course that is never altered or diverted. Allah (swt) said in **Surah Ya- Sin (36: 38-40)**:

وَالشَّمْسُ تَجْرِي لِمُسْتَقَرٍّ لَّهَا ذَٰلِكَ تَقْدِيرُ الْعَزِيزِ الْعَلِيمِ ۝ وَالْقَمَرَ قَدَّرْنَاهُ مَنَازِلَ حَتَّىٰ عَادَ كَالْعُرْجُونِ الْقَدِيمِ ۝ لَا الشَّمْسُ يَنبَغِي لَهَا أَن تُدْرِكَ الْقَمَرَ وَلَا اللَّيْلُ سَابِقُ النَّهَارِ وَكُلٌّ فِي فَلَكٍ يَسْبَحُونَ

And the sun runs on its fixed course for a term [appointed]. That is the decree of the Almighty, the All-Knowing. And the moon - We have determined for it phases, until it returns [appearing] like the old dried curved date stalk. It is not allowable for the sun to overtake the moon, nor does the night outstrip the day but each, in an orbit is swimming.

Do we think that Allah [swt] will be creating trillions of people starting from Adam [as] to the end of this world but none of them [including twins and quadruples] will have the same finger prints? What an amazing creator? Thus, the whole universe is full of the signs of Allah. He is its Creator, Who rules and regulates it. The universe can never function by itself, nor even be regulated by other than Allah. Can there be more than one such creator?

The assumption that there are others besides the one Allah leads to false consequences and must therefore be false. If there is more than one creator, then (a) if every detail of everything in the world was the result of the action of one of the creators, it cannot at the same time be the result of the action of another creator. But if (b) some creators and others by others created some things in the world, then each creator would rule independently over what he created, which means that nothing in his world can even in principle, be influenced by anything outside it. But this contradicts the observed unity and interdependence of the world. And if that is impossible, then (c) each of them would have appropriated to himself what he created, and some would have overcome others." There can, therefore, be no more than one creator.

How does this creator create? Since He is self-sufficient, He cannot be said to depend on anything outside Himself in any actions, and cannot therefore be said to produce His effects the way nature causes do. But if He is not a natural cause, He must be a volitional agent. And since intention implies knowledge, and knowledge and intention imply life, He must be a living being. Since He is an eternal and everlasting being, all His attributes must reflect this quality; thus He must be not only knowing, but all-knowing, not only powerful, but all-powerful.

After the Creation of the Heaven and Earth, What is the function of Allah [swt] now? The answer is given by Allah [swt] in **Surah ar-Rahman (55:29)** as:

$$\text{يَسْـَٔلُهُۥ مَن فِى ٱلسَّمَـٰوَٰتِ وَٱلْأَرْضِ ۚ كُلَّ يَوْمٍ هُوَ فِى شَأْنٍ}$$

"Whosoever is within the heavens and earth asks Him; everyday He is [engaged] in some affair."

It is also important here to mention a few more characteristics of Allah [swt]. Allah [swt] mentions in **Surah al-Baqarah (2:255)**:

$$\text{ٱللَّهُ لَآ إِلَـٰهَ إِلَّا هُوَ ٱلْحَىُّ ٱلْقَيُّومُ ۚ لَا تَأْخُذُهُۥ سِنَةٌ وَلَا نَوْمٌ ۚ لَّهُۥ مَا فِى ٱلسَّمَـٰوَٰتِ وَمَا فِى ٱلْأَرْضِ}$$

Allah, there is no deity except Him, the Ever living, the sustainer of [all] existence. Neither drowsiness overtakes Him nor sleep. To Him belongs whatever is in the heavens and whatever is on the earth.

Having said this let me give one example of a non-Islamic religious belief that the Qur'an considers to be a stupendous blasphemy against Allah [swt], namely that He has children. Now if He is the creator of everything, this necessarily includes the one who is claimed to be His child. But if He creates this, it cannot be His child; it has to be one of His creations. One does not create one's child; one begets it.

Allah [swt] has categorically rejected this claim of the Jews and the Christians; and the idol worshipers, and strongly asserted that He is the only Creator of this Universe and there is none else equal to Him in **Surah al-Ikhlas (112:1-4):**

قُلْ هُوَ اللَّهُ أَحَدٌ - اللَّهُ الصَّمَدُ - لَمْ يَلِدْ وَلَمْ يُولَدْ - وَلَمْ يَكُنْ لَهُ كُفُوًا أَحَدٌ -

Say: "He is Allah, [who is] One, Allah, the Eternal Refuge, He neither begets nor is born, nor is there to Him any equivalent."

Thus, we should be thankful to Allah, praising Him with our tongues and recounting His favors endowed upon us. Give thanks in return for Allah's Favors through complying with His commands and eschewing His prohibitions! Give thanks to Allah through returning to Him in repentance with our hearts, having an unshakable belief that such graces are given by Allah, out of His Bounty, Mercy and Benevolence.

Allah (swt) warns those who, despite the proofs provided by Him, deny His existence and power in **Surah al-Ar'af (7:179)** as:

وَلَقَدْ ذَرَأْنَا لِجَهَنَّمَ كَثِيرًا مِنَ الْجِنِّ وَالْإِنْسِ لَهُمْ قُلُوبٌ لَا يَفْقَهُونَ بِهَا وَلَهُمْ أَعْيُنٌ لَا يُبْصِرُونَ بِهَا وَلَهُمْ ءَاذَانٌ لَا يَسْمَعُونَ بِهَا أُوْلَئِكَ كَالْأَنْعَامِ بَلْ هُمْ أَضَلُّ أُوْلَئِكَ هُمُ الْغَافِلُونَ

And surely, We have created many of the Jinn and mankind for Hell. They have hearts wherewith they understand not, and they have eyes wherewith they see not, and they have ears wherewith they hear not (the truth). They are like cattle, nay even more astray; those! They are the heedless ones.

O Allah! Enable us to remember you, give thanks to You and worship you in the best manner! O Allah! Make your provision to us a means that we use to obey You! O Allah! Forgive all Muslims and us! May Allah guide us to understand His Book and behave accordingly, and protect us against deviation in words and deeds? **Amin!**

Backbiting and Slandering are Major Sins

Unfortunately, on the streets, in official organizations or popular gatherings, one may hear people reviling others, calling them names, or scoffing at them. Allah considers back biting as equivalent to eating the flesh of the dead brother which no people will like in **Surah al-Hujurat (49:12):**

يَٰٓأَيُّهَا ٱلَّذِينَ ءَامَنُوا ٱجْتَنِبُوا كَثِيرًا مِّنَ ٱلظَّنِّ إِنَّ بَعْضَ ٱلظَّنِّ إِثْمٌ وَلَا تَجَسَّسُوا وَلَا يَغْتَب بَّعْضُكُم بَعْضًا أَيُحِبُّ أَحَدُكُمْ أَن يَأْكُلَ لَحْمَ

أَخِيهِ مَيْتًا فَكَرِهْتُمُوهُ وَٱتَّقُوا ٱللَّهَ إِنَّ ٱللَّهَ تَوَّابٌ رَّحِيمٌ.

O you who believed, avoid much [negative] assumption. Indeed, some assumption is sin. And do not spy or backbite each other. Would one of you like to eat the flesh of his dead brother? You would detest it. And have Taqwa of Allah; indeed, Allah is the One Who forgives and accepts repentance, Most Merciful.

The Prophet [sas] said, "Mentioning your brother with something that he hates". This means in the person's absence; so the person asked another question by saying, "O Prophet [sas], what if what he said was true?" He said, "If it was in him then you have actually practiced backbiting, and if it was not then you fabricated lies and slandered him". (Muslim, book #32, hadith #6225)

This is how big of a sin backbiting is looked upon and yet we continue to backbite without a second thought, next time we lie, talk about somebody, remember Allah [swt] and the Prophet [sas] and put them in front of us before we speak.

We may think that it is all right to take the mock out of someone so long as we say it to their face. We will make fun of the way someone talks, walks, or how they look. Allah (swt) warns us against such behavior in **Surah al-Hujurat (49:11):**

يَٰٓأَيُّهَا ٱلَّذِينَ ءَامَنُوا لَا يَسْخَرْ قَوْمٌ مِّن قَوْمٍ عَسَىٰ أَن يَكُونُوا خَيْرًا مِّنْهُمْ وَلَا نِسَآءٌ مِّن نِّسَآءٍ عَسَىٰ أَن يَكُنَّ خَيْرًا مِّنْهُنَّ وَلَا تَلْمِزُوا

أَنفُسَكُمْ وَلَا تَنَابَزُوا بِٱلْأَلْقَٰبِ بِئْسَ ٱلِٱسْمُ ٱلْفُسُوقُ بَعْدَ ٱلْإِيمَانِ وَمَن لَّمْ يَتُبْ فَأُوْلَٰٓئِكَ هُمُ ٱلظَّٰلِمُونَ.

O you who have believed, let not a group scoff at another group; perhaps they may be that the latter is better than the former. Nor let [some] women scoff at other women, it may be that the latter is better than the former; and do not insult one another, and do not call each other by [offensive] nicknames. Evil is the name of wickedness after faith. And whosoever does not repent - then it is those who are the wrongdoers.

Don't forget that Allah made us the way we are, so how can we even think of making fun of his creation? Don't get angry in the first place. Anger is the root of many evil and wrong doings and is instigated by Satan.

A man came to Prophet [sas] one day and said "Advise me". The prophet [sas] said, "Anger is from Satan, and Satan was created from fire. Only water will extinguish fire, so if one of you gets angry, he should perform wudû." (Ahmad, vol.4, page 226).

So let us follow this beautiful advice of the Prophet [sas] and remember that anger is from Satan. If someone angers you or swears at you then don't harm yourself by doing the same but respond in a better way as Allah [swt] says in **Surah Fusssilat (41:34):**

وَلَا تَسْتَوِى الْحَسَنَةُ وَلَا السَّيِّئَةُ ادْفَعْ بِالَّتِى هِىَ أَحْسَنُ فَإِذَا الَّذِى بَيْنَكَ وَبَيْنَهُ عَدَاوَةٌ كَأَنَّهُ وَلِيٌّ حَمِيمٌ ۔

The good deed and the evil deed cannot be equal. Repel [the evil] with one which is better, then verily the one whom between you and him is enmity, [will become] as though he was a devoted friend.

It's one of the greatest sins and yet it is something we do day after day. Sometimes we don't even realize it. We are just chatting away with friends and begin to talk about somebody else. Our lives are soaps based on lying, backbiting etc. But look at what the Prophet [sas] said about it: "A Muslim can never be a liar". Furthermore, he said "Truth leads to virtue and virtue leads to paradise...Lying leads to wickedness and wickedness leads to the hellfire." (Bukhari, book # 73, hadith #116) As we know, one lie leads to another ten lies which lead to bad actions. Remember we can lie and think that we have got away with it but on the Day of Judgment our hands, tongue and feet will bear testimony against us and tell the truth. As Allah [swt] says in **Surah Fussilat (41:20):**

حَتَّى إِذَا مَا جَاءُوهَا شَهِدَ عَلَيْهِمْ سَمْعُهُمْ وَأَبْصَارُهُمْ وَجُلُودُهُم بِمَا كَانُوا يَعْمَلُونَ ۔

Until, when they reach it, their hearing [ears] and their eyes and their skins will testify against them of what they used to do.

Indeed the tongue controls the rest of our body. A well-controlled tongue will keep us within Islam but a loose tongue will destroy us. The Prophet [sas] said, "Whoever can guarantee me two things I can guarantee him Paradise." The companions asked "What O Messenger of Allah?" He replied, "What is between his jaws [his tongue] and his legs [private parts]" (Bukhari, book# 76, hadith #481). A beautiful saying of Prophet [sas] that will ensure the protection of our tongue is "Whoever believes in Allah and the last day, let him either speak well or keep silent".

Fabricating lies and slandering is greater than backbiting as Allah [swt] says in **Surah al-Ahzab (33:58):**

وَالَّذِينَ يُؤْذُونَ الْمُؤْمِنِينَ وَالْمُؤْمِنَاتِ بِغَيْرِ مَا اكْتَسَبُوا فَقَدِ احْتَمَلُوا بُهْتَانًا وَإِثْمًا مُّبِينًا ۔

And those who harm believing men and women for [something] other than what they have earned [deserved] have certainly bore upon themselves a slander and manifest sin.

In another narration, it says he is one of the liars. Allah says in **Surah an-Nahl (16:105):**

إِنَّمَا يَفْتَرِى الْكَذِبَ الَّذِينَ لاَ يُؤْمِنُونَ بِآيَتِ اللَّهِ وَأُوْلِبِكَ هُمُ الْكَذِبُونَ

They only invent falsehoods who do not believe in the verses of Allah, and it is those who are the liars.

Ayesha [ra] reported that the Prophet [sas] said: "Do not revile the dead, because they have already faced their destiny [be it good or bad]." (Bukhari, book #23, hadith #476) The meaning of the hadith is that the dead has already been commissioned with the consequences of his deeds, whether good or bad; accordingly, the hadith warns against reviling them especially if they are Muslims.

Prophet Muhammad [sas] said, "Whoever has oppressed another person concerning his reputation or anything else, he should beg him to forgive him before the Day of Resurrection when there will be no money [to compensate for wrong deeds], but if he has good deeds, those good deeds will be taken from him according to his oppression which he has done, and if he has no good deeds, the sins of the oppressed person will be loaded on him" (Bukhari, book #43, hadith #629). This person whose hasanat [good deeds] are taken from him by the people, and then has their sayi'at [bad or evil deeds] placed on his own back, is the one who is bankrupt, as the Messenger [sas] called him because he will be a great loser in spite of a good collection of good deeds at his credit.

If we do not have a chance to beg forgiveness from those whom we had back bitted, it is better to ask for their forgiveness to Allah [the Exalted].

O Allah! We ask you make our tongues pure and instill love in our hearts for the believers. Do not make us have enmity nor hatred for them. O Allah, make us among those who say good when they speak and we take refuge in You from tongues that will lead us to the hellfire. **Amin!**

Belief in Destiny is a Part of Our Religious Faith

Allah has recorded in His Preserved Tablet the decree of everything that will occur until the Day of Resurrection, fifty thousand years before the creation of the heavens and the earth. The Prophet [sas] said: "The first thing which Allah created was the Pen. Then He ordered it to write. The Pen asked 'What should I write?' Allah said: 'Write down everything that will occur until the Day of Judgment."(Tirmidhi)

What is ordained for man will definitely befall him, and that which is not ordained for him shall never befall him. The records have dried and the pen has been lifted after recording the destinies of humanity and the destinies have begun to become realised.

Allah, the Exalted and Glorified, said in **Surah al-Hadeed (57:22-23):**

مَآ أَصَابَ مِن مُّصِيبَةٍ فِى ٱلْأَرْضِ وَلَا فِى أَنفُسِكُمْ إِلَّا فِى كِتَٰبٍ مِّن قَبْلِ أَن نَّبْرَأَهَآ إِنَّ ذَٰلِكَ عَلَى ٱللَّهِ يَسِيرٌ ۝ لِّكَيْلَا تَأْسَوْا۟ عَلَىٰ مَا

فَاتَكُمْ وَلَا تَفْرَحُوا۟ بِمَآ ءَاتَىٰكُمْ ۗ وَٱللَّهُ لَا يُحِبُّ كُلَّ مُخْتَالٍ فَخُورٍ

No disaster strikes upon the earth or among yourselves except that it is in a register the persevered slate [al-Lawh al-Mahfuth] before We bring it into being – indeed that, for Allah is easy. In order that you may not despair over what has eluded you and not exult [in pride] over what He has given you. And Allah is the Free of need, the praiseworthy.

Therefore, a servant should be content with Allah's Decree, even if it goes against his wishes, as Allah's Decree can never be averted. Gratification lies in receiving the decree of Allah with contentment whilst acknowledging that all things come from Allah and that He has the ultimate command and absolute power over His creatures.

When a person accepts Allah as his Lord and is content with Him, he gets an immense reward in this life and the Hereafter. If a man observes patience during afflictions, Allah will guide his heart and give him comfort and contentment. He will alleviate the effect of the afflictions on him due to the man's anticipation of Allah's reward for his patience. On the Day of Resurrection, he will find the reward for his patience at a time when rewards are most desperately needed.

Allah also decrees the destiny of a person whilst he/she is in the womb of the mother. Prophet Muhammad [sas] said: "The matter of the creation of a human being is put together in the womb of the mother in forty days, and then he becomes a clot of thick blood for a similar period, and then a piece of flesh for a similar period. Then Allah sends an angel who is ordered to write four things. He is ordered to write down his [i.e. the new creature's] deeds, his livelihood, his [date of] death, and whether he will be blessed or wretched [in the Hereafter]. Then the soul is breathed into him. So a man amongst you may do [good] deeds till there is only a cubit between him and Paradise and then what has been written for him decides his behaviour and he starts doing [evil] deeds characteristic of the people of the Hellfire. And similarly a man amongst you may do [evil] deeds till there is only a cubit between him and the Hellfire, and then what has been written for him decides his behaviour, and he starts doing deeds characteristic of the people of Paradise."(Tafsir-Ibn-Kathir)

O Believers! Just as our lives contain problems, afflictions and disasters, they also have great bounties and favours from Allah, who is the Most Generous. In addition Allah has blessed our lives by giving us ease through times of grief and hardships as well as and protecting us from other trials and tribulations that did not affect us.

This life is the abode of hardship and ease, sorrow and joy, happiness and sadness and laughter and weeping. Things are constantly changing and the trials that we face are always different. People are tested in different ways so that the wise can learn lessons from this and the successful can take advantage of them. Through these trials, the heedless become deceived and those who are doomed will go into further destruction.

Therefore, it is saddening to observe in life so many different types of people who always seem to be complaining. They complain and weep about sickness, poverty, hardship, being away from loved ones, deaths of relatives or missing out on the riches of this world. These people do not seem to have any faith, nor do they seem to believe in the Divine Decree of Allah and his Pre-Destiny.

O Muslims! Complaining about Allah to His creatures and weeping about things that one has missed out on in life is either an indication of weak faith, or something that leads it. It is also either an indication of despairing of the mercy of Allah or something that would lead to it.

Allah says in **Surah Yunus (10:106-7):**

وَلاَ تَدْعُ مِن دُونِ اللَّهِ مَا لاَ يَنفَعُكَ وَلاَ يَضُرُّكَ فَإِن فَعَلْتَ فَإِنَّكَ إِذًا مِّنَ الظَّـٰلِمِينَ - وَإِن يَمْسَسْكَ اللَّهُ بِضُرٍّ فَلاَ كَاشِفَ لَهُ إِلاَّ هُوَ وَإِن

يُرِدْكَ بِخَيْرٍ فَلاَ رَآدَّ لِفَضْلِهِ يُصِيبُ بِهِ مَن يَشَآءُ مِنْ عِبَادِهِ وَهُوَ الْغَفُورُ الرَّحِيمُ

And do not invoke besides Allah that which neither benefits you nor harms you, for if you did, then you would certainly be among the wrongdoers. And if Allah touches you with adversity, there is none who can lift it; and if He does for you good, there is no repeller of His bounty. He causes to reach whom He wills among His servants. And He is the Pardoning, the Merciful.

O Believers! As for those who believe in Allah, realise the insignificance of this life and fully submit to their Rabb in all that He has decreed and predestined; we grateful at times of ease. These people remember Allah at all times and know very well that Allah is with His servants whenever they mention and remember Him; we know that Allah will be exactly as His servants think of him. We realise that Allah tests his slaves with good and evil to check their patience and purify their faith and to make them practice reliance on Him, as well as to see if they maintain a good opinion of Him.

The Prophet [sas] said, "No fatigue, nor disease, nor sorrow, nor sadness, nor hurt, nor distress befalls a Muslim, even if it were the prick he receives from a thorn, but that Allah expiates some of his sins for that." (Bukhari, book #70, hadith #545)

Servants of Allah! How many hardships carry blessings and mercy and how many adversities befall a slave of Allah, due to which he reaches an exalted rank and becomes honorable in the sight of Allah? Allah [swt] also said in **Surah az-Zumar (39:10):**

قُل يَـٰعِبَادِيَ الَّذِينَ ءَامَنُوا اتَّقُوا رَبَّكُمْ لِلَّذِينَ أَحْسَنُوا فِى هَـٰذِهِ الدُّنْيَا حَسَنَةٌ وَأَرْضُ اللَّهِ وَاسِعَةٌ إِنَّمَا يُوَفَّى الصَّـٰبِرُونَ أَجْرَهُم بِغَيْرِ

حِسَابٍ

Say: "O, My servants who believe! Fear your Rabb. For those who do good in this world is good, and Allah's earth is spacious. Indeed, the patient shall receive their reward in full, without limit."

Allah [swt] also says in **Surah Fatir (35:2):**

مَا يَفْتَحِ اللَّهُ لِلنَّاسِ مِن رَّحْمَةٍ فَلَا مُمْسِكَ لَهَا وَمَا يُمْسِكْ فَلَا مُرْسِلَ لَهُ مِنْ بَعْدِهِ وَهُوَ الْعَزِيزُ الْحَكِيمُ

Whatever of mercy, Allah may grant to mankind - none can withhold it; and whatever He withholds - none can grant it thereafter. And He is the Almighty, the All-Wise.

O Muslims! Fear Allah and believe in His Divine Decree and Destiny. Belief in the Divine Decree of Allah is one of the pillars of faith. The faith of a servant will be incomplete unless he believes in the Divine Decree, whether good or bad.

O believers! Fear Allah and have sound belief in Him. We must believe in destiny, His might and His will. This is because belief in Allah's decree on destiny is one of the pillars of faith, without which a person's belief will be incomplete. **Amin!**

Caring for Earth is Essential for Our existence

There are more than 500 verses in the Qur'an dealing directly with nature, the environment and natural phenomena. In fact, there are 18 chapters [Surahs] titled after either animals or natural phenomena. These are: Surah 2: Al-Baqarah [The Cow], Surah 6: Al-An'am [The Cattle], Surah 13: Ar-Ra'd [The Thunder], Surah 16: An-Nahl [The Bee], Surah 24: An-Nur [the Light], Surah 27: An-Naml [the Ant], Surah 29: Al-'Ankabut [the Spider], Surah 52: At-Tur ([he Mountain], Surah 53: An-Najm [the Star], Surah 54: Al-Qamar [the Moon], Surah 85: Al-Buruj [the Constellation of Stars], Surah 86: At-Tariq [the Night Star], Surah 89: Al-Fajr [the Dawn], Surah 91: Ash-Shams [the Sun], Surah 92: Al-Layl the Night], Surah 93: Ad-Duha the Morning], Surah 95 :At-Tin the Fig], and Surah 105: Al-Fil [the Elephant]. It is astonishing to note that the smallest animal Ant has not escaped the attention of Allah [swt] and so as the biggest animal Elephant among His creations in making revelations in the Holy Qura'n.

Allah [swt] says in **Surah al-Hijr (15:19):**

وَالأَرْضَ مَدَدْنَاهَا وَأَلْقَيْنَا فِيهَا رَوَاسِيَ وَأَنبَتْنَا فِيهَا مِن كُلِّ شَيْءٍ مَّوْزُونٍ

And We have spread out the earth, and cast therein firmly set mountains, and caused to grow therein of every things in due proportion.

Allah [swt] says in **Surah al-Qamar (54:49):**

إِنَّا كُلَّ شَيْءٍ خَلَقْنَاهُ بِقَدَرٍ

Indeed, We have created all things with predestination.

Allah created the creation with destined limits before they were created. The above ayahs provide clear evidence that Allah [swt] has created everything in due proportions and destined limits. If these limits and proportions are violated or destroyed by the activities of mankind or any other force, then it will imbalance the whole creation and will bring catastrophic consequences as is happening now -a -days on the land and the sea.

In **Surah al-Naml (27:61)** Allah [swt] says:

أَمَّن جَعَلَ الأَرْضَ قَرَارًا وَجَعَلَ خِلاَلَهَا أَنْهَارًا وَجَعَلَ لَهَا رَوَاسِيَ وَجَعَلَ بَيْنَ الْبَحْرَيْنِ حَاجِزًا أَءِلَهٌ مَّعَ اللهِ بَلْ أَكْثَرُهُمْ لاَ يَعْلَمُونَ

Is He [not best] who made the earth a stable ground, and placed within it rivers and placed firm mountains therein, and set a barrier between the two seas [of salt and sweet water]. Is there any other *ilah* but Allah? [No], but most of them do not know!

The Millennium Ecosystem Assessment [MA] formed in 2000 engaged 1,360 experts from 95 nations to do a survey into the state of the planet concludes in its report published in March 2005 revealed that human activities threaten the Earth's ability to sustain future generations.

Results show that 60 % of the world ecosystems have been degraded. Of 24 evaluated ecosystems, 15 are being damaged. The World Conservation Union [IUCN] latest report shows that species threatened with extinction are: 25% of mammal, 20% of reptiles, and 11% of bird species, 34% of fish, and 12.5% of all plant species.

The report indicates that human abuse of the environment through pollution, deforestation and indiscriminate exploitation of the natural resources has caused irreversible changes that are degrading the natural processes that support life on Earth. This will impact on hunger, poverty and healthcare.

If present trends continue one half of all species of life on earth could be extinct in 100 years. Nearly seven out of 10 of the biologists polled said they believed a "mass extinction" was underway and almost all attributed the losses to human activity, especially the destruction of plant and animal habitats.

We are commanded in the Qur'an not to cause disruption /corruption/ mischief/chaos on earth after it has been so well ordered/organized. Allah [swt] says in **Surah al-A'raf (7:56):**

$$وَلَا تُفْسِدُوا فِي الْأَرْضِ بَعْدَ إِصْلَاحِهَا وَادْعُوهُ خَوْفًا وَطَمَعًا إِنَّ رَحْمَتَ اللَّهِ قَرِيبٌ مِّنَ الْمُحْسِنِينَ$$

And do not do mischief on the earth, after it has been set in order. And invoke Him in fear and hope. Indeed, Allah's mercy is [ever] near to the good-doers.

Currently over one billion people lack a reliable supply of water while 2.4 billion people - or just under half the world's population - have no adequate water supply for daily needs. Human pollution is one of the main factors seriously undermining the quality and availability of freshwater, says the report. About 2 million tons of wastes are dumped every day into rivers, lakes and streams. One gallon of wastewater pollutes about eight gallons of freshwater [UN World Water Development Report, 2003]. As a result, more than 2.2 million people die each year from diseases owing to contaminated drinking water and poor sanitation. Everyday around 6,000 people, mainly children under the age of five, die from water-related diseases.

In **Surah al-Naml (27:61)** Allah [swt] says:

$$أَمَّن جَعَلَ الْأَرْضَ قَرَارًا وَجَعَلَ خِلَالَهَا أَنْهَارًا وَجَعَلَ لَهَا رَوَاسِيَ وَجَعَلَ بَيْنَ الْبَحْرَيْنِ حَاجِزًا أَإِلَهٌ مَّعَ اللَّهِ بَلْ أَكْثَرُهُمْ لَا يَعْلَمُونَ$$

Is He [not best] who has made the earth as a stable ground and has placed within it rivers, and has placed firm mountains therein, and has set a barrier between the two seas [of salt and sweet water]. Is there any other *ilah* than Allah? [No], but most of them do not know.

He has placed rivers that are fresh and sweet, cutting through the earth, and He has made them of different types, large rivers, small rivers and some in between. He has caused them to flow in all directions, east, west, south, north, according to the needs of mankind in different areas and regions, as He has created them throughout the world and sends them their provision according to their needs

He has placed a barrier between the fresh water and the salt water, to prevent them from mixing lest they corrupt one another. Divine wisdom dictates that each of them should stay as it is meant to be. The sweet water is that which flows in rivers among mankind, and it is meant to be fresh and palatable so that it may be used to water animals and plants and fruits. The salt water is that which surrounds the continents on all sides, and its water is meant to be salty and undrinkable lest the air be corrupted by its smell, as Allah says in **Surah al-Fatir (35:12):**

وَمَا يَسْتَوِى الْبَحْرَانِ هَـذَا عَذْبٌ فُرَاتٌ سَآئِغٌ شَرَابُهُ وَهَـذَا مِلْحٌ أُجَاجٌ وَمِن كُلٍّ تَأْكُلُونَ لَحْمًا طَرِيًّا وَتَسْتَخْرِجُونَ حِلْيَةً تَلْبَسُونَهَا وَتَرَى الْفُلْكَ فِيهِ مَوَاخِرَ لِتَبْتَغُوا مِن فَضْلِهِ وَلَعَلَّكُمْ تَشْكُرُونَ

And the two seas [kinds of water] are not alike. One is fresh and sweet, and pleasant to drink, and one is salty and bitter. And from each you eat fresh tender meat [fish], and extract ornaments that you wear. And you see the ships plowing through [them] that you may seek of His bounty, and perhaps you will be grateful.

UN World Water Development Report [WWDR] warns that water resources will steadily decline because of population growth, pollution and expected climate change. Human pollution is one of the main factors seriously undermining the quality and availability of freshwater, says the report. About 2 million tons of wastes are dumped every day into rivers, lakes and streams. One liter of wastewater pollutes about eight liters of freshwater. The World Resources Institute predicts that by 2025, at least 3.5 billion people, or nearly 60 percent of the world's population, will face water scarcity.

Pollution of the air from factories, automobiles, and homes causes environmental illnesses from cancer to lung diseases. Pollution of the water in rivers and lakes and now oceans makes conditions unsafe for fish and other water creatures. Humans cannot eat the fish and the water cannot be used for recreational purposes.

Pollution of the land from the garbage and other waste produced by humans, toxic dumps and nuclear waste are a threat to the health of many communities, as well as to the plants and animals of the area.

Allah has placed on the earth, the various plants, animals, valleys, mountains, deserts, rivers and oceans. Allah [swt] says in **Surah ar-R'ad (13:4):**

وَفِى الْأَرْضِ قِطَعٌ مُّتَجَاوِرَاتٌ وَجَنَّاتٌ مِّنْ أَعْنَابٍ وَزَرْعٌ وَنَخِيلٌ صِنْوَانٌ وَغَيْرُ صِنْوَانٍ يُسْقَى بِمَآءٍ وَاحِدٍ وَنُفَضِّلُ بَعْضَهَا عَلَى بَعْضٍ فِى الْأُكُلِ إِنَّ فِى ذَلِكَ لَآيَاتٍ لِّقَوْمٍ يَعْقِلُونَ

And in the earth are neighboring plots and gardens of grapevines and green crops [fields], and palm trees, [growing] several from a single stem root, or otherwise, watered with the same water; but We make some of them exceed others in [quality of] fruit. Indeed in that are signs for the people who understand.

Loss of ground water reserves from overuse for personal and agricultural purposes will lead to food losses, lifestyle changes, and conflicts over limited resources. Loss of biological diversity due to encroachment of humans causes destruction of plant and animal species. The loss of species goes hand in glove with the loss of diverse ecosystems that support many forms of life. The result is the loss of sources for medicine, as well as a diminishment of the gene pool of animals and plant strains that allow life to survive and adapt to changing conditions.

The destruction of forests changes the temperature of the earth and diminishes the earth's capacity to provide the carbon dioxide that enables humans and other animals to breathe. The loss of arable land to desert from erosion and overuse leaves people without sustainable levels of food and water. Global warming from the trapping of heat due to pollution of the air threatens to cause the oceans to expand, which will inundate population areas and fresh water reserves, create extreme weather patterns, move the food belts to different areas of the globe, and bring on outbreaks of infectious disease.

The depletion of the ozone layer due to the use of certain refrigerants and other dangerous products will allow greater exposure to ultraviolet rays and will cause chemical and genetic changes in the entire food chain from the plankton in the sea to the cattle in the fields. It will also greatly increase the cases of skin cancer.

Sunday December 26, 2004, we witnessed the largest natural tragedy to strike the human race in modern times. A 9.0-magnitude quake struck 6 miles beneath the ocean and ruptured a 600-mile stretch of fault running north and south off the coast of Sumatra. The quake moved the entire island of Sumatra about 100 feet to the southwest. Such a large earthquake beneath the sea floor causes a large region of the seabed to drop which in turn results in the whole sea above -- perhaps over an area of hundreds of square miles -- to drop by the same amount, setting off a train of massive waves known as tsunamis which can accelerate to 600 mph and stretch up to 100 miles long. Such a Tsunami developed and the result … within hours - over 130 000 dead, over 40 million displaced, over a million injured, thousands missing, leaving up to five million people across 12 countries without access to the basic requirements for life - water, food and sanitation.

We are indeed witnessing devastation of biblical proportions, suffering unprecedented in contemporary times; death and destruction beyond belief, affecting the most heavily populated areas of the world. The images of the aftermath of the Tsunami and earthquake are shocking and by comparison with past disasters, this one has not been confined to just one country or region, neither in terms of impact nor in news worthiness. This is the first cataclysmic tragedy in which the entire Indian Ocean region is both shocked spectator and direct victim.

The epicenter of the quake was in Indonesia; its shockwaves and the subsequent tsunami spread to Sri Lanka and as far as the eastern seaboard of Africa. Amateur videotape played on television showed terrifying scenes from several countries of huge walls of water crashing through palm trees and over the tops of buildings and roaring up coastal streets with cars and debris bobbing on the surface. The wave arrives like a great, big, huge tide coming in quickly, with the tall wave washing everything away before it for hundreds of yards inland, then the wave washes out, ripping down buildings and dragging debris and people out to sea with an inescapable pull. The receding wave is often the deadliest part of the tsunami, particularly hard on the elderly and infants too weak to hold onto anything. To backdrops of screams and shouts, people were shown clinging to buildings, being swept away by the current, running for their lives, weeping, carrying the injured and cradling dead children. The images we see are moving. In the aftermath, hundreds were buried in mass graves, millions were displaced from their destroyed homes, hospitals ran out of medicine, and food and water are scarce.

We live in a universe of cause and effect and the consequences of certain causes are inescapable. As for the seemingly solid earth, the planet's interior has an inner core of molten elements. It surely would not be an exaggeration to call this part of the earth, which remains invisible to our eyes, "a flaming core". There also exists an atmosphere surrounding the earth, which is a "shield" against external threats. Yet, no part of the earth is immune against the effects of atmospheric forces like thunderstorms, storms, or hurricanes or celestial dangers like meteors. Any of these hazards may strike at any time. They can cause considerable loss of life and property. What is common to all these disasters is that in just moments they can reduce a city, with all its inhabitants, to ruin.

We must realize and acknowledge that all this corruption occurs upon the earth as a result of mankind's evil deeds. Allah [swt] says in **Surah ar-Rum (30:41):**

ظَهَرَ الْفَسَادُ فِي الْبَرِّ وَالْبَحْرِ بِمَا كَسَبَتْ أَيْدِى النَّاسِ لِيُذِيقَهُم بَعْضَ الَّذِى عَمِلُوا الْعَلَّهُمْ يَرْجِعُونَ

Corruption has appeared throughout the land and sea by [reason of] what the hands of men have earned, so He may let them taste part of [the consequence of] what they have done, in order that they may return [i.e., refrain].

These outbursts of nature are reminders to all mankind that we have no control whatsoever over the planet. Likewise, each disaster serves the purpose of reminding us of our inherent weakness. These are surely warnings to those who can contemplate the significance of such events and draw lessons from the experience of others.

Each one of these events is important in the sense that it reminds man that wealth, power, science, nor technology has any power to resist the forces greater than us. Allah did not make this world a permanent world. This is a temporary world and everything here is finite and has a time limit. When its times comes it will die, come to an end and finish. Neither the good things of this world are forever, or the bad things eternal.

One has the challenge to frame the terrible traumatic events into a new crucible of meaning. Having been helpless does not mean that one is a helpless person; having witnessed or experienced evil does not that the world as a whole is evil; witnessing the devastation caused by earthquakes and tsunami does not imply that nature is destructive; the fact that Allah allows nature to take its course does not imply a lack of compassion. Rather, all this is a challenge to us as to what we do in the face of such challenges.

Satan will also make his evil deeds fair seeming to him so much so that he will actually view the evil and corruption that he does as good deeds; just like the hypocrites whom Allah describes in **Surah al-Baqarah (2:11-12):**

وَإِذَا قِيلَ لَهُمْ لَا تُفْسِدُوا فِي الْأَرْضِ قَالُوا إِنَّمَا نَحْنُ مُصْلِحُونَ - أَلَا إِنَّهُمْ هُمُ الْمُفْسِدُونَ وَلَكِن لَّا يَشْعُرُونَ

And when it is said to them, "Do not cause corruption on the earth," they say, "We are the reformers". Unquestionably, it is they who are the corrupters, but they perceive [it] not.

We abuse land and water because we regard it as a commodity, when we see land and water as a community to which we belong, we may begin to use it with love and respect. Environmental pollution with its widespread destruction is another form of causing corruption upon the earth in modern times. This pollution has caused immense and unnecessary damage to human beings, animals, plants and aquatic creatures. This harm is caused by man's selfish desire to hasten productivity, a result of his selfish materialism and his craving for wealth that has no limit.

Therefore fellow Muslims, fear Allah and be among the righteous so that we will earn the pleasure of our Rabb and be successful and victorious with the help of Allah. May Allah [swt] gives us the guidance to use our sanity in using His creations in the best way that will benefit us all and will not cause chaos and corruption in this world. **Amin!**

Characteristics of the Successful Believers

Allah [swt] reminds us in **Surah al-Ahzab (33:72)** that we, the human being, are the custodians of an amanah:

$$إِنَّا عَرَضْنَا الْأَمَانَةَ عَلَى السَّمَوَاتِ وَالْأَرْضِ وَالْجِبَالِ فَأَبَيْنَ أَنْ يَحْمِلْنَهَا وَأَشْفَقْنَ مِنْهَا وَحَمَلَهَا الْإِنْسَانُ إِنَّهُ كَانَ ظَلُومًا جَهُولًا$$

Indeed, We offered the [Amanah] the trust to the heavens and the earth, and the mountains, and they declined to bear it; but man [undertook to] bear it. Indeed, he was unjust and ignorant.

In order to successfully carry out that trust and be rewarded, we must believe, without any doubt, and follow the instructions of Allah [swt] and the Sunnah of prophet [sas].

Allah [swt] says in **Surah al-Mu'minun (23):**

$$قَدْ أَفْلَحَ الْمُؤْمِنُونَ$$

"Certainly will the believers have succeeded" means, they have attained victory and are blessed, for they have succeeded in the day of final judgment Believing is not only by saying only, but also to believe wholeheartedly about it without any hesitation or doubt These are the believers who have the following characteristics:

$$الَّذِينَ هُمْ فِي صَلَاتِهِمْ خَاشِعُونَ$$

[Those who are during their prayer are humbly submissive]. Ali bin Abi Talhah reported that Ibn `Abbas said:

$$خَاشِعُون$$

"(khashi`un) means those with fear and with tranquility." "al-khushoo" means calmness, serenity, tranquility, dignity, and humility." Al-khushoo is a necessary component of salah khushoo is very easily lost and Allah's Messenger said: "The first thing to be lifted up [taken away] from this Ummah is khushoo [saheehal-Targheeb]. The site of Khushoo is in the heart and heart is the king of the limbs, so if one intends to pray wholeheartedly, the limbs will follow the heart as Allah says in **Surah al-Baqarah (2:45):**

$$وَاسْتَعِينُوا بِالصَّبْرِ وَالصَّلَوةِ وَإِنَّهَا لَكَبِيرَةٌ إِلَّا عَلَى الْخَاشِعِين$$

And seek help through patience and prayer, and indeed, it is extremely heavy and hard [difficult], except for the humbly submissive [to Allah]. The meaning is that the burden of prayer is heavy indeed; except for those who have khushoo. To attain khushoo one must forget everything about the world and concentrate in the prayer acts, reciting the Qur'an and thinking of the verses one reads and bearing death, grave and the torment in mind so that he never loses concentration. Imam Ibn Kathir writes, 'khushoo is gained by the fear of Allah and the sense that He is always watching.'

وَالَّذِينَ هُمْ عَنِ اللَّغْوِ مُعْرِضُونَ-

And they who turn away from ill speech refers to falsehood, which includes shirk and sin, and any words or deeds that are of no benefit: evil play or evil talks.

As Allah says in **Surah al- Furqan (25:72):**

وَإِذَا مَرُّواْ بِاللَّغْوِ مَرُّواْ كِرَاماً-

And when they pass by evil play or evil talks, they pass by it with dignity

وَالَّذِينَ هُمْ لِلزَّكَوةِ فَعِلُونَ-

And they who are observant of zakah. Most commentators say that the meaning here is the zakah that is paid on wealth; It could be that what is meant here by zakah is purification of the soul from Shirk and filth, as in **Surah ash-shams (91:9-10):**

قَدْ أَفْلَحَ مَن زَكَّهَا-وَقَدْ خَابَ مَن دَسَّهَا-

He has succeeded who purifies it [zakah]. And he has failed who instills it with corruption [disobeys that Allah has ordered]. It could be that both meanings are intended, purification of the soul and of one's wealth, because that is part of the purification of the soul, and the true believer is one who pays attention to both matters. And Allah knows best.

وَالَّذِينَ هُمْ لِفُرُوجِهِمْ حَفِظُونَ-إِلاَّ عَلَى أَزْوَجِهِمْ أَوْ مَا مَلَكَتْ أَيْمَنُهُمْ فَإِنَّهُمْ غَيْرُ مَلُومِينَ-فَمَنِ ابْتَغَى وَرَاءَ ذلِكَ فَأُوْلَئِكَ هُمُ الْعَادُونَ

And those who guard their private parts. Except from their wives or those right hand possess, for indeed, they will not be blamed. But whoever seeks beyond that, and then those are the transgressors - mean those who protect their private parts from unlawful actions and do not do that which Allah has forbidden; fornication and homosexuality, and do not approach anyone except the wives whom Allah has made permissible for them or their right hand possessions from the captives. One who seeks what Allah has made permissible for him is not to be blamed and there is no sin on him. Zina [fornication/adultery] is one of the major sins, concerning which Allah and His Messenger [sas] have issued stern warnings.

$$ وَلَا تَقْرَبُوا الزِّنَى إِنَّهُ كَانَ فَاحِشَةً ۗ - وَسَاءَ سَبِيلًا $$

And do not approach unlawful sexual intercourse [avoid all situations that might possibly lead to it]. Indeed, it is ever an immorality and is evil as a way (Surah al-Isra 17: 32). We are living here in a society where homosexuality, pre-marital and extra-marital sexual activities [which are responsible for STD, HIV, and AIDS] are part of societal norms, we should be very careful, and especially our youngsters must be kept under strict watch so that they do not engage themselves in such evil activity. May Allah [swt] save us and our youngsters from such forbidden acts?

$$ وَالَّذِينَ هُمْ لِأَمَانَاتِهِمْ وَعَهْدِهِمْ رَاعُونَ $$

And they who are to their trust and their promises attentive. When they are entrusted with something, they do not betray that trust, but they fulfill it, and when they make a promise or make a pledge, they are true to their word. This is not like the hypocrites about whom the Messenger of Allah said:

$$ آيَةُ الْمُنَافِقِ ثَلَاثٌ: إِذَا حَدَّثَ كَذَبَ، وَ إِذَا وَعَدَ أَخْلَفَ، وَ إِذَا اؤْتُمِنَ خَانَ $$

The signs of the hypocrite are three: when he speaks he lies, when he makes a promise he breaks it, and when he is entrusted with something he betrays that trust.

Scholars have explained the amanah to mean, all the duties which Allah has ordained: honesty, moral responsibility and trusts, etc. based on the hadith of Hudhaifah [ra.] who narrated: Allah's Messenger [sas] said to us: "Honesty descended from the Heavens and settled in the roots of the hearts of men [faithful believers], and then the Quran was revealed and the people read the Quran, [and learnt it from it] and also learnt it from the Sunnah." Both Quran and Sunnah strengthened their [the faithful believers'] honesty (Bukhari, book #92, hadith #381)

$$ وَالَّذِينَ هُمْ عَلَى صَلَوَاتِهِمْ يُحَافِظُونَ $$

And they who carefully maintain their prayers - means they persistently offer their prayers at their appointed times, as Ibn Mas`ud said: "I asked the Messenger of Allah, `O Messenger of Allah, which deed is most beloved to Allah' He said,

$$ الصَّلَاةُ عَلَى وَقْتِهَا $$

[Prayer at the appointed time], I said, `Then what' He said,

Kindness to one's parents, I said, `Then what' He said,

«الْجِهَادُ فِي سَبِيلِ الله»

Jihad in the way of Allah. It was recorded in the two sahihs. Qatadah said: "At the fixed times, with the proper bowing and prostration." Allah begins and ends this list of praiseworthy qualities with salah, which is indicative of its virtue, as the Prophet said: Adhere to righteousness, you will never be able encompass it all. Know that the best of your deeds is salah. Allah's forgiveness and pleasure is closely related to the prayers. The Messenger of Allah [sws] said, "Allah, the Exalted, has made five prayers obligatory. If anyone performs ablution for them well, offers them at their [right] time, and observes perfectly their bowing and submissiveness in them, it is the guarantee of Allah that He will pardon him; if anyone does not do so, there is no guarantee for him on the part of Allah; He may pardon him if He wills, and punish him if He wills" (Abu Dawud, book #2, hadith #0425).

Allah [swt] says in **Surah al-Ankaboot (29:45)**:

إِنَّ الصَّلَوةَ تَنْهَى عَنِ الْفَحْشَاءِ وَالْمُنْكَرِ

Indeed, prayers prohibit immorality and wrongdoing.

Having described them with these praiseworthy characteristics and righteous deeds, Allah then says:

أُوْلَـئِكَ هُمُ الْوَرِثُونَ - الَّذِينَ يَرِثُونَ الْفِرْدَوْسَ هُمْ فِيهَا خَـلِدُونَ -

Those are the inheritors who will inherit al-Firdaus [the highest part of paradise]. They will abide therein eternally [forever]. The Messenger of Allah said: If you ask Allah for Paradise, then ask him for Al-firdaus, for it is the highest part of Paradise, in the middle of Paradise, and from it spring the rivers of Paradise, and above it is the [Mighty] Throne of the Most Merciful (Tafsir-Ibn-Kathir).

May Allah [swt] forgive our sins and bestow on us His rahmat and give us His hidayat [proper guidance] so that we can achieve all the seven characteristics of successful mumin and inherit al-firdaus. **Amin!**

Cheating in Measurement is a Sinful Act

Allah [swt] has made trade legal as He says in **Surah al-Baqarah (2:275):**

وَأَحَلَّ اللَّهُ الْبَيْعَ وَحَرَّمَ الرِّبَواْ

But Allah has permitted trade and has forbidden Riba [interest].

Our prophet [sas] was also engaged in trade during the early part of his life. Allah [swt] encourages us to make legal transactions in trade. Allah [swt] says in **Surah al-Isra' (17:35):**

وَأَوْفُوا الْكَيْلَ إِذَا كِلْتُمْ وَزِنُوا بِالقِسْطَاسِ الْمُسْتَقِيمِ ذَلِكَ خَيْرٌ وَأَحْسَنُ تَأْوِيلاً

And give full measure when you measure, and weigh with an even [honest] balance. That is the best [way] and best in the result, meaning, do not try to make it weigh less nor wrong people with their belongings meaning that which is not distorted nor that which will cause confusion. Sa`id narrated that Qatadah said that this means "Better in reward and a better end. " Ibn `Abbas used to say: "O people, you are entrusted with two things for which the people who came before you were destroyed - these weights and measures.'"

And also in **Surah ash-Shu'ara (26:181-3)** Allah [swt] instructs:

أَوْفُوا الْكَيْلَ وَلاَ تَكُونُوا مِنَ الْمُخْسِرِينَ - وَزِنُوا بِالقِسْطَاسِ الْمُسْتَقِيمِ وَلاَ تَبْخَسُوا النَّاسَ أَشْيَاءَهُمْ وَلاَ تَعْثَوْا فِي الأَرْضِ

مُفْسِدِينَ

Give full measure, and cause no loss [to others]. And weigh with an even [honest] balance. And do not deprive people of their due and do not commit abuse on earth, spreading corruption."`When you give to people, give them full measure, and do not cause loss to them by giving them short measure, while taking full measure when you are the ones who are taking. Give as you take, and take as you give.'

Allah [swt] says in **Surah ar-Rahman (55:9):**

وَأَقِيمُوا الْوَزْنَ بِالقِسْطِ وَلاَ تُخْسِرُوا الْمِيزَانَ

And establish weight in justice and do not make deficient in balance. Allah destroyed the people of Shu`ayb and wiped them out because of their cheating in weights and measurements." meaning, they take their right by demanding full measure and extra as well.

Allah [swt] commands us in **Surah al-An'am (6:152):**

وَأَوْفُوا الْكَيْلَ وَالْمِيزَانَ بِالْقِسْطِ

And give full measure and full weight with justice. It is a command to establish justice while giving and taking. Allah has also warned against abandoning this commandment, when He said in **Surah al-Mutaffifin (83:1-6):**

وَيْلٌ لِّلْمُطَفِّفِينَ - الَّذِينَ إِذَا اكْتَالُوا عَلَى النَّاسِ يَسْتَوْفُونَ - وَإِذَا كَالُوهُمْ أَو وَّزَنُوهُمْ يُخْسِرُونَ - أَلَا يَظُنُّ أُولَئِكَ أَنَّهُم مَّبْعُوثُونَ - لِيَوْمٍ عَظِيمٍ - يَوْمَ يَقُومُ النَّاسُ لِرَبِّ الْعَالَمِينَ -

Woe to those who give less [than due], who when they take a measure from people take in full. But if they give by measure or weight to [other] people, give less than due. Do they not think that they will be resurrected [for reckoning] for a tremendous Day - The Day when [all] mankind will stand before the Lord of the worlds?

In **Surah HUD (11:84-6)**, Allah [swt] describes the case of the Madyan people as:

وَإِلَى مَدْيَنَ أَخَاهُمْ شُعَيْبًا قَالَ يَا قَوْمِ اعْبُدُوا اللَّهَ مَا لَكُم مِّنْ إِلَهٍ غَيْرُهُ وَلَا تَنقُصُوا الْمِكْيَالَ وَالْمِيزَانَ إِنِّي أَرَاكُم بِخَيْرٍ وَإِنِّي أَخَافُ عَلَيْكُمْ عَذَابَ يَوْمٍ مُّحِيطٍ - وَيَا قَوْمِ أَوْفُوا الْمِكْيَالَ وَالْمِيزَانَ بِالْقِسْطِ وَلَا تَبْخَسُوا النَّاسَ أَشْيَاءَهُمْ وَلَا تَعْثَوْا فِي الْأَرْضِ مُفْسِدِينَ - بَقِيَّتُ اللَّهِ خَيْرٌ لَّكُمْ إِن كُنتُم مُّؤْمِنِينَ وَمَا أَنَا عَلَيْكُم بِحَفِيظٍ -

And to the Madyan people [We sent] their brother Shu`ayb. He said: "O my people! Worship Allah, you have no deity other than Him. And do not decrease from the measure and the scale. I see you in prosperity, but indeed, I fear for you the punishment of an all encompassing day. And O my people! Give full measure and weight in justice and do not deprive the the people of their due and do not commit mischief on the earth, spreading corruption. What remains [lawful] from Allah is best for you, if you are believers. And I am not a guardian over you."

He [Shu`ayb] prohibited them from cheating in business by decreasing the weights whenever they gave [products] to people. He commanded them to give just measure and weight whether they were giving or receiving [in transactions]. He also forbade them from causing mischief and corruption in the land. The Prophet [sas] said: "The Muslim is the brother of his fellow Muslim. The Muslim is not permitted to sell to his brother anything which is faulty without pointing out the faults to him." (Ibn Maajah, 2/754)

But the people of Madyan denied the advice and command of Shu'ayb [as] and challenged Shu'ayb [as] to bring punishment on them if he is truly a messenger of Allah [swt]. This is what they asked for, when they asked for a part of the heaven to fall upon them as described **in Surah ash-Shu'ara (26:187):**

فَأَسْقِطْ عَلَيْنَا كِسَفًا مِّنَ السَّمَاءِ إِن كُنتَ مِنَ الصَّادِقِينَ

So cause to fall upon us a piece of the sky, if you are of the truthful!

In **Surah ash–Shu'ara (26:189),** Allah [swt] describes how the people of Madyan were punished:

$$فَكَذَّبُوهُ فَأَخَذَهُمْ عَذَابُ يَوْمِ الظُّلَّةِ إِنَّهُ كَانَ عَذَابَ يَوْمٍ عَظِيمٍ$$

But they denied him, so the punishment of the day of the black cloud seized them. Indeed it was the punishment of a terrible day.

Allah destroyed an entire nation that was accustomed to giving less in weights and measures. Allah [swt] elaborates in **Surah HUD (11:94-5)** how the people of Madayan were punished:

$$وَلَمَّا جَاءَ أَمْرُنَا نَجَّيْنَا شُعَيْبًا وَالَّذِينَ آمَنُوا مَعَهُ بِرَحْمَةٍ مِّنَّا وَأَخَذَتِ الَّذِينَ ظَلَمُوا الصَّيْحَةُ فَأَصْبَحُوا فِي دِيَارِهِمْ جَاثِمِينَ ۔ كَأَن لَّمْ يَغْنَوْا فِيهَا أَلَا بُعْدًا لِّمَدْيَنَ كَمَا بَعِدَتْ ثَمُودُ ۔$$

And when Our commandment came, We saved Shu`ayb and those who believed with him by a mercy from Us. And As-Sayhah [awful cry] seized the wrongdoers, and they lay [Jathimin] in their homes [corpses]. As if they had never lived there! Then away with Madyan just as Thamud was taken away! And As-Sayhah [awful cry] seized the wrongdoers, and they lay [Jathimin] in their homes. His saying Jathimin means extinct and lifeless without any movement. Here Allah mentions that a loud cry [Sayhah] came to them. In **Surah al-A`raf (7:91-2):**

$$فَأَخَذَتْهُمُ الرَّجْفَةُ فَأَصْبَحُوا فِي دَارِهِمْ جَاثِمِينَ ۔ الَّذِينَ كَذَّبُوا شُعَيْبًا كَأَن لَّمْ يَغْنَوْا فِيهَا الَّذِينَ كَذَّبُوا شُعَيْبًا كَانُوا هُمُ الْخَاسِرِينَ$$

So the earthquake seized them, and they became within their homes [corpses] fallen prone. Those who denied Shu`ayb – it was as though they had never resided there. Those who denied Shu`ayb - they were the losers. Allah describes the enormity of disbelief, rebellion, transgression and misguidance [of Shu`ayb's people] and the defiance of truth encrypted in their hearts. He says a severe quake [Rajfah] came to them.

Allah made their punishment in the form of intense heat that overwhelmed them for seven days, and nothing could protect them from it. Then He sent a cloud to shade them, so they ran towards it to seek its shade from the heat. When all of them had gathered underneath it, Allah sent sparks of fire and flames and intense heat upon them, and caused the earth to convulse beneath them, and He sent against them a mighty Sayhah that destroyed their souls. What a terrible punishment the people of Madyan had witnessed for cheating in weight in trade?

For those brothers and sisters in Islam whose trade and business is attached to measurement, be aware of the severe punishment of the Day of Judgment for cheating in measurement when dealing with people. May Allah [swt] give us the proper guidance to take lessons from the destruction of the people of Madyan for disbelieving the advice and command of the messenger of Allah [swt]? **Amin!**

Creation of Heaven and Earth

Allah [swt] has planned and created the Universe without any help from any other and there was none as a witness in this creation. So nobody knows what materials were used in creating the universe and the time of its creation. Those who indulge in studying the creation of the heavens and the earth; of which material it has been created, when and how it was created - is a study based on speculation that might be right or wrong. Very little is still known about the mysteries of this creation as yet. Whatever is known about this creation is only known through the revelation of Allah [swt] in the Holy Qur'an. Almighty Allah says in **Surah al-Kahf (18:51):**

مَّآ أَشْهَدتُّهُمْ خَلْقَ السَّمَوَتِ وَالْأَرْضِ وَلَا خَلْقَ أَنفُسِهِمْ وَمَا كُنتُ مُتَّخِذَ الْمُضِلِّينَ عَضُداً

I did not make them witness to the creation of the heavens and the earth or to [even] their own creation; I would not have taken the misguides as assistant.

O Muslims! Almighty Allah created the heavens and the earth in six days and made the heavens seven and the earth seven in layers one above the other. Allah [swt] says in **Surah as-Sajdah (32:4):**

اللَّهُ الَّذِى خَلَقَ السَّمَوَتِ وَالْأَرْضَ وَمَا بَيْنَهُمَا فِى سِتَّةِ أَيَّامٍ

It is Allah who has created the heavens and the earth and whatever in between them in six days.

About the creation of Heaven and Earth Allah [swt] says in **Surah al-Anbiya (21:30):**

أَوَلَمْ يَرَ الَّذِينَ كَفَرُوا أَنَّ السَّمَوَتِ وَالْأَرْضَ كَانَتَا رَتْقاً فَفَتَقْنَهُمَا وَجَعَلْنَا مِنَ الْمَاءِ كُلَّ شَىْءٍ حَىٍّ أَفَلَا يُؤْمِنُونَ

Have not those who disbelieve consider that the heavens and the earth were a joined entity [as one united piece], and We separated them and have made from water every living thing. Then will they not believe?

And also in **Surah Fussilat (41:9-12):**

قُلْ أَئِنَّكُمْ لَتَكْفُرُونَ بِالَّذِى خَلَقَ الْأَرْضَ فِى يَوْمَيْنِ وَتَجْعَلُونَ لَهُ أَندَاداً ذَلِكَ رَبُّ الْعَلَمِينَ - وَجَعَلَ فِيهَا رَوَاسِىَ مِن فَوْقِهَا وَبَرَكَ

فِيهَا وَقَدَّرَ فِيهَا أَقْوَتَهَا فِى أَرْبَعَةِ أَيَّامٍ سَوَآءً لِّلسَّآئِلِينَ - ثُمَّ اسْتَوَى إِلَى السَّمَاءِ وَهِىَ دُخَانٌ فَقَالَ لَهَا وَلِلْأَرْضِ ائْتِيَا طَوْعاً أَوْ كَرْهاً قَالَتَا

أَتَيْنَا طَآئِعِينَ - فَقَضَاهُنَّ سَبْعَ سَمَوَتٍ فِى يَوْمَيْنِ وَأَوْحَى فِى كُلِّ سَمَآءٍ أَمْرَهَا وَزَيَّنَّا السَّمَآءَ الدُّنْيَا بِمَصَبِيحَ وَحِفْظاً ذَلِكَ تَقْدِيرُ

الْعَزِيزِ الْعَلِيمِ

Say: "Do you verily disbelieve in Him who created the earth in two days and attribute to Him equals? That is the Rabb of the worlds. And He placed on it [the earth] firmly set mountains over its surface, and He blessed it and determined therein its [creatures'] sustenance in four days without distinction – for [the information] of those who ask." Then He directed Himself [Istawa ila] [turned towards] to the heaven when it was smoke and said to it and to the earth: "Come [into being] willingly or by compulsion." They both said: "We come willingly." And He completed them as seven heavens in two Days and inspired in each heaven its command. And We adorned the nearest [lowest] heaven with lamps [stars] to be an adornment as well as protection. That is the determination of the Exalted, the Almighty, and the All-Knower.

The above Ayahs clearly state the order of creation: the Earth was created first and then the Heaven. Allah [swt] explains in **Surah an-Nahl (16:15-8),** why mountains were created on the Earth:

وَأَلْقَىٰ فِي ٱلْأَرْضِ رَوَاسِيَ أَن تَمِيدَ بِكُمْ وَأَنْهَٰرًا وَسُبُلًا لَّعَلَّكُمْ تَهْتَدُونَ ۞ وَعَلَامَٰتٍ ۚ وَبِٱلنَّجْمِ هُمْ يَهْتَدُونَ ۞ أَفَمَن يَخْلُقُ كَمَن لاَّ يَخْلُقُ ۗ أَفَلَا تَذَكَّرُونَ ۞ وَإِن تَعُدُّوا۟ نِعْمَةَ ٱللَّهِ لَا تُحْصُوهَآ ۗ إِنَّ ٱللَّهَ لَغَفُورٌ رَّحِيمٌ

And He has cast into the earth firmly set mountains, lest it shift with you, and [made] rivers and roads, that you may be guided. And [by the] landmarks; and by the stars, they are [also] guided. Then is He who creates like one who does not create? So will you not be reminded? And if you would try to count the favors of Allah, you would never be able to enumerate them. Indeed, Allah is Forgiving and the Merciful.

Allah [swt] describes the creation of Heaven in **Surah Nuh (71:15):**

أَلَمْ تَرَوْا۟ كَيْفَ خَلَقَ ٱللَّهُ سَبْعَ سَمَٰوَٰتٍ طِبَاقًا

Do you not consider how Allah has created the seven heavens in layers?

Allah [swt] says in **Surah Qaf (50:38):**

وَلَقَدْ خَلَقْنَا ٱلسَّمَٰوَٰتِ وَٱلْأَرْضَ وَمَا بَيْنَهُمَا فِى سِتَّةِ أَيَّامٍ وَمَا مَسَّنَا مِن لُّغُوبٍ

And indeed We created the heavens and the earth and all between them in six Days and there touched Us no weariness.

He also says in **Surah Qaf (50:6):**

أَفَلَمْ يَنظُرُوٓا۟ إِلَى ٱلسَّمَآءِ فَوْقَهُمْ كَيْفَ بَنَيْنَٰهَا وَزَيَّنَّٰهَا وَمَا لَهَا مِن فُرُوجٍ

Have they not looked at the heaven above them - how We structured it and adorned it, and there are no Furuj [flaws] in it.

And also in **Surah Adh-Dhariyat (51:47-8):**

$$\text{وَالسَّمَاءَ بَنَيْنَاهَا بِأَيْدٍ وَإِنَّا لَمُوسِعُونَ - وَالأَرْضَ فَرَشْنَاهَا فَنِعْمَ الْمَاهِدُونَ}$$

And the heaven We constructed with strength, and indeed, We are able to expand the vastness of space thereof. And the earth We have spread out [a Firash]; how excellent spreader.

Allah has separated Heaven and Earth by spaces, so Gabriel ascended with the Prophet [sas] from one heaven to the other until they reached the seventh. Almighty Allah raised it in a fabulous way. He says **in Surah an-Nazi'at (79:27-8)** in the form of a question that the creation of Heaven was more difficult than the creation of mankind:

$$\text{أَأَنْتُمْ أَشَدُّ خَلْقًا أَمِ السَّمَاءُ بَنَاهَا - رَفَعَ سَمْكَهَا فَسَوَّاهَا}$$

Are you more difficult to create or is the heaven that He constructed? He raised its ceiling and has perfected it.

Allah [swt] also challenges in **Surah Al-Mulk (67:3)** that nobody will find any flaws in His creation of the Heavens one above the other:

$$\text{الَّذِي خَلَقَ سَبْعَ سَمَوَاتٍ طِبَاقًا مَا تَرَى فِي خَلْقِ الرَّحْمَنِ مِنْ تَفَاوُتٍ فَارْجِعِ الْبَصَرَ هَلْ تَرَى مِنْ فُطُورٍ}$$

Who has created the seven heavens one above the other; you can see no fault in the creation of the Most Gracious. Then look again. Can you see any rifts?

He, glorified be He, raised it without pillars and sustained it with His might. He says in **Surah al-Hajj (22:65):**

$$\text{وَيُمْسِكُ السَّمَاءَ أَنْ تَقَعَ عَلَى الأَرْضِ إِلَّا بِإِذْنِهِ إِنَّ اللَّهَ بِالنَّاسِ لَرَؤُوفٌ رَحِيمٌ}$$

He withholds the heaven from falling on the earth except by His leave. Verily, Allah is for mankind, full of kindness, Most Merciful.

Allah [swt] says in **Surah ar-Ra'd (13:2):**

$$\text{اللَّهُ الَّذِي رَفَعَ السَّمَوَاتِ بِغَيْرِ عَمَدٍ تَرَوْنَهَا}$$

Allah is He Who raised the heavens without any pillars that you can see…Allah has made the cover of the sky protected from devils. He says in **Surah al-Anbiya' (21:32):**

$$\text{وَجَعَلْنَا السَّمَاءَ سَقْفًا مَحْفُوظًا وَهُمْ عَنْ آيَاتِهَا مُعْرِضُونَ}$$

And We have made the heaven a roof, safe and well-guarded. Yet they turn away from its signs.

And in **Surah al-Hijr (15:16-9)** Allah [swt] says how He beautified the Heaven after its creation:

$$وَلَقَدْ جَعَلْنَا فِى السَّمَاءِ بُرُوجًا وَزَيَّنَّاهَا لِلنَّاظِرِينَ - وَحَفِظْنَاهَا مِن كُلِّ شَيْطَنٍ رَّجِيمٍ - إِلَّا مَنِ اسْتَرَقَ السَّمْعَ فَأَتْبَعَهُ شِهَابٌ مُّبِينٌ -$$

$$وَالْأَرْضَ مَدَدْنَاهَا وَأَلْقَيْنَا فِيهَا رَوَاسِيَ وَأَنبَتْنَا فِيهَا مِن كُلِّ شَيْءٍ مَّوْزُونٍ$$

And indeed, We have put the big stars in the heaven and We beautified it for the beholders. And We have guarded it [near heaven] from every outcast Shaytan [devil], except him [devil] who steals the hearing, then he is pursued by a clear flaming fire. And We have spread out the earth, and have placed firm mountains in it, and caused all kinds of things to grow in it, in due proportion.

On the Resurrection Day, Allah will roll up the heavens by His right Hand. In this regard He says in **Surah al-Anbiya' (21:104):**

$$يَوْمَ نَطْوِى السَّمَاءَ كَطَيِّ السِّجِلِّ لِلْكُتُبِ كَمَا بَدَأْنَا أَوَّلَ خَلْقٍ نُّعِيدُهُ وَعْدًا عَلَيْنَا إِنَّا كُنَّا فَاعِلِينَ$$

And [remember] the Day when We shall roll up the heaven like [Sijill] the folding of a [written] sheet for books. As We began the first creation, We will repeat it. [That is] a promise binding upon Us. Indeed, We will do it.

O Muslims! These great decisive verses indicate beyond any doubt that the seven heavens are actual bodies, which are sustained, and no one can approach except by Allah's leave. Do you not know that the Prophet [sas] who is the best among humans and Gabriel who is the best among angels could not enter the heavens during ascension except by Allah's leave? What about other creatures?

O people! How can believers after all these references say that the heavens are developed from the earth or to say that what we see is a limitless space? Whoever believe in this is either ignorant of the revelation or denying it out of arrogance and opposing Allah and His Messenger.

Therefore, whoever denies the creation or the existence of the heavens is denying Allah. As to the earth, it was created seven according to the explicit text of the holy Qur'an and Sunnah of the Prophet [sas].

Allah says in **Surah at-Talaq (65:12):**

$$اللَّهُ الَّذِى خَلَقَ سَبْعَ سَمَوَاتٍ وَمِنَ الْأَرْضِ مِثْلَهُنَّ يَتَنَزَّلُ الْأَمْرُ بَيْنَهُنَّ لِتَعْلَمُوا أَنَّ اللَّهَ عَلَى كُلِّ شَيْءٍ قَدِيرٌ وَأَنَّ اللَّهَ قَدْ أَحَاطَ بِكُلِّ شَيْءٍ عِلْمًا$$

It is Allah Who has created seven heavens and of the earth, the like of them [seven]. [His] command descends among them so you may know that Allah has power over all things and that Allah surrounds all things with [His] knowledge.

The earth is similar to the heavens as being in layers one above the other. The Prophet [sas] is reported to have said: "He who took a span of earth wrongly would be made to wear around his neck seven earths on the Day of Resurrection. (Bukhari, book #43, hadith #632)

May Allah guide us to understand His Book and behave accordingly, and protect us against deviation in words and deeds? **Amin!**

Death: the First Stage of Eternal Life

Death is a very well known fact. It has always been indisputable. No one has ever doubted death, although human beings rarely agree on anything, they have never disagreed on their mortality.

Death is mentioned in the Qur`an almost everywhere. The word *"death"* and its derivatives *"die, dying, dead"* is mentioned more than 160 times in the Qur`an. The Qur'an has put a lot of emphasis on death. Why is it that the Qur`an is consistently reminding the believers about their own mortality while they already take it for granted? To understand why we have to take a close look at the verses that mention death in the Qur`an and reflect upon them? Let us explore some of these verses:

In **Surah al -'Imrân (3:185)**, Allah [swt] says:

كُلُّ نَفْسٍ ذَآئِقَةُ الْمَوْتِ وَإِنَّمَا تُوَفَّوْنَ أُجُورَكُمْ يَوْمَ الْقِيَـٰمَةِ فَمَن زُحْزِحَ عَنِ النَّارِ وَأُدْخِلَ الْجَنَّةَ فَقَدْ فَازَ وَمَا الْحَيَوٰةُ الدُّنْيَا إِلَّا مَتَـٰعُ الْغُرُورِ

Every soul will taste death, and you will only given your [full] on the Day of resurrection. So he who is saved far from the Fire and admitted to Paradise has attained [his desire] of Life . And what is the life of this world except the enjoyment of delusion.

The verse is clear and emphatic. The massage it conveys to us is: Make no mistake about death, it is a foregone conclusion. Every soul shall taste it no matter what.

This verse represents one of the important Tenets of Islam that there is another life after death? Thus, for us death is not the end but just the Start of an ever-lasting life. The other fact stated in this verse with no uncertainty is that the true measure of success is not in this life. Success is not having a huge sum of money, or a large family, or a prestigious job, or an impressive title, or a degree from a respected university, or a big house, or a nice car, all these are nothing but goods of deception. The real success is to be saved from the hell fire and be admitted to paradise. Anything short of this is a mere deception.

In another verse that conveys a similar meaning in **Surah al-Anbiya' (21:35)** is:

كُلُّ نَفْسٍ ذَآئِقَةُ الْمَوْتِ وَنَبْلُوكُم بِالشَّرِّ وَالْخَيْرِ فِتْنَةً وَإِلَيْنَا تُرْجَعُونَ

Every soul will taste death. And We test you with evil and with good as trial; To Us you will be returned.

The message is clear: everyone will die and this life is just many things will test probation on this earth, our faith. There is no escape from death. Allah [swt] says in **Surah an-Nis`a (4:78):**

أَيْنَمَا تَكُونُواْ يُدْرِككُّمُ الْمَوْتُ وَلَوْ كُنتُمْ فِي بُرُوجٍ مُّشَيَّدَةٍ -

Wherever you may be, death will overtake you, even if you are within towers of lofty construction.

No matter how long one lives, nothing will save him/her from death. Strong towers won't save him. Progress of science will never overcome death. Advanced health care systems will never overcome death. Family, friends, money, power, prestige, all are of no avail.

Listen to the following verse of **Surah al-Waqi'ah (56: 83-87)** which describes our helplessness when death comes:

فَلَوْلاَ إِذَا بَلَغَتِ الْحُلْقُومَ - وَأَنتُمْ حِينَئِذٍ تَنظُرُونَ - وَنَحْنُ أَقْرَبُ إِلَيْهِ مِنكُمْ وَلَـكِن لاَّ تُبْصِرُونَ - فَلَوْلاَ إِن كُنتُمْ غَيْرَ مَدِينِينَ - تَرْجِعُونَهَا إِن كُنتُمْ صَادِقِينَ -

Why don't you intervene when the soul of the dying man reaches the throat and you are at that time looking on - and We [Our angels] are nearer to him, but you do not see - Then why do you not, if you are exempt from future account, bring it back [the soul to the body] if you are truthful?

One also finds in the Qur`an many verses which adenosines the believers of their obligations in this life before they die. Allah says in **Surah al-`Imran (3:102):**

يَـأَيُّهَا الَّذِينَ ءَامَنُواْ اتَّقُواْ اللَّهَ حَقَّ تُقَاتِهِ وَلاَ تَمُوتُنَّ إِلاَّ وَأَنتُم مُّسْلِمُونَ -

O you who have believed, fear Allah as He should be feared and do not die except in the state of Islam.

Allah is commanding us not to die except as Muslims. But we are never sure when death will come to us. Therefore, we have to be Muslims all the time. That is, the message is be Muslim today, tomorrow and forever, be Muslim in faith and in behavior, be Muslim in private and in public. Be Muslim with others and with your own self, be Muslim when at ease and be Muslim when in hardship. Always be in a state of Islam, in a state of submission to your Allah, so that when death comes, you will be ready.

Allah is reminding us to watch out: whatever good you might do, does it now, don't delay it, and don't postpone it. If you fail to do good now, it is your mistake, you have already been warned and all the loss will be yours.

Allah says in **Surah al-An'âm (6:61):**

وَهُوَ الْقَاهِرُ فَوْقَ عِبَادِهِ وَيُرْسِلُ عَلَيْكُم حَفَظَةً حَتَّى إِذَا جَاءَ أَحَدَكُمُ الْمَوْتُ تَوَفَّتْهُ رُسُلُنَا وَهُمْ لاَ يُفَرِّطُونَ -

He is the subjugator over His servants, and He sent over you guardian- angels until, when death comes to

you, Our messengers [angels of death] take his soul, and they never fail [in their duties].

There is no doubt that the disbeliever and the hypocrite suffer a greater agony than the believer. This happens when the angels are informing him of the punishment awaiting him, as Allah says in **Surah al -An'âm (6:93):**

وَلَوْ تَرَىٰ إِذِ الظَّالِمُونَ فِي غَمَرَاتِ الْمَوْتِ وَالْمَلَائِكَةُ بَاسِطُوا أَيْدِيهِمْ أَخْرِجُوا أَنفُسَكُمُ الْيَوْمَ تُجْزَوْنَ عَذَابَ الْهُونِ بِمَا كُنتُمْ

تَقُولُونَ عَلَى اللَّهِ غَيْرَ الْحَقِّ وَكُنتُمْ عَنْ آيَاتِهِ تَسْتَكْبِرُونَ

And if you could but see how the wicked are in the agonies of death, while the angels are stretching forth their hands, saying: `Deliver your soul! This day you shall be recompensed with the torment of degradation.

Allah [swt] also said in **Surah Al-An'âm (6:94)**, which means:

وَلَقَدْ جِئْتُمُونَا فُرَادَىٰ كَمَا خَلَقْنَاكُمْ أَوَّلَ مَرَّةٍ وَتَرَكْتُم مَّا خَوَّلْنَاكُمْ وَرَاءَ ظُهُورِكُمْ وَمَا نَرَىٰ مَعَكُمْ شُفَعَاءَكُمُ الَّذِينَ

زَعَمْتُمْ أَنَّهُمْ فِيكُمْ شُرَكَاءُ لَقَد تَّقَطَّعَ بَيْنَكُمْ وَضَلَّ عَنكُم مَّا كُنتُمْ تَزْعُمُونَ

[It will be said to them], "And you have certainly come to US alone [individually] as We created you the first time, and you have left whatever We bestowed upon you behind. And We do not see with you your intercessors which you claimed that they were among you associates [of Allah], it has [all] been severed between you, and lost from you is what you used to claim."

Allah [swt] describes in **Surah al -Mutaffifeen (83:7-9):**

كَلَّا إِنَّ كِتَابَ الْفُجَّارِ لَفِي سِجِّينٍ ۛ وَمَا أَدْرَاكَ مَا سِجِّينٌ ۛ كِتَابٌ مَّرْقُومٌ

No! Indeed, the Record of the wicked is in Sijjeen. And what will make you know what Sijjin is? It is [their destination [the lowest depth of Hell] recorded in] a register inscribed.

[And what will make you know what Sijjin is?] Meaning, it is a great matter, an eternal prison, and a painful torment. Some have said that it is beneath the seventh earth. It has been mentioned in a lengthy Hadith of Al-Bara' bin `Azib that the Prophet said, (Allah says concerning the soul of the disbeliever, `Record his book in Sijjin.' And Sijjin is beneath the seventh earth.)" it is known that the destination of the wicked people will be Hell, and it is the lowest of the low (Tafsir-Ibn-Kathir). Does seventh earth exist? Yes. As Allah (swt) states in **Surah at-Talaq (65:12):**

اللَّهُ الَّذِى خَلَقَ سَبْعَ سَمَوَاتٍ وَمِنَ الْأَرْضِ مِثْلَهُنَّ يَتَنَزَّلُ الْأَمْرُ بَيْنَهُنَّ لِتَعْلَمُوا أَنَّ اللَّهَ عَلَى كُلِّ شَىْءٍ قَدِيرٌ وَأَنَّ اللَّهَ قَدْ أَحَاطَ بِكُلِّ شَىْءٍ عِلْمًا

It is Allah Who has created seven heavens and of the earth, the like of them [seven]. [His] command descends among them so you may know that Allah has power over all things and that Allah surrounds all things with [His] knowledge.

Allah [swt] then says in **Surah al -Mutaffifeen (83:18-21):**

كَلَّا إِنَّ كِتَبَ الْأَبْرَارِ لَفِى عِلِّيِّينَ - وَمَآ أَدْرَاكَ مَا عِلِّيُّونَ كِتَبٌ مَّرْقُومٌ يَشْهَدُهُ الْمُقَرَّبُونَ

No! The record of the righteous is preserved in `Illiyyun. And what can make you know what `Illyyun is? It is [their destination] [the highest elevation of Paradise] recorded in an inscribed.

Ali bin Abi Talhah reported that Ibn `Abbas said concerning Allah's statement,

[كَلَّا إِنَّ كِتَبَ الْأَبْرَارِ لَفِى عِلِّيِّينَ]

**N0! Verily, the Record of Al-Abrar (the righteous believers is in `Illiyyin)** [This means Paradise]. Others besides him have said, "`Iliyyin is located at *Sidrat Al-Muntaha.* The obvious meaning is that the word `Illiyyin is taken from the word `*Uluw*, which means highness. The more something ascends and rises, the more it becomes greater and increases (Tafsir –Ibn- Kathir).

Thus the "*ruh*'s" journey to heaven starts right after death. This happens while the person is lying dead and his family is around him, but they neither hear nor see the process. As if the "*ruh*" of the righteous is on bail unto the day of final judgment. When the dead person is put in the grave, it will embrace him, exerting a pressure on him. The grave will be an embrace from which neither believer nor disbeliever can escape. Afterwards, the believer will be relieved of its pressure while the disbeliever will remain in punishment. When the dead body will be placed in the grave, the "ruh" will be inserted again between the body and the shroud so that questioning can take place. The dead person then will hear the receding footfall of the last person.

The inter space [*Barzakh*] is what separates the world we are living in, from the Eternal Domain which comprises Paradise and Hell. A person who dies is neither in this world nor in the Eternal Domain. He is in the inter space and remains there until the Day of Resurrection. In the inter space, he experiences either happiness or torment. Happiness or torment in the grave is what is meant by happiness or torment in the inter space. Many verses in the Quran show us the reality of punishment in the grave. For example, Allah said in **Surah Ghâfir (40:45-6):**

فَوَقَاهُ اللَّهُ سَيِّئَاتِ مَا مَكَرُوا وَحَاقَ بِالِ فِرْعَوْنَ سُوءُ الْعَذَابِ - النَّارُ يُعْرَضُونَ عَلَيْهَا غُدُوًّا وَعَشِيًّا وَيَوْمَ تَقُومُ السَّاعَةُ أَدْخِلُوا ءَالَ

فِرْعَوْنَ أَشَدَّ الْعَذَابِ

So, Allah protected him from the evils they plotted [against him], and the people of Pharaoh were enveloped by the worst of punishment - The Fire; they are exposed to it morning and evening [from the time of their death until the day of Resurrection, when they will be driven into it]. And on the Day when the Hour will be established [it will be said to the angels]: "Admit the people of Pharaoh into the severest punishment."

Sayedna 'Ali [ra] advised: "Socialize with people in such a way that when you die, they mourn for you; and when you live, they desire your company". No human being is perfect, but every single one has a work in progress. Commit yourself to excellence in everything you do, but do not seek perfection; and have the wisdom to know the difference. Remember that man can attain excellence, while perfection is the domain of the Divine.

Allah clearly indicates in **Surah al-Kahf (18:46)** that only our good deeds are of any avail in the after life:

الْمَالُ وَالْبَنُونَ زِينَةُ الْحَيَوةِ الدُّنْيَا وَالْبَقِيَاتُ الصَّالِحَاتُ خَيْرٌ عِندَرَبِّكَ ثَوَابًا وَخَيْرٌ أَمَلًا

Wealth and children are [but] adornment of the worldly life. But the things that endure, good deeds, are best in the sight of your Creator, as rewards, and best as [the foundation for] hopes.

The dead are made to be lonely after having lived with their families; they live in darkness after having been in the light; in tightness after having lived in wide space, and under the soil after having walked the earth. They become bare-footed, naked and alone. The grave is their dwelling, dust is their shroud, and mortal remains are their neighbours, who cannot hear a call nor respond to it.

Contemplate death, for it prevents one from disobedience, softens a hard heart, stops one from trusting this life and makes one feel ease at the time of hardships. Remember death so that you may be saved at the time of regret.

The Prophet [sas] said, "Do not abuse the dead; for they have gone to meet the consequences of their deeds." (Bukhari, book #23, hadith #476)

O Allah [swt] gives us the proper guidance so that we can die in peace and our soul is placed in "*Illiyun*". O Allah [swt] gives us the fortune not to die without being a Muslim. Forgive all our sins and we ask for your blessings and forgiveness. **Amin!**

Du'aa: Asking for Allah's [swt] Favor

Allah [swt] becomes angry when we abandon asking Him, while the Son of Adam becomes angry, when we ask him for something. Du'aa is the most superior form of worship: "Du'aa is worship", then Prophet [sas] recited the saying of Allah as in **Surah Ghafir (40:60):**

وَقَالَ رَبُّكُمُ ادْعُونِي أَسْتَجِبْ لَكُمْ إِنَّ الَّذِينَ يَسْتَكْبِرُونَ عَنْ عِبَادَتِي سَيَدْخُلُونَ جَهَنَّمَ دَاخِرِينَ

And your Creator said: "Call upon Me; I will respond to you. Indeed, those who scorn My worship they will surely enter Hell in humiliation!"(Abu Dawood, book #8, hadith #1474)

In spite of Allah's having in no need of His creatures; He commanded men and women to make D'uaa [supplicate Him], because they are the ones who are in need of Him as in **Surah Fatir (35:15):**

يَا أَيُّهَا النَّاسُ أَنْتُمُ الْفُقَرَاءُ إِلَى اللَّهِ وَاللَّهُ هُوَ الْغَنِيُّ الْحَمِيدُ

O mankind, you are those in need of Allah, while Allah is the Free of need, worthy of all praise.

In addition, He said in **Surah Muhammad (47:38):**

وَاللَّهُ الْغَنِيُّ وَأَنْتُمُ الْفُقَرَاءُ وَإِنْ تَتَوَلَّوْا يَسْتَبْدِلْ قَوْمًا غَيْرَكُمْ ثُمَّ لَا يَكُونُوا أَمْثَالَكُمْ

Allah is free of needs, while you are the needy. And if you turn away [refuse], He will replace you with another people; then they will not be likes of you.

And also in **Surah Muhammad (47:19)**, Allah [swt] advises Prophet Muhammad [sas] to pray to Allah [swt] for forgiveness and to make duaa for the believers:

فَاعْلَمْ أَنَّهُ لَا إِلَهَ إِلَّا اللَّهُ وَاسْتَغْفِرْ لِذَنْبِكَ وَلِلْمُؤْمِنِينَ وَالْمُؤْمِنَاتِ وَاللَّهُ يَعْلَمُ مُتَقَلَّبَكُمْ وَمَثْوَاكُمْ

So know, [O Muhammad], that there is no deity except Allah, and ask forgiveness for your sin and for the believing men and women. Allah knows of your movement and your resting place.

Of all the 99 beautiful names of Alláh, it is Ar-Rahmán and Ar-Rahím that we use most frequently, in our prayers and du'aas. There is hardly any important thing that a Muslim does, without first invoking these names of Alláh, in saying بِسْمِ اللَّهِ الرَّحْمَنِ الرَّحِيمِ. Ar-Rahmán and Ar-Rahím are both derived from the same Arabic root word Rahma, meaning mercy, compassion. Most of us, unfortunately, take Alláh's mercy and compassion for granted.

But if we stop for a moment, and just reflect on the depth and extent of Alláh's mercy, we will be astonished beyond words.

All life on this planet earth is suspended, precariously, on the thin crust of a huge ball of boiling lava, covered by a thin membrane of oxygen, floating through space, passing deadly showers of meteors and comets and all kinds of deadly radiation. The mind just boggles. Any rock larger than about 1 or 2 miles thick, striking the earth head-on, like the comet Schumacher-Levy that struck Jupiter a few years ago, would wipe out all life on this planet. The scientists and astronomers [some of them claim to be atheists, they don't believe in Allah], they tell us that we living creatures survive on this planet, only by the narrowest of margins. Statistically, the dangers are so great, they say, and the mathematical probabilities of our survival are so small, that we should really not have been here at all! We Muslims as believers would say, that our creation and continued existence on this planet is due entirely to the mercy of Alláh [swt], glorified and exalted is He. The Holy Qur'an makes this point in many beautiful verses. For example, in **Súrah Saba (34:9)** we read:

أَفَلَمْ يَرَوْا إِلَى مَا بَيْنَ أَيْدِيهِمْ وَمَا خَلْفَهُم مِّنَ السَّمَآءِ وَالْأَرْضِ إِن نَّشَأْ نَخْسِفْ بِهِمُ الْأَرْضَ أَوْ نُسْقِطْ عَلَيْهِمْ كِسَفًا مِّنَ السَّمَآءِ إِنَّ فِي ذَلِكَ لَآيَةً لِّكُلِّ عَبْدٍ مُّنِيب.

Then, do they not look what is before them and what is behind them of the heaven and the earth. We could cause the earth to swallow them, or [could] let fall upon them fragments from the sky. Indeed, in that is a sign for every servant turning back [to Allah] in repentance.

In **Surah Fátir (35: 41)** Allah [swt] said:

إِنَّ اللَّهَ يُمْسِكُ السَّمَوَاتِ وَالْأَرْضَ أَن تَزُولَا وَلَئِن زَالَتَا إِنْ أَمْسَكَهُمَا مِنْ أَحَدٍ مِّن بَعْدِهِ إِنَّهُ كَانَ حَلِيمًا غَفُورًا.

Indeed, Allah holds the heavens and the earth, lest they cease. And if they should cease, no one could hold them [in place] after Him. Indeed, He is Most Forbearing and Forgiving.

And further in the same surah (45):

وَلَوْ يُؤَاخِذُ اللَّهُ النَّاسَ بِمَا كَسَبُوا مَا تَرَكَ عَلَى ظَهْرِهَا مِن دَآبَّةٍ وَلَكِن يُؤَخِّرُهُمْ إِلَى أَجَلٍ مُّسَمًّى فَإِذَا جَآءَ أَجَلُهُمْ فَإِنَّ اللَّهَ كَانَ بِعِبَادِهِ بَصِيرًا.

And if Allah were to punish men for what they have earned, He would not leave upon it [the earth] any creature. But He defers them for an appointed term. And when their term comes, then indeed, Allah has ever been, of His servants, seeing.

How do we become worthy of Alláh's [swt] Mercy? We become worthy of His Mercy when we begin that long journey from doing what pleases us, to doing what pleases Alláh [swt]. We should also remember, that part of

Alláh's [swt] mercy, is that he is very patient with our shortcomings. We all have many faults, but Alláh's anger does not just descend on us like a bolt of lightning, as soon as we step out of line. He always gives us time, lots of time, to recognize the error of our ways, and to put things right, to ask for mercy.

In the same way, we must not be impatient with others. We must also show mercy, wherever we have power and authority. This is especially towards our wives and our children. We expect Alláh's mercy and patience for ourselves. Why then we should not show mercy and patience for others, especially our women and children? Allah's Apostle said, "When Allah completed the Creation, He wrote in His Book which is with Him on His Throne, "My Mercy overpowers My Anger." (Bukhari, book #54, hadith #416)

Also Allah [swt] has told His Prophet [sas] that He is nearby and answers the prayers of any supplicant who calls Him. He said in **Surah al-Baqarah (2:186):**

وَ إِذَا سَأَلَكَ عِبَادِي عَنِّي فَإِنِّي قَرِيبٌ أُجِيبُ دَعْوَةَ الدَّاعِ إِذَا دَعَانِ فَلْيَسْتَجِيبُوا لِي وَلْيُؤْمِنُوا بِي لَعَلَّهُمْ يَرْشُدُونَ-

And when My servants ask you [O Muhammad], concerning Me – then indeed I am near. I respond to the invocations of the supplicant when he calls upon Me [without any mediator or intercessor]. So let them respond to Me [by obedience] and believe in Me that they may be [rightly] guided.

Those who associate partners with Him, such as idols, tombs, the dead people in tombs, saints, etc., like the grave-worshippers do now-a-days by seeking refuge with the dead - Allah does not answer their supplications because they have gone far away from Him and broken off their relationship with Him. When they supplicate to Allah in times of adversity, they will never be answered.

Du'aas are not automatically accepted by Allah [swt]. Among the main reasons for Du'aas not being accepted is the use of unlawful food, drink and clothing [bought out of unlawful income]. Abu Huraira reported, Allah's Messenger [sas] as saying: "0 people, Allah is good and He, therefore, accepts only that which is good". And Allah commanded the believers as He commanded the Messengers by saying, "O Messengers, eat of the good things, and do good deeds; verily I am aware of what you do" (Surah23: 51). And He said: "0 those who believe, eat of the good things that We gave you" (Surah al-Baqarah, 2:172) He then made a mention of a person who travels widely, his hair disheveled and covered with dust. He lifts his hand towards the sky (and thus makes the supplication): "O Lord, 0 Lord" whereas his diet is unlawful, his drink is unlawful, and his clothes are unlawful and his nourishment is unlawful. How can then his supplication be accepted? (Muslim, book #005, hadith #2214)

O people, be aware of ourselves and review the sources of our livelihood, food and drink so that Allah may answer our Du'aa and invocations. The Du'aa may not be answered if the servant is disobeying or ignoring Allah's commands and obligations upon him, committing sins and doing what has been forbidden. In the above-mentioned Hadith, the Prophet [sws] indicates that the enjoyment of unlawful food, drink or clothing is the greatest reason preventing the acceptance of Du'aa.

Also, among the reasons of the non-acceptance of Du'aa 'is insincerity in supplication: Allah [swt] said in **Surah Ghafir (40:14):**

فَادْعُوا اللَّهَ مُخْلِصِينَ لَهُ الدِّينَ وَلَوْ كَرِهَ الْكَافِرُونَ-

So, call you upon Allah, [being] sincere to Him in religion, although the disbelievers dislike it.

Whoever fears Allah and obeys Him in prosperity, Allah will relieve his affliction and fade away his sorrow during calamity. As Allah said concerning His Prophet Yunus [as], when the whale swallowed him in **Surah as-Saffat (37:143-144):**

فَلَوْلَا أَنَّهُ كَانَ مِنَ الْمُسَبِّحِينَ-لَلَبِثَ فِي بَطْنِهِ إِلَى يَوْمِ يُبْعَثُونَ-

And had he not been of those who glorify Allah, He would have remained inside its belly [the fish] until the Day they are resurrected.

Negligence in advocating good actions and forbidding evil acts is surely one of the causes of the no acceptance of Du'aa. The Prophet [sas] said: "Your Lord – blessed and elevated He is – is shy and generous. He is shy from His servant to raise his hands to Him and turn them away empty and disappointed." [Sunan al-Tirmidhî (3556)]

Islam is a Mercy which Allah the Rabb [Cherisher and Sustainer] of the worlds bestows only to whom He likes. We Muslims must thank and praise Allah for guiding us to Islam. As part of Allah's divine guidance, we read in the Qur'an the following brief but comprehensive supplication for a well-balanced life in **Surah al-Baqarah (2:201):**

رَبَّنَا آتِنَا فِي الدُّنْيَا حَسَنَةً وَفِي الْآخِرَةِ حَسَنَةً وَقِنَا عَذَابَ النَّارِ-

Our Sustainer, Give us in this world [that which is] good and in the Hereafter [that which is] good, and protect us from the punishment of Fire.

We Muslims want to be successful and happy in the eternal world. We will not only enjoy all the blessings of Paradise but above all reap Allah's supreme reward and that is to be able to see Allah [swt], our Creator and Sustainer. As Allah [swt] said in **Surah at-Tawbah (9:72):**

وَعَدَ اللَّهُ الْمُؤْمِنِينَ وَالْمُؤْمِنَاتِ جَنَّاتٍ تَجْرِي مِنْ تَحْتِهَا الْأَنْهَارُ خَالِدِينَ فِيهَا وَمَسَاكِنَ طَيِّبَةً فِي جَنَّاتِ عَدْنٍ وَرِضْوَانٌ مِنَ اللَّهِ أَكْبَرُ

ذَلِكَ هُوَ الْفَوْزُ الْعَظِيمُ

Allah has promised the believing -- men and women, gardens under which rivers flow, to dwell therein forever, and beautiful mansions in gardens of perpetual residence; but approval from Allah is greater. It is that which the great attainment is.

There are elements that make the Du'aa to be answered:

I. Reason related to the one making Du'aa, or a state in which he is in that makes him more likely to be answered include: the just ruler, the fasting person until breaking the fast, and the supplication of the oppressed person.

II. A Reason related to the Du'aa itself; meaning the etiquettes of Du'aa are adhered to so that the Du'aa may be perfected: 1) begin by praising Allah and sending prayers and blessings upon Rasulullah [sas]; 2. End your Du'aa with praise of Allah and prayers upon Rasulullah [sas].

III. Some special times when Du'aa is most likely to be answered: 1) Standing at mount Arafat [part of Hajj]; 2) Lailatul Qadr; 3) Friday after Asr till Maghrib; 4) When a fasting person breaks his fast; 5) Before drinking Zam-Zam; 6) Right after Salah [prayer]; 7) In sujood [prostrations].

Supplications can be made in supplicates own mother tongue. But it is better to make supplication by reciting duaas mentioned in the Holy Quran in Arabic because those are the duaas the prophets used, and those are in Allah's language. Supplications for disbelievers and hypocrites are prohibited even they are among the parents.

Let us pray to Alláh [swt] May His mercy descend into our homes and in our hearts Insh-Alláh. May we all show greater mercy and compassion to one another, especially to those over whom we have some authority. May Alláh guide our leaders to show mercy to their citizens, our employers to their workers, our parents to their children? And May He reward us all, according to the best of our deeds that is the supreme success. **Amin!**

Effects of Sin

It is essential to know that sins and acts of disobedience are, necessarily, very harmful. Their harmful effects upon the heart are akin to the harmful effects of poison upon the body, though the effects vary in their levels and intensities. So is there any evil or harm in this world, or in the Hereafter, except that it is due to sins and disobedience?

What caused the destruction with a single overwhelming punishment as happened to 'Aad, when they were destroyed by the violent wind which He unleashed upon them for seven nights and eight days in succession so that they were left lying like the hollow trunks of palm trees? What was it that caused the piercing shrieks to be set loose upon the Thamood people who were seized by the terrible shout and the earthquake so that they lay prostrate corpses in their homes such that their hearts were severed within their very bodies, by which they all perished? What was it that caused the town of the homosexuals to be raised up and turned upside down, such that they were all destroyed during the time of Lut [as]? Then stones from the sky pelted down upon them so that they suffered a combined punishment, the like of which was not given to any other nation! What was it that caused the Pharaoh and his people to be drowned in the ocean, and caused their souls to be transported to the Hellfire, so their bodies drowned and their souls burned? What was it that caused Qaaroon, his dwelling, wealth and family to sink down into the earth? What was it that caused the destruction of those generations after Noah, and how they were afflicted with various punishments that caused their annihilation?

All these punishments were because of their denying the creator Allah [swt] and for not believing and listening to the advices of the prophets sent to them. As Allah [swt] says in **Surah Luqman (31:13):**

$$\text{وَإِذْ قَالَ لُقْمَانُ لِابْنِهِ وَهُوَ يَعِظُهُ يَا بُنَيَّ لَا تُشْرِكْ بِاللَّهِ إِنَّ الشِّرْكَ لَظُلْمٌ عَظِيمٌ}$$

And [mention, O Muhammad], when Luqman said to his son when he was instructing him: "O my son! Do not associate [anything] with Allah. Indeed, association [with Him] is a great Zulm [injustice]." The greatest of all sins is disbelief in Allah [swt] and joining others as partner in His worship.

Allah [swt] also says in **Surah an-Nisa' (4:79):**

$$\text{مَا أَصَابَكَ مِنْ حَسَنَةٍ فَمِنَ اللَّهِ وَمَا أَصَابَكَ مِنْ سَيِّئَةٍ فَمِنْ نَفْسِكَ}$$

What comes to you of good is from Allah, but what comes to you of evil, [O man], is from yourself.

Whatever good comes upon us - blessing or security - it is from Allah, it is He who provided that, its beginning and end, from his beneficence. It is He who granted us from his bounty that we should carry out that which would lead to it, and it is He who granted us His blessing and completed that for us. Many people today attribute the misfortunes that befall them, whether relating to wealth and economics, or security and political affairs to purely materialistic causes.

Behind these reasons are causes prescribed as such by Allah [swt]. However the material reasons may be a means of bringing about what is due to the causes prescribed by Allah that necessitates the misfortune and punishment. Allah, the Mighty and Majestic say in **Surah ar-Rum (30:41)**:

ظَهَرَ الْفَسَادُ فِى الْبَرِّ وَالْبَحْرِ بِمَا كَسَبَتْ أَيْدِى النَّاسِ لِيُذِيقَهُمْ بَعْضَ الَّذِى عَمِلُوا لَعَلَّهُمْ يَرْجِعُونَ ٠

Corruption [sins and disobedience of Allah] has appeared through the land and sea [by reason of] what the hands of people have earned [by oppression and evil deeds etc.] so Allah may let them taste part of [the consequence] what they have done perhaps they will return [by repenting to Allah].

O, Muslims! Allah, from His Wisdom and his Mercy, punishes this nation for its sins and disobedience by setting some part of it upon the others so that they destroy one another and take each other prisoner. Allah, the Mighty and Majestic, says in **Surah al-An'am (6:65)**:

قُلْ هُوَ الْقَادِرُ عَلَى أَن يَبْعَثَ عَلَيْكُمْ عَذَابًا مِّن فَوْقِكُمْ أَوْ مِن تَحْتِ أَرْجُلِكُمْ أَوْ يَلْبِسَكُمْ شِيَعًا وَيُذِيقَ بَعْضَكُم بَأْسَ بَعْضٍ انظُرْ كَيْفَ نُصَرِّفُ الْآيَتِ لَعَلَّهُمْ يَفْقَهُونَ ٠

Say: "He is the [one] able to send upon you affliction from above you or from beneath your feet or to confuse you [so you become] sects [following your inclination rather than the truth, biased and hostile towards each other] and make you taste the violence of one another. Look how We diversify the signs that they may understand."

It is also reported by Sa'd ibn Abee Waqqaas, on the authority of his father that one day Allah's Messenger [may peace be upon him] came from a high land. He passed by the mosque of Banu Mu'awiya, went in and observed two rak'ahs there and we also observed prayer along with him and he made a long supplication to his Lord. He then came to us and said: I asked my Lord three things and He has granted me two but has withheld one. I begged my Lord that my Ummah should not be destroyed because of famine and He granted me this. And I begged my Lord that my Ummah should not be destroyed by drowning [by deluge] and He granted me this. And I begged my Lord that there should be no bloodshed among the people of my Ummah. But He did not grant it. (Muslim, book #41, hadith #6906) .

Sins are results of activities that people do by refusing what Allah [swt] told us not to do, and not doing those that Allah [swt] advised us to do. There are some people who doubt and seek to cause doubts that sins are a cause of misfortunes, and that is because of the weakness of their Iman and their negligence in reflecting upon the book of Allah as He says in **Surah al-Ar'af (7:96-9)**:

وَلَوْ أَنَّ أَهْلَ الْقُرَى ءَامَنُوا وَاتَّقَوا لَفَتَحْنَا عَلَيْهِم بَرَكَتٍ مِّنَ السَّمَاءِ وَالأَرْضِ وَلَكِن كَذَّبُوا فَأَخَذْنَـٰهُم بِمَا كَانُوا يَكْسِبُونَ - أَفَأَمِنَ

أَهْلُ الْقُرَى أَن يَأْتِيَهُم بَأْسُنَا بَيَـٰتًا وَهُمْ نَائِمُونَ - أَوَ أَمِنَ أَهْلُ الْقُرَى أَن يَأْتِيَهُم بَأْسُنَا ضُحًى وَهُمْ يَلْعَبُونَ - أَفَأَمِنُوا مَكْرَ اللَّهِ فَلاَ يَأْمَنُ

مَكْرَ اللَّهِ إِلاَّ الْقَوْمُ الْخَـٰسِرُونَ -

And if only the people of the cities had believed and feared Allah, We would have opened [bestowed] upon them blessings from the heavens and the earth; but they belied [the messengers], So We seized them [with punishment] for what they were earning [polytheism and crimes etc]. Then did the people of the cities feel secure from Our punishment coming to them at night while they were asleep? Or did the people of the cities feel secure from Our punishment coming to them in the morning while they are at play? Then did they feel secure from the plan of Allah? But no one feels secure from the plan of Allah except the loosing people.

Sins affect the security of a land; they affect its prosperity, economy and also the hearts of its people. Sins cause alienation between the people. Sins cause one Muslim to regard his Muslim brother as enemy. But if we sought to rectify ourselves, our families, our neighbors and those in our areas, and everyone we are able to rectify , if we mutually encourage good and forbade evil, if we assist those who do this with wisdom and wise admonition then it would produce unity and harmony.

The Prophet [sas] said, "Avoid the seven great destructive sins." They [the people!] asked, "O Allah's Apostle! What are they" He said, "To join partners in worship with Allah; to practice sorcery; to kill the life which Allah has forbidden except for a just cause [according to Islamic law]; to eat up usury [Riba], to eat up the property of an orphan; to give one's back to the enemy and freeing from the battle-field at the time of fighting and to accuse chaste women who never even think of anything touching chastity and are good believers." (Bukhari, book #82, hadith #840) The Messenger of Allah [sas] said: 'The curse of Allah be upon the one who gives a bribe and the one who accepts it." (Ibn Maajah, 2313)

Allah [swt] says in **Surah an-Nisa (4:31):**

إِن تَجْتَنِبُوا كَبَآئِرَ مَا تُنْهَوْنَ عَنْهُ نُكَفِّرْ عَنكُمْ سَيِّئَاتِكُمْ وَنُدْخِلْكُم مُّدْخَلاً كَرِيما -

If you avoid the major sins which you are forbidden, We shall remove from you your [small] sins, and admit you to a noble entrance [into Paradise.]

From among the teachings of Allah's Messenger [sas] is to keep sins a secret matter. If someone commits a sinful act that is against the Commandments of Allah, or is against the moral character, or is such an act that may cause harm to one's honor, then he should keep it a secret and seek forgiveness from Allah in the darkness of night. The Prophet used to invoke Allah at night, saying, "O Allah: All the Praises are for You: You are the Lord of the Heavens and the Earth. All the Praises are for You; You are the Maintainer of the Heaven and the Earth and whatever is in them. All the Praises are for You; You are the Light of the Heavens and the Earth. Your Word is the Truth, and Your Promise is the Truth, and the Meeting with You is the Truth, and Paradise is the Truth, and the [Hell] Fire is the Truth, and the Hour is the Truth. O Allah! I surrender myself to You, and I believe in You and I depend upon You, and I repent to You and with You [Your evidences] I stand against my opponents, and to you I leave the judgment [for those who refuse my message]. O Allah! Forgive me my sins that I did in the past or will do in the future, and also the sins I did in secret or in public. You are my only God [Whom I worship] and there is no other God for me [i.e. I worship none but You]." (Bukhari, book #93, hadith #482)

Allah [swt] says in **Surah an-Nisa (4:111-2):**

وَمَن يَكۡسِبۡ إِثۡمًا فَإِنَّمَا يَكۡسِبُهُۥ عَلَىٰ نَفۡسِهِۦ وَكَانَ ٱللَّهُ عَلِيمًا حَكِيمًا - وَمَن يَكۡسِبۡ خَطِيٓئَةً أَوۡ إِثۡمًا ثُمَّ يَرۡمِ بِهِۦ بَرِيٓئًا فَقَدِ ٱحۡتَمَلَ

بُهۡتَـٰنًا وَإِثۡمًا مُّبِينًا -

And whoever earns [commits] a sin only earns it against him. And Allah is Ever All-Knowing, All-Wise. But whoever earns an offense or a sin and then blames it on an innocent [person] has taken upon him a slander and manifest sin.

Exposing sins lead to humiliation and embarrassment, which ceases the possibility that the sinner might someday regret his mistake, seek forgiveness from Allah and purify his soul from sins because one of the things that prevent one from committing sins is the fear of humiliation. However, if the sinner knows that the people are already aware of his sins, then he does not experience the shame and distraction that he used to feel before and this might encourage him to commit sins openly!

Secondly, when sins are repeatedly mentioned in gatherings, etc. the fear of committing sins vanishes from the people's hearts. First the sin will become easy on people's tongue and gradually he, who does not feel any shame in mentioning the sin, will not find it difficult to even commit the sin. This is how, sins spread in the society!

So, if someone becomes aware of his brother's sins and realizes that nobody except him has seen him committing the sin, then he should keep the sin a secret. He should not encourage people towards sins by exposing his faults. Allah, the Exalted, has not only condemned committing sins in the Qur'an but He has also condemned those people who mention sins in public. He said in **Surah an-Nur (24:19):**

إِنَّ ٱلَّذِينَ يُحِبُّونَ أَن تَشِيعَ ٱلۡفَـٰحِشَةُ فِى ٱلَّذِينَ ءَامَنُوا۟ لَهُمۡ عَذَابٌ أَلِيمٌ فِى ٱلدُّنۡيَا وَٱلۡـَٔاخِرَةِ وَٱللَّهُ يَعۡلَمُ وَأَنتُمۡ لَا تَعۡلَمُونَ -

Indeed, those who like that immorality [unlawful sexual relations] should be circulated have [publicized] among those who believed will have a painful punishment in this world and the Hereafter. And Allah knows and you do not know.

Allah [swt] says in **Surah an-Nisa (4:148):**

لاَّ يُحِبُّ اللَّهُ الْجَهْرَ بِالسُّوءِ مِنَ الْقَوْلِ إِلاَّ مَن ظُلِمَ -

Allah does not like the public mention of evil except by one who has been wronged.

Today sins have become widespread in the society because we have forgotten the teachings of Allah's Messenger [sas] who discouraged people from revealing one's mistakes and sins as well as others. As a result, people have lost the fear of committing not only minor sins but even major sins - moreover, we find people proudly attributing sins to them!!

Today, there are also many novel channels through which sins are propagated in the society; like such book, magazines and television programs that mention the crimes of others, illicit acts, and immorality under the name of creating awareness among the people. These programs that are meant to help the people against the crimes are in reality, helping the crime to spread fast in the society! Crimes which were previously unknown to people have become common offense! It is therefore necessary for the Muslims to avoid all such avenues which may lead to the destruction of our Muslim Ummah.

We ask Allah (swt) to turn the misguided of this Ummah back to guidance, and that He makes us all to support one another and aid one another in carrying out good and righteousness until we return to this Ummah its lost glory and honor, Indeed He is fully able and having the power to do that. **Amin!**

Existence of Allah: Myth or Reality

We believe in science and knowledge because some orderliness which we perceived in the artifacts [a building, scientific discovery] forces us to recognize the knowledge of their constructors. Now let us consider the construction and work modules of the latest devices of cellular phones.

For the cell phones to work, we make use of electricity, magnetism, infrared radiations, and ultra - violet phenomenon. We cannot see light, the magnetic effects, infrared or ultra-violet radiations. But in the absence of any of these, cell phones will not work. We can feel their existence through each of their effects. So cell phones are not creations because materials that are used in cell phones existed before, they only changed the form of the existing materials, and it is created.

In our worldly life, the architect or the designers on the basis of his imagination design something, but they are not necessarily the implementer of his design. Somebody else work out on the basis of the design. But in the case of the creation of this universe, the architect/ designer, the planner, and the implementer is the same, Allah [the best designer and the creator].

Intelligence is not something visible or audible in the sense that man can see it or hear it. But, in fact, although it is intangible, every one finds it in him/her in addition to the powers of the sight and hearing and other external faculties. Moreover, people can construct in their imagination any form of objects and things they wish. All the materials for the imagined things are made by the one who imagined it. But they remain in our minds as long as we want them to, and when we forget about them they become nothing again.

This is the condition of the entire universe of creation. If Allah ceased which is completely from Allah, created by Him, and in no way independent. It is always in need of the creator Allah. Also, if Allah ceases to will its existence, it will return to nothings.

Love, hate, determination are not visible or tangible things which can be perceived through the external senses. Again, life is not an object of the senses. We discover its existence through movements, feeding etc. [from effects we discover the existence]. Thus we can deduce that there can be no effect without a cause, nothing orderly without wise and knowledgeable designer.

It is not right for us to reject something which we do not see because it is not visible, because, being not visible is different from not existing, and the way of discovering something is not confined to the eyes or other external senses.

Allah [the Guardian] is an unlimited being Who possess every perfection, and is free from all imperfections. Allah is a creator, not created. Now the question is - does Allah [the most Exalted] exist? Let us see what Allah [the Most Gracious] says in the Holy book Quran the way to feel His existence in **Surah al-Isra' (17:36):**

وَلَا تَقْفُ مَا لَيْسَ لَكَ بِهِ عِلْمٌ إِنَّ السَّمْعَ وَالْبَصَرَ وَالْفُؤَادَ كُلُّ أُولَٰئِكَ كَانَ عَنْهُ مَسْؤُولًا

And do not pursue [do not assume or do not say] that of which you have no knowledge. Indeed, the hearing, and the sight, and the heart – about those entire one will be questioned [by Allah].

And He warns in **Surah al-A'raf (7:179):**

وَلَقَدْ ذَرَأْنَا لِجَهَنَّمَ كَثِيرًا مِّنَ الْجِنِّ وَالْإِنسِ لَهُمْ قُلُوبٌ لَّا يَفْقَهُونَ بِهَا وَلَهُمْ أَعْيُنٌ لَّا يُبْصِرُونَ بِهَا وَلَهُمْ ءَاذَانٌ لَّا يَسْمَعُونَ بِهَا أُوْلَئِكَ كَالْأَنْعَامِ بَلْ هُمْ أَضَلُّ أُوْلَئِكَ هُمُ الْغَافِلُونَ

And We have certainly created for Hell many of the Jinn and mankind. They have hearts, with which they do not understand, and they have eyes with which they do not see, and they have ears with which they do not hear [the truth]. Those are like livestock; rather they are more astray. It is they who are the heedless.

Allah [the Most High] tells us the purpose behind the creation of Jinn and mankind in **Surah adh-Dhariyat (51:56)** as:

وَمَا خَلَقْتُ الْجِنَّ وَالْإِنسَ إِلَّا لِيَعْبُدُونِ

And I did not create the Jinn and mankind except to worship Me.

Once again, the chronology of our creation has been described as follows in **Surah al-A'raf (7: 172):**

وَإِذْ أَخَذَ رَبُّكَ مِن بَنِي ءَادَمَ مِن ظُهُورِهِمْ ذُرِّيَّتَهُمْ وَأَشْهَدَهُمْ عَلَى أَنفُسِهِمْ أَلَسْتُ بِرَبِّكُمْ قَالُوا بَلَى شَهِدْنَا أَن تَقُولُوا يَوْمَ الْقِيَامَةِ إِنَّا كُنَّا عَنْ هَذَا غَافِلِينَ

And [mention] when your Lord took from the Children of Adam - from their loins – their descendents and made them testify of themselves, [saying to them], "Am I not your Lord?" They said: "Yes, We have testified." [This] - Lest you should say on the Day of Resurrection, "Indeed, we were of the unaware."

Allah (The Perfectly Wise) reminds us that we testified ourselves that Allah is our creator.

Allah (the Best Creator) reminds us the process of our creation in **Surah al-Mu'minun (23: 12-16):**

وَلَقَدْ خَلَقْنَا الْإِنسَانَ مِن سُلَالَةٍ مِّن طِينٍ ثُمَّ جَعَلْنَاهُ نُطْفَةً فِي قَرَارٍ مَّكِينٍ ثُمَّ خَلَقْنَا النُّطْفَةَ عَلَقَةً فَخَلَقْنَا الْعَلَقَةَ مُضْغَةً فَخَلَقْنَا الْمُضْغَةَ عِظَامًا فَكَسَوْنَا الْعِظَامَ لَحْمًا ثُمَّ أَنشَأْنَاهُ خَلْقًا ءَاخَرَ فَتَبَارَكَ اللَّهُ أَحْسَنُ الْخَالِقِينَ ثُمَّ إِنَّكُم بَعْدَ ذَلِكَ لَمَيِّتُونَ ثُمَّ إِنَّكُمْ يَوْمَ الْقِيَامَةِ تُبْعَثُونَ

And indeed We created man out of an extract of Tin [clay]. Then We placed him as a sperm-drop [as a zygote] in a firm lodging [the womb]. Then We made the sperm-drop into a clinging clot, then We made the clot into a little lump [of flesh], and We made [from] the lump, bones, and We clothed the bones with flesh; and then We developed him into another creation. So Blessed is Allah, the best of creators [the most skillful and only true creator]. Then indeed, after that you have to die. Then indeed [again] you will be resurrected on the Day of Resurrection.

And once again in **Surah Ghafir (40:67)** as:

هُوَ الَّذِى خَلَقَكُم مِّن تُرَابٍ ثُمَّ مِن نُّطْفَةٍ ثُمَّ مِنْ عَلَقَةٍ ثُمَّ يُخْرِجُكُمْ طِفْلاً ثُمَّ لِتَبْلُغُوا أَشُدَّكُمْ ثُمَّ لِتَكُونُوا شُيُوخاً وَمِنكُم مَّن

يُتَوَفَّى مِن قَبْلُ وَلِتَبْلُغُوا أَجَلاً مُّسَمًّى وَلَعَلَّكُمْ تَعْقِلُونَ - هُوَ الَّذِى يُحْىِ وَيُمِيتُ فَإِذَا قَضَى أَمْراً فَإِنَّمَا يَقُولُ لَهُ كُن فَيَكُونُ

It is He Who has created you from dust, then from a sperm-drop, then from a clinging clot [a piece of coagulated blood]; then He brings you out as an infant; then [He develops you] that you reach your [time of] maturity,, and then [further] that you become elders. And among you is He who is taken in death before [that], so that you reach a specified term [time decreed for your death]; and perhaps you will use reason."

And also in **Surah al-Infitar (82:7-8):**

الَّذِى خَلَقَكَ فَسَوَّاكَ فَعَدَلَكَ - فِى أَىِّ صُورَةٍ مَّا شَاءَ رَكَّبَكَ

Who created you, proportioned you, and balanced you? In whatever form He willed has He assembled you.

Life is not an object of senses, we only perceive the effects of it which are movement, and eating, etc. are from these effects we discover its existence.

The body of a human being is a like a building. It is composed of small building blocks called cells, each of which is itself a living entity. Each cell, therefore, is alive, and its nourishment, digestion, absorption, elimination and reproduction, for example, are as in other organisms, and are perfectly carried out. The number of cells in human body is about 10^{16} which is equivalent to ten thousand, million, million. Blood, with the help of heart, performs the duty of supplying nourishment to the cells, absorbs poisonous substances which have accumulated there and returns to the heart with a dull color.Our heart works round the clock – 35 millions of beats (lub dub) a year – for as long as we live, without ever taking a rest. The heart delivers it to the lungs, a filtering apparatus for the blood, whereupon it is resupplied to the whole body with a bright color and greater freshness. While passing through the kidneys, another part of the poisonous matters are removed, so that no kind of disturbance arises in the general working of the body. The blood in our body is produced from the food and drink we consume through the digestive apparatus set inside, and the waste products are removed from the body through a built in mechanism sewerage system. No doubt, it is a plan of a perfect and superior designer and creator.

Now imagine if our heads are placed where it is, but the mouth was in the back side of the head; or our arms and legs were interchanged, how we had been looked like? What would have happened to us? That would have been undue proportions.

The wonderful design and orderliness which is observed in the brains, the nerves, the digestive system, the heart, the eyes, the ears and thousands of other examples constitute complete evidence and a living proof that the world of creation has a wise and powerful designer and creator, and whatever attracts our attention among the secrets of the way the creation [who raised up the heavens without pillars, subjected the sun and the moon each one running to a term stated] is arranged, permits us to become more aware of the greatness of the creator. Allah [the Magnificent Creator] states in the Holy Book **Surah al- An`am (6:59):**

وَعِندَهُ مَفَاتِحُ الْغَيْبِ لَا يَعْلَمُهَا إِلَّا هُوَ وَيَعْلَمُ مَا فِي الْبَرِّ وَالْبَحْرِ وَمَا تَسْقُطُ مِن وَرَقَةٍ إِلَّا يَعْلَمُهَا وَلَا حَبَّةٍ فِي ظُلُمَاتِ الْأَرْضِ وَلَا

رَطْبٍ وَلَا يَابِسٍ إِلَّا فِي كِتَابٍ مُّبِينٍ

And with Him are the keys of the unseen; none knows them except Him. And He knows what is on the land and in the sea. Not a leaf falls but that He knows it. And no grain in the darkness of the earth and no moist or dry [thing] but it is [written] in a clear record.

In developing the system of communication, we see the use from tiny screws to big studios, and big towers. The world of creation thus owes its existence to variety, and if there had not been any variety there would not have been any universe, there would have been one big uniformity. It was this variety that brought into existence atoms, molecules, solar systems, galaxies, trees, plants and animals. In the creation of plants, animals, and insects; we see ants, elephants, from tiny to big trees. Diversity in man is not an exception to this general principle of variety in its creation.

Those who find difficulty in understanding the creation of things, and ask why Allah has not created all people equal and without distinction, and why He does not behave towards everyone with equal measure, and imagine that Allah's justice has been proved to non-existent and completely imaginary have not understood the real meaning of justice. If Allah does not create anyone at all, or if He distinguishes between beings, nobody's rights have been violated so that we can say there is injustice.

If human beings were created uniform, there would have been a chaos in running the worldly affairs – no division of labor would have been possible. No one would have the power to rule or order the others, resulting in a chaos. Thus Allah [the Wise] has created human beings in classes: rich, poor, powerful and powerless. Alongside Allah [the Just] has warned us not to do any sort of injustice to anybody. Moreover, Allah [the Resurrect or] has made it mandatory to help and be kind and helpful to those who are poor, disadvantaged, orphans in the religion of Islam. Allah [the Most Gracious], thus, will not make people accountable on the day of Final Judgment those who does not have sufficient wealth to give Zakat and perform Hajj [the two of the five pillars of Islam].

Another point to notice is that Allah demands from everyone according to his ability and responsibility, and no-one is asked do more than his bodily and mental powers. This is justice itself.

Allah [The Most Kind] assures that He will not make us accountable for anything beyond our power and capacity of which He is very much aware of on the day of final judgment in **Surah al-Baqarah (2:286)** as:

$$لَا يُكَلِّفُ اللَّهُ نَفْسًا إِلَّا وُسْعَهَا$$

Allah does not charge a soul except [with that within] its capacity.

Islam is the continuation of the teaching of previous Prophets, some of whom were also given divine books. Muslims believe that the message brought by all prophets was the same, to believe in one Allah [God], and not to associate partners with Him, to remind us of what we have testified, and stay away from wrong doings [sins] and to lead a life devoted to earning Allah's pleasure. All Prophets taught about life after death, and gave glad tidings of Paradise for those who obey Allah, but warned of severe punishment in Hell for those who choose to disobey Him.

Allah [The All-Aware] advises the Prophet not to be disappointed when people fail to respond to his call to believe Allah [the Mightiest] and do good deeds in **Surah al-Ma'idah (5:41)** as:

$$يَا أَيُّهَا الرَّسُولُ لَا يَحْزُنكَ الَّذِينَ يُسَارِعُونَ فِي الْكُفْرِ مِنَ الَّذِينَ قَالُوا آمَنَّا بِأَفْوَاهِهِمْ وَلَمْ تُؤْمِن قُلُوبُهُمْ$$

O Messenger! Let them not grieve you who hasten into disbeliefs of those who say, "We believe" with their mouths, but their hearts believe not.

Allah [the Creator] describes in **Surah al-An`am (6:101)** that:

$$بَدِيعُ السَّمَاوَاتِ وَالْأَرْضِ أَنَّى يَكُونُ لَهُ وَلَدٌ وَلَمْ تَكُن لَّهُ صَاحِبَةٌ وَخَلَقَ كُلَّ شَيْءٍ وَهُوَ بِكُلِّ شَيْءٍ عَلِيمٌ$$

He is the Badi` [Originator/creator] of the heavens and the earth. How could He have a son when He does not have a companion [wife] and He created all things? And He is, of all things, knowing.

And again in **Surah al-Ma'idah (5:120)** says:

$$لِّلَّهِ مُلْكُ السَّمَاوَاتِ وَالْأَرْضِ وَمَا فِيهِنَّ وَهُوَ عَلَى كُلِّ شَيْءٍ قَدِيرٌ$$

To Allah belongs the dominion of the heavens and the earth and whatever is within them. And He is over all things competent.

$$لَهُ مَا فِي السَّمَاوَاتِ وَمَا فِي الْأَرْضِ وَمَا بَيْنَهُمَا وَمَا تَحْتَ الثَّرَى$$

To Him belongs what is in the heavens and what is on the earth and what is between them and is under the soil.

And also in **Surah al-`Imran (3:5)**:

$$إِنَّ اللَّهَ لاَ يَخْفَى عَلَيْهِ شَىْءٌ فِى الأَرْضِ وَلاَ فِى السَّمَآءِ$$

Indeed, from Allah nothing is hidden in the earth or in the heaven.

Again in **Surah al-Baqarah (2:284)**:

$$لِلَّهِ مَا فِى السَّمَـوَتِ وَمَا فِى الأَرْضِ$$

To Allah belongs whatever is in the heavens and whatever is in the earth.

The marvelous order and harmony that we see in the motion of the sun, the moon, the outer space around us cannot be the result of an aimless accident. It must have a founder and creator. There is no doubt that the study of even one of the parts of creation or even just a fragment of that part is sufficient to lead man to the knowing Designer and Builder of the universe. The atmosphere, most of whose constituent elements are life saving gases, is sufficiently viscous that it can, like a shield or armor, protect the deadly attack of 200 million meteors every day, which approach the earth with a speed of 50 kilometers per second.

The responsibility for regulating the temperature of the earth's surface within limits which maintain life also belong to the atmosphere, if it did not exists, inhabited world, like the dry deserts, become incapable of supporting life. For example, a minute change in the emission of Carbon monoxide has increased the temperature of the atmosphere to a danger level. Is it possible to create such a balanced order by anyone but the Almighty Allah? Scientists fear that even any tiny change in the orderly movement of the heavenly bodies would call the end of this world. Who guards all these, Allah [the Maker of Order]?

Allah [The Seer and Hearer of All] warns that He is very much aware of what we do or we think and nothing is out of His knowledge saying in **Surah al-Qasas (28:69-70)**:

$$وَرَبُّكَ يَعْلَمُ مَا تُكِنُّ صُدُورُهُمْ وَمَا يُعْلِنُونَ - وَهُوَ اللَّهُ لا إِلَـهَ إِلاَّ هُوَ لَهُ الْحَمْدُ فِى الإِّولَى وَالأُّخِرَةِ وَلَهُ الْحُكْمُ وَإِلَيْهِ تُرْجَعُونَ$$

And your Lord knows what their hearts conceal and what they reveal. And He is Allah; La ilaha illa Huwa. To Him is [due all] praise in the first [life] and the Hereafter. And His is the [final] decision, and to Him you will be returned.

And again in **Surah al-`Imran (3:29)**:

$$قُلْ إِن تُخْفُواْ مَا فِى صُدُورِكُمْ أَوْ تُبْدُوهُ يَعْلَمْهُ اللَّهُ وَيَعْلَمُ مَا فِى السَّمَـوَتِ وَمَا فِى الأَرْضِ وَاللَّهُ عَلَى كُلِّ شَىْءٍ قَدِيرٌ$$

Say [O Muhammad]: "Whether you conceal what is in your hearts or reveal it, Allah knows it. And He knows that which is in the heavens and that which is on the earth. And Allah is over all things competent."

Allah [The Just] assures us that He will do Justice and nothing but Justice on the day of final judgment in **Surah al-Isra'** (17:15) as:

مَّنِ اهْتَدَى فَإِنَّمَا يَهْتَدِى لِنَفْسِهِ وَمَن ضَلَّ فَإِنَّمَا يَضِلُّ عَلَيْهَا وَلَا تَزِرُ وَازِرَةٌ وِزْرَ أُخْرَى وَمَا كُنَّا مُعَذِّبِينَ حَتَّى نَبْعَثَ رَسُولاً

Whoever is guided is only guided [for the benefit of] his soul. And whoever errs only errs against it. No bearer of burdens will bear the burden of another. And never would We punish until We sent a Messenger [to give warning].

The question that may bother us is how Allah [The All Knower] is aware of all the happenings in the heavens and earth when He is far away from us. The answer is given by Allah in **Surah al-Baqarah (2:255)** as under:

وَسِعَ كُرْسِيُّهُ السَّمَوَاتِ وَالْأَرْضَ وَلَا يَؤُودُهُ حِفْظُهُمَا وَهُوَ الْعَلِيُّ الْعَظِيمُ

His Kursi [chair or footstool] extends over the heavens and the earth, and their preservation tires Him not. And He is the Most High, the Most Great.

To the question that comes to our mind about Allah, Allah directs Prophet Muhammad [sas] to tell people as in **Surah al-Baqarah (92:186):**

وَإِذَا سَأَلَكَ عِبَادِي عَنِّي فَإِنِّي قَرِيبٌ أُجِيبُ دَعْوَةَ الدَّاعِ إِذَا دَعَانِ فَلْيَسْتَجِيبُوا لِى وَلْيُؤْمِنُوا بِى لَعَلَّهُمْ يَرْشُدُونَ

And when My servants ask you, [O Muhammad], concerning Me, then answer them], indeed I am nearer [to them by My knowledge]. I respond to the invocations of the supplicant when he calls upon Me [without any mediator or intercessor]. So let them respond to Me [by obedience] and believe in Me that they may be led [rightly] guided.

Being with Allah [the Most Powerful] is possible wherever we are, there is no need to travel or to pass by a doorman. He is nearest to us than anything when He says in **Surah Qaf (50:16-18):**

وَلَقَدْ خَلَقْنَا الْإِنسَانَ وَنَعْلَمُ مَا تُوَسْوِسُ بِهِ نَفْسُهُ وَنَحْنُ أَقْرَبُ إِلَيْهِ مِنْ حَبْلِ الْوَرِيدِ - إِذْ يَتَلَقَّى الْمُتَلَقِّيَانِ عَنِ الْيَمِينِ وَعَنِ الشِّمَالِ قَعِيدٌ - مَا يَلْفِظُ مِن قَوْلٍ إِلَّا لَدَيْهِ رَقِيبٌ عَتِيدٌ

And We have already created man and know what his self whispers to him, and We are nearer to him than [his] jugular vein. When the two receivers [recording angels] receive [and record each word and deed] one sitting on the right and one on the left, He [or she] does not utter any word except that with him/her is an observer prepared [to record].

Allah [The Subduer] of the whole universe, we should turn to Him and be saved before it is too late. Before Him no Allah was formed, nor there any after Him. He is the Lord, and besides Him there is no savior. Allah [the Most Powerful] says in **Surah al-Ikhlas (112:4):**

$$ وَلَمْ يَكُن لَّهُ كُفُوًا أَحَدٌ $$

And there is none equivalent to Him.

Thus the world of existence is firm on the foundation of perfect orderliness, and undoubtedly, every orderliness and design is the creation and accomplishment of a wise and powerful maker, He is Allah [The Preserver]. If you ask an atheist why he does not believe in Allah, he will say like a scientist, I cannot see, feel, hear, or sense Allah. You then tell him, you have no brain. The answer will be, yes I have a brain. Then ask him, do you see, feel, hear, or sense your brain? No? So you are brainless creature.

These are some of the proofs that Allah [the Supreme One] exists in reality. As Allah [the Most Exalted] mentioned, you must use your *hearing, sight, heart, and other faculties* to search around you and within yourselves the existence of this wonderful, exotic, and unique creator, Allah. O Allah! Give us the ability to understand your presence all the time we are in this world, and guide us to obey You and the Prophet so that we may become successful on the day of Final Judgment. **Amin!**

Good Conduct Is the Right Weapon against Islamophobes

Whatever we do, whatever we say or even think, we must harmonize our actions and behavior, with the Will of Allah, we must conform to the values of Islam! Truthfulness, justice, sincerity and honesty all flow from the same fountain. We cannot be trustworthy and sincere unless we are truthful. We cannot love and practice justice unless we love truth.

Another virtue flowing from a truthful personality is courage. After our commitment to truth, our personality is free of fear and we would courageously stand up for truth and justice. Prophet Muhammad [sas] said: The best fighting [Jihad] in the path of Allah is [to speak] a word of justice to an oppressive ruler. (Abu Dawud, book #37, hadith #4330, Tirmidhi-Miskat: 17)

Ignorance breeds fear. When people begin to know and understand, their confidence increases. Gradually, trust is established and fear is removed. So we as Muslims must acquire true and perfect knowledge about Islam and its teachings properly so that we can overpower others by the beauties of Islam. Courage is very important in every day of our lives to face the problems confronting us. How can we regain courage? Allah [swt] gives us the answer in **Surah Ta-Ha (20:46):**

[Allah] said: "Fear not, indeed I am with you both; I hear and see [everything]." As Muslims our courage comes from Allah [swt]. It is our salah that has taught us to be humble. We are ever-thankful to Allah [swt] for the gifts He is constantly bestowing on us. Our achievements in all spheres of life are nothing but the results of our honest personal efforts along with the blessings of Allah [swt]. The very fact that Allah [swt] has honored us with success should make us more humble. We must try to respect the opinion of others even if we don't agree. Let others also have an opinion. We may try to convince others by putting arguments in a respectful manner. The Prophet [sas] said: "Allah hates the obscene and vulgar." (Tirmidhî (2003))

Brothers and Sisters! Let us make a pledge to be true in our words as well as in our deeds. It is so easy to promise but more often so difficult to fulfill that promise. So why promise unless we are very certain that we can keep our word. One simple way to remain truthful is to speak little, but always the truth, offer little but honor your offers. Make few promises, but keep everyone. May Allah [swt] open our hearts to the truth and let the truth remain our beacon in life, Insha-Allah,

Muslims must not simply people who claim to hold certain beliefs, but do very little to demonstrate in action. How should we defend the good name of Islam from the attacks of slanderers and Islamophobes? Should we retaliate in the same way? Should we become abusive and trade insult with insult? Should we resort to violence?

It is high time that we behave like the true representatives of a universal faith. Even if we don't yet know how to get others to love us, we can at least try not to let them hate us. We can at least treat our host community with courtesy; we can at least refrain from behaving in an insulting and ungrateful manner. Surely we must accept some responsibility for our troubles instead of trying to blame everything on the merchants of Islamophobia. If as Muslims we cannot become Islamic role models following the footsteps of our beloved Prophet and his followers how can we become real ambassadors of Islam?

Dear Brothers and sisters, the sooner we start practicing Islam in our lives, in our neighborhoods and in our country as a whole, the better for everyone. We need to show by example that in Islam, holiness is about wholeness, about being complete. Having beard or wearing hijab does not in itself make our faith complete. A true Muslim is a good citizen, a helpful neighbor, a trustworthy employee. A true Muslim is courteous, fair and honest in business affairs. When people know and understand healthy Islam and when Muslims become better role models of their faith, then Islamophobia will automatically disappear for good.

The greatest thing in life is to remember the One [Allah] who gave us life, to remember the goal of our life and to work hard to achieve that goal. Let us not forget that Prophet Muhammad [sas] was the leader of the first Muslim minority in a very hostile non-Muslim society. As a precaution, Prophet Muhammad [sas] sent a small delegation to Abyssinia...They became the 1st Muslim minority in a friendly non-Muslim society. There, a wise, just and tolerant Christian king, accepted them and guaranteed their safety.

 Muslims coming to the West have one of 3 options: assimilation, isolation, or selective interaction with the host community. In more than one sense, we are living in two cultures, two civilizations, at one and the same time.

Those who choose to assimilate, abandon their own identity, imitate the non-Muslims in every way and become little Englishmen or Little Europeans.

Those who choose isolation are horrified with what has become of the first group. They want to preserve their Islamic identity, which they often confuse with their cultural and ethnic identity. Further, they think the best way to protect Islam is to maintain little or no contact with non-Muslims around them. This fear of the isolationists is understandable, but it cannot be a solution. Islam was never intended to be a religion of the ghetto, or a religion only for "ethnic minorities."

The third group has adopted selective interaction. They believe that, by freely associating with non-Muslims at home, work and leisure, they can cultivate a friendship that benefits both sides. This group seeks to adapt to western society by absorbing good influences and avoiding bad influence. Also, this interaction allows Muslims to generate an Islamic influence on our neighbors and fellow citizens.

 What is the correct choice for us?

In **Surah al –Anbiya (21:107)** Allah [swt] describes the mission of our Prophet [sas] as:

$$وَمَآأَرْسَلْنَٰكَ إِلَّا رَحْمَةً لِّلْعَٰلَمِينَ$$

We have not sent you [O Muhammad], except as a mercy to the worlds.

The only way we can address the ignorance and hostility that breeds Islam phobia is to promote the beauty of Islam. By far the most eloquent message will be through our own living example. Just live in Islam as a good Muslim. That's all. Part of being a good Muslim is being a good neighbor, being a trustworthy and honest person in our business and social life, and being a loving and caring member of our family. It's as simple as that. But, first we must ensure that Islam becomes a living reality in our lives.

In the same way, for us, the best invitation to Islam is to set a shining personal example, which will convince others to follow. Debates and discussions have their place, but even there, we must be careful. As Muslims, we must at all times follow the Islamic ethics of debate. How should we discuss religion with non-Muslims?

The Holy Qur'an offers some eloquent advice in **Surah an-Nahl (16:125):**

ادْعُ إِلَى سَبِيلِ رَبِّكَ بِالْحِكْمَةِ وَالْمَوْعِظَةِ الْحَسَنَةِ وَجَادِلْهُمْ بِالَّتِي هِيَ أَحْسَنُ إِنَّ رَبَّكَ هُوَ أَعْلَمُ بِمَن ضَلَّ عَن سَبِيلِهِ وَهُوَ أَعْلَمُ بِالْمُهْتَدِينَ-

Invite to the Way of your Lord with wisdom and good instruction, and argue with them in a way that is best. Indeed your Lord is most knowing of who has strayed from His way, and He is the most knowing of who is [rightly] guided.

Allah does not expect us to perform wonders. He will hold us accountable for our intention and effort, not for the results. The results are entirely in Allah's hand. It is often not our planned and deliberate efforts that will bring anyone to Islam. It is Allah who works through us, if he deems our efforts fit for His Plan. Allah [swt] says in **Surah al-Baqarah (2:12):**

أَلَا إِنَّهُمْ هُمُ الْمُفْسِدُونَ وَلَكِن لَّا يَشْعُرُونَ-

Unquestionably, it is they who are the corrupters, but they perceive [it] not.

O Allah! Help us to live as true and worthy examples to those who are not yet Muslim. May Islam make its greatest conquest, not by physical force, but by winning the hearts and minds of all who love truth, beauty and justice? Our purpose of life is therefore perfectly clear. We are created as the Ambassadors of Allah. We are here to serve him, and like good ambassadors, we must work to please our Creator. Anything less would be a betrayal of the Trust. It is vital that we understand and accept this great responsibility.

The beauty of men does not only apply to physical appearance, but it applies especially to moral and spiritual values. The character of the Muslims and the quality of conduct has a special beauty that attracts the appreciation of even the non-Muslims. The Prophet [sas] regarded the praise or criticism of a neighbor as a measure of a person's goodness or badness. Ibn Mas'ood [ra.] reported that a man said to the Prophet [sas]: "O Messenger of Allah, how may I know if I am doing well or not" The Prophet [sas] said: "If you hear your neighbor say that you are good, then you are doing well, and if you hear him saying that you are bad, you are not doing well" (Ahmad, 1/402)

We can find two groups of people who hate Islam and Muslims. One-who are born to hate anything good, actually they do not believe in any religion. We cannot change them. Other- They hate Islam from ignorance and watching the activities of the followers of Islam. We can change them and their attitude by changing our life style as Muslim. Muslims should try to Islamize themselves, their houses, their trades, their societies, and their environment.

Let us pray to Allah, to help us all to increase our awareness and consciousness of Him at all times. Help us to keep our hearts and our minds focused on what pleases you. Help us to be mindful of our priorities, and to keep us away from anything that might lead us to shame and humiliation or that may invite your displeasure. O Allah! Transform our lives and activities as Your successful Ambassadors should have. O Allah, help us to live and die as Muslims. **Amin!**

Hajj: The Legacy of Prophet Ibrahim [as] and Hajera [ra]

Ibrahim [as] was the first to "announce the pilgrimage" as stated in **Surah al-Hajj (22:27)**:

وَأَذِّن فِى النَّاسِ بِالْحَجِّ يَأْتُوكَ رِجَالاً وَعَلَى كُلِّ ضَامِرٍ يَأْتِينَ مِن كُلِّ فَجٍّ عَمِيقٍ

And proclaim to the people the hajj [Pilgrimage]; they will come to you on foot and [mounted] on every kind of camel, lean on account of journeys through deep and distant mountain highways.

According to the correct view, hajj was made obligatory in 9 AH [i.e. after Hijrah, migration to Medina], the year of the delegations, in which the **Surah al-`Imran** was revealed; it is this Surah in which Allah [swt] says **(3:97)**:

فِيهِ ءَايَـتٌ بَيِّنَـتٌ مَّقَامُ إِبْرَهِيمَ وَمَن دَخَلَهُ كَانَ ءَامِناً وَلِلَّهِ عَلَى النَّاسِ حِجُّ الْبَيْتِ مَنِ اسْتَطَاعَ إِلَيْهِ سَبِيلاً وَمَن كَفَرَ فَإِنَّ اللهَ غَنِيٌّ عَنِ الْعَلَمِينَ-

In it are clear signs [such as] the standing place of Ibrahim. And whoever enters it [the Haram] shall be safe. And [due] to Allah, from the people is a pilgrimage to the House – for whoever is able to find thereto a way. But whoever disbelieves [refuses] - then indeed, Allah is free from need of the worlds [He has no need for His servant's worship; it is they who are in need of Him].

Allah [swt] says in **Surah al-Hajj (22:26)**:

وَإِذْ بَوَّأْنَا لإِبْرَهِيمَ مَكَانَ الْبَيْتِ أَن لاَّ تُشْرِكْ بِى شَيْئاً وَطَهِّرْ بَيْتِىَ لِلطَّآئِفِينَ وَالْقَآئِمِينَ وَالرُّكَّعِ السُّجُودِ-

And [mention, O Muhammad], when We designated for Ibrahim the site of the House, [saying], "do not associate anything with Me and purify My House for those who perform tawaf and those who stand [in prayer], and those who bow and prostrate."

O Muslims! Our great religion [Islam] commands us to perform Hajj, and considers it as one of its pillars. Not finding the way to Hajj, could mean not finding ticket reservations, the car breaking down on the way, or anything else.

Ibn 'Abbas [ra] reported that the Allah's Messenger [sas] said,"He who intends to perform hajj should hasten to do so". (Abu Dawud, book #10, hadith #1728) Abu Hurayrah [ra] also reported that the Prophet [sas] said, "An Umrah is expiation for the sins committed between it and the next, and Hajj which is accepted will receive no other reward than paradise" (Bukhari, book #007, hadith #3127).

Allah is the transcendent stage manager of this annual show 'Hajj'. The theme portrayed is the actions of the main characters involved ... Adam [as], Ibrahim [as], Hajera [ra], Ismai'l [as] and Muhammad [sws]. The scenes are Masjid-ul Haram, Masa between the hills, the plain of Arafah, Mash'ar at Muzdalifah, and the vicinity of Mina. Important symbols in this show are the Kaba, Safa, Marwa, day, night, sunshine, sunset, and ritual of sacrifice. The clothing and make up are ihram, halaq and taqsir. Importantly, the player of this role in this "show" is only one; and that is YOU! Regardless of whether you are a man or a woman, young or old, you are the main feature of the performance. In accordance with the teachings of Islam - all are one and one is all.

It is obligatory for the pilgrims to be aware of the rituals of hajj and to perform its pillars accordingly. The pillars of hajj are: Ihram [the state of a pilgrim in which he performs hajj and Umrah, and during which he is prohibited from certain acts that are lawful otherwise], staying at 'Arafah, the Tawaf Al-Ifadhah [circumambulation of the Ka'bah on the tenth day of Dhul-Hijjah] and the pacing between Safa and Marwah. He should also perform the obligatory acts of Hajj which are: Ihram from the Meeqaat [the place from where people must get into the state of Ihram], standing at 'Arafah till sunset, passing the night at Muzdalifah, throwing the stones [at the Jamarat, i.e., three stone-built pillars in Mina], shaving or trimming of the hair, spending the nights at Mina, sacrificing an animal if necessary [according to the type of hajj one is performing] and doing the farewell Tawaaf [circumambulation]. Ibn 'Umar reported, when the Messenger of Allāh, peace and blessings of Allāh be on him, made circuits in the hajj and the 'Umrah, on first coming [to Makkah], he started with three circuits at a fast pace, and made four circuits walking; then he said two rak'as of prayer; then he ran between the Safā and the Marwah. (Bayhaqi, 25:62)

The pilgrims should, while reciting the Talbiyah [a prayer recited by pilgrims going to Makkah], feel the real sense of liberation from the worship of fellow creatures to the worship of the Creator alone, by answering Allah's call and submitting to His authority.

We note that all three figures; Ibrahim, Hajera and Isma'il, played a major role in the re-establishment of tawhid/monotheism in Makkah and much of the annual hajj undertaken by believers are symbolic re-enactments of significant phases in their life; and this include the tawaaf [circumambulation of the Ka'bah], the sa'iy [running between the hills of Safa and Marwa], the udhiyah [sacrifice of animals].

Indeed, what Qur'an refers to the Millat of Ibrahim is essentially rooted in the legacy of a model family. Allah [swt] says in **Surah al-Imran (3:95):**

$$\text{قُلْ صَدَقَ اللّهُ فَاتَّبِعُوا مِلَّةَ إِبْرَهِيمَ حَنِيفاً وَمَا كَانَ مِنَ الْمُشْرِكِينَ}$$

Say: "Allah has told the truth. So follow the religion of Ibrahim, inclining toward truth; and he was not of the Mushrikin [polytheists]."

We are all too familiar with the story of Ibrahim [as] unwavering faith and conviction, and his supreme sacrifice as embodied in the event when he was ready to sacrifice his dear and only son to fulfill the wish of his creator. Allah [swt] says in **Surah al-Baqarah (2:131):**

إِذْ قَالَ لَهُ رَبُّهُ أَسْلِمْ قَالَ أَسْلَمْتُ لِرَبِّ الْعَالَمِينَ-

When his Lord said to him, "Submit [i.e. be a Muslim]", he said, "I have submitted [in Islam i.e. to the will of Allah] to the Lord of the worlds."

Ibrahim [as] is mentioned by name 69 times in the Qur'an with an entire Surah titled Ibrahim. Muslims consider Ibrahim the khalil [friend of Allah] as Allah states in **Surah an-Nisa (4:125):**

وَمَنْ أَحْسَنُ دِيناً مِمَّنْ أَسْلَمَ وَجْهَهُ لله وَهُوَ مُحْسِنٌ وَاتَّبَعَ مِلَّةَ إِبْرَاهِيمَ حَنِيفاً وَاتَّخَذَ اللّهُ إِبْرَاهِيمَ خَلِيلاً

And who is better in religion than one who submits himself to Allah while being a doer of good and follows the religion of Ibrahim, inclining toward truth? And Allah took Ibrahim as a Khalil [an intimate friend].

Another verse in the Qur'an portrays Ibrahim [as] as father of all believers as portrayed in **Surah al-Hajj (22:78):**

وَجَاهِدُوا فِي اللَّهِ حَقَّ جِهَادِهِ هُوَ اجْتَبَاكُمْ وَمَا جَعَلَ عَلَيْكُمْ فِي الدِّينِ مِنْ حَرَجٍ مِّلَّةَ أَبِيكُمْ إِبْرَاهِيمَ-

And strive for Allah with the striving due to Him. He has chosen you, and has not placed upon you in the religion any difficulty. It is the religion of your father, Ibrahim.

Faithful worshippers send [durud-e-Ibrahim] salutation on Ibrahim [as] and his family along with the Prophet Muhammad [sas] and his family in every one of their daily prayers.

We want to focus on the not-so-familiar legacy of a great woman, Mother Hajera [ra] the wife of Ibrahim [as] and the mother of Ismail [as]. Indeed, she is an integral and as important part of the legacy of Tawheed and the Millat of Ibrahim. Her submission to the will of her Creator and her sacrifice were as ideal as that of Ibrahim [as] and Ismail [as]. Allah has ennobled her in the Qur'an by making Safa and Marwah integral part to the performance of hajj, one of the five pillars of Islam. These are the two hills between which she ran back and forth in search of water for her beloved infant son, while she was all alone according to the plan of Allah [swt] Himself as described in **Surah al-Baqarah (2:158):**

إِنَّ الصَّفَا وَالْمَرْوَةَ مِن شَعَآئِرِ اللّهِ فَمَنْ حَجَّ الْبَيْتَ أَوِ اعْتَمَرَ فَلاَ جُنَاحَ عَلَيْهِ أَن يَطَّوَّفَ بِهِمَا وَمَن تَطَوَّعَ خَيْراً فَإِنَّ اللّهَ شَاكِرٌ عَلِيمٌ-

Indeed, As-Safa and Al-Marwah are among the symbols [places designated for the rites of [*hajj* and *'umrah*] of Allah. So whoever makes hajj [pilgrimage] to the House or performs 'umrah – there is no blame upon him for walking between [*Sa`i*] them. And whoever volunteers good – then indeed, Allah is Appreciative and Knowing.

Mother Hajera [ra] was not just wife of Ibrahim [as] but she was deeply loved by him. But, once again, to fulfill the wish of Allah [swt], he brought Mother Hajera [ra] and their beloved infant son, Ismail [as], to this abandoned, desolate, barren valley of Makkah. There was no such inhabited place called Makkah at that time. As Ibrahim [as] brought Mother Hajera [ra] and Ismail [as] to that barren, rugged valley, she asks [as in the hadith]: "O Ibrahim! Where are you going, leaving us in this valley where there is neither any person nor anything else [to survive]?" She repeated that to him many times, but he did not look back at her. Then she asked him, "Has Allah [swt)] instructed you to do so?" He replied, 'Yes.' That was enough for Mother Hajera [ra]. Now she knew that it was according to the Divine Will. With the same nobility and dignity of faith as it ran in that family, she said, "Then Allah (swt) will not neglect us." [In another version]: "'am pleased to be [left] with Allah [swt]." (Bukhari, book #55, hadith #583-4)

Then Ibrahim [as] left and she were alone with her infant. Makka was not an inhabited place yet. Food and water, that Ibrahim [as] provided them with were finished. Then, she started searching for water running back and forth through the valley between the hills of Safa and Marwah. Finally, she was visited by the arch-angel Jibril [as]. [This is an important point for Muslims to ponder: What kind of persons is visited individually by Jibril [as]?

Then, water, in the form of an ever flowing spring, the Zamzam, was made available to them by direct intervention of Allah [swt]. Right during that time, the tribe of Jurhum, passing by the valley saw birds flying. Realizing that water must be available, they searched and discovered Mother Hajera [ra] and Ismail [as]. They sought permission to settle there. Thus, the desolate valley of Makkah became an inhabited area. Hazrat Ibrahim [as] later returned there and laid the foundation of Ka'ba. Makkah ultimately was to emerge as a city; no, even greater than that, the perennial heartland of Tawhid, the belief in oneness of Allah [swt].

Subhanallah, Allah is glorified. He took such a significant and noble service from a woman. But consider another aspect. What kind of situation Mother Hajera [ra] was placed into? In that desolate, uninhabited valley, what might have been going on in her mind?

She, while whole-heartedly submitted to her Creator, was constantly searching, moving and struggling not remembering her any longer, but to find some water and save her infant. What could she think about herself? Once she was slave only to be given away by her Master, a King representing the owning class; now a victim and a stranger, exiled and abandoned by her family all alone with her child in her arms! She hardly ever had a dignified identity. Had she not been the mother of Ismail [as], who would have recognized her for anything worth? There, in that barren place, her identity did not matter any further. Yet, she reposed her complete trust in her Creator and was determined to pursue whatever she could in the way of Allah [swt].

It is so unfortunate that so little about Hajera [ra] is talked about even on such pertinent occasion of which she is an integral part. We can hardly recall ourselves listening to any discussion that highlighted her faith, sacrifice, and contribution that were second to none.

What men and women can learn from a woman, whose service and contribution enabled the hills of Safa and Marwah to the status of "among the Sign of Allah," which must be visited, and whose quest for saving the object of her love must be reenacted.

When we do the Sa'ie [running between Safa and Marwah], we are reminded of the trial that afflicted Hajera [ra], Since this woman was patient in the face of this adversity and turned to her creator, this teaches the man that doing this is better and more appropriate. When a man remembers the struggle and patience of this woman, it makes it easier for him to bear his own problems and a woman, who is of the same gender [as Hajera (ra)], will also find her problems easier to put up with.

Another member of this ideal family was the first son of Ibrahim [as], Ismail [as]. The Qur'an presents him as like father, like son as mentioned in **Surah as-Saffat (37:102)**:

فَلَمَّا بَلَغَ مَعَهُ السَّعْيَ قَالَ يَبُنَيَّ إِنِّي أَرَى فِي الْمَنَامِ أَنِّي أَذْبَحُكَ فَانظُرْ مَاذَا تَرَى قَالَ يَأَبَتِ افْعَلْ مَا تُؤْمَرُ سَتَجِدُنِي إِن شَاءَاللَّهُ مِنَ الصَّبِرِينَ-

And, when he reached [the age of] exertion [the ability to work and be of assistance], he said, "O my son! Indeed I have seen in a dream that I [must] sacrifice you, so what you think.'" He said: "O my father! Do as you are commanded. You will find me, if Allah wills, of the steadfast."

In his submission to the will of his Creator Ismail [as] were no fewer ideals. He submitted to the will of Allah whole-heartedly and with a heart full of peace and tranquility. Once again, there are very few among us who are not already familiar with the role and position of Ismail [as] in the heritage of Tawheed and the eternal truth.

Allah says in **Surah al-Hajj (22:28)**:

لِيَشْهَدُوا مَنَفِعَ لَهُمْ وَيَذْكُرُوا اسْمَ اللَّهِ فِي أَيَّامٍ مَّعْلُومَتٍ عَلَى مَارَزَقَهُم مِّن بَهِيمَةِ الْأَنْعَامِ فَكُلُوا مِنْهَا وَأَطْعِمُوا الْبَآئِسَ الْفَقِيرَ-

That they may witness [i.e. attend] benefits for themselves and mention the name of Allah on known [specific] days over what He has provided for them of [sacrificial] animals. So eat of them and feed the miserable and poor.

When we slaughter our sacrificial animals, we are reminded of the great incident when our father Ibrahim [as] submitted to the command of Allah to sacrifice his only son Ismail [as], after he had grown up and become a helping hand for him. He is also reminded that there is no room for sentiments, which go against the commands of Allah [swt]. This teaches him to respond to what Allah orders, as Allah tells us that Ismail [as] said: "…'O my father, do as you are commanded. You will find me, if Allah wills, of the steadfast." **(As-Saffat: 102)**

The essence of hajj is the pilgrim's evolution toward a higher degree of submission to Allah in Islam, all that is demanded as a sacrifice is one's personal willingness to submit one's ego and to Allah as described in **Surah al-Hajj (22:37)**:

لَن يَنَالَ اللَّهَ لُحُومُهَا وَلَا دِمَآؤُهَا وَلَكِن يَنَالُهُ التَّقْوَى مِنكُمْ كَذَلِكَ سَخَّرَهَا لَكُمْ لِتُكَبِّرُوا اللَّهَ عَلَى مَا هَدَا كُمْ وَبَشِّرِ الْمُحْسِنِينَ-

Their meat will not reach Allah, nor will their bloods, but what reaches Him is deity from you. Thus We have subjected them to you that you may magnify Allah for that [to] which He has guided you; and give glad tidings to the doers of good.

True purpose of sacrifice is not appeasing of higher powers, for Allah is Supreme, free of all wants and does not delight in flesh and blood. Sacrifice is a symbol of thanksgiving to Allah and of promoting goodwill by sharing sustenance with fellow human beings.

The benefits of hajj are both worldly and religious [spiritual]. With regards to the religious benefits, the one who goes for Hajj, earns the pleasure of his Lord and comes back with all his sins forgiven. He also earns immense reward, which he cannot earn in any other place; one prayer in Al-Masjid al-Haram [i.e., the Sacred Mosque in Makkah], for instance, is equal to a hundred thousand prayers elsewhere, and Tawaaf [circumambulation of the Ka'bah] and Sa'i [pacing between Safa and Marwah] cannot be done anywhere else. Whereas, the worldly benefits include trade and business, as well as other kinds of earnings that have to do with Hajj.

Brethren in faith! Social gatherings and assemblies, however high and noble their objectives may be, can never reach the sublimity of the goal of this gathering of pilgrimage to the House of Allah in this sacred land, which Allah has sanctified, protected and bestowed with complete and comprehensive security in which men, animals and plants are all guaranteed protection; [this land] in which tranquility has descended and the banner of Islam is raised.

The Pilgrim should endeavor to read the Qur'an and supplicate much, especially on the day of Arafah. for the Messenger of Allah [swt] said, "The best supplication is that of [the day of] Arafah, and the best word that I and all Prophets have said on the day of Arafah is, 'Laa ilaaha illallaah wahdahu laa shareeka lahu lahul-mulk walahul hamd, wahuwa 'alaa kulli shay'in qadeer' [None has the right to be worshipped but Allah alone, Who has no partner. His is the dominion and His is the praise, and He is Able to do all things]."(Tirmidhi) Some people believe that hajj is annulled if a pilgrim does not touch or kiss the Black Stone. But this is not true because touching the black stone or kissing it is recommended when it is affordable to do so, but is preferable to be overlooked amidst dense crowding. Narrated 'Abis bin Rabia: 'Umar came near the Black stone and kissed it and said "No doubt, I know that you are a stone and can neither benefit anyone nor harm anyone. Had I not seen Allah's Apostle kissing you I would not have kissed you" (Bukhari, book #26, hadith #667)?

It is the Sunnah to recite Takbeer, "Allahu Akbar" generally in these days, and particularly after the obligatory Salah starting Fajr of the day of Arafah [9th day] for those not in Hajj, and Dhuhr of the day of sacrifice for those in Hajj; Both continue until the Asr prayer of the thirteenth of Dhul -Hijjah.

O Muslims, let those who fulfill the conditions of Hajj perform it without delay before he is overtaken by death and then regret when it will be too late for regret.

The mercy of Allah is overwhelming and sins don't hinder it. To realise this, it is enough to know that Allah [swt] ordered His slaves to expose themselves to His mercy regardless of the extent of sinfulness that they have reached. Allah (swt) says in **Surah az-Zumar (39:53):**

$$\text{قُلْ يَٰعِبَادِىَ الَّذِينَ أَسْرَفُوا عَلَىٰ أَنفُسِهِمْ لَا تَقْنَطُوا مِن رَّحْمَةِ اللَّهِ إِنَّ اللَّهَ يَغْفِرُ الذُّنُوبَ جَمِيعًا إِنَّهُ هُوَ الْغَفُورُ الرَّحِيمُ}$$

Say: "O, My servants who have transgressed against themselves [by sinning], do not despair of the mercy of Allah. Indeed, it is He who is the Forgiving, the Merciful.'"

May Allah guide us to establish His ordinances and to abide by their limits, out of His Bounty and Generosity, for He is most bounteous and most generous?

We ask Allah's [swt] forgiveness for all of us, for all Muslims from all sins. So, seek His forgiveness, for He is Oft-Forgiving, Most Merciful. **Amin!**

Iblees: Clear Enemy of Mankind Designated by Allah [swt]

Who is Iblees? `Abbas said, "Before he undertook the path of sin, Ibleess was with the angels and was called `Azazil.' He was among the residents of the earth and was one of the most active worshippers and knowledgeable one among the angels. This fact caused him to be arrogant. Ibleess was from a genus called Jinn (Tafir Ibn Kathir). Iblees is also called Shaytan. In the Arabic language, Shaytan is derived from Shatana, which means the far thing.

We, as Muslims, know that after the creation of Adam and Hawwa, Allah [swt] allowed them to live in paradise and also know why and how both of them were expelled from Paradise.

Allah [swt] describes the event in Surah **al-Baqarah (2:34-5)** as:

وَقُلْنَا يَاءَادَمُ اسْكُنْ أَنْتَ وَزَوْجُكَ وَ إِذْقُلْنَا لِلْمَلَـٰئِكَةِ اسْجُدُوا لِلْأَدَمَ فَسَجَدُوا إِلَّا إِبْلِيسَ أَبَى وَاسْتَكْبَرَ وَ كَانَ مِنَ الْكَـٰفِرِينَ-

الْجَنَّةَ وَ كُلَا مِنْهَا رَغَدًا حَيْثُ شِئْتُمَا وَلَا تَقْرَبَا هَـٰذِهِ الشَّجَرَةَ فَتَكُونَا مِنَ الظَّـٰلِمِينَ-فَأَزَلَّهُمَا الشَّيْطَـٰنُ عَنْهَا فَأَخْرَجَهُمَا مِمَّا كَانَا فِيهِ

وَقُلْنَا اهْبِطُوا بَعْضُكُمْ لِبَعْضٍ عَدُوٌّ وَ لَكُمْ فِي الْأَرْضِ مُسْتَقَرٌّ وَ مَتَـٰعٌ إِلَى حِينٍ-

And [mention] when We said to the angels: "Prostrate before Adam"; so they prostrated except for Iblees [Satan]. He refused and was arrogant and became of the disbelievers [disobedient to Allah]. And We said: "O Adam, dwell, you and your wife in the Paradise and eat there from in [ease and] abundance from wherever you will. But do not approach this tree, lest you among the the Zalimin [wrongdoers]". But Satan caused them to slip out of it and removed them from that [condition] in which they had been. And We said: "Go down, [all of you], as enemies to one another, and you will have upon the earth a place of settlement and provision for a time."

What made Iblees deny the order of Allah [swt] and what had happened to him is described in **Surah Saad (38:73-78)** as:

فَسَجَدَ الْمَلَـٰئِكَةُ كُلُّهُمْ أَجْمَعُونَ إِلَّا إِبْلِيسَ اسْتَكْبَرَ وَ كَانَ مِنَ الْكَـٰفِرِينَ قَالَ يَا إِبْلِيسُ مَا مَنَعَكَ أَنْ تَسْجُدَ لِمَا خَلَقْتُ بِيَدَيَّ

أَسْتَكْبَرْتَ أَمْ كُنْتَ مِنَ الْعَـٰلِينَ قَالَ أَنَا خَيْرٌ مِنْهُ خَلَقْتَنِي مِنْ نَارٍ وَ خَلَقْتَهُ مِنْ طِينٍ قَالَ فَاخْرُجْ مِنْهَا فَإِنَّكَ رَجِيمٌ وَ إِنَّ عَلَيْكَ لَعْنَتِي إِلَى

يَوْمِ الدِّينِ-

So, the angels prostrated – all of them entirely, except Iblees, he was arrogant and became among the disbelievers. [Allah] said: "O Iblees, what prevented you from prostrating to that which I have created with My hands? Were you arrogant [then], or were you [already] among the haughty?'" [Iblees] said: "I am better than him. You created me from fire and created him from clay." [Allah] said: "Then get out of it

[the Paradise], for indeed, you are expelled. "And indeed, upon you is My curse until the Day of Recompense."

The Messenger of Allah said,

«خُلِقَتِ الْمَلَائِكَةُ مِنْ نُورٍ وَخُلِقَ إِبْلِيسُ مِنْ مَارِجٍ مِنْ نَارٍ وَخُلِقَ آدَمُ مِمَّا وُصِفَ لَكُمْ»

The angels were created from light, Shaytan from a smokeless flame of fire, while Adam was created from what was described to you (Muslim, book#o42, hadith#7134).

Allah [swt] created the angels from light and they were created only to worship Allah [swt] and carry out His orders without any power of denying and they will not have to face trial on the Day of Judgment. But Iblees was created from smokeless flame of fire [like other Jinns] and were given the authority to deny or accept the order of Allah [swt] and will be under trail on the Day of Judgment with other Jinns and mankind.

Allah [swt] was very angry with the decision of Iblees and cursed him as described in **Surah al-Ar'af (7: 18):**

قَالَ اخْرُجْ مِنْهَا مَذْءُومًا مَّدْحُورًا لَّمَن تَبِعَكَ مِنْهُمْ لَأَمْلَأَنَّ جَهَنَّمَ مِنكُمْ أَجْمَعِينَ

[Allah] said [to Iblees], "Get out of it [Paradise], Madh'uman Madhura [reproached and expelled]. Whoever follows you among them- I will surely fill hell with you, all together."

How Iblees convinced Adam and Hawwa to go against the advice of Allah [swt] is enunciated **in Surah al-Ar`af (7:20-1):**

فَوَسْوَسَ لَهُمَا الشَّيْطَنُ لِيُبْدِيَ لَهُمَا مَا وُورِيَ عَنْهُمَا مِن سَوْءَتِهِمَا وَقَالَ مَا نَهَىٰكُمَا رَبُّكُمَا عَنْ هَـٰذِهِ الشَّجَرَةِ إِلَّا أَن تَكُونَا مَلَكَيْنِ أَوْ تَكُونَا مِنَ الْخَـٰلِدِينَ - وَقَاسَمَهُمَا إِنِّي لَكُمَا لَمِنَ النَّصِحِينَ

But Satan whispered to them to make apparent to them that which was concealed from them of their private parts. He said, "Your Lord did not forbid you this tree except that you become angels or become of the immortals." And he Qasamahuma [swore to them by Allah], "Indeed, I am to you from among the sincere advisor."

Adam and Hawwa ate fruits from the forbidden tree and the consequence was - they were expelled from Heaven [where they stayed for one hour] as mentioned in **Surah al-`Araf (7:22):**

فَدَلَّهُمَا بِغُرُورٍ فَلَمَّا ذَاقَا الشَّجَرَةَ بَدَتْ لَهُمَا سَوْءَتُهُمَا وَطَفِقَا يَخْصِفَانِ عَلَيْهِمَا مِن وَرَقِ الْجَنَّةِ وَنَادَاهُمَا رَبُّهُمَا أَلَمْ أَنْهَكُمَا عَن تِلْكُمَا الشَّجَرَةِ وَأَقُل لَّكُمَا إِنَّ الشَّيْطَنَ لَكُمَا عَدُوٌّ مُّبِينٌ-

So he misled them with deception. And when they tasted of the tree, their private parts became apparent to them, and they began to cover themselves with the leaves of Paradise. And their Lord called to them [saying], "Did I not forbid you from the tree and tell you that Satan to you a clear enemy?"

Iblees could not tolerate his insult and expulsion from the Heaven. So he asked Allah [swt] to grant him time till the appointed hour, and Allah [swt] granted his Prayer as described in **Surah al-Hijr (15: 36-40):**

قَالَ رَبِّ فَأَنظِرْنِى إِلَى يَوْمِ يُبْعَثُونَ - قَالَ فَإِنَّكَ مِنَ الْمُنظَرِينَ - إِلَى يَوْمِ الْوَقْتِ الْمَعْلُومِ - قَالَ رَبِّ بِمَا أَغْوَيْتَنِى لَأُزَيِّنَنَّ لَهُمْ فِى الْأَرْضِ وَلَأُغْوِيَنَّهُمْ أَجْمَعِينَ - إِلَّا عِبَادَكَ مِنْهُمُ الْمُخْلَصِينَ

[Iblees] said: "My Lord, then reprieve me until the Day they [the dead] will be resurrected." [Allah] said, "So indeed, you are of those reprieved until the Day of the time well-known." [Iblees] said: "My Lord, because You have put me in error, I will surely make [disobedience] attractive to them [mankind], and I will mislead them all except among them your chosen servants."

And Allah (swt) also said in **Surah Sad (38: 79 - 85):**

قَالَ رَبِّ فَأَنظِرْنِى إِلَى يَوْمِ يُبْعَثُونَ - قَالَ فَإِنَّكَ مِنَ الْمُنظَرِينَ - إِلَى يَوْمِ الْوَقْتِ الْمَعْلُومِ - قَالَ فَبِعِزَّتِكَ لَأُغْوِيَنَّهُمْ أَجْمَعِينَ - إِلَّا عِبَادَكَ مِنْهُمُ الْمُخْلَصِينَ - قَالَ فَالْحَقُّ وَالْحَقَّ أَقُولُ لَأَمْلَأَنَّ جَهَنَّمَ مِنكَ وَمِمَّن تَبِعَكَ مِنْهُمْ أَجْمَعِينَ -

[Iblees] said: "My Lord! Then reprieve until the Day the [dead] are resurrected." [Allah] said: "So indeed, you are of those reprieved until the Day of the time well-known." [Iblees] said, "By Your might, I will surely mislead them all except, among them, Your chosen servants." [Allah] said: "The truth [is My oath], and the truth I say [That] I will surely fill Hell with you and those of them that follow you all together."

How Iblees, because of his anguish, will try to mislead mankind expressed in the ayah of **Surah al-`Araf (7:16-17)** as:

قَالَ فَبِمَا أَغْوَيْتَنِى لَأَقْعُدَنَّ لَهُمْ صِرَاطَكَ الْمُسْتَقِيمَ - ثُمَّ لَآتِيَنَّهُم مِّن بَيْنِ أَيْدِيهِمْ وَمِنْ خَلْفِهِمْ وَعَنْ أَيْمَانِهِمْ وَعَن شَمَائِلِهِمْ وَلَا تَجِدُ أَكْثَرَهُمْ شَاكِرِينَ -

[Ibleess] said, "Because You have [Aghwaytni] put me in error, I will surely sit in wait for them [mankind] on Your straight path. Then I will come to them from before and from behind them, and on their right and on their left, and You will not find most of them grateful [to You]."

And also in **Surah an-Nisa (4:118-120):**

لَعَنَهُ اللَّهُ وَقَالَ لَأَتَّخِذَنَّ مِنْ عِبَادِكَ نَصِيبًا مَّفْرُوضًا ۔ وَلَأُضِلَّنَّهُمْ وَلَأُمَنِّيَنَّهُمْ وَلَأَمُرَنَّهُمْ فَلَيُبَتِّكُنَّ ءَاذَانَ الْأَنْعَمِ وَلَأَمُرَنَّهُمْ فَلَيُغَيِّرُنَّ
خَلْقَ اللَّهِ وَمَن يَتَّخِذِ الشَّيْطَنَ وَلِيًّا مِّن دُونِ اللَّهِ فَقَدْ خَسِرَ خُسْرَانًا مُّبِينًا ۔ يَعِدُهُمْ وَيُمَنِّيهِمْ وَمَا يَعِدُهُمُ الشَّيْطَنُ إِلَّا غُرُورًا

Allah cursed him. For he [Satan] said: "I will surely from among Your servants a specific portion. And I will mislead them, and I will arouse in them [sinful] desires, and I will command them to slit the ears of cattle, and indeed I will order them to change the nature created by Allah." And whoever takes Satan as an ally instead of Allah has certainly sustained a clear loss. He [Satan] promises them, and arouses desire in them. But Satan promises are does not promise them except delusion.

Prophet [sas] said, "Satan circulates in the body of Adam's offspring as his blood circulates in it." (Bukhari, book # 33; Hadith # 255).

Allah [swt] also describes to the believers how Iblees will try to mislead them in **Surah al-Baqarah (2:268)** as:

الشَّيْطَنُ يَعِدُكُمُ الْفَقْرَ وَيَأْمُرُكُم بِالْفَحْشَاءِ وَاللَّهُ يَعِدُكُم مَّغْفِرَةً مِّنْهُ وَفَضْلًا وَاللَّهُ وَسِعٌ عَلِيمٌ

Satan threatens you with poverty and orders you to immorality [evil deeds], while Allah promises you forgiveness from Himself and bounty. And Allah is all encompassing and knowing.

And also in **Surah al-Maidah (5:91)** as:

إِنَّمَا يُرِيدُ الشَّيْطَنُ أَن يُوقِعَ بَيْنَكُمُ الْعَدَاوَةَ وَالْبَغْضَاءَ فِي الْخَمْرِ وَالْمَيْسِرِ وَيَصُدَّكُمْ عَن ذِكْرِ اللَّهِ وَعَنِ الصَّلَوةِ فَهَلْ أَنتُم مُّنتَهُونَ

Satan only wants to cause between you animosity and hatred through Khamr [intoxicants] and Maysir [gambling], and to avert you from the remembrance of Allah and from Salah [the prayer]. So will you not desist?

Allah [swt] warns us not to be tempted by the evil desires prompted by Iblees in **Surah an-Nur (24:21)** as:

يَأَيُّهَا الَّذِينَ ءَامَنُوا لَا تَتَّبِعُوا خُطُوَتِ الشَّيْطَنِ وَمَن يَتَّبِعْ خُطُوَتِ الشَّيْطَنِ فَإِنَّهُ يَأْمُرُ بِالْفَحْشَاءِ وَالْمُنكَرِ وَلَوْلَا فَضْلُ اللَّهِ
عَلَيْكُمْ وَرَحْمَتُهُ مَا زَكَى مِنكُم مِّنْ أَحَدٍ أَبَدًا وَلَكِنَّ اللَّهَ يُزَكِّى مَن يَشَاءُ وَاللَّهُ سَمِيعٌ عَلِيمٌ

O, you who have believed, do not follow not the Khutuwat [footstep] of Satan. And whoever follows the footsteps of Satan -indeed, he enjoins Al-Fahsha'[immorality] and wrong doing. And if not for the favor of

Allah upon you and His mercy, not one of you would have been pure, ever, but Allah purifies whom He wills, and Allah is All-Hearer, All-Knower.

Allah [swt] warns us in **Surah al-Araf (7:27)** to be vigilant against the evil design of Iblees as:

يَٰبَنِىٓ ءَادَمَ لَا يَفْتِنَنَّكُمُ ٱلشَّيْطَٰنُ كَمَآ أَخْرَجَ أَبَوَيْكُم مِّنَ ٱلْجَنَّةِ يَنزِعُ عَنْهُمَا لِبَاسَهُمَا لِيُرِيَهُمَا سَوْءَٰتِهِمَآ إِنَّهُۥ يَرَىٰكُمْ هُوَ وَقَبِيلُهُۥ مِنْ حَيْثُ لَا تَرَوْنَهُمْ إِنَّا جَعَلْنَا ٱلشَّيَٰطِينَ أَوْلِيَآءَ لِلَّذِينَ لَا يُؤْمِنُونَ

O Children of Adam, let not Satan tempt you as he removed your parents from Paradise, stripping them of their clothing [the garments of Paradise] to show them their private parts. Indeed, he [Satan], and his tribe from where you do not see them. Indeed, We have made the devils allies to those who do not believe.

And also in **Surah al-Fatir (35:6)** and the consequence of following the footstep of Iblees as:

إِنَّ ٱلشَّيْطَٰنَ لَكُمْ عَدُوٌّ فَٱتَّخِذُوهُ عَدُوًّا إِنَّمَا يَدْعُو حِزْبَهُۥ لِيَكُونُوا مِنْ أَصْحَٰبِ ٱلسَّعِيرِ

Indeed, Satan is an enemy to you; so take [treat] him as an enemy. He only invites his party to be among the companions of Blaze.

In **Surah al-Isra (17:63-5)**, Allah [swt] threw challenge to Iblees that he will not be able to mislead those who are true believers as:

قَالَ ٱذْهَبْ فَمَن تَبِعَكَ مِنْهُمْ فَإِنَّ جَهَنَّمَ جَزَآؤُكُمْ جَزَآءً مَّوْفُورًا وَٱسْتَفْزِزْ مَنِ ٱسْتَطَعْتَ مِنْهُم بِصَوْتِكَ وَأَجْلِبْ عَلَيْهِم بِخَيْلِكَ وَرَجِلِكَ وَشَارِكْهُمْ فِى ٱلْأَمْوَٰلِ وَٱلْأَوْلَٰدِ وَعِدْهُمْ وَمَا يَعِدُهُمُ ٱلشَّيْطَٰنُ إِلَّا غُرُورًا إِنَّ عِبَادِى لَيْسَ لَكَ عَلَيْهِمْ سُلْطَٰنٌ وَكَفَىٰ بِرَبِّكَ وَكِيلًا

[Allah] said: "Go, for whoever of them follows you, indeed, Hell will be the recompense of [all of] you – an ample recompense. And incite [to senselessness] whoever you can among them with your voice and assault them with your horses and your infantry, and become a partner in their wealth and their children, and promise them. But Satan does not promise them anything except delusion. Indeed, over My [believing] servants there is for you no authority. And Sufficient is your Lord as a Disposer of affairs."

Allah [swt] mentions in ayah of **Surah al-`Imran (3:14)** those things beautifying and tempting for human being, especially, for men:

زُيِّنَ لِلنَّاسِ حُبُّ الشَّهَوَاتِ مِنَ النِّسَآءِ وَالْبَنِينَ وَالْقَنَاطِيرِ الْمُقَنطَرَةِ مِنَ الذَّهَبِ وَالْفِضَّةِ وَالْخَيْلِ الْمُسَوَّمَةِ وَالْاَنْعَمِ وَالْحَرْثِ ذَلِكَ مَتَعُ الْحَيَوةِ الدُّنْيَا وَاللَّهُ عِندَهُ حُسْنُ الْمَأَبِ ۔

Beautified for people is the love of that which they desire – of women and children, heaped-up sums of gold and silver, fine branded horses, and cattle and fertile land. That is the enjoyment of worldly life; but Allah has with Him the best return [Paradise].

Iblees and his associates tempt us through things mentioned in the above ayah. Main armor for Iblees and his associates are women, wealth, and wine [the three Ws].

Finally, after Iblees misguide those who will follow him, what will be the stand of Iblees is expressed in **Surah al-Hashr (59:16-17)**:

كَمَثَلِ الشَّيْطَنِ إِذْ قَالَ لِلْإِنسَنِ اكْفُرْ فَلَمَّا كَفَرَ قَالَ إِنِّى بَرِىٓءٌ مِّنكَ إِنِّى أَخَافُ اللَّهَ رَبَّ الْعَلَمِينَ ۔ فَكَانَ عَقِبَتَهُمَآ أَنَّهُمَا فِى النَّارِ خَلِدِينَ فِيهَا وَذَلِكَ جَزَآءُ الظَّلِمِينَ ۔

[The hypocrites are] like example of Satan, when he says to man: "Disbelieve." But when he disbelieves, Satan says: "Indeed, I am disassociated from you. Indeed, I fear Allah, the Lord of the worlds." So, the outcome for both of them will be in Hell Fire, abiding eternally therein. And that is the recompense of the wrongdoers.

And also in **Surah Ibrahim (14:22)** as:

وَقَالَ الشَّيْطَنُ لَمَّا قُضِىَ الْأَمْرُ إِنَّ اللَّهَ وَعَدَكُمْ وَعْدَ الْحَقِّ وَوَعَدتُّكُمْ فَأَخْلَفْتُكُمْ وَمَا كَانَ لِىَ عَلَيْكُم مِّن سُلْطَنٍ إِلَّآ أَن دَعَوْتُكُمْ فَاسْتَجَبْتُمْ لِى فَلَا تَلُومُونِى وَلُومُوٓا أَنفُسَكُم مَّآ أَنَا۠ بِمُصْرِخِكُمْ وَمَآ أَنتُم بِمُصْرِخِىَّ إِنِّى كَفَرْتُ بِمَآ أَشْرَكْتُمُونِ مِن قَبْلُ إِنَّ الظَّلِمِينَ لَهُمْ عَذَابٌ أَلِيمٌ ۔ وَأُدْخِلَ الَّذِينَ ءَامَنُوا وَعَمِلُوا الصَّلِحَتِ جَنَّتٍ تَجْرِى مِن تَحْتِهَا الْأَنْهَرُ خَلِدِينَ فِيهَا بِإِذْنِ رَبِّهِمْ تَحِيَّتُهُمْ فِيهَا سَلَمٌ

And Satan will say when the matter has been decided, "Indeed, Allah has promised you the promise of truth. And I too promised you, but I betrayed you. But I had no authority over you except that I invited you, and you responded to me. So do not blame me, but blame yourselves. I cannot be called to your aid, nor can you called to my aid. Indeed, I deny your association of me [with Allah] before [by obeying me in the life of the world]. Indeed, for the wrong-doers is a painful punishment."

Allah [swt] teaches the true believers the way of facing the evil temptation of Iblees in **Surah al-A'raf (7:200)** as:

وَإِمَّا يَنزَغَنَّكَ مِنَ الشَّيْطَنِ نَزْغٌ فَاسْتَعِذْ بِاللَّهِ إِنَّهُ سَمِيعٌ عَلِيمٌ

And if an evil suggestion comes to you from Satan, then seek refuge in Allah. Indeed, He is Hearing and Knowing.

Brothers and sisters in Islam, always be aware of the evil designs of Iblees and his associates, otherwise we will also be in hellfire with him and his associates. O Allah! Provide us the proper guidance and the hikmah, so that we may remain as true believers, die as true believers and give us the strength to face all temptations of Iblees. **Amin!**

Iman: the Fundamental Pillar of Islam

Iman is a general term that includes affirming and believing in Allah, His Books and His Messengers, and realizing this affirmation through adhering to the implications of what the tongue utters and affirms. As Allah [swt] has affirmed in **Surah al -Hujurât (49:15):**

إِنَّمَا الْمُؤْمِنُونَ الَّذِينَ ءَامَنُوا بِاللَّهِ وَرَسُولِهِ ثُمَّ لَمْ يَرْتَابُوا وَجَهَدُوا بِأَمْوَلِهِمْ وَأَنفُسِهِمْ فِى هُمُ الصَّدِقُون-

The believers are only those who have believed in Allah and His Messenger and then doubt not but strive with their properties and their lives for the cause of Allah. It is those who are the truthful.

Fear is the core of Iman and knowledge, just as Allah [the Exalted] said in **Surah Fatir (35:28):**

إِنَّمَا يَخْشَى اللَّهَ مِنْ عِبَادِهِ الْعُلَمَاء-

Only those fear Allah, among His servants who have knowledge.

Why I am a Muslim is more important than how I am a Muslim. Many of us are Muslim because we are born in a Muslim family. Or we uttered «لَا إِلَهَ إِلَّا اللهُ» when we were very young without knowing the meaning of what we had uttered. The religion of Islam cannot be attained by inheritance. One can become a true Muslim by choice, which means he must know what Islam is all about. Absence of becoming a Muslim by choice is the reason for the lack of commitment to the religion of Islam. That to me is the main problem of the Muslims all over the world. A person who is born in a Muslim family, who has a Muslim name and calls himself a Muslim, is not necessarily a Muslim if he does not know what Islam stands for and affirms his faith with full consciousness.

The real difference between a Kafir and a Muslim is not that of a name that one is called John and the other is called Abdullah, so, one is a Kafir and the other is a Muslim. How many Muhammads do we know who do not deserve to carry this beautiful name? How many Davids and Richards are there who are better as human beings than many of us are? Nor in the way do they dress the color of their eyes or hair or the length of their beards. The real difference between the two is in their knowledge, the knowledge that leads to strong faith, commitment and action.

We must understand that the gain or loss of Allah's greatest gift of Islam depends entirely on this knowledge. If there is no knowledge then one cannot get this gift. Even if there is little bit of knowledge, there is always the risk of losing the magnificent gift of Islam due to ignorance.

The person who is totally unaware of the difference between Islam and Kufr and the difference between Islam and Shirk is like one who is walking in darkness on a track. Maybe while following a straight line, his steps serve to another path and he is unaware of this deviation from the right course.

It is not necessary to read so much to become a Muslim. Each one of us should try to spend one hour or even half an hour out of the twenty four hours of the day and night to acquire the knowledge of Deen. At least that much knowledge should be acquired by every Muslim youth, adult and old person as may enable him or her to understand the essence of the teaching of Qur'an and the purpose for which it was revealed.

Not much time is required to acquire this amount of knowledge. And if Iman is dear to us, it is not so difficult to find a little time every day to acquire it. We spend so much time on mundane matters. In a life of an average length, How much time do we spend in sleeping, in eating, in watching TV, and waiting for the bus.

The Islamic attitude towards the pursuit of knowledge and education is summarized in the following Qur'anic verse in **Surah Ta-Ha (20:114):**

وَقُل رَّبِّ زِدْنِي عِلْمًا.

And say [O Mohammad]: My Lord! Increase me in knowledge.

And in **Surah az-zumar (39:9):**

أَمَّنْ هُوَ قَانِتٌ ءَانَاءَ الَّيْلِ سَاجِدًا وَقَآئِمًا يَحْذَرُ الْأَخِرَةَ وَيَرْجُوا رَحْمَةَ رَبِّهِ قُلْ هَلْ يَسْتَوِى الَّذِينَ يَعْلَمُونَ وَالَّذِينَ لاَ يَعْلَمُونَ إِنَّمَا يَتَذَكَّرُ أُوْلُوا الْأَلْبَبِ.

Is one who is devoutly obedient during the periods of the night, prostrating and standing [in prayer], fearing the Hereafter and hoping for the mercy of his Lord, - [like one who does not]? Say: "Are those who know equal to those who do not know?" Only they will remember [who are] people of understanding.

And also says in **Surah al-'Imran (3:18):**

شَهِدَ اللَّهُ أَنَّهُ لاَ إِلَهَ إِلاَّ هُوَ وَالْمَلَئِكَةُ وَأُوْلُوا الْعِلْمِ قَآئِمًا بِالْقِسْطِ لاَ إِلَهَ إِلاَّ هُوَ الْعَزِيزُ الْحَكِيمُ.

Allah witnesses that there is no deity except Him, and [so do] the angels and those of knowledge - [that He is] maintaining [creation] in justice. There is no deity except Him, the Exalted in might, the Wise.

If Allah, the Most High, His Angels and those with knowledge witness to this, those who do not are either ignorant or transgressors. Allah might forgive the former group depending on whether they did seek the knowledge and He knows best but the latter group may not be forgiven for we read in **Surah Ibrahim (14:27):**

يُثَبِّتُ اللَّهُ الَّذِينَ ءَامَنُوا بِالْقَوْلِ الثَّابِتِ فِي الْحَيَوةِ الدُّنْيَا وَفِي الْأَخِرَةِ وَيُضِلُّ اللَّهُ الظَّلِمِينَ وَيَفْعَلُ اللَّهُ مَا يَشَآءُ.

Allah keeps firm those who believe, with the firm word there is no deity except Allah and that Muhammad [sas] is the messenger of Allah], in worldly life and in the Hereafter [when questioned in their graves by the angels after death]. And Allah sends astray the wrongdoers and Allah does what He wills.

In **Surah al-Baqarah (2:138),** Allah [swt] says:

صِبْغَةَ اللَّهِ وَمَنْ أَحْسَنُ مِنَ اللَّهِ صِبْغَةً وَنَحْنُ لَهُ عَـٰبِدُونَ ۞

[Ours is] the religion of Allah [Islam]. And who is better than Allah [in ordaining] religion? And we are His worshippers.

If a Muslim is asked who is a Muslim? He unhesitatingly replies that whoever recites and believes in «لَا إِلَهَ إِلَّا اللهُ» is a Muslim. This affirmation sums up the whole of Islam. Its limits are marked out very clearly. It leaves no one in doubt about itself.

The question remains, does by the recitation of «لَا إِلَهَ إِلَّا اللهُ» alone, can we really claim to be a believer. Once a group of Bedouins came to the Prophet [sas] and said – we believe [they were not hypocrites, but true believers]. Then Allah [swt] revealed the ayah of **Surah al-Hujurrat (49:14)** which states:

قَالَتِ الْأَعْرَابُ ءَامَنَّا قُل لَّمْ تُؤْمِنُوا وَلَـٰكِن قُولُوا أَسْلَمْنَا وَلَمَّا يَدْخُلِ الْإِيمَـٰنُ فِى قُلُوبِكُمْ

The Bedouins say: "We have believed." Say, "You have not [yet] believed, but say [instead], "we have submitted," for faith has not yet entered your hearts.

Dear Brothers and sisters, just ponder! To be a true believer, we must have firm belief in our intensions [not wishful thinking) then in our proclamation by the tongue, and finally above all in our heart.

As Islam is a "color" and a program of life, as it stands so forcefully for a condition of feeling and awareness and requires change in life-values and ideals, the responsibility of Muslims settled in the west is a complex and serious matter. Allah [swt] says in **Surah al-'Imran (3:102):**

يَـٰٓأَيُّهَا الَّذِينَ ءَامَنُوا اتَّقُوا اللَّهَ حَقَّ تُقَاتِهِ وَلَا تَمُوتُنَّ إِلَّا وَأَنتُم مُّسْلِمُونَ ۞

O, you who have believed, fear Allah as He should be feared and do not die except as Muslims [in submission to Him].

O, you who have believed! The message is clearly directed to us as believers. It is not a general statement but addressed specifically to the believers and hence the emphasis – O you who have believed – Fear Allah. Fear

Allah as He should be feared and die not but as Muslims. This ayah from Surah Al Imran states a simple and straightforward message that forms the basis of our Iman i.e. having Taqwa. .

Today as Muslims - both in America and beyond, our Iman is weak and this fear that we should have for the creator today is displaced by the fear for the created. The created, people, wealth ... We fear people, we fear poverty, we fear humiliation, we fear death and we fear and fear everything but Allah [swt] as He should be feared- the most prominent fear and only fear that we should have is deficient. This overpowering fear of created things rather than for The Creator of all has subjected us [as a collective Ummah] to one humiliation after another with subsequent loss of our pride, our dignity, and our self-respect.

The phenomenon of weak faith has become so widespread among Muslims today. So often we feel this hardness in our heart, in that we do not find any joy in worship, reading Qur'an does not move us and we fall into sin so easily. It is unfortunate that this entity of weakness often goes by our entire existence without us being consciously aware of its destructive nature – and how it is detrimental to the spiritual and the moral aspects of our lives. As Muslims this is not acceptable. We need to recognize and acknowledge this weakness and make a sincere effort to channel this weakness to become our strength to serve Allah [swt] and His cause.

What causes weakness of faith? Three broad categories include:

1. Failing to seek knowledge on a constant basis:

Many of us have abandoned reading the Qur'an and Hadith on a daily basis and when we do we seldom reflect on its message or seek guidance. Our minds are not focused on the virtue of its message. We starve ourselves in the knowledge of deen by allowing our attention to be diverted by feasting on daily talk shows on TV, or other forms of destructive activities for the passing of time. We miss out on that breeze of Iman that softens hearts.

2. Living in an environment surrounded with sin is conducive to weakening the faith.

In this environment temptation exists, continuously at every point. We need to guard our prayers and our Iman. We are not as Allah conscious as we ought to be, we allow ourselves to be swayed and distracted by temptations. We have been devoid of a faith-filled environment for too long. We've become de-sensitized and lost sight of the world of the Prophet [sas]. We are oblivious to the good as taught by the Prophet [sws]. -- Moral and spiritual values that elevate man are replaced by the worldly pleasures of today's society. We fail to protect our families and ourselves from acts of disobedience and often we accept them as the norm. And seldom do we turn to Allah [swt] in repentance [tawbah]. This is our ignorance, our weakness.

And last but not the least,

3. Preoccupation with our worldly life, while neglecting the hereafter.

Our day to day activities centre on our material world - our business, our work, our money, our bills, the sizes of our homes, our cars, and so on. These take preference both in our minds and speech. This preoccupation with the world enslaves our hearts.

We have allowed the diseases of the heart to flourish such as vanity, pride, fame, glory. We tend to get lost in these illusions, fooled by the worldly glamour and fail to illuminate our hearts with Allah's Noor.

We remain pre-occupied with our worldly life. Allah says in **Surah al-Hijr (15:3):**

ذَرْهُمْ يَأْكُلُوا وَيَتَمَتَّعُوا وَيُلْهِهِمُ الْأَمَلُ فَسَوْفَ يَعْلَمُون

Let them eat and enjoy themselves and be diverted by [false] hope, for they will come to know!

And Allah [swt] created us only for His worship alone, as His slaves but today we have become slaves to this duniya, this world, slaves of our desires and ambitions, slaves of our wealth.

We must analyze and reflect where we are in terms of our knowledge, our environment, our desires, our hopes and dreams and our level of Iman. A weak Iman is a disease of the heart. And like all diseases this too has it's this lax attitude, and where are we in terms of our acts of worship?

Strengthening our Iman:

We need to value that we are Muslims. No other creation has been as blessed as us, and no other creation is shielded by Allah's Mercy as we Muslims are. Allah [swt] bestowed us with His best blessings and made us the Ummah of the Prophet [sas]. He granted this special favor, this high honor and privilege to us. He guides whom He wills.

For us to strengthen our Iman we must reflect on our relationship with Allah [swt] and His commandments Allah's messenger [sas] taught us that Faith is never static. It increases and decreases, or waxes and wanes. It is our responsibility to assess where our faith is, and make it our duty to constantly work towards improving it.

Allah mentions in **Surah al-Fath (48:4):**

هُوَ الَّذِى أَنزَلَ السَّكِينَةَ فِى قُلُوبِ الْمُؤْمِنِينَ لِيَزْدَادُوا إِيمَانًا مَّعَ إِيمَانِهِمْ وَلِلَّهِ جُنُودُ السَّمَوَتِ وَالْأَرْضِ وَكَانَ اللَّهُ عَلِيمًا حَكِيمًا ـ

It is He who sent down tranquility into the hearts of the believers that they would increase in faith along with their [present] faith. And to Allah belong the soldiers of the heavens and the earth, and ever is Allah Knowing and Wise.

Faith increases with obedience and decreases with disobedience. There is a very good reason for this. Good deeds, good conduct and good behavior are but a reflection of one's Iman.

Iman is a favor from Allah [swt] as mentioned in **Surah al -Hujurât (49:17):**

يَمُنُّونَ عَلَيْكَ أَنْ أَسْلَمُوا قُل لَّا تَمُنُّوا عَلَىَّ إِسْلَمَكُمْ بَلِ اللَّهُ يَمُنُّ عَلَيْكُمْ أَنْ هَدَاكُمْ لِلايمَنِ إِن كُنتُمْ صَدِقِين ـ

They consider it a favor to you that they have accepted Islam. Say: "Do not consider your Islam a favor to me. Rather, Allah has conferred favor upon you that He has guided you to the faith, if you should be truthful".

O Allah, we ask You by Your beautiful names and magnificent attributes to renew the faith in our hearts. O Allah, make faith appear beautiful to us and adorn our hearts with it, and make kefir, sin and disobedience abhorrent to us. Make us of those who are rightly guided. Glorified be the Lord of Might above what they ascribe to Him. Allah [swt] says in **Surah al-Baqarah (2:165):**

But those who believe are stronger in love for Allah [more than anything else]. Amin!

Interfaith Movement: Towards Infidelity or Reality?

The specific meaning of Islam can only be applied to those who testify that there is no God but Allah and that Muhammad [sas] is the Messenger of Allah. Islam, in this special meaning, which Muhammad [sas] came with, overruled all past laws and annulled them. So, whoever believes in it, believes in Allah and His messengers, and whoever disbelieves in it, then he disbelieves in Allah and His messengers. Allah says in **Surah an-Nisa (4:150-1)**:

إِنَّ الَّذِينَ يَكْفُرُونَ بِاللّهِ وَرُسُلِهِ وَيُرِيدُونَ أَن يُفَرِّقُواْ بَيْنَ اللّهِ وَرُسُلِهِ وَيقُولُونَ نُؤْمِنُ بِبَعْضٍ وَنَكْفُرُ بِبَعْضٍ وَيُرِيدُونَ أَن يَتَّخِذُواْ بَيْنَ ذَلِكَ سَبِيلاً ۞ أُوْلَـئِكَ هُمُ الْكَافِرُونَ حَقّاً وَأَعْتَدْنَا لِلْكَافِرِينَ عَذَاباً مُّهِيناً

Indeed, those who disbelieve in Allah and His messengers and wish to discriminate between Allah and His messengers and say, "We believe in some and disbelieve in others," and wish to adopt a way in between – Those are the disbelievers, truly. And We have prepared for the disbelievers a humiliating punishment.

The Prophet [sas] said, "If anyone testifies that None has the right to be worshipped but Allah Alone Who has no partners, and that Muhammad is His Slave and His Apostle, and that Jesus is Allah's Slave and His Apostle and His Word which He bestowed on Mary and a Spirit created by Him, and that Paradise is true, and Hell is true, Allah will admit him into Paradise with the deeds which he had done even if those deeds were few." (Junada, the sub-narrator said, "'Ubada added, 'such a person can enter Paradise through any of its eight gates he likes".) (Bukhari, book #55, hadith #644)

'Religious brotherhood', 'Islamic-Christian friendship', 'unity of the three religions' and the so-called 'global religion' call was so active and extensive that the Pope even held a collective prayer between representatives of the three [major] religions – Islam, Judaism and Christianity – in a village in Italy, on October 27, 1986. This prayer is called [the Spirit of Al-Quds]. By performing it, the Pope presented himself to the world as the spiritual leader of all religions and the carrier of the message of 'international peace' to humanity. He later announced the twenty-seventh of October to be a holiday for all religions. The call for interfaith is one for the elimination of religious differences between people, so that there is no such thing as a believer and an infidel and that they all come under the banner of the 'unity of brotherhood of mankind'. The propagators of this idea call for the necessity of printing the Torah, Gospel and Qur'an under one cover, and for building a mosque, church and synagogue in one place.

The purpose of this call was: (a) Giving rise to a period of confusion regarding Islam and causing chaos among the Muslims, (b) Controlling and containing the reach of Islam, (c) Destroying Islam from its roots, (d) Detaching one from faith under the guise of interfaith cooperation, (e) Overthrowing the essence of Islam by undermining its distinction.

Considering Islam just like the other distorted religions; that there is no difference whether one follows it or not and that it has no distinction above other religions.

Destruction of Islam in the hearts of its followers because whoever is satisfied with or calls towards interfaith, distorts his own religion while the others hold on to their beliefs as they are the ones urging for interfaith.

The callers of interfaith movement have forgotten that this Pope is the head of the Catholic Church and alongside him are the callers for interfaith, the offspring of those who made the Inquisition tribunals occur in Spain and committed the bloodiest and worst acts of torture against Muslims; they are the grandsons of those who led the Crusades against the Eastern Islamic countries in which thousands of not only Muslims, but also Jews and non-Catholic Christians in some instance, were slaughtered and countless numbers of women and children were captured as slaves. Can the callers provide a single evidence of organized Muslim atrocities against any religious groups not to speak of the Christians alone?

Let us look at what the Qur'an says in **Surah al-Ma'idah (5:77):**

قُلْ يَاأَهْلَ الْكِتَابِ لَا تَغْلُوا فِي دِينِكُمْ غَيْرَ الْحَقِّ وَلَا تَتَّبِعُوا أَهْوَاءَ قَوْمٍ قَدْ ضَلُّوا مِن قَبْلُ وَأَضَلُّوا كَثِيرًا وَضَلُّوا عَن سَوَاءِ السَّبِيلِ-

Say, "O People of the Scripture, do not exceed limits in your religion beyond the truth and do not follow the inclination of a people who had gone astray before and misled many and have strayed from the soundness of the way".

Allah [swt] also says in **Surah al-Baqarah (2:135-7):**

وَقَالُوا كُونُوا هُودًا أَوْ نَصَارَى تَهْتَدُوا قُلْ بَلْ مِلَّةَ إِبْرَاهِيمَ حَنِيفًا وَمَا كَانَ مِنَ الْمُشْرِكِينَ-قُولُوا آمَنَّا بِاللهِ وَمَا أُنزِلَ إِلَيْنَا وَمَا أُنزِلَ إِلَى إِبْرَاهِيمَ وَإِسْمَاعِيلَ وَإِسْحَاقَ وَيَعْقُوبَ وَالْأَسْبَاطِ وَمَا أُوتِيَ مُوسَى وَعِيسَى وَمَا أُوتِيَ النَّبِيُّونَ مِن رَّبِّهِمْ لَا نُفَرِّقُ بَيْنَ أَحَدٍ مِّنْهُمْ وَنَحْنُ لَهُ مُسْلِمُونَ-فَإِنْ آمَنُوا بِمِثْلِ مَا آمَنتُم بِهِ فَقَدِ اهْتَدَوا وَإِن تَوَلَّوْا فَإِنَّمَا هُمْ فِي شِقَاقٍ فَسَيَكْفِيكَهُمُ اللهُ وَهُوَ السَّمِيعُ الْعَلِيمُ-

And they say, "Be Jews or Christians [so] you will be guided". Say, "Rather, [We follow] the religion of Ibrâhim [Abraham], inclining toward truth [Islâmic Monotheism, i.e. to worship none but Allâh (Alone)], and he was not of the polythesists [Those who associate others with Allah in worship]". Say, [O believers], "We have believed in Allâh and what has been revealed to us and that has been revealed to Ibrâhim [Abraham], Ismâ'il [Ishmael], Ishâq [Isaac], Ya'qûb [Jacob], and the dscendents [the twelve tribes of Israel descended from Ya'qûb [Jacob], and what was given to Mûsa [Moses] and 'Isa [Jesus], and what was given to the Prophets from their Rabb. We make no distinction between any of them, and we are submitted Muslims [in submission] to Him". So if they believe in the same as you believe in, then they have been [rightly] guided; but if they turn away, they are only in dissension, and Allâh will be sufficient for you against them. And He is the Hearing, the All-Knowing.

Confirmation of the origin of belief: the religion of all the prophets is one though their laws are many; those laws are all from Allah and the Law of Islam revokes all other laws. Belief in Allah: In contradiction with Jewish and Christian beliefs.

Belief in the Holy Books: Contradictions in belief in the Holy Books by the Jews and Christians, who have falsified and replaced parts of these Sacred Books, with a high percentage of fabrications regarding the prophets of Allah, examples of which are:

Accusations of the Jews that Prophet Solomon [as] committed apostasy and worshipped statues/idols – in their Kings I: 1/5.

Accusations of the Jews about Prophet Aaron [Harun] that he created the calf and worshipped it.

Accusations of the Jews about the prophet Abraham Ibrahim [as] that he offered his wife to the Pharaoh to gain favor – in their Genesis: 12/14.

Accusations of the Jews that prophet Lot [as] drank alcohol and whilst intoxicated, had sexual intercourse with his daughter – in their Genesis: 19/30.

Accusations of the Jews about Prophet David Dawud [as] that his son Solomon [Sulaiman (as)] was an illegitimate child – in their Samuel II: 11/11.

Accusations of the Christians – God curse them – which the grandfather of David and Solomon [as] is from the lineage of Yahootha, the son of Jacob [Yakub (as)] who was born out of wedlock – in their Gospel: 1/10.

Accusations of the Christians – God curse them – that all the prophets among the sons of Israel are thieves and pickpockets – in their Jonah: 10/8.

The total number of prophets is 124,000. Of which 315, are messengers:25 of them are named in the Holy Qur'an; 4 of them are Arabs: Hud, Salih, Shu'ayb and Muhammad [sas].The Jews and Christians Deny that Uzair [Ezra] and Jesus [as] were mere human beings and they disbelieve in the entire message of Muhammad [sas].

The theory of integrating the religions or interfaith was first initiated by the non-Muslims during the time of Prophet Muhammad [sas] and the answer to the theory is also recorded in the Holy Qur'an as mentioned in **Surah al-Baqarah (2:109):**

$$ وَدَّ كَثِيرٌ مِّنْ أَهْلِ الْكِتَابِ لَوْ يَرُدُّونَكُم مِّن بَعْدِ إِيمَانِكُمْ كُفَّارًا حَسَدًا مِّنْ عِندِ أَنفُسِهِم مِّن بَعْدِ مَا تَبَيَّنَ لَهُمُ الْحَقُّ فَاعْفُواْ $$

$$ وَاصْفَحُواْ حَتَّى يَأْتِيَ اللهُ بِأَمْرِهِ إِنَّ اللهَ عَلَى كُلِّ شَيْءٍ قَدِيرٌ ـ $$

Many of the people of the Scripture [Jews and Christians] wish they could turn you away back to disbelief after you have believed, out of envy from themselves [even] after the truth that Muhammad [Peace be upon him] is Allâh's Messenger has become clear to them. So pardon and overlook until Allâh delivers His Command. Indeed, Allâh is over all things competent.

And also in **Surah al-Baqarah (2:111-2):**

وَقَالُواْ لَن يَدْخُلَ الْجَنَّةَ إِلاَّ مَن كَانَ هُودًا أَوْ نَصَارَى تِلْكَ أَمَانِيُّهُمْ قُلْ هَاتُواْ بُرْهَانَكُمْ إِن كُنتُمْ صَادِقِينَ - بَلَى مَنْ أَسْلَمَ وَجْهَهُ لِلّهِ

وَهُوَ مُحْسِنٌ فَلَهُ أَجْرُهُ عِندَ رَبِّهِ وَلاَ خَوْفٌ عَلَيْهِمْ وَلاَ هُمْ يَحْزَنُونَ -

And they say, "None will enter Paradise except one who is a Jew or a Christian". That is [merely] their wishful thinking. Say, "Produce your proof if you should be truthful". Yes, [on the contrary] whoever submits his face [self] in Islam to Allah while being a doer of good will has his reward with his Lord? And no fears will there be concerning them, nor will they grieve.

And also in **Surah al-Baqarah (2:120):**

وَلَن تَرْضَى عَنكَ الْيَهُودُ وَلاَ النَّصَارَى حَتَّى تَتَّبِعَ مِلَّتَهُمْ قُلْ إِنَّ هُدَى اللّهِ هُوَ الْهُدَى وَلَئِنِ اتَّبَعْتَ أَهْوَاءهُم بَعْدَ الَّذِي جَاءكَ مِنَ الْعِلْمِ مَا

لَكَ مِنَ اللّهِ مِن وَلِيٍّ وَلاَ نَصِيرٍ -

And never will the Jews and the Christians approve of you until you follow their religion. Say, "Indeed, the guidance of Allah is the [only] guidance." If you were to follow their desires after what has come to you of knowledge, you would have against Allah no protector or helper.

And also in **Surah al-Kafirun (109)** Allah [swt] says:

قُلْ يَا أَيُّهَا الْكَافِرُونَ - لاَ أَعْبُدُ مَا تَعْبُدُونَ - وَلاَ أَنتُمْ عَابِدُونَ مَا أَعْبُدُ - وَلاَ أَنَا عَابِدٌ مَّا عَبَدتُّمْ - وَلاَ أَنتُمْ عَابِدُونَ مَا أَعْبُدُ - لَكُمْ

دِينُكُمْ وَلِيَ دِينِ

Say: "O disbelievers, I do not worship what you worship. Nor are you worshippers of what I worship. Nor will I worshipper of you worship. Nor will you worshippers of what I worship. For you is your religion, and for me is my religion [Islâmic Monotheism]".

Allah [swt] says in **Surah al-Ma'idah (5:17):**

لَّقَدْ كَفَرَ الَّذِينَ قَالُواْ إِنَّ اللّهَ هُوَ الْمَسِيحُ ابْنُ مَرْيَمَ قُلْ فَمَن يَمْلِكُ مِنَ اللّهِ شَيْئًا إِنْ أَرَادَ أَن يُهْلِكَ الْمَسِيحَ ابْنَ مَرْيَمَ وَأُمَّهُ وَمَن فِي الأَرْضِ

جَمِيعًا وَلِلّهِ مُلْكُ السَّمَاوَاتِ وَالأَرْضِ وَمَا بَيْنَهُمَا يَخْلُقُ مَا يَشَاءُ وَاللّهُ عَلَى كُلِّ شَيْءٍ قَدِيرٌ

They have certainly disbelieved who say that Allah is Christ, the son of Mary. Say: "Then who could prevent Allah at all if He had indeed to destroy Christ, the son of Mary, or his mother, or everyone on the earth?" And to Allah belongs the dominion of the heavens and the earth and whatever in between them. He creates what He wills, and Allah is over all things competent.

The call for interfaith is thus a call for infidelity with which there can be no trace of faith. Can an agreement be reached with those who attribute lies to Allah; for they claim that Jesus [as] is the son of God? Therefore, Muslims must reject this theory – the theory of interfaith – and the unity of any and every fabricated and abrogated religion with the religion of Islam, the true religion of Allah which He preserved from falsification and alteration, and which abrogates [all] other religions before it.

Indeed, there is nothing after Islam except infidelity and there is nothing after guidance except error. Let those people know that Islam is the religion of moderation and Muslims are witnesses over all nations on the Day of Judgment; Allah says in **Surah al-Baqarah (2:143):**

وَكَذَلِكَ جَعَلْنَاكُمْ أُمَّةً وَسَطًا لِتَكُونُوا شُهَدَاءَ عَلَى النَّاسِ وَيَكُونَ الرَّسُولُ عَلَيْكُمْ شَهِيدًا وَمَا جَعَلْنَا الْقِبْلَةَ الَّتِي كُنْتَ عَلَيْهَا إِلَّا لِنَعْلَمَ مَنْ يَتَّبِعُ الرَّسُولَ مِمَّنْ يَنْقَلِبُ عَلَى عَقِبَيْهِ وَإِنْ كَانَتْ لَكَبِيرَةً إِلَّا عَلَى الَّذِينَ هَدَى اللَّهُ وَمَا كَانَ اللَّهُ لِيُضِيعَ إِيمَانَكُمْ إِنَّ اللَّهَ بِالنَّاسِ لَرَؤُوفٌ رَحِيمٌ

And thus We have made you a median [just] community that you will be witnesses over the people and the messenger will be a witness over you. And We did not make the Qiblah which you used to face except that We might make evident who would follow the messenger from who would turn back on his heels. And indeed, it is difficult except for those whom Allah has guided. And never would Allah have caused you to lose your faith [your previous prayers]. Indeed Allah is, to the people, kind and Merciful.

And also in **Surah al-Ma'idah (5:3)** Allah (swt) declares Islam as His Selected religion:

الْيَوْمَ أَكْمَلْتُ لَكُمْ دِينَكُمْ وَأَتْمَمْتُ عَلَيْكُمْ نِعْمَتِي وَرَضِيتُ لَكُمُ الْإِسْلَامَ دِينًا

This day I have perfected for you your religion and completed My favor upon you and have approved for you Islam as religion.

If the religious leaders can guarantee that the arrogant and unjust rulers of the concerned religions will listen to them, and the rulers will be punished if they kill or instigate to kill people, and do unjust things, create chaos on the Earth; then there may be a consensuses of unity among the religions with each religion having its own identity.

Finally I will end the discussion by giving another quote from **Surah az-Zukhruf (43:33-5):**

وَلَوۡلَآ أَن يَكُونَ النَّاسُ أُمَّةً وَاحِدَةً لَّجَعَلۡنَا لِمَن يَكۡفُرُ بِالرَّحۡمَٰنِ لِبُيُوتِهِمۡ سُقُفًا مِّن فَضَّةٍ وَمَعَارِجَ عَلَيۡهَا يَظۡهَرُونَ ۰ وَلِبُيُوتِهِمۡ أَبۡوَابًا

وَسُرُرًا عَلَيۡهَا يَتَّكِؤُونَ ۰ وَزُخۡرُفًا وَإِن كُلُّ ذَٰلِكَ لَمَّا مَتَاعُ الۡحَيَاةِ الدُّنۡيَا وَالۡآخِرَةُ عِندَ رَبِّكَ لِلۡمُتَّقِينَ ۰

And if it were not that the people would become one community [of disbelievers], We would have made of those who disbelieve in the Most Merciful – for their houses – ceiling and stairways of silver upon which to mount. And for their houses – doors and couches [of silver] upon which to recline and gold ornaments. But all that is not but the enjoyment of worldly life. And the Hereafter with your Lord is for the righteous.

O, Allah! Give us the proper guidance to be perfectly true to Your nominated religion Islam, and protect us from the allurement of the enemies of Islam in their effort to destroy our faith. **Amin!**

Is Al-Mawlid Bid'ah?

The word bid'ah in Arabic is taken from 'Al-Bada', that is to create something without precedence. A bid'ah is a new, innovated practice introduced into the religion of Islam that deceivingly appears to be lawful in Islam with the intention of being a form of worship. The companions of the Prophet said, "Some men from my companions will come to my Lake-Fount and they will be driven away from it, and I will say, 'O Lord, my companions!' It will be said, 'You have no knowledge of what they innovated after you left: they turned apostate as renegades [reverted from Islam] (Bukhari, book #76, hadith #586).

The Prophet [sas] also said: "If somebody innovates something which is not in harmony with the principles of our religion, that thing is rejected" (Bukhari, book #49, hadith #861). And he [sas] said: Medina is a sacred territory, so he who made any innovation in it. Or gave protection to an innovator, there is upon him the curse of Allah, that of the angels and that of all the people. There would not be accepted on the Day of Resurrection either obligatory acts or supererogatory acts from him. (Muslim, book #007, hadith #3166) Ibn Hajar [ra] commenting on the hadith said: "It is anything introduced into the religion of Islam as an innovation through any means without any legitimacy from the Shari'ah". He also said: "This hadith is considered to be one of the fundamentals and foundations of Islam, because one who innovates will have this deed disregarded by Allah. It is also a misguidance and Islam is free from it."

Bid'ah is not acceptable, no matter who does it. A good intention does not justify a bad deed and even if a person died as a knowledgeable and righteous person, this does not mean that he was infallible. There is nothing good in innovation.

Evidence that is put forward in support of Al-Mawlud is the following hadith:

Jareer Ibn 'Abdullah [ra], narrated that the Prophet [sas] said: "He who introduced some good practice in Islam which was followed after him [by people] he would be assured of reward like one who followed it, without their rewards being diminished in any respect. And he who introduced some evil practice in Islam which had been followed subsequently [by others], he would be required to bear the burden like that of one who followed this [evil practice] without their's being diminished in any respect". (Muslim, book #034, hadith #6466)

 Evidence put forward in support of Al-Mawlid is the following saying of Umar [ra]:

Abdur Rahman bin 'Abdul Qari said, "I went out in the company of 'Umar bin al-Khattab one night in Ramadan to the mosque and found the people praying in different groups. A man praying alone or a man praying with a little group behind him; so, 'Umar said, 'In my opinion I would better collect these [people] under the leadership of one Qari [Reciter] [i.e. let them pray in congregation!]". So, he made up his mind to congregate them behind Ubai bin Ka'b. Then on another night I went again in his company and the people were praying behind their reciter. On that, Umar remarked, "what an excellent Bid'a [i.e. innovation in religion] this is; but the prayer which they do not perform, but sleep at its time is better than the one they are offering.' He meant the prayer in the last part of the night. [In those days] people used to pray in the early part of the night" (Bukhari, book #32, hadith #227).

Narrated Zaid bin Thabit: Allah's Apostle made a small room [with a palm leaf mat]. Allah's Apostle came out [of his house] and prayed in it. Some men came and joined him in his prayer. Then again the next night they came for the prayer, but Allah's Apostle delayed and did not come out to them. So they raised their voices and knocked the door with small stones [to draw his attention]. He came out to them in a state of anger, saying, "You are still insisting [on your deed, i.e. Tarawih prayer in the mosque] that I thought that this prayer [Tarawih] might become obligatory on you. So you people, offer this prayer at your homes, for the best prayer of a person is the one which he offers at home, except the compulsory [congregational] prayer" (Bukhari, book #73, hadith #134).

Imam Ibn Rajab [ra] said: "Any words from the Salaf considering something as a good bid'ah were meant in the linguistic and not the Islamic sense, such as the saying of 'Umar, may Allah be pleased with him, when he saw people praying Tarawih in congregation, that "This is a good Bid'ah". Prophet Muhammad [sas] also prayed Tarawih in congregation for some time. Thus, it was not a new innovation.

Another evidence put forward in defence of Al-Mawlid is: Ibn Mas'ood [ra] said: "What the Muslims see as good in the sight of Allah is good and what they see as bad is bad in the sight of Allah."

As-Sindi [ra] said: "It is obvious that he was referring to the companions of the Prophet [sas] and he was talking exclusively about those things that they had a unanimous consensus on, it does not include others. This is besides the fact that these were the words of a companion and not of the Prophet [sas]."

Al-Maqrizi and Al-Qalqashandi, the famous Muslim historians said: "During the Fatimi era, the rulers were celebrating many events on a yearly basis through which they would grant people gifts and grants, these events were; The New Year, 'Aashura', Al-Mawlid, the birthday of 'Ali Ibn Abu Talib, the birthday of Al-Hasan, the birthday of Al-Husain, the birthday of Fatimah, he birthday of their present leader, …etc".

From among the contemporary scholars who confirmed that it was the Fatimi rulers who initiated Al-Mawlid was Sheikh Muhammad Al-Mutee'i [ra], who was the grand Mufti of Egypt before his death in 1354 AH. He mentioned that the person who initiated this celebration was the Fatimi ruler Al-Mu'iz Li Dinillaah Al-Fatimi. Sheikh Muhammad Al-Mutee'i [ra] also stated that King Al-Muthaffar Aba Sa'id revived Al-Mawlid in the city of Irbel during the seventh hijri century.

Al-Fatimi people were not recognised by any of the trustworthy Muslim historians to descend from the Prophet [sas]. On the contrary, Muslim scholars wrote books challenging this claim and dispraised the Fatimi people by saying that they were nothing but a bunch of atheists.

Undoubtedly, this celebration was innovated after the blessed first three generations of Muslims, and the ones who introduced it are one of the most evil sects that ever claimed to be Muslims. They did this for political purpose in order to have an effect on the common Muslims and show them that they are indeed descended from the Prophet [sas] although this of course was far from the truth.

Allah says in **Surah an-Nisa (4:115):**

وَمَن يُشَاقِقِ الرَّسُولَ مِنْ بَعْدِ مَا تَبَيَّنَ لَهُ الْهُدَى وَيَتَّبِعْ غَيْرَ سَبِيلِ الْمُؤْمِنِينَ نُوَلِّهِ مَا تَوَلَّى وَنُصْلِهِ جَهَنَّمَ وَسَاءَتْ مَصِيرًا

And whoever opposes the Messenger after guidance has become clear to him and follows other than the way of the believers - We will give him what he has taken [make him responsible for his choice] and drive him into Hell, evil it is as a destination.

Imam Ibn Kathir [ra] said concerning this verse: "This refers to those who take a path other than the one which the Messenger [sas] came with; so they became on one side and the Shari'ah on the other, despite the fact that the truth had become clear to them and they knew this" (Tafsir-Ibn-Kathir).

Allah [swt] says in **Surah al-Ma'idah (5:3):**

الْيَوْمَ أَكْمَلْتُ لَكُمْ دِينَكُمْ وَأَتْمَمْتُ عَلَيْكُمْ نِعْمَتِى وَرَضِيتُ لَكُمُ الْأِسْلاَمَ دِيناً -

This day I have perfected for you your religion and completed My favor upon you and have approved for you Islam as religion.

Imam Malik [ra], said concerning this verse: "He who innovates a new Bid'ah in Islam considering it to be something good is in effect claiming that Muhammad [sas] did not fully convey the message of Islam. So whatever was not a part of the religion at that time [i.e., the time of the Prophet and his companions] cannot be considered as a part of the religion today." Imam Ibn Kathir [ra] also said: "One of the greatest bounties from Allah upon the Muslim nation is that He completed and perfected the religion of Islam for them, so they have no need of any other religion or Prophet other than their Prophet. This is precisely why Allah made Muhammad [sas] the seal of all Prophets and sent him to the Jinn as well as mankind. The only matters that are lawful are those that the Messenger [sas] made lawful and the only matters that are unlawful are those that he made unlawful. The only things that can be considered as part of the religion of Islam are those that he conveyed; and that which he did not convey can never and will never be part of the religion. Everything that the Messenger [sas] said was true and correct without even a trace of error or dishonesty."

Sufyan Ath-Thawri [ra] said: "An innovation is dearer to Satan than a sin, for one can easily repent from a sin, but an innovation is not easily repented from [as an innovator thinks that he is on the correct path".

Allah [swt] also says in **Surah al-'Imran (3:31-2):**

قُلْ إِن كُنتُمْ تُحِبُّونَ اللَّهَ فَاتَّبِعُونِى يُحْبِبْكُمُ اللَّهُ وَيَغْفِرْ لَكُمْ ذُنُوبَكُمْ وَاللَّهُ غَفُورٌ رَّحِيمٌ - قُلْ أَطِيعُواْ اللَّهَ وَالرَّسُولَ فَإِن تَوَلَّوْا فَإِنَّ اللَّهَ لاَ يُحِبُّ الْكَافِرِينَ -

Say, [O Muhammad to mankind]: "If you [really] love Allah, then follow me [Muhammad], [so] Allah will love you and forgive you your sins. And Allah is Oft-Forgiving, Most Merciful". Say, "Obey Allah and the Messenger." But if they turn away - then indeed, Allah does not like the disbelievers.

This love is confirmed when one gives preference to their love of the Prophet [sas] over the love of anything or anyone else. This love cannot be perfected unless it leads a person to follow and obey Prophet [sas].

The companions of the Prophet [sas] achieved perfection in following, imitating and loving the Prophet [sas] and the best of them was Abu Bakr [ra], yet none of them celebrated the birthday of the Prophet [sas] nor did any of them consider its celebration as a sign of loving him.

There is nothing in the Qur'an to say that we should celebrate Al-Mawlid, or the birthday of the Prophet [sas]. The Prophet [sas] himself did not do this or command anyone to do it, either during his lifetime or after his death. Indeed, he told us not to exaggerate about him as the Christians had exaggerated about Jesus [as]. Narrated 'Umar: I heard the Prophet saying, "Do not exaggerate in praising me as the Christians praised the son of Mary, for I am only a Slave. So, call me the Slave of Allah and His Apostle" (Bukhari, book #55, hadith #654).

Did any of the Imams – Abu Hanifah, Malik, Al-Shafi'i, Ahmad [ra], do this or command others to do it or say that it was good? By Allah, no! It was not even mentioned during the first and best three centuries of Islam. The Prophet [sas] warned us of the dangers of disobeying him, and the danger of adding to what he brought. The celebration of Al-Mawlid or his birthday is indeed an addition to what he brought – as all the scholars agree. Jabir b. Abdullah said: When Allah's Messenger [sas] delivered the sermon, his eyes became red, his voice rose. and his anger increased so that he was like one giving a warning against the enemy and saying: "The enemy has made a morning attack on you and in the evening too." He would also say: "The last Hour and I have been sent like these two." and he would join his forefinger and middle finger; and would further say: "The best of the speech is embodied in the book of Allah, and the beet of the guidance is the guidance given by Muhammad. And the most evil affairs are their innovations; and every innovation is error." He would further say, I am dearer to a Muslim even than his self; and he who left behind property that is for his family. And he who dies under debt or leaves children [in helplessness] the responsibility [of paying his debt and bringing up his children] lies on me." (Muslim, book #004, hadith #1885)

There are many other verses from the Qur'an that convey the same meaning. Innovating things like Al-Mawlid implies that Allah did not complete the religion for the Muslim nation, and that the Messenger [sas] failed to convey to this nation that he should have done. In fact, it implies that the religion was not completed until these people came along later and innovated in the religion things that Allah [swt] had not permitted, claiming that these were things that would bring them closer to Allah [swt]. There is no doubt that celebration of Al-Mawlid is due to weakness of faith, lack of understanding and the effects of sins piling up on one's heart. We ask Allah to keep all the Muslims and us safe from that.

In conclusion, celebrating the birthday of the Prophet [sas], whatever form it takes, is a reprehensible innovation. The Muslims should put a stop to this and other kinds of bid'ah, and occupy themselves with reviving and adhering to the Sunnah.

Righteous deeds are those, which are loved by Allah and His Messenger [sas], those which are prescribed in Islam and in the Sunnah. Thus, Umar ibn al-Khattab [ra] used to say in his du'aa: "O Allah, make all of my deeds righteous and make them purely for Your sake, and do not let there be any share for anyone or anything else in them."

The Qur'an and Sunnah are the reference point in cases of dispute. Where in the Qur'an or Sunnah does it indicate that it is prescribed in Islam to celebrate the Prophet's birthday? Whoever does that or thinks that it is good must repent to Allah [swt] from this and from other kinds of bid'ah. This is the attitude of the Muslims who is seeking the truth. But whoever is too stubborn and arrogant after proof has been established, then his reckoning will be with his Creator. **Amin!**

Islam as a Religion has no Contestant

Islam is the most recent religion revealed by Allah to all humanity. Prophet Muhammad [*peace be on him*] was not sent to abolish any religion, but to purify, admonish, approve, correct, and to complete the previous messages revealed to the prophets sent before him, and the last one before him *Isa* [Jesus].

We and people of the scriptures believe in the oneness of Allah [God] used interchangeably and not to associate any partner with Him [*monotheism*]. Christians from the Arabian Peninsula always called Allah [not God] and all Arabic translations of *Injil* also used Allah instead of God. We all believe in strong family bondage, and moral standing. We also commonly believe that we will be resurrected for trail, the sinners will be punished, and the good doers will be rewarded. We pray to Allah and also observe fasting, and make charity for the sake of Allah [according to our religions]. Allah has no feminine. That is why we say Allah, rather than God [the feminine of God is Goddess]. In running the affairs, Allah does not need any help from anybody and none is comparable to Him.

In addition, Muslims believe that Allah [He] begets not, nor was He begotten and has no partner. The creation of Jesus, as far as Allah [swt] is concerned, is equal to the creation of Adam. Allah [swt] created Adam from clay, and then said to him, "Be," and he was. As Allah [swt] says in **Surah al-'Imran (3:59-60):**

إِنَّ مَثَلَ عِيسَى عِندَ اللَّهِ كَمَثَلِ ءَادَمَ خَلَقَهُ مِن تُرَابٍ ثُمَّ قَالَ لَهُ كُن فَيَكُونُ -- الْحَقُّ مِن رَّبِّكَ فَلاَ تَكُن مِّنَ الْمُمْتَرِينَ

Indeed, the example of 'Isa' to Allah [regarding His creation of him] is like that of Adam. He created him from dust; then He said to him, "Be," and he was. The truth is from your Lord, so do not be among the doubters.

Then Allah [swt] advised Prophet Muhammad [sas] to through challenge to those who believed in the creation of Isa [as] by some other means in **Surah al-'Imran (3:61):**

فَمَنْ حَآجَّكَ فِيهِ مِن بَعْدِ مَا جَآءَكَ مِنَ الْعِلْمِ فَقُلْ تَعَالَوْاْ نَدْعُ أَبْنَآءَنَا وَأَبْنَآءَكُمْ وَنِسَآءَنَا وَنِسَآءَكُمْ وَأَنفُسَنَا وَأَنفُسَكُمْ ثُمَّ نَبْتَهِلْ فَنَجْعَل لَّعْنَتَ اللَّهِ عَلَى الْكَاذِبِينَ --

Then whoever argues with you about it after [this] knowledge has come to you - say: "Come, let us call our sons and your sons, our women and your women, ourselves and yourselves, then supplicate earnestly [together] and invoke the curse of Allah upon the liars [among us]". But none took that challenge.

Faith of a Muslim will be incomplete if he/she does not believe in all the prophets [25 Prophets are mentioned in *holy Quran*] sent by Allah including Muhammad [*peace be upon him*] as the last Prophet. It is thus mandatory for a Muslim to believe in prophets *Musa* [Moses], *Isa* [Jesus], *Ibrahim* [Abraham] to mention a few. It is also a mandatory part of a Muslim's belief that *Tawrah* was sent to Prophet *Musa* [*peace be on him*] and *Injil* [Bible] was sent to Prophet *Isa* [*peace be on him*].

Allah [the All-Aware] informed the Muslims in **Surah al- Baqrah (2:136):**

قُولُوٓاْ ءَامَنَّا بِاللَّهِ وَمَآ أُنزِلَ إِلَيْنَا وَمَآ أُنزِلَ إِلَىٰٓ إِبْرَٰهِيمَ وَإِسْمَٰعِيلَ وَإِسْحَٰقَ وَيَعْقُوبَ وَالْأَسْبَاطِ وَمَآ أُوتِىَ مُوسَىٰ وَعِيسَىٰ وَمَآ أُوتِىَ النَّبِيُّونَ مِن رَّبِّهِمْ لَا نُفَرِّقُ بَيْنَ أَحَدٍ مِّنْهُمْ وَنَحْنُ لَهُ مُسْلِمُونَ

Say, [O believers], "We have believed in Allah and what has been revealed to us and what has been revealed to Ibrahim [Abraham], Isma`il [Ishmael], Ishaq [Isaac], Ya`qub [Jacob], and the descendents [the offspring of the twelve sons of Ya`qub], and what was given to Musa [Moses] and `Isa [Jesus], and what was given to Prophets from their Lord. We make no distinction between any of them, and we are Muslims [in submission] to Him".

In **Surah al-Ma'idah (5:46)**, Allah [swt] informs us that Isa [as] was given the knowledge of both Tawrah and Injil.

وَقَفَّيْنَا عَلَىٰٓ ءَاثَٰرِهِم بِعِيسَى ابْنِ مَرْيَمَ مُصَدِّقًا لِّمَا بَيْنَ يَدَيْهِ مِنَ التَّوْرَىٰةِ وَءَاتَيْنَٰهُ الْإِنجِيلَ فِيهِ هُدًى وَنُورٌ وَمُصَدِّقًا لِّمَا بَيْنَ يَدَيْهِ مِنَ التَّوْرَىٰةِ وَهُدًى وَمَوْعِظَةً لِّلْمُتَّقِينَ-

And We sent, following in their footsteps, Isa, the son of Maryam, confirming that which came before him in the Torah; and We gave him the Injil, in which was guidance and light and confirming that which preceded it of the Torah as guidance and instruction for the righteous.

One may ask why Allah [the Most Gracious] had not sent only one Prophet and only one divine book. The reason is, after the departure of a Prophet, his followers distorted [corrupted] the messages of the Prophet by adding and/or deleting some portions of the messages sent by Allah to serve the worldly interest of the privileged/power groups. So Allah had to send next another Prophet with new/revised directions. For example, prostrating a person out of respect was allowed before the last Prophet. But this practice has been declared illegal in Islam. And Islam gave right of inheritance to women, not by the earlier religions. Fats of animals were made haram [forbidden], but it was made halal for the Muslims. In original Torah and Injil, Allah [the Most Gracious] mentioned that a Prophet named Muhammad will come after Isa [as] that have been omitted intentionally by the writers of Old and New Testaments. Allah [the Almighty] said in **Surah al-'Imran (3:70-1):**

يَٰٓأَهْلَ الْكِتَٰبِ لِمَ تَكْفُرُونَ بِـَٔايَٰتِ اللَّهِ وَأَنتُمْ تَشْهَدُونَ - يَٰٓأَهْلَ الْكِتَٰبِ لِمَ تَلْبِسُونَ الْحَقَّ بِالْبَٰطِلِ وَتَكْتُمُونَ الْحَقَّ وَأَنتُمْ تَعْلَمُونَ

O people of the Scripture, why do you disbelieve in the verses of Allah [deliberately reject them] while you witness [to their truth]? O people of the Scripture, why do you mix [confuse] the truth with falsehood and conceal the truth while you know [it]?

Also in **Surah al-Anam (6:20-1):**

$$ الَّذِينَ ءَاتَيْنَـٰهُمُ الْكِتَـٰبَ يَعْرِفُونَهُ كَمَا يَعْرِفُونَ أَبْنَاءَهُمُ الَّذِينَ خَسِرُوا أَنفُسَهُمْ فَهُمْ لاَ يُؤْمِنُونَ - وَمَنْ أَظْلَمُ مِمَّنِ افْتَرَى عَلَى اللَّهِ كَذِباً $$

$$ أَوْ كَذَّبَ بِـَايَـٰتِهِ إِنَّهُ لاَ يُفْلِحُ الظَّـٰلِمُونَ $$

Those to whom We have given the Scripture [Jews and Christians] recognize him [Muhammad or the Ka`bah at Makkah] as they recognize their [own] sons. Those who will lose themselves [in the Hereafter] do not believe. And who is more unjust than one who invents about Allah a lie or denies His verses? Indeed, the wrongdoers will not succeed.

All the prophets were sent with one mission, to invite people to Allah Almighty, the creator, not the created. We must recognize that we are all going to die, and we are going back to Allah. At that point in time, all of us are going to realize that we have no choice but to face reality, we will be rewarded by Allah for our good deeds, and punished for the bad ones. No one will share the punishment of others even if he is the most loved ones in this worldly life. The punishment will be severe that is beyond our realization, rewards will also be beyond our comprehension.

Let us look at some of the miraculous and dynamic creations of Allah. Allah has created men and women with a rainbow of colors, races, languages, nationalities or regions so that we can recognize each other, to work, help and respect one another. In the Holy Quran, Allah [the Most Gracious] says in **Surah al-Hujuraat (49:13):**

$$ يَـٰأَيُّهَا النَّاسُ إِنَّا خَلَقْنَـٰكُم مِّن ذَكَرٍ وَأُنثَى وَجَعَلْنَـٰكُمْ شُعُوباً وَقَبَائِلَ لِتَعَارَفُوا إِنَّ أَكْرَمَكُمْ عِندَ اللَّهِ أَتْقَـٰكُمْ إِنَّ اللَّهَ عَلِيمٌ $$

$$ خَبِيرٌ $$

O mankind, We have created you from a male [father Adam] and a female [mother Hawaa (Eve)] and made you peoples and tribes that you may know one another. Indeed, the most noble of you in the sight of Allah is the most righteous of you. Indeed, Allah is Knowing and Acquainted. Thus Islam has denounced all sorts of discrimination by color, race, nationality, and language.

A black slave of Abyssinian origin, Bilal Ibn Rabah was the second male adult Muslim- first *Mua'dhdhin* [caller for prayer] and *Mua'dhdhin* of Prophet Muhammad [*sas*] and the leader of *Muadhdhins*, treasurer of the first Muslim state. Bilal was also the first one to greet Prophet Muhammad in Medina when he reached Medina after migration –hugged the Prophet and kissed his head. After the conquest of Mecca, Bilal was one of the three persons who accompanied the Prophet inside *Kaba* for the first time and on Prophet's order he climbed the roof of *Kaba* to recite the *adhan*. A black slave rose to the position of one of the closet associates of the most powerful head of the first Muslim state and thus turned into a "*black diamond*", Masa-Allah [*may Allah bestow His mercy on Bila]).* Islam, thus, at the beginning of this great religion buried discrimination by color.

Allah has also created the father of mankind *Adam* (*peace be on him*) without a father and a mother; *Hawaa* [Eve] [*peace be on her*] without a mother, *Isa* [*as*] without a father and was introduced as the son of *Mariam* [Mary] in the holy book Quran. Thus we are all the children of *Adam* and *Eve*. We do not call people of other religious faiths to embrace Islam or convert anyone. Islam does not believe in baptizing, preaching, or teaching. Islam is all about presenting correct information about this great religion to others. Everyone is educated enough to distinguish right from wrong, and make judicial choice.

Few examples how Islam has honored the brothers and sisters of scriptures and their Prophets are described in the Holy Quran as:

1. There is a chapter in Quran [Chapter 3] by the name *Al-'Imran* father of *Mariam*. Only woman mentioned by name in our holy book Quran is *Mariam*. There is a complete chapter after the name of *Mariam* in the holy Quran (Chapter # 19). Allah (swt) mentioned about Mariam (Mary), in **Surah Al-'Imran (3:42):**

وَإِذْ قَالَتِ الْمَلَائِكَةُ يَا مَرْيَمُ إِنَّ اللهَ اصْطَفَاكِ وَطَهَّرَكِ وَاصْطَفَاكِ عَلَى نِسَاءِ الْعَالَمِينَ

"And (remember) when the angels said: "O Maryam! Verily, Allah has chosen you, purified you, and chosen you above the women of the nations."

2. of all the 25 Prophets, maximum number of times Holy Quran discussed about Prophet *Musa* and the children of Israel. It is also mentioned in the Quran that only Prophet with whom Allah talked directly is *Musa* [*as*]. Allah [the Great] said in **Surah an-Nisa (4:164):**

وَكَلَّمَ اللهُ مُوسَى تَكْلِيمًا

And Allah spoke to Musa [peace be on him] with [direct] speech.

3. The one who was preferred and selected as a guide during the migration of Prophet Muhammad [*peace be on him*] and his companion Hazrat Abu Bakr [*as*] from Mecca to Medina was a Christian.

4. The man who first saw Prophet Muhammad [*peace be on him*] entering Medina from the roof of his high building and rejoiced and sent the message to the people of Medina was a Jew who later embraced Islam.

5. Prophet of Islam honored the Christians of Najran from Yemen who visited him in his Medina mosque. The Christians prayed according to their religious fashion while inside the mosque, and the Prophet and his followers prayed in Muslim tradition.

6. During the time of the Prophet [*peace be on him*], super powers Persians [*atheistic, Godless believers*] and Romans [*adopted Christianity*] were at war with each other. Muslims prayed to Allah for the Romans so that they can win the war. The reason was that Romans were part of the people of the book. A complete chapter of the Quran titled the Romans [Quran, Chapter 30] was revealed at that time

7. In the early stage of the Islamic history, Muslims with only 20% of the total population of Medina had a Muslim state with majority being Jews and Christians. None of the non-Muslim population was forced to embrace Islam. Muslims made lots of treaties even with the Jews.

Islam is not to be called *Muhammadanism*. The word Islam is an Arabic word with root "*Silm*" which means Peace, Greetings, and obedience to Allah. Muslims do not worship Muhammad, and Muhammad is not the founder of Islam. The founder is Allah Himself, and the name Islam as a religion was given by *Ibrahim* [Abraham].

There is no place of *Pope, Priesthood or Nunhood, or monarchy* in Islam. Moreover, there is neither *original sin* [no concept of such sin in Islam], system of confession, nor religious hierarchy in Islam. In Islam every individual is a pope, a priest. It is thus obligatory on every Muslim to spread his knowledge on fundamentals of Islam to the larger mankind. There is no sect system in Islam. Muslims are the followers of the Quran and the teachings of our beloved Prophet. Islam does not recognize in *divinity*. Islam does neither support *fanaticism, nor radicalism*.

About killing of innocent people Allah says in **Surah al-Ma'idah (5:32):**

مِنْ أَجْلِ ذَلِكَ كَتَبْنَا عَلَى بَنِى إِسْرَءِيلَ أَنَّهُ مَن قَتَلَ نَفْسًا بِغَيْرِ نَفْسٍ أَوْ فَسَادٍ فِى الْأَرْضِ فَكَأَنَّمَا قَتَلَ النَّاسَ جَمِيعًا وَمَنْ أَحْيَهَا فَكَأَنَّمَا أَحْيَا النَّاسَ جَمِيعًا وَلَقَدْ جَاءَتْهُمْ رُسُلُنَا بِالْبَيِّنَتِ ثُمَّ إِنَّ كَثِيرًا مِّنْهُمْ بَعْدَ ذَلِكَ فِى الْأَرْضِ لَمُسْرِفُونَ

Because of that, We decreed upon the children of Israel that whoever kills a soul unless for a soul [in legal retribution for murder] or for corruption [done] in the land [that requiring the death penalty] – it is as if he had slain mankind entirely. And whoever saves one [or refrains from killing] – it is as if he had saved mankind entirely. And our messengers had certainly come to them with clear proofs. Then, indeed, many of them, [even] after that, throughout the land, were transgressors [negligent of their duties].

Killing people because of personal differences [differences is a sign of vitality, dynamism, and healthy atmosphere] is strictly prohibited in Islam.

Allah also says in **Surah ash-Shura (42:40):**

وَجَزَآؤُاْ سَيِّئَةٍ سَيِّئَةٌ مِّثْلُهَا فَمَنْ عَفَا وَأَصْلَحَ فَأَجْرُهُ عَلَى اللَّهِ إِنَّهُ لاَ يُحِبُّ الظَّلِمِينَ

The retribution of an evil act is an evil one like it, but whoever pardons and makes reconciliation - his reward is [due] from Allah. Indeed, He does not like the wrongdoers.

In **Surah al-'Imran (3:64)** Allah [the Warner] teaches us how to invite the people of scriptures:

قُلْ يَا أَهْلَ الْكِتَابِ تَعَالَوْا إِلَى كَلِمَةٍ سَوَآءٍ بَيْنَنَا وَبَيْنَكُمْ أَلَّا نَعْبُدَ إِلَّا اللَّهَ وَلَا نُشْرِكَ بِهِ شَيْئًا وَلَا يَتَّخِذَ بَعْضُنَا بَعْضًا أَرْبَابًا مِّن

دُونِ اللَّهِ فَإِن تَوَلَّوْا فَقُولُوا اشْهَدُوا بِأَنَّا مُسْلِمُونَ-

Say, "O the people of the Scripture, Come to a word that is just between us and you - that we will worship none except Allah and not associate anything with Him, and not take one another as lord instead Allah". But if they turn away, say: "Bear witness that we are Muslims".

And also in **Surah al-'Ankabut (29:46):**

وَلَا تُجَادِلُوا أَهْلَ الْكِتَابِ إِلَّا بِالَّتِي هِيَ أَحْسَنُ إِلَّا الَّذِينَ ظَلَمُوا مِنْهُمْ وَقُولُوا ءَامَنَّا بِالَّذِي أُنزِلَ إِلَيْنَا وَأُنزِلَ إِلَيْكُمْ وَإِلَـٰهُنَا

وَإِلَـٰهُكُمْ وَاحِدٌ وَنَحْنُ لَهُ مُسْلِمُونَ-

And do not argue with the People of the Scripture except in a way that is best, except for those who commit injustice among them, and say [to them], We believe in that which has been revealed to us and revealed to you by our Allah.

This is, in very brief, what Islam is all about.

We must remember that on the day of final judgment, each individual will be pardoned or rewarded on the basis of his/her activity in this worldly life. There is none accept Allah who can pardon our sins, not to speak of any individual.

Brothers and sisters of the books, your perception about Islam is mainly based on media reports, blogs, and talk shows in television that are being presented in a biased way to humiliate the religion of Islam. I will request you to read books on Islam and Islamic principles, and then you will be able to know what true Islam is all about. Moreover, you listen from news and discussions on the media about terrorism and Islam, and see videos in this connection. These, of course, are not Islam, but a few are doing all these in the name of Islam. For acts of a few deviants, it will be unjust to form your opinion about 1.5 billion followers of this great religion. So be judicious in forming your opinion about Islam.

Finally, in the final verse of the Quran revealed to Prophet Muhammad [*peace be on hmi), Allah [*the Most Gracious*] Confirmed Islam as final religion for mankind as proclaimed in Holy Quran **Surah al-Miadah (5:3):**

الْيَوْمَ أَكْمَلْتُ لَكُمْ دِينَكُمْ وَأَتْمَمْتُ عَلَيْكُمْ نِعْمَتِي وَرَضِيتُ لَكُمُ الْأِسْلَامَ دِينًا

This day I have perfected for you your religion and completed My favor upon you and have approved for

you Islam as religion.

In Islam, Muslims while praying 5 compulsory salaat everyday, they have to recite a part from the   Holy book. So, if there are 1.5 billion Muslims in the World, 5 billion Muslims had a part of the Holy book Quran in their memory. No religious group of the world had ever to memorize a part from their scriptures. Is not that astounding?

So Islam as a religion has no competitor as it is the last religion prescribed by Allah (the Most Gracious) and announced through the last Prophet Muhammad [peace be on him] for the whole mankind till the day of final judgment. Burning copies of the Quran by a few insane can, in no way, wipe out the faith from the heart of more than 1.5 billion Muslims. May Allah (the Most Powerful) guide all of the humanity in the true and right path? **Amin!!**

Islam: The Misinterpreted Religion

Maurice Bucaille, a French doctor, who writes, shares the feeling that there is a general ignorance of Islam in the West:

"When one mentions Islam to the materialist atheist, he smiles with a complacency that is only equal to his ignorance of the subject. In common with the majority of Western intellectuals, of whatever religious persuasion, he has an impressive collection of false notions about Islam. One must, on this point, allow him one or two excuses. Firstly, apart from the newly adopted attitudes prevailing among the highest Catholic authorities, Islam has always been subject in the West to a so-called 'secular slander'. Anyone in the West who has acquired a deep knowledge of Islam knows just to what extent its history, dogma and aims have been distorted. One must also take into account the fact that documents published in European languages on this subject (leaving aside highly specialized studies) do not make the work of a person willing to learn any easier." (From The Bible, the Qur'an and Science, by Maurice Bucaille, page 118)

The misinterpretation of Islam by Christians was mainly due to the fact that they consider Islam as the rival religion. Many Christian writers tried to defame Islam that ranges from willful distortion to simple ignorance by misinterpreting it. During the Colonial period of the British [most of the Muslim countries], the colonial regime, for political reasons, used the Church for propaganda against Islam.

Even today there are many Westerners for whom Islam can be reduced to three ideas: fanaticism, fatalism and polygamy. One symptom of this ignorance is the fact that in the imagination of most Europeans, Allah refers to the divinity of the Muslims, not the God of the Christians and Jews; they are all surprised to hear, when one takes the trouble to explain things to them, that 'Allah' means 'God', and that even Arab Christians know him by no other name. Today, most Muslims in the West would probably agree that the largest volume of distorted information about Islam comes from the media, whether in newspapers, magazines or on television. In terms of the number of people who are reached by such information, the mass media certainly has more of a widespread impact on the West's view of Islam than do the academic publications.

The religion of Islam is not named after a person as in the case of Christianity that was named after Jesus Christ, Buddhism after Gotama Buddha, and Confucianism after Confucius. Nor was it named after a tribe like Judaism after the tribe of Judah and Hinduism after the Hindus. Islam is the religion that was given to Adam, the first man and the first prophet of Allah, and it was the religion of all the prophets sent by Allah to mankind. The name of Allah's religion --- Islam --- was not decided upon by later generations of man. It was chosen by Allah Himself and clearly mentioned in His final revelation to man. In the final book of divine revelation, the Qur'an, Almighty Allah states in **Surah al-Mai'dah (5:3)** the following:

الْيَوْمَ أَكْمَلْتُ لَكُمْ دِينَكُمْ وَأَتْمَمْتُ عَلَيْكُمْ نِعْمَتِي وَرَضِيتُ لَكُمُ الإِسْلاَمَ دِينًا

This day I have perfected for you your religion and completed My favor upon you and have approved for you Islam as religion.

Due to this fact, and since the teachings of Islam are straightforward, profound and logical, Islam is the "Natural Religion" of all human beings. The name of no other religion carries any significant message, or conveys the true sense of its outlook on life, as does the name "Islam". Islam is truly unique among the religions of the world because it is addressed to all of mankind. The scripture of Islam, called the Qur'an, repeatedly addresses all human beings by saying: "O mankind!" Additionally, in the Qur'an, Almighty Allah is never addressed as the Allah of a particular people or nation.

Allah (swt) also declares in **Surah al-'Imran (3:85):**

وَمَن يَبْتَغِ غَيْرَ الإِسْلَامِ دِينًا فَلَن يُقْبَلَ مِنْهُ وَهُوَ فِي الآخِرَةِ مِنَ الْخَاسِرِين.

And whoever desires other than Islam as religion, - never will it be accepted from him, and he, in the Hereafter will be among the losers.

And also in **Surah al-'Imran (3:67)** Allah (swt) says:

مَا كَانَ إِبْرَاهِيمُ يَهُودِيًّا وَلَا نَصْرَانِيًّا وَلَكِن كَانَ حَنِيفًا مُّسْلِمًا وَمَا كَانَ مِنَ الْمُشْرِكِين.

Abraham was, neither a Jew nor Christian, but he was one inclining toward truth - a Muslim [submitting to Allah]. And he was not of the polytheists.

Nowhere in the Bible will we find God saying to Prophet Moses' people or their descendants that their religion is Judaism, nor to the followers of Christ that their religion is Christianity. In fact, Christ was not even his name, nor was it Jesus! The name "Christ" comes from the Greek word Christos that means "the anointed". That is, Christ is a Greek translation of the Hebrew title "Messiah". The name "Jesus" on the other hand, is a Latinized version of the Hebrew name *Esau.*

Some non-Muslims have come to incorrectly believe that Muslims worship a different God than Jews and Christians. This might be due to the fact that Muslims refer to God as "Allah", but also because over the centuries there have been many lies and distortions spread by the enemies of Islam. Moreover, the word God has a feminine 'Goddess' in English language, but Allah has no feminine word. In actuality, Muslims worship the God of Noah, Abraham, Moses and Jesus - the same God as Christians and Jews. The word "Allah" is simply the Arabic word for Almighty God and it is the same word that Arabic speaking Christians and Jews use to refer to God. If you pick up an Arabic translation of the Christian Bible, you will see the word "Allah" where "God" is used in English.

But even though Muslims, Jews and Christians believe in the same God, their concepts about Him differ quite a bit. For example, Muslims reject the idea of the Trinity or that God has become "incarnate" in the world. Also, the teachings of Islam do not rely on or appeal to "mystery" or "paradox" --- they are straightforward and clear. Islam teaches that Allah is Merciful, Loving and Compassionate and that He has no need to become man [nor do humans need for Him to].

One of the unique aspects of Islam is that it teaches that man can have a personal and fulfilling relationship with Almighty Allah without compromising the transcendence of God. In Islam there is no ambiguity in Divinity --- Allah is Allah and man is man. Muslims believe that Allah is the "Most Merciful", and that he deals directly with human beings without the need of any intermediary.

According to Islamic belief, the Prophet Muhammad was the last Messenger of Allah. He, like all of Allah's prophets and messengers - such as Noah, Abraham, Moses and Jesus -- was only a human being. Christians came to the mistaken assumption that Muslims worship Muhammad by formulating an incorrect analogy - they worship Jesus so they assumed Muslims worship Muhammad.

This is one of the reasons that they called Muslims by the incorrect name "Mohammedans" for so many years! Muhammad, like Jesus, never claimed divine status. He called people to worship only Almighty God, and he continually emphasized his humanity so that people would not fall into the same errors as Christians did in regards to Jesus. In order to prevent his deification, the Prophet Muhammad always said to refer to him as "the Messenger of Allah and His slave". Muhammad was chosen to be Allah's final messenger --- to communicate the message not only in words but to be a living example of the message. Muslims love and respect him because he was of the highest moral character and he brought the Truth from Allah- which is the Pure Monotheism of Islam.

Islam teaches Muslims to respect all of Allah's prophets and messengers - but respecting and loving them does not mean worshipping them. All true Muslims realize that all worship and prayer must be directed to Almighty Allah alone. Suffice it to say that worshipping Muhammad --- or anyone else --- along with Almighty Allah is considered to be the worst sin in Islam.

Another misinterpretation that all Muslims are Arabs is completely false. The fact is that only about 15% to 20% of the Muslims in the world are Arabs. There are more Indian Muslims than Arab Muslims, and more Indonesian Muslims than Indian Muslims! Believing that Islam is only a religion for Arabs is a myth that was spread by the enemies of Islam early in its history. This mistaken assumption is possibly based on the fact that most of the first generation of Muslims was Arabs, the Qur'an is in Arabic and the Prophet Muhammad was an Arab. Furthermore, it should be clarified that not all Arabs are Muslims and not all Muslims are Arabs. An Arab can be a Muslim, Christian, Jew, atheist - or of any other religion or ideology. Also, many countries that some people consider to be "Arab" are not "Arab" at all -- such as Turkey and Iran [Persia].

It is important to realize that from the very beginning of the mission of Prophet Muhammad [sas] his followers came from a wide spectrum of individuals -- there was Bilal, the African slave; Suhaib, the Byzantine Roman; Ibn Sailam, the Jewish Rabbi; and Salman Farsi, the Persian. The Truth of Islam is meant for all people regardless of race, nationality or linguistic background. Taking a look at the Muslim World, from Nigeria to Bosnia and from Malaysia to Afghanistan is enough to prove that Islam is a Universal message for all of mankind --- not to mention the fact that significant numbers of Europeans and Americans of all races and ethnic backgrounds are coming into Islam.

Even though many aspects of Islam are misunderstood by non-Muslims, the ignorance, misinformation and incorrect assumptions that are made in regards to Islam's treatment of women are probably the most severe. Numerous verses of the Qur'an make it clear that men and women are equal in the site of Allah. According to the teachings of Islam, the only thing that distinguishes people in the site of Allah is their level of Allah-consciousness.

Due to this, many people are surprised to find that Islamic Law guaranteed rights to women over 1400 years ago, where as women in the Europe and America only obtained the right very recently. Actually, the rights that Islam gave to women over 1400 years ago were almost unheard of in the West until the 1900s. Less than fifty years ago, in England and America, a woman could not buy a house or car without the co-signature of her father or husband! Additionally, Islam gives great respect to women and their role in society --- it gives them the right to own property, marry whom they want and many other rights. If women in the Muslim World today don't have their rights, it is not because Islam did not give these to them. The problem is that in many places alien traditions have come to overshadow the teachings of Islam, either through ignorance or due to the impact of colonialization.

Even then, while in Bangladesh, the third populous Muslim country in the world, both the Prime Minister and the Leader of the Opposition are Women for the last 12 years and hope to continue in future also; in Pakistan the second populous Muslim country in the world had a woman as Prime Minister and leader of the opposition, as well; and also in Indonesia, the most populous Muslim country in the world had a woman as President; but even today majority of the Ammericans can not yet conceive of having a woman as President of USA or a woman as president or Prime Minister in majority of the European Countries.

 It is interesting to note that no other religious scripture claims to be the direct word of Almighty in to to as clear and as often as the Holy Qur'an. Allah [swt] says in **Surah al-Baqara (2:23-4):**

وَإِن كُنتُمْ فِى رَيْبٍ مِّمَّا نَزَّلْنَا عَلَى عَبْدِنَا فَأْتُوا بِسُورَةٍ مِّن مِّثْلِهِ وَادْعُوا شُهَدَاءَكُم مِّن دُونِ اللَّهِ إِن كُنتُمْ صَادِقِينَ ۛ فَإِن لَّمْ تَفْعَلُوا وَلَن

تَفْعَلُوا فَاتَّقُوا النَّارَ الَّتِى وَقُودُهَا النَّاسُ وَالْحِجَارَةُ ۖ أُعِدَّتْ لِلْكَافِرِينَ ۛ

And if you [Arab pagans, Jews, and Christians] are in doubt about what We have sent down [i.e. the Qur'an] upon Our servant [Muhammad], then produce a Surah [chapter] the like thereof and call upon your witnesses [supporters and helpers] other than Allah, if you should be truthful. But if you do not - and you will never be able to - then fear the Fire [Hell], whose fuel is people and stones, prepared for the disbelievers. Suffice it to say that not only is the Qur'an the most memorized and well preserved scripture on earth, it is also unequaled in eloquence, spiritual impact, clarity of message and the purity of its truth.

Many non-Muslims, when they think about Islam, picture religious fanatics on camels with a sword in one hand and a Qur'an in the other. This myth, which was made popular in Europe during the Crusades, is totally baseless. First of all, the Holy Qur'an clearly says in **Surah al-Baqarah (2:256):**

لاَ إِكْرَاهَ فِى الدِّينِ

There will be no compulsion in [acceptance of] religion. In debunking the myth that Islam was "spread by the sword", the [non-Muslim] historian De Lacy O' Leary wrote: "History makes it clear, however, that the legend of fanatical Muslims sweeping through the world and forcing Islam at the point of the sword upon conquered races is one of the most fantastically absurd myths that historians have ever accepted." (Islam at the Crossroads, London, 1923, p. 8). That is why in all the eighty-two encounters between the Muslims and the non-Muslims during the life of the Holy Prophet [sas], only 1018 persons lost their lives on both sides. Out of which 259 were Muslims, whereas the remaining 759 belonged to the opposite camp. History provides testimony to the fact that during the Muslim rule in most of the world, the non-Muslims used to live happy and normal life, and were not forced to change their religion.

Many non-Muslims are surprised to see that according to Muslim belief, Jesus, the son of Mary, is one of the greatest messengers' of Allah. Muslims are taught to love Jesus, and a person cannot be a Muslim without believing in the virgin birth and miracles of Jesus Christ [as]. Muslims believe these things about Jesus not because of the Bible or any other religion, but simply because the Holy Qur'an says these things about him. However, Muslims always emphasize that the miracles of Jesus, and all other prophets, were by "Allah's permission". This is because the Qur'an clearly says that Almighty Allah does not have a "Son" --- neither allegorically, physically, metaphorically or metaphysically. Muslims are the true followers of Jesus [as] because they defend him from the exaggerations of the Christians and teach the Pure Monotheism that Jesus himself followed. Prophet Muhammad [sas] said about Jesus: "By Him in Whose Hands my soul is, son of Mary (Jesus) will shortly descend amongst you people [Muslims] as a just ruler and will break the Cross and kill the pig and abolish the Jizya [a tax taken from the non-Muslims, who are in the protection, of the Muslim government". Then there will be abundance of money and no-body will accept charitable gifts. (Bukhari, book #34, hadith #425)

Most Muslims find it rather odd that their religion, which strikes a beautiful balance between faith and action, could be accused of being "fatalistic". Perhaps this misconception came about because Muslims are taught to say "Praise be to Allah!" whenever anything good or bad happens. This is because Muslims know that everything comes from Almighty Allah, who is the All-Knowing Sustainer of the Universe, and that since a Muslim should rely completely on Allah, whatever happened must have been for the better. Far from being "fatalistic", Islam teaches that a human being's main purpose in life is to be Allah-conscious.

In recent years, great deals of attention in the media have been given to the threat of "Islamic Fundamentalism". Unfortunately, due to a twisted mixture of biased reporting in the Western media and the actions of some ignorant Muslims, the word "Islam" has become almost synonymous with "terrorism". It should be remembered that all religions have cults and misguided followers, so it is their teachings that should be looked at, not the actions of a few individuals. Unfortunately, in the media, whenever a Muslim commits a heinous act, he is labeled a "Muslim terrorist". However, when Serbs murder and rape innocent women in Bosnia, they are not called "Christian terrorists" or the Crusaders who killed millions of Muslims are not called "Christian terrorists".

While other religions have either mixed man-made doctrines with divine revelation, or ignored the divine revelation almost completely, Islam's concept of Allah is based totally on what Allah has said about Himself. Islam's concept of Allah can be called pure and straightforward because there is a clear distinction made between the Creator and the created. As such, there is no ambiguity in divinity -- it is made clear that there is nothing divine or worthy of being worshipped except for Almighty Allah. The only Creator -- Almighty Allah -- is Unique, Eternal and Transcendent above His Creation. Everything else besides Almighty Allah -- meaning anything that you can see or even imagine -- is part of Allah's creation, and thus not worthy of worship.

In other religions, even the ones which claim belief in "One God", people often approach Allah through an intermediary, such as a saint, an angel, the Virgin Mary or Jesus. However, it is only in Islam that a person is required only to pray to Allah. Additionally, in Islam there are no priests or clergy -- each worshipper, man or woman, has a direct relationship with their Merciful Creator -- Almighty Allah. Even more importantly, all rites of formal worship in Islam are based on Divine revelation, while the modes of worship in other religions are a mixture of Divine revelation, man-made traditions, opinions of clergymen and religious councils

Elsewhere, in the final book of revelation, the Qur'an Allah [swt] also said in **Surah Ghafir (40:60)**:

وَقَالَ رَبُّكُمُ ادْعُونِي أَسْتَجِبْ لَكُمْ إِنَّ الَّذِينَ يَسْتَكْبِرُونَ عَنْ عِبَادَتِي سَيَدْخُلُونَ جَهَنَّمَ دَاخِرِينَ-

And your Lord says, "Call upon Me; I will respond to you. Indeed, those who disdain My worship will enter Hell [rendered] contemptible."

In the Qur'an, Almighty Allah clearly states in **Surah an-Nahl (16:36)**:

مَّنْ حَقَّتْ عَلَيْهِ الضَّلَالَةُ فَسِيرُوا فِي الْأَرْضِ فَانظُرُوا كَيْفَ كَانَ عَاقِبَةُ الْمُكَذِّبِينَ-

And We certainly sent into every nation a messenger, [saying], "Worship Allah, and avoid [false objects of worship]. And among them were those whom Allah guided, and among them were those upon whom error was [deservedly] decreed. So proceed [travel] through the earth and observe how was the end of the deniers."

When the idol worshipper is questioned as to why he or she bows down to idols created by men, the invariable reply is that they are not actually worshipping the stone image, but God who is present within it. They claim that the stone idol is only a focal point for God's essence and is not in itself God! One who has accepted the concept of the presence of God's being within His creation in any way will be obliged to accept this argument of idolatry. Whereas, one who understands the basic message of Islam and its implications would never concede to idolatry no matter how it is rationalized.

False religions all have in common one basic concept with regards to God. They either claim that all men are gods; or that specific men were God; or that nature is God; or that God is a figment of man's imagination. Thus, it may be stated that the basic message of false religion is that God may be worshipped in the form of His creation. False religion invites man to the worship of creation by calling the creation or some aspect of it God. As Allah said **in Surah Yusuf (12:40)**:

مَا تَعْبُدُونَ مِن دُونِهِ إِلَّا أَسْمَاءً سَمَّيْتُمُوهَا أَنتُمْ وَآبَاؤُكُم مَّا أَنزَلَ اللَّهُ بِهَا مِن سُلْطَانٍ إِنِ الْحُكْمُ إِلَّا لِلَّهِ أَمَرَ أَلَّا تَعْبُدُوا إِلَّا إِيَّاهُ ذَلِكَ الدِّينُ الْقَيِّمُ وَلَكِنَّ أَكْثَرَ النَّاسِ لَا يَعْلَمُونَ-

You worship besides Him none except [mere] names you have named them, you and your fathers, for which Allah has sent down no authority. Legislation is not but for Allah. He has commanded that you worship none except Him. That is the correct religion, but most of the people do not know.

It may be argued that all religions teach good things so why should it matter which one we follow. The reply is that all false religions teach the greatest evil, the worship of creation. Creation-worship is the greatest sin that man can commit because it contradicts the very purpose of his creation. Man was created to worship Allah alone as explicitly stated in **Surah adh –Dhariyat (51:56):**

وَمَا خَلَقْتُ الْجِنَّ وَالْإِنسَ إِلَّا لِيَعْبُدُونِ-

And I did not create jinn and mankind except to worship me.

Consequently, the worship of creation, which is the essence of idolatry, is the only unforgivable sin. One who dies in this state of idolatry has sealed his fate in the next life. This is not an opinion, but a revealed fact stated by Allah in his final revelation to man:

Allah (swt) says in **Surah an-Nisa' (4:48):**

إِنَّ اللَّهَ لَا يَغْفِرُ أَن يُشْرَكَ بِهِ وَيَغْفِرُ مَا دُونَ ذَلِكَ لِمَن يَشَاءُ وَمَن يُشْرِكْ بِاللَّهِ فَقَدِ افْتَرَى إِثْمًا عَظِيمًا-

Indeed, Allah does not forgive association with Him, but He forgives what is less than that for whom He wills. And he who associates others with Allah has certainly fabricated a tremendous sin.

In **Surah al-A'raf (7:172-173),** Allah [swt] explained:

وَإِذْ أَخَذَ رَبُّكَ مِن بَنِي آدَمَ مِن ظُهُورِهِمْ ذُرِّيَّتَهُمْ وَأَشْهَدَهُمْ عَلَى أَنفُسِهِمْ أَلَسْتُ بِرَبِّكُمْ قَالُوا بَلَى شَهِدْنَا أَن تَقُولُوا يَوْمَ الْقِيَامَةِ إِنَّا كُنَّا عَنْ هَذَا غَافِلِينَ- أَوْ تَقُولُوا إِنَّمَا أَشْرَكَ آبَاؤُنَا مِن قَبْلُ وَكُنَّا ذُرِّيَّةً مِّن بَعْدِهِمْ أَفَتُهْلِكُنَا بِمَا فَعَلَ الْمُبْطِلُونَ-

And [mention] when your Lord took from the Children of Adam - from their loins - their descendants, and made them testify of themselves, [saying to them] "Am I not your Lord [who cherishes and sustains you]"? They said: "Yea! We have testified"! [This] - Lest you say on the Day of Resurrection, "Indeed, we were of this unaware". Or [lest] you say: "It was only that our forefathers associated [others in worship] with Allah

before, and we were but descendants after them. Then would you destroy us for what the falsifiers have done?"

The Prophet Muhammad [sas] said: "Every child is born with a true faith of Islam [i.e. to worship none but Allah alone] and his parents' convert him to Judaism or Christianity or Paganism, as an animal delivers a perfect baby animal. Do you find it mutilated?" (Bukhari, book #23, hadith #467)

My dear brothers and sisters, Islam is so strong and so self-assured that it does not need to use force to attract others to it. The moral and intellectual superiority of Islam over all other religions has manifested itself so clearly throughout the history of Islam. Despite all of the ills of Muslims everywhere, Islam continues to be the fastest growing religion on earth.

We pray to Almighty Allah, the Exalted, to keep us on the right path to which He has guided us, and to bestow on us a blessing from Him. He is indeed the Most Merciful. Praise and gratitude is to Allah [swt], the Lord of the Worlds, and peace and blessings are on Prophet Muhammad [sas], his Family, his companions, and those who rightly follow them. **Amin!**

Islam is under Terrorist Attack

Honest students of history will tell us that religious tolerance, racial harmony and cultural diversity are not British, American or even European inventions. For more than a thousand years, churches and synagogues rested peacefully alongside the mosques throughout the Islamic world. Now, ask ourselves, while we're on the subject of tolerance, how many mosques were there anywhere in Christian Europe during that time? Who can forget the Crusades, and the Spanish Inquisition? Are they branded as Christian terrorists?

History will once again testify that the noble character achieved the global spread of Islam and the personal example set by remarkable human beings. Our noble and illustrious ancestors were men and women of courage, honesty and personal integrity. As teachers, traders, soldiers and administrators, they took Islám to the far corners of the world. The enemies of Islám are today militarily strong, but they are spiritually and morally weak, as they always have been. These days, when religion has become marginalized, our modern world has also lost its sense of what is sacred. That is where our real strength lies, and that is where we must intensify our struggle: to win hearts and minds, and to help rebuild a spiritual and moral framework for human affairs.

It seems there is still some confusion about where Islám stands in relation to Terrorism. Sadly, terrorism and Islám have become so closely connected in the Western mindset these days, and this is not by accident. There are some people and media with a dark agenda, which seek to discredit the good name of Islám, and who consider Islám to be a threat to their global ambitions. There are, sadly, also some misguided Muslims who are playing directly into their hands, by committing acts of violence that are totally forbidden by The Holy Qur'an and the prophetic Sunnah. As to why they commit these acts of terror, the reasons can be debated, but never justified. Wisdom, Justice, Allah-awareness and gallantry: these were the core values that underpinned that great civilization, when the Islámic world had political authority and military power for more than a thousand years, "Terrorist attacks" by 'freedom fighters' are attacks by the weak designed to draw attention to a just cause and are usually resorted to by people who have exhausted all other means to draw attention to injustices and oppression.

Let us first define what we mean by Terrorism. Chambers English Dictionary defines it as 'the systematic use of violence and intimidation to achieve some goal'. In practice, the term is rarely used neutrally. One man's terrorist is usually another man's freedom fighter. In Britain, some people regarded the IRA as terrorists, in the USA they were mostly seen as freedom fighters. When the Palestinians are in Jjihd to regain their motherland from the Israelis they are branded as terrorists by the Americans and some Western leaders. In South Africa during the Apartheid era, the whites regarded Nelson Mandela and the African National Congress as terrorists, the blacks regarded them as freedom fighters, and so on. Therefore, 'terrorism' is often used selectively to describe the actions of an enemy, whereas the same actions by one's friends may be regarded as heroic and justified, much hypocrisy and double standards surround this term. As Muslims, our only point of reference is our Holy Qur'an and Sunnah. What does Islám say about terrorism?

One of the great moral debates in history has been the question of means and ends. Does the end justify the means? Can one achieve moral ends by immoral means? The ends and the means are inextricably integrated with each other. Only moral means can achieve moral ends. This was the way of the Prophets and of all Allah's beloved servants, throughout the ages. However much we are provoked, however much we might be tempted to retaliate or to defend ourselves with forbidden actions, and we cannot do so. Terrorism is evil. Terrorism is indiscriminate. An act of terror does not distinguish between soldier and civilian, innocent or guilty. By its very nature it is an act of cowardice. Islám does not promote or condone cowardice.

It seems rather strange and unnecessary that one should need to explain why Islám condemns terrorism. After all, the very word, Islám, is derived from the Arabic letters 'seen' 'laam' and 'meem' which form the root word "salaam" meaning 'Peace.' Islám therefore means the state of being at peace, or to bring into peace. In its very root, therefore, there is nothing in common between a way of life that stands for peace, harmony, order, justice and compassion on the one hand, and acts of hatred, vengeance and evil on the other. Indeed, Islám and terrorism stand at the very opposite ends of the moral spectrum. In Islám, life is so sacred; it is a gift from Allah that He alone has the right to take back. Murder, suicide and the killing of innocent civilians in warfare, is strictly forbidden. In **Surah al-Ma'idah (5:32),** Allah [swt] says:

$$\text{مَن قَتَلَ نَفْسَاً بِغَيْرِ نَفْسٍ أَوْ فَسَادٍ فِي الأَرْضِ فَكَأَنَّمَا قَتَلَ النَّاسَ جَمِيعاً وَمَنْ أَحْيَاهَا فَكَأَنَّمَا أَحْيَا النَّاسَ جَمِيعا"}$$

Whoever killed a soul unless for a soul [in real retribution of murder] or for corruption [done] in the land [that requiring a death penalty] -- it is as if he has slained mankind entirely. And whoever saves one [or refrains from killing] – it is as if he saved he had saved mankind entirely.

The word Jihad is derived from the verb jahada that means: "he exerted himself". Thus literally, Jihad means exertion, striving; but in juridical-religious sense, it signifies the exertion of one's power to the utmost of one's capacity in the cause of Allah. Thus Jihad in Islam is not an act of violence directed indiscriminately against the non-Muslims; it is the name given to an all-round struggle that a Muslim should launch against evil in whatever form or shape it appears. A Muslim is saddled with the responsibilities to protect him and all those who seek his protection. He cannot afford to abandon the defenseless people, old man, women and children to privation, suffering and moral peril. Fighting in Islam, therefore, represents in Islamic law what is known among Western jurists as "just war".

A Muslim is only permitted to take up arms for Jihad as described in **Surah an-Nisâ'(4:75)** as:

$$\text{وَمَا لَكُمْ لاَ تُقَاتِلُونَ فِي سَبِيلِ اللَّهِ وَالْمُسْتَضْعَفِينَ مِنَ الرِّجَالِ وَالنِّسَاءِ وَالْوِلْدَانِ الَّذِينَ يَقُولُونَ رَبَّنَا أَخْرِجْنَا مِنْ هَـذِهِ الْقَرْيَةِ}$$
$$\text{الظَّـالِمِ أَهْلُهَا وَاجْعَل لَّنَا مِن لَّدُنْكَ وَلِيَّاً وَاجْعَل لَّنَا مِن لَّدُنْكَ}$$

And is [the matter] with you that you fight not in the cause of Allah and [for] the oppressed men, women, and children, who say, "Our Creator, take us out of this city of oppressive people and appoint for us from Yourself a protector and appoint for us from Yourself a helper".

In this case, striving in this effort, against an oppressor, is known as Jihad. It does not matter who the oppressor is – all Muslims have a duty to fight all forms of oppression, discrimination and slavery [whether it is social, political or economic]. If a Muslim is oppressing a Muslim, then all Muslims must perform Jihad against the Muslim ruler to fight on behalf of the silent masses. If a Jewish government is oppressing its Jewish citizens, then Muslims have a duty to perform Jihad against the oppressor. If a Christian government or a Hindu government or a Communist government or any other oppressive government is oppressing its citizens, then Muslims are duty bound to assist and free the victims of oppression.

Islam places great emphasis on the rules of conduct in any war. War is the last resort, when all other measures fail. Discussion and negotiation win more wars and battles than military conflict- "jaw-jaw" is better than "war-war." In the extreme scenario when war is inevitable, then Muslims are duty bound to abide to the following very strict conditions of warfare: Muslims cannot dishonor a treaty; they cannot mutilate the dead; they cannot kill women, children, the elderly or any person who does not carry weapons. A Muslim cannot kill those engaged in worship, like monks or priests or Rabbis; we cannot cut down trees or burn crops or poison water supplies [i.e. use chemical weapons]; we are only allowed to kill those who physically attack us, intending to kill us.

Islam has purified even war of all its cruelty and horrors and has made it a "reformative process" to deal with evil. The Holy Qur'an observes in **Surah al-Baqarah (2:190):**

وَقَـٰتِلُواْ فِى سَبِيلِ اللَّهِ الَّذِينَ يُقَـٰتِلُونَكُمْ وَلاَ تَعْتَدُواْ إِنَّ اللَّهَ لاَ يُحِبُّ الْمُعْتَدِينَ۔

Fight in the way of Allah those who fight you but do not commit aggression. Indeed, Allah does not like the aggressors.

Mohammad [sas] was persecuted and forced to flee from the land of his birth. He came back victorious after 10 years – in that moment of victory, he was the Superpower of Arabia and he could have annihilated all his enemies – yet, not a single drop of blood was shed – he performed Jihad of the highest order, when he forgave his enemies. The Prophet Jesus [as] did not pray for revenge-he controlled his inner desire [*'nafs'*] for revenge, sympathy and sense of justice.

That is why in all the eighty-two encounters between the Muslims and the non-Muslims during the life of the Holy Prophet [sas], only 1018 persons lost their lives on both sides. Out of them 259 were Muslims, whereas the remaining 759 belonged to the opposite camp. One wonders at the audacity of these writers only when one compares the religious wars of Charles the Great, in which 4300 pagan Saxons were killed in cold blood.

It is indeed strange that the criticism on the use of sword by Muslims emanates from those whose hands are soiled in the blood of countless innocent human beings, by those who exult in the techniques of homicide, who have depersonalized warfare to such an extent that millions of innocent men and women are put to death and numberless are thrown into concentration camps and flogged with steel rods and ox-hide whips, and all this is done without any qualm of conscience. As human being, we hang our heads down in shame when we think of the horrifying atrocities that have been perpetrated by the modern civilized world. It is estimated that, in the First World War, ten million soldiers were killed and an equal number of civilians lost their lives, and twenty million died on account of widespread epidemics and famines throughout the world as an aftermath of this war. Economic costs are estimated at $338b of which $186b were direct costs.

The losses in the Second World War were staggeringly greater compared to those in the first one. Twenty-two million persons were killed and thirty-four million were wounded. The estimated cost of the war was $1.348 trillion of which $1.167 trillion consisted of direct military costs.

It is significant that in the Korean War, the first instance in which an international organization for establishing peace utilized military force to suppress aggression, more than one million persons were killed which added to the civilian deaths in Korea and totaled about five millions.

This is what makes war in Islam a '*holy*' war – that is, a war that is conducted with the highest morality, ethics and a code of conduct of behavior. Muslims are fully aware that Allah, the one and Only, Who will judge between all humanity will judge all their actions one day. This is the Day of accountability where every action of every person will be displayed. No Muslim will dare utter that he is performing an action "for the sake of Allah", when his actions are against the Code of Conduct laid down in the Qur'an and shown by the Prophet Mohamed [sas]. Thus the word "holy" simply means that it is a war with ethics, compassion and the highest moral conduct by all combatants.

Over the centuries, in Ottoman Turkey and Muslim Spain, it was such true believers who cared for the wretched and persecuted, like the Jews were in Europe. If we study the history of Islam, we will find that Muslims were the protectors of persecuted minorities like the Jews. While Jewish people were persecuted in Europe, Muslims not only gave them shelter, but also employed their talents at the highest levels of the empire, in great Islámic cities like Istanbul, Cairo, Fez, Granada and Cordoba.

It is often said that 'the pen is mightier than the sword'. Part of our Jihad, therefore, is in the field of information. We must engage the propaganda and misinformation about our faith, with truthful, articulate and sincere words and actions. We have to purify our hearts and minds, and struggle towards establishing truth over falsehood.

If we ask what motives, what values underpin the foreign policies of the USA, Britain and in fact, we will find phrases like 'to pursue our national interests abroad', 'to liberate and restore democracy' we will look in vain, to find words like justice, human rights, or fairness or compassion towards disadvantaged people. If the most powerful nations on earth could set a good example, they would adopt foreign policies based on human rights, justice and compassion towards weaker nations. This will recognize the frailties and vulnerabilities of others, rather than exploit them. We believe that such a wise, compassionate and farsighted policy will make the world a much safer place for everyone. It will certainly drain the swamp of misery and despair that today still nourishes the evil of hatred and terror.

We must not lose sight of the important distinction between a "freedom fighter" and a "terrorist" or we will fall into the US and UK propaganda trap of demonizing all people who have no other option but to use "terrorist activity" as a political weapon against Isla'm. And, they call us terrorists! "Islámic Terrorist", is a contradiction; a vulgar and mischievous travesty of language. Moreover, American rulers and their principal ally Britain created Frankenstein to serve their purpose, but now they are branded as Islamic terrorists- what an irony of fate? Muslims and Muslim states strongly condemn attributing terrorism to Islam. One should not condemn a nation or a religion or a country, based on the actions of a few individuals. Generalizations breed hatred. Hatred is a cancer that destroys the bearer of this disease. Unfortunately, many world media organizations mischievously spread this unjust accusation against Islam without evidence or proof. Actually Islam is under terrorist attack by a few rulers, their associates, and of their media. Allah says in **Surah an-Nur (24:13):**

لَّوْلَا جَآءُو عَلَيْهِ بِأَرْبَعَةِ شُهَدَآءَ فَإِذْ لَمْ يَأْتُوا بِالشُّهَدَآءِ فَأُوْلَـئِكَ عِندَ اللَّهِ هُمُ الْكَـذِبُونَ

Why did they [who slandered] not produce for it four witnesses? And when they do not produce the witnesses, then it is they, in the sight of Allah, who are the liars.

If individual and group terrorism is regarded as dangerous and inhuman, state terrorism should be regarded as more dangerous and more barbaric, for it is an organized one in which the state perpetrates all kinds of heinous acts against innocent and harmless people with all its apparatuses, power and domination without hindrance.

Latest report on terrorist attacks in European Countries revealed that between 2006-2008 periods – of total terrorist attacks, 84.8% were by separatist; 6.5% by left wing; 8.3% by others; and only 0.4% by Islamists. In 2009, of a total of 294 terrorist attacks – only one was done by Islamists (Source: Europol, The Hague). Now the analysis shows the real face of terrorists. Despite these, those who brand Islam as a terrorist religion; they are the real terrorists and they are inspiring a small fraction of Muslim Ummah to become terrorist to serve the evil purpose of these Satans.

Dear brothers and sisters in Islam, if your country is invaded, your infrastructures including hospitals and bridges are demolished by heavy artillery bombardments and air strikes, if innocent people including men, women and children are indiscriminately killed, if your house is demolished by air strikes or bombardments, and all your relatives including your father, mother are buried under the rubbles of your demolished house and you are the lone survivor of the attack, if you want to take revenge by whatever means you have at your disposal, then if the whole world say that you are a terrorist and you belong to the fascist religion, believe me I am ready to go against the whole world. All terrorism in the world can only be stopped by doing justice and only justice to every nation, individual irrespective of race, color, and religion as emphasized in the religion of Islam.

Let us pray to Alláh [swt] to help us glorify the good name of Islám. As Muslims and as true Believers, let our thoughts, our words and deeds, show convincing proof that Islám, the way of Peace, has no place for terrorism, whether it is individual, group or state terrorism. Muslims must try to Islamize themselves, their houses, their trades, their societies, and their environment. O Alláh! In these difficult times, let us defeat the hate mongers and slanderers. Help us also by giving wisdom and articulate speech. Let us personify noble character and good manners, and win the war of hearts and minds. **Amin!**

Jihad and Quranic Instructions

The root of the word "*jihad*" is "jud" which means "effort." Another related word is "*ijtihad*" which means, "working hard or diligently." There are thirty different verses in total on Jihad and only six of these verses were revealed in Mecca. The remaining twenty-four verses were all revealed in al-Madinah. The Qur'an uses the verb of "*jihad*" in its generic meaning of "exerting the best efforts against something" in the following two verses of **Surah al-'Ankabut (29:8):**

وَوَصَّيْنَا الْإِنسَانَ بِوَالِدَيْهِ حُسْنًا وَإِن جَاهَدَاكَ لِتُشْرِكَ بِي مَالَيْسَ لَكَ بِهِ عِلْمٌ فَلَا تُطِعْهُمَا إِلَيَّ مَرْجِعُكُمْ فَأُنَبِّئُكُم بِمَا كُنتُمْ تَعْمَلُونَ

And We have enjoined upon man goodness to parents. But if they endeavor to make you associate with Me that of which you have no knowledge [of its divinity], do not obey them. To Me is your return [o people] and I will inform you about what you used to do?

Most Muslim scholars consider verse 39 of Surah Al-Hajj to be the first verse that granted Muslims the right to carry arms to defend themselves against their attackers. This is the permission verse, along with verses of **Surah al-Hajj (22:38-40):**

إِنَّ اللَّهَ يُدَافِعُ عَنِ الَّذِينَ آمَنُوا إِنَّ اللَّهَ لَا يُحِبُّ كُلَّ خَوَّانٍ كَفُورٍ - أُذِنَ لِلَّذِينَ يُقَاتَلُونَ بِأَنَّهُمْ ظُلِمُوا وَإِنَّ اللَّهَ عَلَى نَصْرِهِمْ لَقَدِيرٌ - الَّذِينَ أُخْرِجُوا مِن دِيَارِهِم بِغَيْرِ حَقٍّ إِلَّا أَن يَقُولُوا رَبُّنَا اللَّهُ وَلَوْلَا دَفْعُ اللَّهِ النَّاسَ بَعْضَهُم بِبَعْضٍ لَّهُدِّمَتْ صَوَامِعُ وَبِيَعٌ وَصَلَوَاتٌ وَمَسَاجِدُ يُذْكَرُ فِيهَا اسْمُ اللَّهِ كَثِيرًا وَلَيَنصُرَنَّ اللَّهُ مَن يَنصُرُهُ إِنَّ اللَّهَ لَقَوِيٌّ عَزِيزٌ -

Indeed, Allah defends [from evil] those who have believed. Indeed, Allah does not like everyone treacherous and ungrateful. Permission [to fight] has been given to those who are being fought [the prophet's companions], because they are wronged. And indeed, Allah is competent to give them victory. [They are] those who have been evicted from their homes without right - only because they say, "Our Creator is Allah". And was it not that Allah checks the people, some by means of others, there would have been demolished monasteries, churches, synagogues, and mosques in which the name of Allah is much mentioned [praised]. Allah will surely support those who support Him [His cause]. Indeed, Allah is Powerful and Exalted in Might [able to enforce His Will].

However, there are times, in certain circumstances, when Islam [tolerates permits and sometimes even accepts] the practice of war. Islam strongly emphasizes the ideas of justice, freedom and opposition to oppression. There is another condition: fighting for self-defense. War is tolerated in these conditions, but if there is a possibility to avoid war, then this alternative, as long as it is reasonable, must be taken. Self-defense involves oppression, aggression and tyranny; Islam tolerates the use of war in these cases.

The other condition and perhaps the most important and often confused as a holy war, is the war in the name of Allah which actually means in the cause of Allah as Allah does not encourage war but rather encourages peace whenever possible. Fighting an oppressor or aggressor is fighting against oppression or aggression, thus it is fighting for justice and therefore in the name [cause] of Allah.

The fulfillment of the promise of victory in verse 22.39 is one miracle that attests to the divine source of that promise and, therefore, of the Qur'an.

Verse 22.40 stresses that had Allah not instructed people to defend themselves their freedom of worship would have been eroded, as "cloisters, churches, synagogues, and mosques" would have been destroyed. Significantly, Allah does not differentiate between those places, treating them equally as places of worship. Rather than aggression to deprive people of their freedom, as portrayed in its popularized image, armed jihad is a just struggle for freedom.

Note how Allah identifies the enemies of the Muslims. The enemies are not simply those who are not Muslims, but rather those who have waged war against the Muslims and driven them out of their homes for embracing Islam. Significantly, Allah orders the Muslims to be "kind" and "just" to the non-Muslims who did not take part in violence against them. The two verses above remove any possible ambiguity and misunderstanding as to how Muslims should treat non-Muslims who are willing to live in peace with them, and how to identify and treat their enemies.

Allah has explicitly prohibited coercing people to accept religion saying: "there is no compulsion in religion" (from 2.256). : "So turn away from them and say 'Peace,' for they shall come to know" (43.89). Allah instructed the Prophet to turn away from the disbelievers on peaceful terms, reminding him that they will come to know one day that what they rejected is the truth.

History of Jews, Christians, and believers of other faiths who lived under Islam reflects the tolerance of the Qur'an. This Qur'anic tolerance toward other religions, which history tells us Muslims applied wherever they ruled, is in complete contradiction with the extremely intolerant image of Islam in the West today.

Not only the Old Testament, which Christianity considers being the Word of God, but other aspects of Christian thought also undermine the positioning of Christianity as the religion of peace. Christians have always known all too well that responding to violence with peace only is unrealistic, unwise, and impractical. This fact was openly and formally acknowledged as early as four centuries after Jesus Christ by St. Augustine (354-430 CE), one of the most influential Christian thinkers of all time. He introduced the concept of "just war" to complement the "peaceful" nature of Christianity. This has allowed Christianity the convenience of claiming to be a totally peaceful religion, while at the same time permitting its followers to resort to war when they deem it just and necessary!

The attitude of Christianity, or more accurately some of its representatives, toward peace and war, cannot be properly assessed without referring to the crusades. These were certainly religious wars that were instigated and supported by Popes and clerics, and carried out under the name of Jesus and Christianity. Pope Urban II (1088-1099 CE), whose speech at the Council of Clermont in November of 1095 effectively launched the first crusade and set in action this deadly chain of religious wars, promised the immediate remission of all sins of anyone who took part in the crusade. Although the crusaders were supposed to target Muslims, their very long list of victims included at the end many thousands of Jews, and even non-Catholic Christians.

The two biggest wars in the history of humanity, World War I and II, which resulted in tens of millions of deaths, were started by the Christian world. While, unlike the crusades, these two wars, and the many other wars that Christians were involved in, were not religious, they show clearly that the history of Christians is far from being one of peace, certainly not one of responding to aggression with peace. Verses 22:39-40 show clearly that armed jihad is a defensive rather than offensive form of struggle:

Allah commands the Muslims here to fight, in addition to the disbelievers who have declared war against them, the hypocrites who rejoined the forces of disbelievers and fought against the Muslims after having a spell with them. Allah commands the Muslims not to fight those who withdraw, do not fight them, and offer them peace. As for those who side with their people against the Muslims, don't offer peace, and don't restrain their hands, Allah has given the Muslims a clear authority to fight them. It is absolutely clear that armed jihad is defensive reaction rather than offensive action.

There are so many references in the Qur'an instructing the Prophet and the Muslims to establish peace with any enemy once that enemy became interested in peace.

The term jihad actually refers to the more general concept of exerting efforts in the way of Allah, of which fighting the enemy, or armed jihad, is only one aspect. The Qur'an refers in several verses to doing jihad with "one's properties and self," i.e. sacrificing one's properties and self in the cause of Islam, as in **Surah al-Hujurat (49:15):**

إِنَّمَا الْمُؤْمِنُونَ الَّذِينَ آمَنُوا بِاللَّهِ وَرَسُولِهِ ثُمَّ لَمْ يَرْتَابُوا وَجَاهَدُوا بِأَمْوَالِهِمْ وَأَنْفُسِهِمْ فِي سَبِيلِ اللَّهِ أُولَئِكَ هُمُ الصَّادِقُونَ-

The believers are only the ones who have believed in Allah and His Messenger and then doubt not but strive with their properties and their lives in the way of Allah. It is those who are the truthful.

Doing jihad with one's properties and self in the way of Allah covers every effort that the person exerts to please Allah. Even when such efforts are in connection with a war, they would include more than the act of fighting. In other words, jihad is more than armed jihad, which itself is more than just fighting So, one major aspect of the widespread misunderstanding of "jihad" is reducing it to "fighting in the way of Allah." What has made this confusion of "jihad" with "fighting" particularly disastrous is another serious misunderstanding, which is that of the characteristics of Islamic fighting, i.e. "fighting in the way of Allah." The erroneous view of the Qur'anic concept of fighting in the way of Allah has been extended to the Qur'anic concept of jihad. Thus, the true Qur'anic meanings of "*jihad*" and "fighting in the way of Allah" have both been distorted.

Clearly, armed jihad in Islam is not about vengeance. It is the kind of armed struggle that can be truly and fairly described as a war for peace. Then Allah [swt] says in **Surah at-Tawbah (9:6):**

وَإِنْ أَحَدٌ مِّنَ الْمُشْرِكِينَ اسْتَجَارَكَ فَأَجِرْهُ حَتَّى يَسْمَعَ كَلَامَ اللهِ ثُمَّ أَبْلِغْهُ مَأْمَنَهُ ذَلِكَ بِأَنَّهُمْ قَوْمٌ لاَّ يَعْلَمُونَ-

And if anyone of the polytheists seeks your protection [O Muhammad], then grant him protection so that he may hear the words of Allah [the Quran]. And deliver him to his place of safety. That is because they are people who do not know.

The first verse shows that Islam does not consider a peaceful disbeliever an enemy. In fact, the Qur'an commanded the Prophet to give protection to any polytheist who sought his help.

Finally, verse 9.13 urges the Muslims to fight aggression, reminding them of the background of the conflict with the disbelievers. First, it was the polytheists who broke the treaty they had with the Muslims. Second, like the Meccans who forced the Prophet to immigrate to al-Madinah, the polytheists were trying to expel him from al-Madinah. Third, it was the polytheists who attacked the Muslims first.

The Qur'anic concept of jihad refers to exerting efforts, in the form of struggle against or resistance to something, for the sake of Allah. This effort can be fighting back armed aggression, but can also be resisting evil drives and desires in one's self. Even donating money to the needy is a form of jihad, as it involves struggling against one's selfishness and inner desire to keep one's money for one's own pleasures. Jihad can, therefore, be subdivided into armed jihad and peaceful jihad. Armed jihad, which is the subject of Chapter 4, is only temporary and is a response to armed aggression. Once the aggression has ceased, armed jihad comes to an end. Armed jihad, thus, can take place only when there is an aggressive, external enemy. Causes of peaceful jihad, on the other hand, are always existent, which is why this form of jihad is permanent. One major form of peaceful jihad is the war of the Muslim against his "nafs," an Arabic term that may be translated as the "lower self," and which refers to the individual's inferior drives and evil motives. This most dangerous enemy never disappears; hence this war knows no end.

Linguistically, the general term *"jihad"* which refers to "struggle" and "resistance," has almost exactly the opposite meaning of the general term "Islam", which means "surrender" or "submission". The Qur'anic *"jihad"*, however, which is about resisting the lower self and other sources and forms of evil, is the route that the individual must take to attain the state of Qur'anic "Islam". Many Muslims think that *"jihad"* means "holy war". It is a sad but undeniable fact that many Muslims learn about Islamic practices and concepts, such as jihad, from secondary, often unreliable, sources. It is not uncommon even for cultural beliefs and narratives to be among those sources.

By the means of media, Islam has been given a sinister image in the eye of the public opinion; this notorious image is mainly due to the ignorance and misunderstanding of the media and public. A word which is often heard and associated with the acts of certain individuals, claiming to act in the name of Islam, is the Arabic word: Jihad. Its significance plays an extremely crucial role in the image of Islam. But what does this so widely known word mean?

Jihad may also reflect the war aspects in Islam. The fighting of a war in the name of justice or Islam, to deter an aggressor, for self-defense, and/or to establish justice and freedom to practice religion, would also be considered a Jihad. Allah [swt] orders in **Surah al-Hajj (22:78):**

وَجَاهِدُوا فِي اللَّهِ حَقَّ جِهَادِهِ هُوَ اجْتَبَاكُمْ وَمَا جَعَلَ عَلَيْكُمْ فِي الدِّينِ مِنْ حَرَجٍ مِلَّةَ أَبِيكُمْ إِبْرَاهِيمَ هُوَ سَمَّاكُمُ الْمُسْلِمِينَ مِن

قَبْلُ وَفِي هَذَا لِيَكُونَ الرَّسُولُ شَهِيدًا عَلَيْكُمْ وَتَكُونُوا شُهَدَاءَ عَلَى النَّاسِ فَأَقِيمُوا الصَّلَاةَ وَآتُوا الزَّكَاةَ وَاعْتَصِمُوا بِاللَّهِ هُوَ

مَوْلَاكُمْ فَنِعْمَ الْمَوْلَى وَنِعْمَ النَّصِيرُ

And strive for Allah with the striving due to Him [with sincerity and under discipline]. He has chosen you and has not placed upon you in the religion any difficulty. [It is] the religion of your father Ibrahim [Abraham]. He named you Muslims before [in former scriptures] in this [revelation] that the Messenger may be a witness over you, and you may be witnesses over the people. So establish regular Prayer and give [zakah] regular charity and hold fast to Allah. He is your Protector; and excellent is the protector, and excellent is the helper.

Examples of this Jihad would be to exceed in the sincere act of good deeds [to frequent the mosques that worship Allah alone more often; to study the scripture in detail, to help the poor and the orphans, to stand for people's right for freedom, be equitable, never bear witness false testimony, frequent and stay in good terms with friends and neighbors, etc.] and the restraining of the doing of sins [to commit adultery, to steel, to lie, to cheat, to insult people, to gossip, etc.].

Since this verse shows that Allah accepts only justice, fighting in the name of Allah is fighting in the name of justice. But, contrary to many people's interpretation, Jihad is anything but a holy war; the media and public misunderstand this.

In Brief; the meaning the media gives to this word "*Jihad*" is false. This word does not mean a holy war, for there is nothing holy about a war in Islam. There are times when war is tolerated, permitted and even, in some case, to a point accepted, but never considered holy. Islam is a religion of peace, no matter what certain media or deranged individuals say or claim. Islam revolves around the concept of peace. Allah [swt] says in **Surah al-Anfal (8:61):**

وَإِن جَنَحُوا لِلسَّلْمِ فَاجْنَحْ لَهَا وَتَوَكَّلْ عَلَى اللَّهِ إِنَّهُ هُوَ السَّمِيعُ الْعَلِيمُ

And if they incline to peace, then incline to it [also] and rely upon Allah. Indeed, it is He who is the Hearing, the knowing.

O, Allah! Give us the courage and guidance to do Jihad as you have instructed in the Holy Qur'an to defend your religion, justice, freedom and opposition to oppression. **Amin!**

Journey from Here to Hereafter

Duration of human life in this world is very very short compared to our creation as "*ruh*". "*Ruh*" was created millions of billions of years ago. What is the purpose f the creation of our worldly lives? Allah [swt] says in **Surah al-Mulk (67:2):**

الَّذِي خَلَقَ الْمَوْتَ وَالْحَيَاةَ لِيَبْلُوَكُمْ أَيُّكُمْ أَحْسَنُ عَمَلًا وَهُوَ الْعَزِيزُ الْغَفُورُ

[He] who created death and life to test you [as to] which of you is best in deed - and He is the Exalted in Mighty, the Forgiving.

Allah [swt] states that He has created all mankind from Adam, peace be upon him, and from Adam, He created his wife, Hawwa' and from them, people started to spread. Allah [swt] created our "ruh" as stated in **Surah al-A`raf (7:172):**

وَإِذْ أَخَذَ رَبُّكَ مِنْ بَنِي آدَمَ مِنْ ظُهُورِهِمْ ذُرِّيَّتَهُمْ وَأَشْهَدَهُمْ عَلَى أَنْفُسِهِمْ أَلَسْتُ بِرَبِّكُمْ قَالُوا بَلَى

And [mention] when your Lord took from the Children of Adam - from their loins, - their descendants and made them testify of themselves, [saying to them], "Am I not your Lord"? They said: "Yes! We have testified,'"

After the creation of our "*ruhs*", all the "*ruhs*" testified that Allah [swt] is our creator. So Allah [swt] created life and deaths in this world in order to test whether our testification of Allah [swt] as the creator, we truthfully obey His orders. All the "*ruhs*" were kept in the world of "*ruhs*" and the "*ruhs*" were chronologically sent, as per the wish of Allah [swt], and breathed "ruh" when the human being is put together in the womb of the mother as flesh i.e. after 120 days after the Nutfah stage, as Prophet Muhammad [sas] narrated, "…..Then Allah sends an angel who is ordered to write four things. He is ordered to write down his [i.e. the new creature's] deeds, his livelihood, his [date of] death, and whether he will be blessed or wretched [in religion]. Then the soul is breathed into him……" (Bukhari: book # 54, hadith # 430). That is how we came to this world as a live human being. We are alive because there is something in our physical body, which is "*ruh*". When the "*ruh*" is taken out of the human physical body, the human being is declared as dead.

Allah [swt] describes beautifully our life in this world as short lived in **Surah Yunus (10:24)** as:

إِنَّمَا مَثَلُ الْحَيَاةِ الدُّنْيَا كَمَاءٍ أَنْزَلْنَاهُ مِنَ السَّمَاءِ فَاخْتَلَطَ بِهِ نَبَاتُ الْأَرْضِ مِمَّا يَأْكُلُ النَّاسُ وَالْأَنْعَامُ حَتَّى إِذَا أَخَذَتِ الْأَرْضُ

زُخْرُفَهَا وَازَّيَّنَتْ وَظَنَّ أَهْلُهَا أَنَّهُمْ قَادِرُونَ عَلَيْهَا أَتَاهَا أَمْرُنَا لَيْلًا أَوْ نَهَارًا فَجَعَلْنَاهَا حَصِيدًا كَأَنْ لَمْ تَغْنَ بِالْأَمْسِ كَذَلِكَ نُفَصِّلُ

الْآيَاتِ لِقَوْمٍ يَتَفَكَّرُونَ

The example of [this] worldly life is but like rain which We have sent down from the sky that the plants of the earth absorb – [those] from which men and livestock eat – until when the earth its adornment and beautified and its people suppose that they have capability over it, there comes to it Our command by night or by day, and We make it as a harvest [utterly destroyed], as if it had not flourished yesterday. Thus do We explain in detail the signs for people who give thought.

And also as deception as in **Surah Fatir (35:5):**

$$يَا أَيُّهَا النَّاسُ إِنَّ وَعْدَ اللَّهِ حَقٌّ فَلَا تَغُرَّنَّكُمُ الْحَيَاةُ الدُّنْيَا وَلَا يَغُرَّنَّكُم بِاللَّهِ الْغَرُورُ$$

O mankind, indeed, the promise of Allah is truth, so let not the worldly life this present life delude you and be not deceived about Allah by the deceiver [Satan].

Allah [swt] describes our desires in this world in **Surah al-A'la (87:16-17)** as:

$$بَلْ تُؤْثِرُونَ الْحَيَاةَ الدُّنْيَا - وَالْآخِرَةُ خَيْرٌ وَأَبْقَى$$

But you prefer the worldly life, while the Hereafter is better and more lasting.

Our desires and likings in this world over carrying out the orders and commands of Allah [swt] and chance of being rewarded in the life Hereafter is described in **Surah al-`Imran (3:14-15):**

$$زُيِّنَ لِلنَّاسِ حُبُّ الشَّهَوَاتِ مِنَ النِّسَاءِ وَالْبَنِينَ وَالْقَنَاطِيرِ الْمُقَنطَرَةِ مِنَ الذَّهَبِ وَالْفِضَّةِ وَالْخَيْلِ الْمُسَوَّمَةِ وَالْأَنْعَامِ وَالْحَرْثِ ذَلِكَ$$

$$مَتَاعُ الْحَيَاةِ الدُّنْيَا وَاللَّهُ عِندَهُ حُسْنُ الْمَآبِ - قُلْ أَؤُنَبِّئُكُم بِخَيْرٍ مِّن ذَلِكُمْ لِلَّذِينَ اتَّقَوْا عِندَ رَبِّهِمْ جَنَّاتٌ تَجْرِي مِن تَحْتِهَا$$

$$الْأَنْهَارُ خَالِدِينَ فِيهَا وَأَزْوَاجٌ مُّطَهَّرَةٌ وَرِضْوَانٌ مِّنَ اللَّهِ وَاللَّهُ بَصِيرٌ بِالْعِبَادِ$$

Beautified for people is the love of that which they desire - of women and sons, heaped-up sums of gold and silver, fine, branded horses and cattle and tilled land. That is the enjoyment of worldly life, but Allah has with Him the best return [paradise]. Say: "Shall I inform you of [something] far better than that? For those who fear Allah will be gardens [Paradise] in the presence of their Lord beneath which rivers flow, wherein they abide eternally, and purified spouses and approval from Allah. And Allah is seeing [aware] of [His] servants".

The worldly life is a practical examination, where the question is: Do we, without any doubt, believe in Allah [swt] as creator and sustainer? The world is the examination hall, and the duration of examination is our individual lifetime. Satan and his associates whisper in our ears all the time and tempt, and arise our desires to get women, and acquire wealth including gold, silver, other worldly beauties; forgetting our creator Allah [swt] and

His commandments.. The result of the examination is also known. If we pass, we will be given excellent return "*Jannah*"; and if we fail, we will be sent to hellfire [the place of unbearable torment] permanently.

Those of us, who consider the worldly life as the period for making amusements and enjoyment, forgetting the purpose of our life as desired by Allah [swt] and denying His commandments, Allah [swt] clearly and categorically states in **Surah al-Hadeed (57:20):**

اعْلَمُوٓا أَنَّمَا الْحَيَوٰةُ الدُّنْيَا لَعِبٌ وَلَهْوٌ وَزِينَةٌ وَتَفَاخُرٌ بَيْنَكُمْ وَتَكَاثُرٌ فِي الْأَمْوَٰلِ وَالْأَوْلَٰدِ كَمَثَلِ غَيْثٍ أَعْجَبَ الْكُفَّارَ نَبَاتُهُۥ ثُمَّ يَهِيجُ فَتَرَىٰهُ مُصْفَرًّا ثُمَّ يَكُونُ حُطَٰمًا وَفِي الْءَاخِرَةِ عَذَابٌ شَدِيدٌ وَمَغْفِرَةٌ مِّنَ اللَّهِ وَرِضْوَٰنٌ وَمَا الْحَيَوٰةُ الدُّنْيَآ إِلَّا مَتَٰعُ الْغُرُورِ

Know that the life of this world is but amusement and diversion and adornment and boasting to one another and competition in increase of wealth and children – [It is] like the example of a rain whose [resulting] plant growth pleases the tillers; then it dries and you see it turned yellow; then it becomes [scattered] debris. And in the Hereafter [there is] severe punishment, and forgiveness from Allah and approval. And what is the worldly life except the enjoyment of delusion.

The consequences of forgetting the commandments of Allah [swt], and obeying them are described in **Surah al-Baqarah (2:86)** as:

أُو۟لَٰٓئِكَ الَّذِينَ اشْتَرَوُا الْحَيَوٰةَ الدُّنْيَا بِالْءَاخِرَةِ فَلَا يُخَفَّفُ عَنْهُمُ الْعَذَابُ وَلَا هُمْ يُنصَرُونَ

Those are the one who have bought the life of this world [in exchange] for the Hereafter, so the punishment will not be lightened for them, nor will they be aided.

Allah [swt] also warns us about the consequences of our love for children and wealth at the expense for the love of Allah [swt] in **Surah al-Kahf (18:46)** as:

الْمَالُ وَالْبَنُونَ زِينَةُ الْحَيَوٰةِ الدُّنْيَا وَالْبَٰقِيَٰتُ الصَّٰلِحَٰتُ خَيْرٌ عِندَ رَبِّكَ ثَوَابًا وَخَيْرٌ أَمَلًا

Wealth and children are the adornment of the worldly life. But the enduring good deeds are better to your Lord [in His sight or evaluation] for reward and better for [one's] hope.

And also in **Surah at-Taghabun: (64:15):**

إِنَّمَآ أَمْوَٰلُكُمْ وَأَوْلَٰدُكُمْ فِتْنَةٌ وَاللَّهُ عِندَهُۥٓ أَجْرٌ عَظِيمٌ

And also in **Surah al-`Imran (3:185),**

وَمَا الْحَيَوةُ الدُّنْيَا إِلَّا مَتَـٰعُ الْغُرُورِ

 And what is the life of this world except the enjoyment of delusion.

And in **Surah al-Munafiqun (63:9):**

يَـٰٓأَيُّهَا الَّذِينَ ءَامَنُوا لَا تُلْهِكُمْ أَمْوَٰلُكُمْ وَلَآ أَوْلَٰدُكُمْ عَن ذِكْرِ اللَّهِ وَمَن يَفْعَلْ ذَٰلِكَ فَأُوْلَـٰٓئِكَ هُمُ الْخَـٰسِرُون

O you, who have believed, let not your wealth and your children divert you from the remembrance of Allah. And whoever does that, - then those are the losers.

And in **Surah al-Mujadilah (58:17):**

لَّن تُغْنِىَ عَنْهُمْ أَمْوَٰلُهُمْ وَلَآ أَوْلَٰدُهُم مِّنَ اللَّهِ شَيْئًا أُوْلَـٰٓئِكَ أَصْحَـٰبُ النَّارِ هُمْ فِيهَا خَـٰلِدُون

Never will their wealth or their children avail them against Allah at all. Those are being the companions of the Fire; they will abide there in eternally.

Thus, Allah [swt] reminds us of what is waiting for us in the life Hereafter in our journey from this worldly lives, which are nothing but a chance to do good deeds as per the desire of Allah [swt] and acquire hasna for our eternal life Hereafter in **Surah al-Anfal (8:67)** as:

تُرِيدُونَ عَرَضَ الدُّنْيَا وَاللَّهُ يُرِيدُ الْأَّخِرَةَ وَاللَّهُ عَزِيزٌ حَكِيمٌ

You [some Muslims] desire the commodities [material benefit] of this world, but Allah desires [for you] the Hereafter. And Allah is exalted in Might and Wise.

And also in **Surah al-'Ankabut (29:64):**

وَمَا هَـٰذِهِ الْحَيَوةُ الدُّنْيَآ إِلَّا لَهْوٌ وَلَعِبٌ وَإِنَّ الدَّارَ الْأَّخِرَةَ لَهِىَ الْحَيَوَانُ لَوْ كَانُوا يَعْلَمُون

And this worldly life of the world is not but diversion and amusement. And indeed, the home of the Hereafter -- that is the [eternal] life, if only they knew.

Brothers and sisters in Islam, our short stay in this world should not be considered as the end of everything. There will be another life in which we will have to stand before Allah [swt] for accountability of what we have done in this worldly life. May Allah [swt] bestow His mercy and guide us to the right path in this world, so that we will not have to go to Hellfire, instead, we will be pardoned and awarded paradise. **Amin.**

Justice and Truth Go Hand in Hand

Justice is Paramount in Islam. Truthfulness comes at the top of the list of morals and Allah considers it to be the foundation for all principles. A major global escalation of violence is due to the absence of justice and equity. Justice is a pre-requisite for peace. Justice can never be attained without truth. A major mission of all Prophets [as] was the "establishment of justice among people." Allah (swt) says in **Surah al-Hadeed (57:25):**

لَقَدْ أَرْسَلْنَا رُسُلَنَا بِالْبَيِّنَتِ وَأَنزَلْنَا مَعَهُمُ الْكِتَبَ وَالْمِيزَانَ لِيَقُومَ النَّاسُ بِالْقِسْطِ-

We have already sent Our messengers with clear evidences and send down with them the Scripture and the balance that the people may maintain [their affairs] with justice.

Allah certainly commands justice and goodness in everything. This is an individual and collective responsibility. Allah [swt] says in **Surah an-Nahl (16:90):**

إِنَّ اللَّهَ يَأْمُرُ بِالْعَدْلِ وَالْإِحْسَانِ وَإِيتَآءِ ذِى الْقُرْبَى وَيَنْهَى عَنِ الْفَحْشَاءِ وَالْمُنْكَرِ وَالْبَغْىِ يَعِظُكُمْ لَعَلَّكُمْ تَذَكَّرُونَ-

Indeed, Allah orders justice and good conduct and giving [help] to relatives and forbids immorality and bad conduct and oppression. He admonishes you that perhaps you will be reminded.

The suffering of Muslims around the world pains people of conscience very deeply, and we must realize that the way to end that suffering is to work to end injustice across the globe. But remember, "Never let the hatred of a people toward you moves you to commit injustice." Manifesting justice is equated to piety. Allah [swt] says in **Surah al-Mai'dah (5:8):**

يَـٰٓأَيُّهَا الَّذِينَ ءَامَنُوا كُونُوا قَوَّامِينَ لِلَّهِ شُهَدَآءَ بِالْقِسْطِ وَلَا يَجْرِمَنَّكُمْ شَنَآنُ قَوْمٍ عَلَى أَلَّا تَعْدِلُوا اعْدِلُوا هُوَ أَقْرَبُ لِلتَّقْوَى وَاتَّقُوا

اللَّهَ إِنَّ اللَّهَ خَبِيرٌ بِمَا تَعْمَلُونَ-

O you who have believed, be persistently stand firm for Allah, witnesses in justice, and do not let the hatred of a people prevent you from being just. Be just; that is nearer to righteousness. And fear Allah; indeed, Allah is acquainted with what you do.

Allah [swt] also warns against false witness in **Surah al-Baqarah (2:283)** as:

وَلَا تَكْتُمُوا الشَّهَـٰدَةَ وَمَن يَكْتُمْهَا فَإِنَّهُ ءَاثِمٌ قَلْبُهُ وَاللَّهُ بِمَا تَعْمَلُونَ عَلِيمٌ-

And do not conceal testimony, for whoever conceals it - his heart is indeed sinful, and Allah is Knowing of what you do.

Also in **Surah al-Baqarah (2:42),** Allah [swt] warns us not to hide the truth and distorting it with falsehood as:

وَلَا تَلْبِسُوا الْحَقَّ بِالْبَاطِلِ وَتَكْتُمُوا الْحَقَّ وَأَنتُمْ تَعْلَمُونَ-

Do not mix the truth with falsehood or conceal the truth while you know [the truth].

Ironically, it is this very notion of '*adl/justice*', so paramount in Islam and to people of faith; that is so absent when dealing. Islam demands peace, but a peace predicated by Justice. The two fundamental and holistic beacons of the practical philosophy that underlines the expression of Islam are 'Adl and Ihsan', fundamentals never to be compromised.

This Qur'anic principle underpins Justice together with the notion; goodness underpins all Muslim engagement pertaining to every dimensions of the struggle for justice. Abdullah ibn 'Amr [as] said: The Messenger of Allah [sas] said: "The curse of Allah be upon the one who gives a bribe and the one who accepts it." (Ibn Maajah, 2313)

Allah [swt] says in **Surah an-Nisa (4:135):**

يَـٰٓأَيُّهَا الَّذِينَ ءَامَنُوا كُونُوا قَوَّٰمِينَ بِالْقِسْطِ شُهَدَآءَ لِلَّهِ وَلَوْ عَلَىٰ أَنفُسِكُمْ أَوِ الْوَٰلِدَيْنِ وَالْأَقْرَبِينَ إِن يَكُنْ غَنِيًّا أَوْ فَقِيرًا فَاللَّهُ أَوْلَىٰ بِهِمَا فَلَا تَتَّبِعُوا الْهَوَىٰ أَن تَعْدِلُوا وَإِن تَلْوُۥٓا أَوْ تُعْرِضُوا فَإِنَّ اللَّهَ كَانَ بِمَا تَعْمَلُونَ خَبِيرًا-

O, you who have believed, stand out firmly for justice, witness for Allah even if it be against you, or parents and relatives. Whether one is rich or poor, Allah is more worthy of both [more knowledgeable of their best interest]. So follow not [personal] inclination, lest you not be just. And if you distort [your testimony] or refuse [to give it], then indeed Allah is ever, with what you do acquainted.

Allah [swt] also commands people to do Justice in **Surah an-Nisa (4:58):**

إِنَّ اللَّهَ يَأْمُرُكُمْ أَن تُؤَدُّوا الْأَمَٰنَٰتِ إِلَىٰٓ أَهْلِهَا وَإِذَا حَكَمْتُم بَيْنَ النَّاسِ أَن تَحْكُمُوا بِالْعَدْلِ إِنَّ اللَّهَ نِعِمَّا يَعِظُكُم بِهِ إِنَّ اللَّهَ كَانَ سَمِيعًا بَصِيرًا-

Indeed, Allah commands you to render trusts to whom they are due and when you judge between people, you judge with justice. Excellent is that which Allah instructs you. Indeed, Allah is ever Hearing and seeing.

Islam considers truthfulness as the key to righteousness and lying as the key to evil, as the Prophet [sas] said: "Truthfulness leads to righteousness and righteousness leads to Paradise. Lying leads to evil and evil leads to the

Hellfire." (Bukhari, book #73, hadith #116) In fact, lying is one of the major signs of hypocrisy. The Prophet [sas] said: "The signs of a hypocrite are three: When he speaks he lies, when he promises he is unfaithful, and when he is entrusted he betrays."(Bukhari, book #2, hadith #32)

Allah [swt] says in **Surah al-Ahzab (33:70-71):**

يَٰٓأَيُّهَا ٱلَّذِينَ ءَامَنُواْ ٱتَّقُواْ ٱللَّهَ وَقُولُواْ قَوْلًا سَدِيدًا ۞ يُصْلِحْ لَكُمْ أَعْمَٰلَكُمْ وَيَغْفِرْ لَكُمْ ذُنُوبَكُمْ ۗ وَمَن يُطِعِ ٱللَّهَ وَرَسُولَهُ فَقَدْ فَازَ فَوْزًا عَظِيمًا ۞

O you who have believed, fear Allah and speak [always] words of appropriate justice. He will [then] amend for you your deeds and forgive your sins. And whoever obeys Allah and His Messenger has certainly attained a great attainment.

Allah [swt] directs us to speak the truth always *i.e.,* we must not only speak the truth as far as we know it, and when we speak go straight to that which is right in deed as well as in words, meaning, to speak in a straightforward manner, with no crookedness or distortion. He promises that if we do that, He will reward us by making our deeds righteous, i.e., enabling us to do righteous deeds, and He will forgive our past sins. With regard to whatever sins we may commit in the future, He will inspire us to repent from them. This is a salvation, the attainment of our real spiritual desire or ambition, as we are on the high way to nearness to Allah [swt]. What else we can expect from Allah [swt] for speaking the truth? Truthfulness, besides being an honourable trait, is a necessity in all our public lives and perhaps is the greatest gate to happiness of individuals as well as their entire community. For example, when one wishes to make a purchase, they will look for a salesperson known for his honesty.

To find tranquility of the heart, one must stick to truthfulness. The key to blessings in our lives, our business or in our family- is truthfulness. Truthfulness will lead believers to Paradise on the Day of Judgment.

Allah [swt] says in **Surah al-Ma'idah (5:119):**

قَالَ ٱللَّهُ هَٰذَا يَوْمُ يَنفَعُ ٱلصَّٰدِقِينَ صِدْقُهُمْ ۚ لَهُمْ جَنَّٰتٌ تَجْرِى مِن تَحْتِهَا ٱلْأَنْهَٰرُ خَٰلِدِينَ فِيهَآ أَبَدًا ۚ رَّضِىَ ٱللَّهُ عَنْهُمْ وَرَضُواْ عَنْهُ ۚ ذَٰلِكَ ٱلْفَوْزُ ٱلْعَظِيمُ

Allah will say, "This is the Day when the truthful will benefit from their truthfulness. For them are Gardens [in Paradise] beneath which rivers flow, wherein they will abide forever. Allah being pleased with them, and they with Him. That is the great attainment."

The most just and accurate scale of measuring a nation's advancement is in the truthfulness of its people, whether in words or deeds. It is a major crisis when trust is lost and this occurs when people are dishonest in their dealings with one another. When this happens, lying spreads among the people - lying in words, deeds and intentions.

It is no surprise that Islamic law, or the Shari'ah, opposes and prohibits lying and exalts truthfulness; it frequently mentions truthfulness as a pre-condition for piety. In fact, Allah has decreed that truthfulness leads to piety, so whoever loses truthfulness will in turn lose piety. Allah [swt] says in **Surah at-Tawbah (9:119):**

يَـٰٓأَيُّهَا ٱلَّذِينَ ءَامَنُوا ٱتَّقُوا ٱللَّهَ وَكُونُوا مَعَ ٱلصَّـٰدِقِينَ-

O you who have believed, fear Allah and be with those who are true [in words and deeds].

Thus, Muslims must be truthful, even under extremely difficult circumstances; we must realise that nothing except truthfulness will lead to our salvation, both in this life and the life hereafter. It is incumbent upon us that we all be truthful in our words and deeds. This is so that we can regain the complete trust of others, which would bring about security, love, happiness and social-stability. Parents and guardians must raise their children on truthfulness so that they grow up having strong morals such as honesty, chastity and chivalry. Let parents be aware of lying to their children, even if it is only to silence them from crying or to calm them down, as this will get them used to the most despicable action in the scale of Allah. This is besides the fact that children will no longer trust their parent's words or be affected by them.

There are four parts to truthfulness in Islam that are necessary for all Muslims to follow: 1. *Sidq'ul Niya-* Truthfulness of the intention, 2. *Sidq'ul Lisaan-* Truthfulness of the tongue, 3. *Sidq'ul Iman-* Truthfulness of faith, 4. *Sidq'ul Aa'mal-* Truthfulness in actions.

Falsehood is such an evil that it discloses the internal corruption and wickedness of the liar, it is a name of wrong dealing which only acts in spreading evil, so much so that even without the needs that are troublesome or the forcing inclination, it leads people to committing sins.

Beware of lying, even if it is only once, as this will open the door widely for further lying. He who lies once will lose his position and trust in the eyes of the people.

The Prophet [sas] was asked about the great sins. He said, "They are: (1) To join others in worship with Allah, (2) To be undutiful to one's parents, (3) To kill a person [which Allah has forbidden to kill], and (4) to give a false witness." (Bukhari, book #48, hadith #821)

Lying is cowardliness, degradation and a transgression of the boundaries of Allah. The one who practices this evil act deserves the curse of Allah and deprivation of His mercy. Allah says in **Surah al-'Imran (3:61):**

لَّعْنَتَ ٱللَّهِ عَلَى ٱلْكَـٰذِبِينَ-

Allah's curse is upon the liars among us.

May Allah (swt) give us the courage and guidance so that we may always be truthful in our words and deeds, and perform justice when we are entrusted with. **Amin!**

Knowledge is Power

Allah [swt] enjoins us in the Holy Qur'an **Surah al-'Alaq (96:1-5):**

اقْرَأْ بِاسْمِ رَبِّكَ الَّذِى خَلَقَ - خَلَقَ الإِنسَـنَ مِنْ عَلَقٍ - اقْرَأْ وَرَبُّكَ الأُكْرَمُ - الَّذِى عَلَّمَ بِالْقَلَمِ - عَلَّمَ الإِنسَـنَ مَا لَمْ يَعْلَمْ -

Recite in the name of your Lord who created - created man from a clinging substance. Recite and your Lord is the most Generous - Who taught by the pen - taught man that which he knew not.

In these first revealed ayahs, Allah (swt) mentioned thrice about knowledge. First, Read. Second, who taught you by the pen? Third, Allah taught man which he knew not. This exemplifies the importance of gaining knowledge in Islam.

When we hear this First Revelation, the first words revealed by Allah [swt]...*Iqra!* Read! We are moved at the greatness of Allah's Divine Wisdom. Of the infinite number of messages Allah could have given to mankind [for we have so many needs and so many weaknesses], Allah Who knows all man's secrets, and his most intimate needs, chose learning, gaining knowledge or seeking and providing education as the First Message to mankind. Allah [swt] did not say in His First Message: "Go out and get rich!" or "Go out and destroy the enemies of Islam!"

The word *"Iqra"* has a double meaning. It means, *"read"* and it also means *"proclaim."* Furthermore, the very fact that the very first word of the very first revelation is "Iqra" is very significant. Furthermore, before one can *"proclaim"* or spread the message, it logically follows that the proclaimed of the message must first *"read"* – i.e. it is our duty to first acquire the knowledge [i.e. read] and then spread the knowledge [i.e. proclaim]. The Prophet [sas] also warned about a period when ignorance will prevail.

Allah's Apostle said, "From among the portents of the Hour are [the following]: 1. Religious knowledge will be taken away [by the death of Religious learned men], 2. [Religious] ignorance will prevail, 3. Drinking of alcoholic drinks [will be very common], 4. There will be prevalence of open illegal sexual intercourse (Bukhari, book #3, hadith #80).

To avert the above and to show the importance of seeking knowledge and spreading knowledge, the Prophet [sas] urged his followers to spread knowledge as much as possible. The Prophet said, "Convey [my teachings] to the people even if it were a single sentence, and tell others the stories of Bani Israel (which have been taught to you), for it is not sinful to do so. And whoever tells a lie on me intentionally, will surely take his place in the [Hell] Fire." (Bukhari, book #56, hadith #667)

Like food or sleep we have a basic need to know. True knowledge, or knowledge of Allah, gives us the strong motive to believe and to live correctly. Remove our understanding from our belief and we have blind faith or dogmas that can evaporate and disappear as easily as a drop of water on a hot sunny day. On the other hand, without Faith, we cannot gain true knowledge. Knowledge and Faith complement each other. Thus Allah [swt] reminds us in **Surah al-Imran (3:7):**

وَالرَّسِخُونَ فِي الْعِلْمِ يَقُولُونَ ءَامَنَّا بِهِ كُلٌّ مِّنْ عِندِ رَبِّنَا وَمَا يَذَّكَّرُ إِلَّا أُوْلُواْ الْأَلْبَبِ

But those firm in knowledge say, "We believe in it. All [of it] is from our Lord. And no one will be reminded except those of understanding".

Education or the process of seeking knowledge or sharing it with others is part of life itself. Messenger of Allah [sas] said: "When a man dies, his acts come to an end, but three, recurring charity, or knowledge [by which people] benefit, or a pious son, who prays for him [for the deceased". (Muslim, book #013, hadith #4005)

How do we, as Muslims, see education? What are its goals? What kind of knowledge should we seek? What is our role as parents? To help our parents and students gain a clearer understanding of their role in the educational experience The Qur'an is very clear on man's need for a broad-based education. Consider the following verses from **Surah al-Baqarah (2:31):**

وَعَلَّمَ ءَادَمَ الْأَسْمَاءَ كُلَّهَا

And He taught Adam the names - all of them.

Not all knowledge comes from man. There are things which Allah places in our hearts if we sincerely strive in His Path. Our Prophet [sas] further suggests that we must learn and be taught what we need to know. If we like, then all knowledge is religious and sacred. Education is truly an act of '*Ibadah*'. The Messenger of Allâh [sas] said:"He who goes forth in search of knowledge is in the way of Allâh till he returns." (Tirmidhi, 39:2.)

Before we can even consider what kind of knowledge we and our children must learn to live a balanced life, we must ask ourselves the question: What do we ultimately hope to achieve through education?

In an ayah Allah says in **Surah adh-Dhâriyât (51:56):**

وَمَا خَلَقْتُ الْجِنَّ وَالْإِنسَ إِلَّا لِيَعْبُدُونِ-

I did not create Jinn and mankind except to worship ME.

Our purpose on earth is to serve Allah with our different strengths and aptitudes He has given us. As His Vicegerent on earth we have to help our fellowmen in need, care for Allah's creation: the plants and animals, the institutions of the ummah. It stands to reason that all our learning must be directed at Allah, not for self-aggrandizement, not for our personal pride or social status, not to amass money, but to serve Allah and His creation. Education is the process of growing closer to Allah. Our Prophet Muhammad [sas] once said: "[When] the time would draw close to the Last Hour, knowledge would be snatched away, turmoil would be rampant, miserliness would be put [in the hearts of the people] and there would be much bloodshed". They said: "What is al-harj". Thereupon he said: "It is bloodshed". (Muslim, book #034, hadith #6438) The Messenger of Allah [sas] said:"The seeking of knowledge is obligatory upon every Muslim." (Bayhqaqi-Mishkat, 2)

We see it as the process of learning how to live a full life as good Muslims. We realized that we need a comprehensive, all-embracing education to achieve this end. Allah further emphasizes this in the Holy Qur'an in **Surah al-Baqarah (2:44):**

أَتَأْمُرُونَ النَّاسَ بِالْبِرِّ وَتَنسَوْنَ أَنفُسَكُمْ وَأَنتُمْ تَتْلُونَ الْكِتَبَ أَفَلَا تَعْقِلُونَ-

Do you order righteousness for the people and forget [to practice it] yourselves while you recite the Scripture? Then will you not understand?

Our first duty as students is to develop such noble qualities as truthfulness, sincerity, piety and humility. This Imam Ghazzali calls "the adornment and beautification of the inner self." With a *"beautiful inner self"*, with a pure heart, with noble intentions, we approach our learning. We must constantly be aware of why we seek education: not just to get a good job or to be respected by our friends. These are important goals, but they form part of the main agenda, which is to serve Allah through His creation, and ultimately to move closer to Allah [swt]. Even the teacher's guidance means nothing to us: unless we acquire true knowledge, for: "Knowledge humbles the haughty youth, as the flood washes away the hill."

If we dedicate ourselves to the task of studying Allah's creation with a view to serving Him; if our search for Truth is accompanied by a search for Taqwa [piety]; if our knowledge becomes our tools rather than our adornment, then, Insha-Allah, Allah will open our minds and our hearts to His Secrets.

Allah (swt) says in **Surah al-Jâthiyah (45:13):**

وَسَخَّرَ لَكُم مَّا فِى السَّمَوَتِ وَمَا فِى الْأَرْضِ جَمِيعًا مِّنْهُ إِنَّ فِى ذَلِكَ لَآيَتٍ لِّقَوْمٍ يَتَفَكَّرُونَ

And He has subjected to you whatever is in the heavens and whatever on the earth – all from Him. Indeed, in that are signs for people who give thought?

Seek knowledge, since it leads to a supreme status in the worldly life and in the Hereafter. It accrues a continuous reward until the Day of Judgment. Allah says in **Surah al-Mujadilah (58:11):**

يَرْفَعِ اللَّهُ الَّذِينَ ءَامَنُوا مِنكُمْ وَالَّذِينَ أُوتُوا الْعِلْمَ دَرَجَتٍ وَاللَّهُ بِمَا تَعْمَلُونَ خَبِيرٌ-

...Allah will raise those who have believed among you and those who were given knowledge by degrees. And Allah is acquainted with what you do.

Pre - Islamic science was based on the deductive method that is a defective method of inquiry. The Holy Prophet [sas] was the scientific method; he encouraged the experimental or the inductive method.

The foundation of physical science is based on three principles:

1) Unity of mankind; 2) Unity of knowledge; 3) Unity of nature.

The first one to give these principles of unity [*Tawhid*] was the Holy Prophet [sas] Why is it that three-quarters of the verses of the Holy Qur'an refer to natural phenomena? And after these verses we are told in **Surah ar-Ra'd (13:4):**

إِنَّ فِى ذٰلِكَ لَآيٰتٍ لِّقَوۡمٍ يَعۡقِلُوۡنَ-

Indeed, in that are signs for those who use their reasoning powers.

The Holy Prophet [sas] said: "The superiority of a person who cultivates knowledge over the one who does devotional exercises is like my superiority over the meanest of you!" He was the one, amongst the founders of faith, who said, "The ink of the scholar is holier than the blood of the martyr". He also taught, "Every portion of knowledge is the lost property of the believer", and also "Seek knowledge even unto China." They are the followers of him who said: "Seeking knowledge is obligatory upon every Muslim male and female"; but they do not want to learn the Qur'an and Hadith and want to remain in the gutter.

In **Surah az-Zumar (39:9)** Allah (swt) said:

قُلۡ هَلۡ يَسۡتَوِى الَّذِيۡنَ يَعۡلَمُوۡنَ وَالَّذِيۡنَ لَا يَعۡلَمُوۡنَ إِنَّمَا يَتَذَكَّرُ أُولُوا الۡأَلۡبَابِ-

Say, "Are those who know equal to those who do not know?" Only they will remember [who are] people of understanding. And furthermore, Allah advised Prophet (sas) to make supplication for increasing knowledge in **Surah Ta Ha (20:114):**

وَقُلۡ رَّبِّ زِدۡنِىۡ عِلۡما-

And Say, "My Lord, increase me in knowledge."

So we should also ask the favor of Allah (swt) to increase our knowledge. O brothers and sisters! Acquire knowledge and apply it, since acquiring knowledge is a kind of Jihad in the cause of Allah [swt] and acting according to it is a cause of guidance and insight granted by Allah [swt].

Ubayy b. Ka'b said; Allah's Messenger [sas] said: "O Abu' al-Mundhir, do you know the verse from the book of Allah which, according to you, is the greatest"? I said: "Allah and His Apostle [sas] know best". He again said: "Abu'l-Mundhir, do you know the verse from the book of Allah that, according to you, is the greatest"? I said: "Allah, there is no Rabb but He, the Living, the Eternal". Thereupon he struck me on my breast and said: "May knowledge be pleasant for you, O Abu'l-Mundhir!" (Muslim, book #004, hadith #1768)

If we read the history of Islam on Muslim education, we will find that the courses of education were as comprehensive as it could be. Knowledge was arranged in terms of Unity [*Tawhid*]. We think an Alim is one who studies only fiqh, tafsir and Hadith. How wrong it is! Do we know that Imam Abu Hanifa wrote a scientific treatise with mathematical equations and this is available at the International Library in France? Imam Ghazzali, Imam Fakhruddin Ar-Razi, Imam Shafi'i, were intellectual giants in various branches of knowledge and yet they were pious and saintly people.

In his book "The Making of Humanity", R.Briffault says: "Science before Islam was unscientific. The world did not know science before the advent of Islam". Pre - Islamic science was based on the deductive method that is a defective method of inquiry. The Holy Prophet [sws] was the scientific method; he encouraged the experimental or the inductive method.

No wonder Allah [swt] rewarded the Muslim Ummah with such brilliant scholars as Al-Ghazzali [Philosophy and education], Ibn Sina [Medicine], Zakariya Razi [Chemistry], Al-Jahiz [Biology], Ibn Khaldoun [History], Ibn Rushd [Theology], Ibn Arabi [Literature and Philosophy], and so on. These scholars had one ambition...to serve Allah and perpetuate His Deen, not merely through preaching, but through building a body of knowledge of Allah's creation and prove themselves worthy of the honor with which Allah has created them as "Fee ahsani taqweem" *(the best of creation)*.

The above achievements of the early Muslims during the Golden Age of Islam clearly indicate that the Muslims are the intellectual forbearers of the West. Currently, the Muslim world lacks the capacity to produce knowledge, the Muslim world is failing to diffuse knowledge, and the Muslim world is failing to apply knowledge. That is why the Muslim world is falling far behind and lost its supremacy.

O Muslims, take care before Islam becomes a memory of the past. Unless and until we can organize education according to the Islamic concept, and produce Allah- fearing, morally integrated, spiritually elevated, intellectually enlightened Muslims in this community, we will have no future.

O Allah, in these trying times, let us, through education, become a creative and vibrant Ummah. Help us to regain our self-respect and assert our identity in this world. **Amin!**

Lailatul Qadr: The Night of Power

A hundred years ago, the great Ottoman Empire was in its last painful moments. Since its death in 1922, the Muslim world has seen its power and influence removed and placed in the hands of European nations. This was a catastrophic loss. Ever since the time of our beloved prophet Muhammad [sas], from the 7th Century to the early 20th century, Islam and political power went hand in hand with each other. For 1300 years, in one form or another, the Muslim nation had a leader, a Khaleef, whether it was Abbasid or Ummayyad, Seljuk, Moghul, Mamluk, Fatimid or Ottoman. There was always an Amirul-Mu'mineen, a Commander-in-chief of the Faithful, who held power and political authority over the Muslim Ummah. Now, for nearly a century, we have none.

Although we have over 40 nation-states with a population of over one-fourth of the world population, our political power is not even, really, in the hands of our own Muslim governments. Most of them are serving someone else's agenda rather than being the servant of Allah [swt]. Ultimately, these days, it seems as if external forces decide the affairs of the Muslim world.

We may well ask - why are we suffering so much pain and humiliation? What has become of this great Muslim ummah, that a few centuries ago were a superpower, the envy of the world? There was a time when the cry of a single Muslim woman, "where are you, O Mu'tassim?" was enough for the Caliph to launch his entire army to rescue her from the enemies of Islám. Today, whole ummah is crying, and bleeding, and dying, but there is no Mu'tassim to answer their calls for help. Where are commanders of the Muslim army like Khalid bin Al - Walide and Muhammad bin Qasim - rulers like Umar bin Abdul Aziz, Hajjaj bin Yousaf, Salah–ud-Din and the Grand Wizir like Nizam-ul-Mulk Tusi? Has Allah abandoned us? Have we abandoned Allah?

As soon as Muslims neglected their moral and spiritual life, Alláh [swt] removed them from power. So, if we really are once more to regain control over our affairs, and to rebuild our self-esteem, we must begin by removing the pollution, the impurities from our hearts and renewing our faith and rebuilding our fearful awareness of Alláh, our Taqwa.'

Why are we now so powerless, that we cannot defend our own citizens? The answer, as always, is eloquently expressed in The Holy Qur'an in **Surah al-'Imran (3: 26):**

$$
قُلِ اللَّهُمَّ مَـٰلِكَ الْمُلْكِ تُؤْتِى الْمُلْكَ مَن تَشَآءُ وَتَنزِعُ الْمُلْكَ مِمَّن تَشَآءُ وَتُعِزُّ مَن تَشَآءُ وَتُذِلُّ مَن تَشَآءُ بِيَدِكَ الْخَيْرُ إِنَّكَ عَلَىٰ كُلِّ شَىْءٍ قَدِيرٌ
$$

Say, "O Allah, owner of Sovereignty, You give Sovereignty to whom You will and You take Sovereignty away from whom You will. You honor whom you will and You humble whom You will. In Your hand is [all] good. Indeed, You are over all things competent."

Then the next verse continues (3:27):

تُولِجُ الَّيْلَ فِي النَّهَارِ وَتُولِجُ النَّهَارَ فِي الَّيْلِ وَتُخْرِجُ الْحَيَّ مِنَ الْمَيِّتِ وَتُخْرِجُ الْمَيِّتَ مِنَ الْحَيِّ وَتَرْزُقُ مَن تَشَاءُ بِغَيْرِ حِسَابٍ ٠

You cause the night to enter the day, and you cause the day enter the night; and You bring the living out of the dead, and You bring the dead out of the living. And You give provision to whom You will without account [limit or measure].

In these beautiful and eloquent verses, we are reminded that all Power belongs to Alláh, all Honors belong to Him, and He dispenses His grace, and His punishment, and His honor, on whom He pleases. This is why we need to understand Lailatul Qadr, the Night of Power. Allah's Apostle said, "Whoever establishes the prayers on the night of Qadr out of sincere faith and hoping to attain Allah's rewards [not to show off] then all his past sins will be forgiven." (Bukhari, book #2, hadith #34)

Surah al-Qadr (97) of The Holy Qur'an reads:

إِنَّا أَنزَلْنَاهُ فِي لَيْلَةِ الْقَدْرِ ٠ وَمَا أَدْرَاكَ مَا لَيْلَةُ الْقَدْرِ ٠ لَيْلَةُ الْقَدْرِ خَيْرٌ مِّنْ أَلْفِ شَهْرٍ ٠ تَنَزَّلُ الْمَلَائِكَةُ وَالرُّوحُ فِيهَا بِإِذْنِ رَبِّهِم مِّن كُلِّ أَمْرٍ ٠ سَلَامٌ هِيَ حَتَّى مَطْلَعِ الْفَجْرِ ٠

Indeed, We sent it [the Quran] down during the Night of Decree. And what can make you know what the Night of Decree is? The Night of Decree is better than a thousand months. The angels and the Spirit [Gabriel] descend therein by permission of their Lord for every matter [they bring down the decree for everything destined to occur in the coming year]. Peace it is [upon the believers] until the emergence of dawn.

This night is called night of power and decree because: 1. Quran was revealed on this night; 2. this night's *ibadah* is better than thousand months; 3. Decree of everything destined to occur in the coming year is handed over to relevant angels this night.

The first Laylatul Qadr was the night that changed history. It was the night that Jibril [as] brought the first revelation, the first few verses of The Holy Qur'án were pronounced in a cave on Mt Hira, Jabal Thaur. Just imagine, if this event never happened. Imagine if there were no Qur'an today dear brothers and sisters, let us plug our heart and soul into Laylatul Qadr and let us recharge our Imán batteries. If we Muslims hadn't been so lax about our faith over the last few centuries, we would not today have to witness the humiliation and tragedy of Iraq, Afghanistan, Palestine, Chechnya or Kashmir.

Let us spend our night of Power, remembering Alláh [swt], and offering thanks to Him, for his countless blessings that we enjoy each moment of our lives. Let us ask Alláh [swt], glorified and exalted is He, to lift the burden of injustice and oppression from so many Muslim communities around the world. Let us ask him for his Divine power to help us become the dynamic, disciplined and balanced community, the Ummatan wasatan, the Witness to the nations, as described in The Holy Qur'án. Let us spend this historic night asking our Lord and Master, to help us become the model Muslims that our children and all future generations would love to follow.

What can we learn from the history of Islam that will help us build a better future for our children and grandchildren?

The most important lesson is that we Muslims are not Alláh's chosen people, who can do as we please and still enjoy His pleasure. We have to work hard, every day of our lives, to be worthy of the great honor and blessing of being a Muslim. If we succeed, success comes from Alláh. If we fail, we must look to our own hearts to find the reason for failure.

In **Surah ar-Ra'd (13:11)** we read:

$$إِنَّ اللَّهَ لاَ يُغَيِّرُ مَا بِقَوْمٍ حَتَّى يُغَيِّرُواْ مَا بِأَنفُسِهِمْ -$$

Indeed, Allah will not change the condition of a people until they change what is in themselves.

Dear Brothers and Sisters, that mystical and mysterious force that descends by the command of Alláh Most High, during Laylatul Qadr, the Night of Power, has proven itself in history. Its clear evidence is there for all of us to see. Remember that it was during Ramadhán that some of Islam's noblest and greatest victories were achieved, for example, the Battle of Badr, the Conquest of Makka, the Conquest of Spain, and the defeat of the Mongols at Ain Jalut.

In the last ten days of Ramadhan, there is Laylat Al-Qadr [the Night of Revelation] in which every precise matter of wisdom is made distinct and all events of the coming year are decreed. As Allah (swt) asserts in **Surah ad-Dukhân (44:3-5):**

$$إِنَّا أَنزَلْنَاهُ فِي لَيْلَةٍ مُّبَارَكَةٍ إِنَّا كُنَّا مُنذِرِينَ - فِيهَا يُفْرَقُ كُلُّ أَمْرٍ حَكِيمٍ - أَمْراً مِّنْ عِندِنَا إِنَّا كُنَّا مُرْسِلِينَ -$$

Indeed, We sent it down during a blessed night the night of decree. Indeed, We were to warn [mankind]. Therein [on that night] is made distinct [apportioned] every precise matter - [Every] matter [proceeding] from Us. Indeed, We were to send [a messenger].

Allah [swt] reassures this night as a blessed night. [Therein (that night) is decreed every matter, *Hakim*]. Means, on Laylatul-Qadr, the decrees are transferred from Al-Lawh Al-Mahfuz to the [angelic] scribes who write down the decrees of the [coming] year including life span, provision, and what will happen until the end of the year.

It is on this night that angels descend from the heavens and blessings become abundant. Whoever prays its nights, believing in it, and hoping for its reward from Allah, Allah will forgive all his previous sins? Whoever misses this ~~night~~ ~~...~~ people may exert their utmost efforts during all ten Allah [swt] nights in worship, performing optional night prayer, reciting the Holy Qur'an and doing righteous deeds. This is also a means of distinction between those who are active in devotion and those who are not. If Laylat Al-Qadr were identified, many people would have limited themselves to devotion on that night only, neglecting other nights. There would also be no criteria for evaluation between the hardworking people and the lazy ones.

We pray that during this historic time, in this Holy Month, on this Great Night of Power, when Alláh sends His Angels by His Command, that Alláh Most Gracious will accept our commitment. May He also help us to purify our hearts, strengthen our faith, and enable us to meet every challenge, overcome every difficulty in our lives? May Alláh allow us to serve Him in our work, in our leisure, in our study, in our business and professional life, and in our family life and social relations? May Allah help us to re-establish the balance between our inner and outer worlds, and may this find a beautiful flowering in our Adab, in our good conduct. May Allah help us to cultivate the noble and gracious character that was so perfectly worn by our beloved Prophet (sas) and his illustrious followers? This is due to what Imam Ahmad recorded from A'ishah (ra) that she said, "O Messenger of Allah! If I find the Night of Al-Qadr what should I say'." He replied,

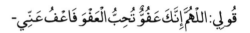

Say: "O Allah! Verily, You are the Oft-Pardoning, You love to pardon, so pardon me." (Tirmidhi)

So, seek the reward of Laylat Al-Qadr by doing good deeds consistently and sincerely. Ask Allah for a share of His reward and to protect us from coming out of Ramadhan empty-handed. **Amin!**

Legal [Halal] Earning is Obligatory

Halal: Halal is a Quranic term which means allowed or lawful. Allah-the Supreme Law Giver permits halal foods and drinks for consumption. Eating Halal food is obligatory on every Muslim.

Haram: Haram is a Quranic term that means prohibited or unlawful. Haram foods and drinks are absolutely prohibited by Allah. Eating Haram food is forbidden for every Muslim.

Mushbooh: Mushbooh is an Arabic term that means suspected. If one does not know the Halal or Haram status of a particular food or drink, such a food or drink is doubtful. A practicing Muslim prevents himself from consuming doubtful things.

Allah [swt] says in **Surah al-Baqarah (2:168):**

يَـٰأَيُّهَا النَّاسُ كُلُوا مِمَّا فِى الْأَرْضِ حَلَـٰلًا طَيِّبًا وَلَا تَتَّبِعُوا خُطُوَٰتِ الشَّيْطَـٰنِ إِنَّهُ لَكُمْ عَدُوٌّ مُّبِينٌ-

O mankind, eat from whatever is on earth [that is lawful] and good and do not follow the footsteps of Satan. Indeed, he is to you a clear enemy.

And also in **(2:188),** Allah [swt] says:

وَلَا تَأْكُلُوا أَمْوَٰلَكُم بَيْنَكُم بِالْبَاطِلِ وَتُدْلُوا بِهَا إِلَى الْحُكَّامِ لِتَأْكُلُوا فَرِيقًا مِّنْ أَمْوَالِ النَّاسِ بِالْإِثْمِ وَأَنتُمْ تَعْلَمُونَ-

And do not consume one another's property unjustly [in any illegal way, e.g., stealing, robbing, deceiving], or send it [in bribery] to the rulers [judges before presenting your cases] in order that [they might aid] you [to] consume a portion of the wealth of the people in sin, while you know [it is unlawful]. Allah [swt] commanded people to walk among the slopes of the earth and eat of His provisions. The Prophet [sas] said: "The reciting of the Zabur (i.e. *Psalms*) was made easy for David. He used to order that his riding animals be saddled, and would finish reciting the Zabur before they were saddled. And he would never eat except from the earnings of his manual work." (Bukhari, book #55, hadith #628) Lawful earnings and sound wealth safe guards the religion, protects one's honor, beautifies one's face, and results in a strong position.

Allah [swt] commanded the believers as He commanded the messengers, when He says in **Surah al-Mu'minun (23:51):**

يَـٰأَيُّهَا الرُّسُلُ كُلُوا مِنَ الطَّيِّبَـٰتِ وَاعْمَلُوا صَـٰلِحًا إِنِّى بِمَا تَعْمَلُونَ عَلِيمٌ-

[Allah said] "**O messengers, eat from the good [lawful] foods and do righteous deeds. Indeed, I, of what you do, am knowing.**" which indicates that eating what is lawful helps one to do righteous deeds.

Allah also says in **Surah al-Baqarah (2:172-3):**

يَـٰٓأَيُّهَا ٱلَّذِينَ ءَامَنُوا۟ كُلُوا۟ مِن طَيِّبَـٰتِ مَا رَزَقْنَـٰكُمْ وَٱشْكُرُوا۟ لِلَّهِ إِن كُنتُمْ إِيَّاهُ تَعْبُدُونَ إِنَّمَا حَرَّمَ عَلَيْكُمُ ٱلْمَيْتَةَ وَٱلدَّمَ وَلَحْمَ

ٱلْخِنزِيرِ وَمَآ أُهِلَّ بِهِۦ لِغَيْرِ ٱللَّهِ فَمَنِ ٱضْطُرَّ غَيْرَ بَاغٍ وَلَا عَادٍ فَلَآ إِثْمَ عَلَيْهِ إِنَّ ٱللَّهَ غَفُورٌ رَّحِيمٌ.

O, you who have believed, eat from the good [lawful] things which We have provided for you and be grateful to Allah, if it is [indeed] Him that you worship. He has only forbidden to you dead animals, blood, the flesh of swine, and that which has been dedicated to other than Allah. But whoever is forced [by necessity], neither desiring [it] not transgressing [its limit], then there is no sin upon him. Indeed, Allah is Forgiving and Merciful.

Eating from pure sources is a cause for the acceptance of supplications and acts of worship, just as eating from impure sources prevents the acceptance of supplications and acts of worship. Dead animals are those that die before being slaughtered; whether they die by strangling, a violent blow, and a headlong fall, the goring of horns or by being partly eaten by a wild animal. Dead animals of the sea are excluded from this ruling. Prophet Muhammad [sas] mentioned, "A man, [who is engaged in a long journey, whose hair is untidy and who is covered in dust, he raises his hands to the sky, and says, `O Lord! O Lord!' Yet, his food is from the unlawful, his drink is from the unlawful, his clothes are from the unlawful, and he was nourished by the unlawful, so how can it (his supplication) be accepted?'" (Muslim, book #005, hadith #2214)

The Prophet [peace be upon him] said: "Feel shame before Allah as you ought to feel shame before him. So guard the head and what it contains, guard the stomach and what you put in it, and think upon death and returning to dust." (Tirmidhî (2458))

Allah (swt) says in **Surah al-Mai'dah (5:96):**

أُحِلَّ لَكُمْ صَيْدُ ٱلْبَحْرِ وَطَعَامُهُ مَتَـٰعًا لَّكُمْ.

Lawful for you is game from the sea and its food as provisions for you and the travelers.

In **Surah al-Baqarah (2:275)** Allah (swt) says:

ٱلَّذِينَ يَأْكُلُونَ ٱلرِّبَوٰا۟ لَا يَقُومُونَ إِلَّا كَمَا يَقُومُ ٱلَّذِى يَتَخَبَّطُهُ ٱلشَّيْطَـٰنُ مِنَ ٱلْمَسِّ.

Those who consume interest [including all types of usury] cannot stand [on the Day of Resurrection] except as one stands who is being beaten by Satan into insanity.

In **Surah al-Mai'dah (5:90)**, Allah (swt) says:

يَـٰٓأَيُّهَا ٱلَّذِينَ ءَامَنُوٓا۟ إِنَّمَا ٱلْخَمْرُ وَٱلْمَيْسِرُ وَٱلْأَنصَابُ وَٱلْأَزْلَـٰمُ رِجْسٌ مِّنْ عَمَلِ ٱلشَّيْطَـٰنِ فَٱجْتَنِبُوهُ لَعَلَّكُمْ تُفْلِحُونَ

O you who have believed, indeed, Khamr [intoxicants], Maysir [gambling], Ansab sacrificing on] stone alerts to other than Allah], and Azlam [divining arrows] are but Rijs [defilement from the work] of Satan, so avoid it that you may be successful.

Seeking lawful provisions and searching for it, is an obligation and a must for no slave's feet will be moved on the Day of Resurrection until he is asked about his wealth. How he earned it? How he spent it? It is incumbent upon every Muslim male and female to look and search for lawful provisions and chaste and pure work, to eat of the lawful and spend on the lawful. Abdullah ibn 'Amr [ra] said: "The Messenger of Allah [sas] said: 'The curse of Allah be upon the one who gives a bribe and the one who accepts it." (Ibn Maajah, 2313)

Some of the Salaf said: "If you stand up in worship like a pole, meaning for a long time without giving up. It will not benefit you, until you watch for what goes in your stomach". The Prophet [sas] said: "Any flesh that grows from ill-gotten gains is more deserving of being touched by Hell-fire . . ." (Reported by Tabaraani in *al-Kabeer*, 19/13)

Lawful provisions are satisfying, bring ease, enlighten the heart, energize the limbs and the body, rectify and reforms the situation of the person, makes the body healthy, and Allah accepts the duaas [supplications] of such a person.

Servants of Allah, eating from unlawful means blinds the insight, weakens the religion, hardens the heart, darkens the mind, prevents the body from worship, entraps one in this life and prevents one's dua [supplication] from being accepted. Allah does not accept except from the righteous.

Unlawful earnings and provisions have bad effects on the individual and the community. It removes blessings and causes the spread of diseases, disasters, financial crisis, unemployment, oppression, and disputes. Buying Halal food using illegal [*haram*] income does not make the income legal.

O Muslims, Woe to the ones who eats from unlawful provisions, raises their children and family by means of unlawful earnings. They enjoy unlawful provisions and they use twisted means - usury, gambling, stealing, forcefully taking, and they give insufficient measures and weights. They conceal deficiency in items. They use magic, fortune telling, they usurp the property of orphans and minors, they lie when they swear, they deceive, they plan, they forge, they betray, - all twisted - dark ways.

On the Day of Resurrection, each person will be asked how he earned money and on what he spent it, and there will be doom and loss. Anyone who still has haram money should hasten to get rid of it; if it is due to anyone else, then he should hasten to return it and ask for his forgiveness before there comes a Day on which *dinars* and *dirhams* will be of no avail, and all that will count will be *hasanaat* and *sayi'aat*. Prophet Muhammad [sas] said: "A time will come on people, when a man will not worry where his earning come from, lawful or unlawful", and in another narration he added, "Such is one whose duas [supplications] are not accepted". (Bukhari, book #34, hadith #275)

O Workers and officers, businessmen, consultants, brokers, Muslim men and Muslim women, it is a duty upon us to seek what is lawful and stay away from the doubtful. Preserve the rights of people. Perform our duties honestly. Fulfill our pledges and our contracts. Refrain from cheating, lying, and fear Allah.

Muslim brothers, the best way is to refrain from unlawful and illegal things is to stay away from doubtful things, and to persevere through devout, pious ways and means, when hesitant So fear Allah, May Allah be merciful us. Fear Allah in ourselves and with our families and guard ourselves from the fire; the fuel of which is people and stones, and has angels harsh and severe, they do not disobey Allah in what he commands them, but do what they are commanded to do. **Amin!**

Luqman's Advice to His Son

Majority of the Salaf favored the view that he was a righteous servant of Allah without being a Prophet. Ibn Jarir recorded that Khalid Ar-Raba`i said: "Luqman [as] was an Ethiopian slave who was a carpenter. His master said to him, `Slaughter this sheep for us,' so he slaughtered it. [His master] said: `Bring the best two pieces from it,' so he brought out the tongue and the heart. Then time passed, as much as Allah willed, and [his master] said: `Slaughter this sheep for us,' so he slaughtered it. [His master] said, `Bring the worst two morsels from it,' so he brought out the tongue and the heart. His master said to him, `I told you to bring out the best two pieces, and you brought these, then I told you to bring out the worst two pieces, and you brought these!' Luqman [as] said, `There is nothing better than these if they are good, and there is nothing worse than these if they are bad." (Tafsir-Ibn-Kathir)

Allah (SWT) said in **Surah Luqman (31:12):**

وَلَقَدْ ءَاتَيْنَا لُقْمَانَ الْحِكْمَةَ أَنِ اشْكُرْ لِلَّهِ وَمَن يَشْكُرْ فَإِنَّمَا يَشْكُرُ لِنَفْسِهِ وَمَن كَفَرَ فَإِنَّ اللَّهَ غَنِيٌّ حَمِيدٌ-

And We had certainly given Luqman wisdom [and said], "Be grateful to Allah. And whoever is grateful is grateful for [the benefit of] himself. And whoever denies [His favor] – then indeed Allah is free of need and Worthy Praiseworthy."

In this verse above there is a reference to Luqman [as] the Wise. *"Wise"* in this sense [*Hakim*] means not only a man versed in knowledge human and divine, but one carrying out in practical conduct [*'amal*] the right course in life to the utmost of his power. His knowledge is correct and practical, but not necessarily complete: for no man is perfect. Such an ideal involves the conception of a man of heroic action as well as of deep and workman-like knowledge of nature and human nature,- not merely dreams or speculation.

The Qur'ân contains some precious advices Luqmân [as] offered his son. Following is the list of the advice offered to Muslim parents, that they may communicate them to their children, family and members of society that they may implement them. If this valuable advice is followed and implemented then we will all be on the straight path leading to Paradise. Luqmân [as] himself summed up in a few words the way to succeed in this life and on the Day of Judgment

Luqmân [as] showed great wisdom in his advice to his son. If Muslim parents take his example, and have their children implement these advices, then by Allâh's permission our Ummah will be successful.

Luqman's sayings and the words of advice he gave to his son, contain rare wisdom, and quite a number of traditions refer to "Luqman's advice to his son". In verse (31:13), Allah [swt] narrates:

1. Luqmân [as] warns his son against the greatest injustice man can do. Allâh said that Luqmân [as] said:

وَإِذْ قَالَ لُقْمَانُ لِابْنِهِ وَهُوَ يَعِظُهُ يَبُنَيَّ لَا تُشْرِكْ بِاللَّهِ إِنَّ الشِّرْكَ لَظُلْمٌ عَظِيمٌ-

When Luqman said to his son while he was instructing him, "O my son, do not associate [anything] with Allâh. Indeed, association [with Him] is a great injustice."

Luqmân [as] calls his son: "My Son". To do so catches his son's attention so that he may listen carefully to his father. Then he calls his son's attention to Tawhid. "Shirk", Luqmân [as] said, "Is a great injustice indeed?"

Let us remind ourselves what Ya`qub's [as] Will and Testament to his children upon His death was as described in **Surah al-Baqarah (2:133):**

$$أَمْ كُنتُمْ شُهَدَآءَ إِذْ حَضَرَ يَعْقُوبَ الْمَوْتُ إِذْ قَالَ لِبَنِيهِ مَا تَعْبُدُونَ مِنْ بَعْدِى قَالُوا نَعْبُدُ إِلَهَكَ وَإِلَهَ آبَآئِكَ إِبْرَهِيمَ وَإِسْمَعِيلَ وَإِسْحَقَ إِلَهًا وَاحِدًا وَنَحْنُ لَهُ مُسْلِمُونَ$$

Or were you witnesses when death approached Ya`qub [Jacob], when he said to his sons, "What will you worship after me?" They said, "We will worship your Allah -and the Allah of your fathers, Ibrahim [Abraham], Isma`il [Ishmael], Ishaq [Isaac] - one Ilah [Allah alone]. And we are Muslims [in submission] to Him."

Therefore, the one who associates others with Allâh in worship does injustice to Allâh, the owner and Creator of the universe. A great injustice is also done to the Mushrik: he subjects himself to Allâh's anger and eternal punishment in Hell.

2. Luqmân [as] reminds his son of the rights of his parents on him (31:14):

$$وَوَصَّيْنَا الْإِنسَنَ بِوَلِدَيْهِ حَمَلَتْهُ أُمُّهُ وَهْنًا عَلَى وَهْنٍ وَفِصَالُهُ فِى عَامَيْنِ أَنِ اشْكُرْ لِى وَلِوَلِدَيْكَ إِلَىَّ الْمَصِيرُ -$$

And We have enjoined upon man [care] for his parents. His mother carried him, [increasing her] in weakness, and his weaning is in two years. Be grateful to Me and to your parents; to Me is the final destination.

He describes hardships mothers face bearing children.

Luqmân [as] mentions the total dependence of infants on their mothers for two years. Thank Allâh, and then your parents. Is not then the final destination is to Allâh?

3. Luqman [as] advises his son on how to behave with Mushrik parents (31:15):

$$وَإِن جَهَدَاكَ عَلَى أَن تُشْرِكَ بِى مَا لَيْسَ لَكَ بِهِ عِلْمٌ فَلَا تُطِعْهُمَا وَصَاحِبْهُمَا فِى الدُّنْيَا مَعْرُوفًا وَاتَّبِعْ سَبِيلَ مَنْ أَنَابَ إِلَىَّ ثُمَّ إِلَىَّ مَرْجِعُكُمْ فَأُنَبِّئُكُم بِمَا كُنتُمْ تَعْمَلُونَ$$

But if they endeavor to make you associate with Me that of which you have no knowledge, do not obey them but accompany them in [this] world with appropriate kindness and follow the way of those who turn back to Me [in repentance]. Then to Me will be your return, and I will inform you about what you used to do.

Luqmân [as] tells his son that if the parents are Mushrikîn, then does not follow their way: Allâh's right comes first by far. Even so far as long as they live, treat your Mushrik parents with kindness.

4. Luqmân [as] then describes some of Allâh's Might (31:16):

يَٰبُنَىَّ إِنَّهَآ إِن تَكُ مِثْقَالَ حَبَّةٍ مِّنْ خَرْدَلٍ فَتَكُن فِى صَخْرَةٍ أَوْ فِى السَّمَٰوَٰتِ أَوْ فِى الْأَرْضِ يَأْتِ بِهَا اللَّهُ إِنَّ اللَّهَ لَطِيفٌ خَبِيرٌ -

[And Luqman said], "O my son, indeed if it [a wrong] be equal to the weight of a grain of mustard seed and should be be within a rock, or [anywhere] in the heavens or the earth, Allâh will bring it forth. Indeed, Allâh is subtle in bringing out that grain, well aware of its place."

Allâh's Knowledge is so perfect that the existence of anything, big or small, is acknowledged and controlled by Him. Luqmân [as] tries to impress his son reminding him of Allâh's absolute control over His kingdom. Such might and power must not be challenged or ignored by anyone

5. A great advice to Luqman's son is to establish regular prayer, on time and with the best possible performance (31:17):

يَٰبُنَىَّ أَقِمِ الصَّلَوٰةَ وَأْمُرْ بِالْمَعْرُوفِ وَانْهَ عَنِ الْمُنْكَرِ وَاصْبِرْ عَلَىٰ مَآ أَصَابَكَ إِنَّ ذَٰلِكَ مِنْ عَزْمِ الْأُمُورِ -

O my son, establish prayer, enjoin what is right forbid what is wrong, and be patient over that befalls you. Indeed, [all] that is of the matters [requiring] determination.

Prayer is the direct connection between a Muslim and his Creator. Parents must take great care to teach and call upon their children to establish prayer

6. Luqmân [as] advises his son to "enjoin [people] for good, and forbid from evil." [31:17]

If every Muslim observes this duty, then evil and mischief will have no place in Muslim society

7. After the useful advice he offered his son, Luqmân [as] recommended patience in implementing them, and in all matters of life,

And bear with patience whatever befalls you. Verily, these are some of the important commandments ordered by Allâh with no exemption [31:17].

Patience is a righteous act ordered, and rewarded by Allâh.

8. Arrogance is an attribute of Allâh alone and not for man.

The Creator and Owner of the universe is the only One who deserves to be arrogant. Allâh threatens arrogant people with punishment in Hellfire. Luqmân [as] said (31:18):

وَلَا تُصَعِّرْ خَدَّكَ لِلنَّاسِ وَلَا تَمْشِ فِي الْأَرْضِ مَرَحًا إِنَّ اللَّهَ لَا يُحِبُّ كُلَّ مُخْتَالٍ فَخُورٍ -

And do not turn your cheek [in contempt] toward people and do not walk through the earth exultantly. Indeed, Allah does not like everyone self-deluded and boastful.

9. To be moderate is a great attitude anyone can possess,

Nor walk in insolence through the earth. Verily Allâh likes not each arrogant boaster.

Allâh does not like that man who is arrogant and proud of themselves.

10. To be moderate in walking and talking is also one of Luqman's advices to his son **(31:19)**:

وَاقْصِدْ فِي مَشْيِكَ وَاغْضُضْ مِن صَوْتِكَ إِنَّ أَنكَرَ الْأَصْوَاتِ لَصَوْتُ الْحَمِيرِ -

And be moderate in walking and lower your voice; indeed, the most disagreeable of sounds is the voice of donkeys.

Islâm offers a code of conduct in every aspect of life. Even the way Muslims walk and talk are regulated. Islam offers guidelines in this regard that will produce the best behavior and generate respect

11. Luqmân [as] reminds his son that being harsh while talking will liken his voice to the braying of a donkey. Shouting does not win hearts; rather, it will offend and alienate people.

And lower your voice. Verily the harshest of all voices is the voice (braying] of a donkey!

May Allah [swt] give us the guidance so that we may follow and pass on the advices and will, the testament of Luqman [as] and Yaqub [as], to our children at the time of our death and build a strong Muslim Ummah? **Amin!**

Lying is an Evil Act

Lying is an evil characteristic, which all religions and systems of ethics warn against and which man's innate common disposition agrees is wrong. Those who possess chivalry and sound reasoning will testify to this fact.

Truthfulness is one of the pillars on which the moral survival of the world depends. It is the foundation of praiseworthy characteristics, the cornerstone of Prophet hood and the fruit of the consciousness of Allah, or Taqwa. Were it not for truthfulness, the rulings of all divinely revealed laws would collapse. Acquiring the characteristic of lying is akin to shedding one's humanity, because speaking is an exclusively human trait.

Our purely monotheistic Islamic Law, or Sharee'ah, warns against lying in the Qur'an and Sunnah, and there is consensus among the Muslims that it is Haram [forbidden]. The liar will have bad consequences in this world and in the Hereafter.

Allah [swt] says in **Surah an-Nahl (16:105):**

إِنَّمَا يَفْتَرِى الْكَذِبَ الَّذِينَ لاَ يُؤْمِنُونَ بِآيَتِ اللَّهِ وَأُوْلَـئِكَ هُمُ الْكَـذِبُون-

They only invent falsehoods who do not believe in the verses of Allah, it is those who are the liars. The kafirs and heretics, who are known amongst the people for telling lies, tell lies about Allah and His Messenger [sas].

Allah [swt] curses the liars in **Surah al-'Imran (3:61):**

لَّعْنَتُ اللَّهِ عَلَى الْكَـذِبِين-

The curse of Allah is upon the liars.

And also in **Surah al-Jathiyah (45:7):**

وَيْلٌ لِّكُلِّ أَفَّاكٍ أَثِيم-

Woe to every sinful liar.

And also in **Surah al-Hajj (22:30):**

وَاجْتَنِبُوا قَوْلَ الزُّور-

And avoid false statement.

Allah [swt] also says in **Surah ash-Shua'ra (26:222)**:

$$تَنَزَّلُ عَلَى كُلِّ أَفَّاكٍ أَثِيم$$

They descend upon every sinful liar.

Athim means one whose speech is lies and fabrication and whose deeds are immoral. This is the person upon whom the Shayatin descend like fortune-tellers and other sinful liars.

The Prophet [sas] said: "The signs of a hypocrite are three: when he speaks he lies; when he makes a promise he breaks it; and when he is entrusted with something he betrays that trust." (Bukhari, book #2, hadith #32)

The most evil kinds of lies are:

1. Lies told about Allah and His Messenger is of the gravest types of lying and the one who does this is subject to severe warning. Some of the scholars have said that the one who does this is to be denounced as a kafir, or disbeliever. Allah says in **Surah Yunus (10:69)**:

$$قُلْ إِنَّ الَّذِينَ يَفْتَرُونَ عَلَى اللّهِ الْكَذِبَ لاَ يُفْلِحُونَ$$

Say, "Indeed, those who invent falsehood about Allah will not succeed".

2. Lying also includes lies told about or to other people, such as lying during buying and selling:

3. The prohibition of lying about visions and dreams: This refers to when some people claim to have seen such and such in a dream, but they are not telling the truth, then in the morning they starts to tell the people about something that they did not see.

4. Lying in jest: Some people think that it is permissible to tell lies if it is in jest. Lying is Haram whether the one who does it is joking or is serious.

5. Lying when playing with children: The Messenger of Allah [sas] said: "Whenever someone says to a child, 'Come here and I will give you this,' then does not give him anything, this is counted as a lie". (Abu Dawud, book #41, hadith #4973)

6. Lying to make people laugh: The Prophet [sas] said: "Woe to him who tells things, speaking falsely, to make people laugh thereby. Woe to him! Woe to him!" (Abu Dawud, book #41, hadith #4972)

The liar is warned of destructive punishment in this world and humiliating punishments in the Hereafter. These include:

1. Hypocrisy entering the heart and flourishing there: Allah says in **Surah at-Tawbah (9:77):**

فَأَعْقَبَهُمْ نِفَاقًا فِي قُلُوبِهِمْ إِلَى يَوْمِ يَلْقَوْنَهُ بِمَا أَخْلَفُوا اللَّهَ مَا وَعَدُوهُ وَبِمَا كَانُوا يَكْذِبُونَ ۔

So He penalized them with hypocrisy in their hearts until the Day they will meet Him - because they failed Allah in which they promised Him and because they [habitually] used to lie.

The lying tongue is like a faculty that is no longer working; indeed it is even worse than that, for the most evil thing a man may possess is a lying tongue.

2. Blackening of the face in this world and in the Hereafter: Allah says in **Surah az-Zumur (39:60):**

وَيَوْمَ الْقِيَامَةِ تَرَى الَّذِينَ كَذَبُوا عَلَى اللَّهِ وُجُوهُهُم مُّسْوَدَّةٌ أَلَيْسَ فِي جَهَنَّمَ مَثْوًى لِّلْمُتَكَبِّرِينَ ۔

And on the Day of Resurrection you will see those who lied about Allah [with] their faces blackened. Is there not in Hell a residence for the arrogant?

We have seen how Islam forbids lying even in jest, and it forbids frightening a Muslim whether in seriousness or in jest, in words or in actions. This is the law of Allah in which is wisdom and care for people's circumstances.

Beware of falsehood in our treatment with other people; do not tell lies, rather, tell the truth and only the truth. A believer can never be a liar, since dishonesty is a quality of the hypocrites.

A believer can never tell lies because he believes in the signs of Allah and His Messenger [sas], and he believes in the Prophet's saying:

«عَلَيْكُمْ بِالصِّدْقِ فَإِنَّ الصِّدْقَ يَهْدِي إِلَى الْبِرِّ، وَإِنَّ الْبِرَّ يَهْدِي إِلَى الْجَنَّةِ، وَلَا يَزَالُ الرَّجُلُ يَصْدُقُ وَيَتَحَرَّى الصِّدْقَ حَتَّى يُكْتَبَ عِنْدَ اللهِ صِدِّيقًا، وَإِيَّاكُمْ وَالْكَذِبَ فَإِنَّ الْكَذِبَ يَهْدِي إِلَى الْفُجُورِ وَإِنَّ الْفُجُورَ يَهْدِي إِلَى النَّارِ، وَلَا يَزَالُ الرَّجُلُ يَكْذِبُ وَيَتَحَرَّى الْكَذِبَ حَتَّى يُكْتَبَ عِنْدَ اللهِ كَذَّابًا»

Hold on to truth, for being truthful leads to righteousness, and righteousness leads to Paradise. Verily, a man will keep saying the truth and striving for truth, until he is written before Allah as very truthful [*Siddiq*]. Beware of lying, for lying leads to sin, and sin leads to the Fire. Verily, the man will keep lying and striving for falsehood until he is written before Allah as a great liar (Bukhari, book #73, hadith #116).

How awful is falsehood and how base is the rank of the liars! Falsehood leads to wickedness, which is the deviation from the straightforward path, which in turn leads to the Fire of Hell, and woe to the denizens of Hell! A liar is never satisfied since he is straining for falsehood in the sight of Allah. How ugly is the description of falsehood, which is always avoided and feared to be known about among people. How can a person feel any peace of mind while he is branded as a liar in the sight of Allah? People, who often suspect his statements and transactions and even dispraise him after his death, always doubt a liar.

Knowing all these, is it appropriate that a Muslim can adopt falsehood as a guide to his behaviour or a mood of life?

So fear Allah, O Muslims, with regard to our community, our religion and us! Do we not know that a religion is reflected and represented by its followers? If the Islamic nation is distinguished by falsehood, blind imitations, and seizing of the properties of others unlawfully, then where will the true Islamic characteristics are? If Muslims are to appear with such disgraceful characteristics then is this not a means of keeping people away from the religion of Islam? This will mean that their enemies, who will feel superior when they realise that the Muslims are adopting their indecencies and bad morals that are condemned by Islam will hold Muslims in contempt. What a disgrace for those who followed the way of those destined to ruin and kept themselves away from the path of those on whom Allah conferred His favours to - the prophets, the trustworthy, the martyrs and the righteous! **Amin!**

Manners and Teachings of Prophet [sas]

Allah [swt] says in **Surah al-'Imrân (3:159):**

فَبِمَا رَحْمَةٍ مِّنَ اللَّهِ لِنتَ لَهُمْ وَلَوْ كُنتَ فَظًّا غَلِيظَ الْقَلْبِ لاَنفَضُّوا مِنْ حَوْلِكَ

So by mercy from Allah [O Muhammad], you are lenient with them. And if you had been rude [in speech] and harsh in heart, they would have disbanded from about you.

By nature he was gentle and kind hearted, always inclined to be gracious and to overlook the faults of others. Politeness and courtesy, compassion and tenderness, simplicity and humility, sympathy and sincerity were some of the keynotes of his character. In the cause of right and justice he could be resolute and severe but more often than not, his severity was tempered with generosity. He had charming manners that won him the affection of his followers and secured their devotion. Though virtual king of Arabia and an apostle of Allah, he never assumed an air of superiority. Not that he had to conceal any such vein by practice and artifice: with fear of Allah, sincere humility was ingrained in his heart.

"He was always the first to greet another and would not withdraw his hand from a handshake till the other man withdrew his. If one wanted to say something in his ears, he would not turn away till one had finished" (Abu Dawud, book #41, hadith #4906). He did not like people to get up for him and used to say, "Let him who likes people to stand up in his honor, he should seek a place in hell." (Abu Dawud, book #41, hadith #5210)

He would himself, however, stand up when any dignitary came to him. He had stood up to receive the wet nurse Halima who had reared him in infancy and had spread his own sheet for her. His foster brother was given similar treatment He used to visit the poorest of ailing persons and exhorted all Muslims to do likewise [Bukhari]. Whenever he visited a person he would first greet him and then take his permission to enter the house. He advised the people to follow this etiquette and not to get annoyed if anyone declined to give permission, for it was quite likely the person concerned was busy otherwise and did not mean any disrespect [Bukhari].

He was especially fond of children and used to get into the spirit of childish games in their company. He would have fun with the children who had come back from Abyssinia and tried to speak in Abyssinian with them. It was his practice to give lifts on his camel to children when he returned from journeys [Bukhari]. He would pick up children in his arms, play with them, and kiss them.

Muhammad [sas] preached to the people to trust in Allah [swt]. His whole life was a sublime example of the precept. In the loneliness of Makkah, in the midst of persecution and danger, in adversity and tribulations, and in the thick of enemies in the battles of Uhud and Hunain, complete faith and trust in Allah [swt] appears as the dominant feature in his life. However great the danger that confronted him, he never lost hope and never allowed him to be unduly agitated The Prophet [sas] asked people to be just and kind.

As the supreme judge and arbiter, as the leader of men, as generalissimo of a rising power, as a reformer and apostle, he had always to deal with men and their affairs In administering justice, he made no distinction between believers and nonbelievers, friends and foes, high and low Muhammad [sas] asked people to shun notions of racial, family or any other form of superiority based on mundane things and said that righteousness alone was the criterion of one's superiority over another

The Prophet [sas] not only preached to the people to show kindness to each other but also to all living souls. He forbade the practice of cutting tails and manes of horses, of branding animals at any soft spot, and of keeping horses saddled unnecessarily (Muslim). The Apostle of Allah [sas] came upon an emaciated camel and said: Fear Allah regarding these dumb animals. Ride them when they are in good condition and feed them when they are in good condition. (Abu Dawud, Book #14, hadith #2542)

Teachings

The Prophet [sas] enjoined upon Muslims to treat the poor kindly and to help them with alms, zakah, and in other ways. He did not prohibit or discourage the acquisition of wealth but insisted that it be lawfully acquired by honest means and that a portion of it would go to the poor. He advised his followers "To give the laborer his wages before his perspiration dried up."

Prayers lighten the heart, and charity is proof of Iman [Faith], and abstinence from sin is perfect splendor; the Qur'an is a proof of gain to you, if you do good, and it is a detriment to you if you do wrong; and every man who rises in the morning either does that which will be the means of his redemption or his ruin When you speak, speak the truth; perform when you promise; discharge your trust; commit not fornication; be chaste; have no impure desires; withhold your hands from striking, and from taking that which is unlawful and bad.

Doing justice between two people is charity; and assisting a man upon his beast, and lifting his baggage is charity; and pure, comforting words are charity; and answering a questioner with mildness, is charity; and removing that which is an inconvenience to wayfarers, such as thorns and stones, is a charity.

Your smiling in your brother's face is charity; and your exhorting man to virtuous deeds is charity; and your prohibiting the forbidden is charity; and your showing men the road, in the land in which they lose it, is charity; and your assisting the blind is charity Modesty and chastity are part of the faith Do not exceed bounds in praising me, as the Christians do in praising Jesus, the son of Mary, by calling Him God, and the Son of God; I am only the Lord's servant; then call me the servant of God and His messenger.

Were it not for fear of troubling my disciples, verily I would order them to clean their teeth before every prayer.

Allah [swt] is pure and loves purity and cleanliness. There is no reward but Paradise for a Muslim who suffers with patience when the 'ruh' of his affectionate friend is taken. The Prophet [sas] said: "The most perfect believer in respect of faith is he who is best of them in manners" (Abu Dawud, book #40, hadith #4665).

All actions are judged by the motive prompting them.

Keep yourselves far from envy; it eats up and takes away good actions,   like as fire eats up and burnt wood.

Do not say, that if the people do well to us, we will do good to them; and if the people oppress us, we will oppress them; but determine that if people do you good, you will do good to them; and if they oppress you, you will not oppress them.

Verily you have two qualities which God and His Messenger love - fortitude and gentleness.

Narrated Abu Huraira: I heard Allah's Apostle saying; "The good deeds of any person will not make him enter Paradise" [i.e., none can enter Paradise through his good deeds]. They [the Prophet's companions] said, "Not even you, O Allah's Apostle?" He said, "Not even myself, unless Allah bestows His favor and mercy on me. So be moderate in your religious deeds and do the deeds that are within your ability: and none of you should wish for death, for if he is a good doer, he may increase his good deeds, and if he is an evil doer, he may repent to Allah" (Bukhari, book #70, hadith #577).

That person who relieves a Mumin [Muslim] from distress in this world, Allah will in like manner relieve him in the next; and he who shall do well to the indigent, Allah will do good to him in this world and the next.

Be persistent in good actions.

Beware! Verily there is a piece of flesh in the body of man, which when good, the whole body is good; and when bad, the whole body is bad, and that is the heart.

Hell is veiled in delights, and Heaven in hardships and miseries Paradise is nearer to you than the thongs of your sandals; and the Fire likewise.

He who believes in one Allah, and a future life, let him honor his guest It is not right for a guest to stay so long as to incommode his host. Humility and courtesy are acts of piety.

The most excellent Jihad is that for the conquest of self.

The ink of the scholar is more holy than the blood of the martyr. He who is not kind to Allah's creatures and to his own children Allah will not be kind to him.

Kindness is a mark of faith and whoever has not kindness has not faith The Qur'an consists of five heads, things lawful, things unlawful, clear and positive precepts, mysteries, and examples. Then consider that lawful which is there declared to be so, and that which is forbidden as unlawful; obey the precepts, believe in the mysteries, and take warning from the examples

Those who earn an honest living are the beloved of Allah. All kinds of modesty are best.

Shall I tell you the very worst among you? Those who eat alone, whip the slaves, and give to nobody.

No misfortune or vexation befalls a servant of Allah, small or great, but on account of his faults committed: and most of these Allah forgives.

The bringers of grain to the city to sell at a cheap rate gain immense advantage by it, and that who keeps back grain in order to sell at a high rate is cursed.

Heaven lies at the feet of mothers.

The best of persons in Allah's sight is the best amongst his friends; and the best of neighbors near Allah is the best person in his own neighborhood.

Of my disciples who will enter Paradise are those who do not use shells [do not consult oracles], and are not influenced by omens, like the people of Ignorance, and who put their whole trust in Allah.

The best Muslim house is that in which there is an orphan, who is benefited; and the worst Muslim house is that in which an orphan is ill-treated.

There is no child, a doer of good to his parents, who looks on them with kindness and affection, but Allah will grant with every look the rewards for an approved pilgrimage Shall I not inform you of a better act than fasting, alms, and prayers? Making peace between one another: enmity and malice tear up heavenly rewards by the roots.

The key of Paradise is Prayer, and the key of prayer is ablution. Neither the proud will enter Paradise, nor a violent speaker.

The best of good acts in Allah's sight is that which is constantly attended to although in a small degree.

The time is near in which nothing will remain of Islam but its name, and of the Qur'an but its mere appearance, and the mosques of Muslims will be destitute of knowledge and worship; and the learned will be the worst people under the heavens; and contention and strife will issue from them, and it will return upon themselves.

Allah does not remove anyone out of the world, but that he wishes to pardon him; and by the diseases of his body and distress for food, He exacts the punishment of every fault that lies on his shoulder.

They will enter the Garden of Bliss who has a true, pure, and merciful heart.

Religion is admonition, and it means being pure He is the most perfect of Muslims, whose disposition is most liked by his own family.

A sincere repenter of faults is like him who has committed none. Riches are not from an abundance of worldly goods but from a contented mind.

Wealth, properly employed, is a blessing; and a man may lawfully endeavor to increase it by honest means.

Allah's Apostle said thrice, "Shall I not inform you of the biggest of the great sins?" We said, "Yes, O Allah's Apostle!" He said, "To join partners in worship with Allah: to be undutiful to one's parents". The Prophet sat up after he had been reclining and added, "And I warn you against giving forged statement and a false witness; I warn you against giving a forged statement and a false witness". The Prophet kept on saying that warning till we thought that he would not stop. (Bukhari, book #73, hadith #7)

To those of your servants who please you give to eat what you eat yourself; and clothe them as yourself; but those who do not please you, part with them; and punish not Allah's creatures Feed the hungry and visit a sick person, and free the captive, if he be unjustly confined. Assist any person oppressed, whether Muslim or non-Muslim. Much silence and a good disposition, there are no two works better than those.

Abu Huraira reported Allah's Messenger [sas] as saying. Allah fixed the very portion of adultery that a man will indulge in. There would be no escape from it. The adultery of the eye is the lustful look and the adultery of the ears is listening to voluptuous [song or talk] and the adultery of the tongue is licentious speech and the adultery of the hand is the lustful grip [embrace] and the adultery of the feet is to walk [to the place] where he intends to

hadith #6422)

Verily, a man has performed prayers, fasts, charity, pilgrimage and all other good works; but he will not be rewarded except by the proportion of his understanding

The taker of usury and the giver of it, and the writer of its papers and the witness to it, are equal in crime

A giver of maintenance to widows and the poor is like a bestowed in the way of Allah, an uttered of prayers all the night, and a keeper of constant fast. Admonish your wives with kindness.

A virtuous wife is a man's best treasure. The best women are the virtuous; they are the most affectionate to infants, and the most careful of their husband's property Allah enjoins you to treat women well, for they are your mothers, daughters, aunts. Do not prevent your women from coming to the mosque.

The love of the world is the root of all evil. This world is a prison for the faithful, but a Paradise for unbelievers.

May Allah [swt] give us the proper guidance to follow the teachings of our prophet Muhammad [sass] and achieve the mercy and forgiveness of Allah [swt]? **Amin!**

Marriage in Islam: A Solemn Agreement

Allah [swt] disclosed in **Surah al-`Araf (7:189)** why and how He has created mother Hawwa [ra]:

هُوَ الَّذِى خَلَقَكُم مِّن نَّفْسٍ وَحِدَةٍ وَجَعَلَ مِنْهَا زَوْجَهَا لِيَسْكُنَ إِلَيْهَا فَلَمَّا تَغَشَّاهَا حَمَلَتْ حَمْلاً خَفِيفًا فَمَرَّتْ بِهِ فَلَمَّا أَثْقَلَت دَّعَوَا اللَّهَ رَبَّهُمَا لَئِنْ ءَاتَيْتَنَا صَلِحًا لَّنَكُونَنَّ مِنَ الشَّكِرِينَ

It is He Who created you from one soul and [then] created from it its mate [wife] that he might enjoy the pleasure of living with her. And when he [man] covers [had sexual relation with] her, she carries a light burden [a pregnancy] and continues therein. And when it becomes heavy, they both invoke Allah, their Lord [saying], If You give us a good child [physically sound and righteous], we will surely be grateful.

Allah has created everything in pairs, each endowed with physical and psychological characteristics to complement and complete one another. The human species has included male and female since its existence as stated in **Surah an-Nisa' (4:1)** as:

يَـٰأَيُّهَا النَّاسُ اتَّقُوا رَبَّكُمُ الَّذِى خَلَقَكُم مِّن نَّفْسٍ وَحِدَةٍ وَخَلَقَ مِنْهَا زَوْجَهَا وَبَثَّ مِنْهُمَا رِجَالاً كَثِيرًا وَنِسَآءً وَاتَّقُوا اللَّهَ الَّذِى تَسَآءَلُونَ بِهِ وَالأَرْحَامَ إِنَّ اللَّهَ كَانَ عَلَيْكُمْ رَقِيبًا

O mankind! Fear your Lord, who created you from one soul and created from it its mate and dispersed from both of them many men and women, And fear Allah, through whom [in whose name] you ask one another [rights], and the wombs. Indeed, Allah is ever, over you, an observer." And the "mating" of male and female is original in human nature and it is out of this instinctive relationship that the human race develops, continues and spreads.

Chastity is the core of a noble life. In Islam Sexual chastity is highly valued. Fornication and homosexuality are forbidden, and is considered one of the major sins, Marriage provides the only legal means of having sexual intimacy with the wife, and also it helps to attain tranquility of the heart and to enjoy the pleasures of life. The marital home organizes one's life and establishes chastity and protection.

The role of family in the overall social structure of Islam is great. In Islam there is no family without union or marriage and there is no marriage without love and respect. The family in Islam is a unit in which two independent persons unite and share life together. The husband's dignity is an integral part of his wife's dignity. Accordingly, neither of them is better than the other. To unite and share, there must be mutual love and compassion - a genuine feeling which, unless translated into action and behavior, would be mere illusion.

When Allah mentions marriage or the relationship between husband and wife in the Qur'an, He describes it as a relationship of love, compassion, mercy, and harmony between two human beings who have entered into a mutual contract in **Surah ar-Rum (30:21):**

وَمِنْ ءَايَتِهِ أَنْ خَلَقَ لَكُم مِّنْ أَنفُسِكُمْ أَزْوَجًا لِّتَسْكُنُوا إِلَيْهَا وَجَعَلَ بَيْنَكُم مَّوَدَّةً وَرَحْمَةً إِنَّ فِى ذَلِكَ لَأَيَتٍ لِّقَوْمٍ يَتَفَكَّرُونَ

And of His signs is this that He created for you from yourselves mate that you may find tranquility in them; and He placed between you affection and mercy. Indeed, in that are signs for people who give thought?

A contract referred to in **Surah an- Nisa' (4:21)** as:

وَكَيْفَ تَأْخُذُونَهُ وَقَدْ أَفْضَى بَعْضُكُمْ إِلَى بَعْضٍ وَأَخَذْنَ مِنكُم مِّيثَقًا غَلِيظًا

And how could you take it [back] while you have gone in unto each other and they have taken from you a solemn covenant.

The Qur'an speaks of the intimate and close relationship of the two spouses in an eloquent way in **Surah al-Baqarah (2:187):**

هُنَّ لِبَاسٌ لَّكُمْ وَأَنتُمْ لِبَاسٌ لَّهُنَّ

They are Libas [garments] [i.e., body-cover, or screen] for you and you are Libas for them.

By using the simile of 'garments', Allah [swt] highlights the significant dimensions of the marital relationship as:

Garments are considered to be one of the most fundamental needs of human beings in all stages of life. They protect us, at times of necessity, from cold or heat. Garments cover the nakedness of the body and hide those parts which are supposed to be kept hidden. They are also the closest things that constantly touch our bare skin with highest levels of intimacy. They are also adornment and enhance one's beauty.

Like garments, the two partners [husband and wife] join together not only for sexual intimacy, but also to cover each other's weakness and frailty, enhance each other's capabilities and help each other make up their deficiencies. Like garments they protect each other at times of hardship, and increase love and intimacy between them. Spouses must be generous and liberal in their treatment of each other under all circumstances, especially when the relations between the two are not very amicable. And do not forget liberality between yourselves. Even in divorce, we are enjoined to be just and fair [ma'ruf]; take them back honorably on equitable terms or set them free with kindness and goodness.

Marriage should be a continuous gateway to a caring relationship and it is through this institution true expression is given to what the Qur'an refers to as وَرَحْمَةً مَّوَدَّةً "love and mercy" in Surah ar-Rum (30:21) between men and women, بَعْضٍ مِن بَعْضُكُم أُنثَى أَوْ ذَكَرٍ مِن that be you male or female, you are members of one another in

Surah al-ʿImran (3:195), and بَعْضٍ أَوْلِيَاءُ بَعْضُهُمْ that men and women are protectors, one of another Surah at-Tauba (9:71).

To meet the needs and take on the challenges that come with relationships, each person needs to make an inventory of characteristics that will help him/her to get closer to the people he/she cares about. Love and care are necessary requirements for sustaining any meaningful relationship.

Witnessing disrespect in action is always an unpleasant experience and when the disrespect or insult emanates from those who supposedly love us it is most painful. People who humiliate their dear ones allow familiarity to breed contempt.

Many people consider themselves 'good' despite their despicable behavior. This is possible only because they try to rationalize their wrongs. When we make rational decisions - that is reasoning before deciding it is commendable when we rationalize, however, we invent reasons to justify our decisions and actions. Often rationalizing is nothing more than self-convincing justification for improper conduct.

The Prophet [sas] said: "Shall I inform you of the best among you? The respectful gentleman is he who has good manners and honors his wife as best as he can. The Prophet [sas] also said, "The most perfect of the believers in faith is he who is the most excellent of them in morals and the best of you are they who are best to their wives."(Tirmidhi, 10:11)

Married couples have many worries, but good treatment and kindness to one another make them disappear; Allah says in **Surah an-Nisa' (4:19):**

يَـٰٓأَيُّهَا ٱلَّذِينَ ءَامَنُوا۟ لَا يَحِلُّ لَكُمْ أَن تَرِثُوا۟ ٱلنِّسَآءَ كَرْهًا ۖ وَلَا تَعْضُلُوهُنَّ لِتَذْهَبُوا۟ بِبَعْضِ مَآ ءَاتَيْتُمُوهُنَّ إِلَّآ أَن يَأْتِينَ بِفَـٰحِشَةٍ مُّبَيِّنَةٍ
وَعَاشِرُوهُنَّ بِٱلْمَعْرُوفِ ۚ فَإِن كَرِهْتُمُوهُنَّ فَعَسَىٰٓ أَن تَكْرَهُوا۟ شَيْئًا وَيَجْعَلَ ٱللَّهُ فِيهِ خَيْرًا كَثِيرًا

O you who have believed, it is not lawful for you to inherit women by compulsion. And do not make difficulties for them in order to take [back] part of what you gave them [mehr] unless they commit a clear immorality [adultery]. And live with them in kindness. For if you dislike them - perhaps you dislike a thing Allah makes therein much good.

The condition of one's family is constantly fluctuating between calm and complaint and contentment and discontent; man should always forgive mistakes and overlook shortcomings and be kind and compassionate, because woman was created from a bent rib. It is by persevering and being patient through that which the husband hates of the wife's behavior that things improve. The Prophet [sas] said: "Treat women nicely, for a woman is created from a rib and the most curved portion of the rib is its upper portion, so, if you should try to straighten it, it will break, but if you leave it as it is, it will remain crooked. So treat women nicely." (Bukhari, book #55, hadith #548)

Exchanging gifts is the key to winning a heart and is a reflection of one's love. Being easy upon ones wife, abandoning ambiguity and bad communication and arrogance are ways to achieve a lasting happy marital life. Be an upright and straightforward man and your wife will thereby also improve and become more righteous, by the will of Allah. Deal with our wives as we would like them to deal with us at all times, because it is natural that she would like you to be with her as you would like her to be with you.

We should listen to our wife's criticism with an open mind and heart. Also a husband should not take from his wife's wealth without her permission, because it belongs to her; treat her kindly and be generous with her and do not be stingy; remember that our wives like to talk to us regarding all her affairs, so be attentive and listen to them, indeed this is a reflection of perfect manners.

Never remind our wives with mistakes that they may have made, nor hint about their shortcomings; conceal problems from the children because it has a negative effect on them and reduces the respect they have towards their parents. Anger is the cause of all disputes, and the relation between a man and his wife is far too valuable to ruin in a moment of anger; remain silent whenever you become upset and remember that forgiveness is closer to piety and wisdom. The rights of the wife are great and only a noble man will fully honor his wife and respect her.

The intelligent wife is she who makes her heart an abode of relaxation and tranquility for her husband, and who makes him feel joy just by talking to her. She lives with him in contentment and deals with him kindly. She obeys him in all matters except when it entails disobedience to Allah and she acknowledges the favors that he has done for her. Also, she fulfils all her rights and accepts that he has a superior standing and a higher rank than her.

She helps him through the hardships of life and never exposes his secrets. She always obeys him and supports him in his duties to his parents because they were the ones who raised and cultivated him. She seeks Allah's pleasure by pleasing her husband, she honors him when he is around and defends him when he is absent; she never overburdens him with unnecessary expenses; her main concern is to please Allah by It is narrated on the authority of Abdullah (b. Umar) that when the Messenger of Allah [may peace be upon him] was taken for the Night journey, he was taken to Sidrat-ul-Muntaha, which is situated on the sixth heaven, where terminates everything that ascends from the earth and is held there, and where terminates every- thing that descends from above it and is held there. [It is with reference to this that Allah said: "When that which covers covered the lote-tree" (Al-Qur'an, 3:16). He [the narrator] said: "[It was] gold moths." He [the narrator further] said: "The Messenger of Allah [sas]] was given three [things]: he was given five prayers; he was given the concluding verses of Surah al-Baqara, and remission of serious sins for those among his Ummah who associate not anything with Allah (Muslim, book #001, hadith#0329).

May Allah [swt] help and guide us in fulfilling the solemn agreement we make at the time of marriage and be faithful, loving, caring, and helpful to each other throughout our married life. **Amin!**

Miraj: The Night Journey by Prophet Muhammad [sas]

Allah [swt] says in **Surah al-Isra' (17:1):**

$$سُبْحَانَ الَّذِى أَسْرَى بِعَبْدِهِ لَيْلًا مِّنَ الْمَسْجِدِ الْحَرَامِ إِلَى الْمَسْجِدِ الْأَقْصَى الَّذِى بَارَكْنَا حَوْلَهُ لِنُرِيَهُ مِنْ ءَايَتِنَآ إِنَّهُ هُوَ السَّمِيعُ الْبَصِيرُ$$

Exalted is He who took His servant [Prophet Muhammad [sas] by night from Al-Masjid Al-Haram to Al-Masjid Al-Aqsa [in Jerusalem] whose surroundings We have blessed, to show him Our signs. Indeed, He is the Hearing, the seeing.

The above-mentioned verses clearly establish a conceptual link between the auspicious "journey" [al-Mi`raj and al-Isra] undertaken by the Holy Prophet [sas] and the notion of deliberative rationality. This claim is supported by the Qur'an's reference to Allah Almighty's attributes of Hearing and seeing and humankind's cognitive capacities of hearing [sam`a], seeing [basr] and spiritual cognition [fuad]. These cognitive human capacities ought to be the basis of any type of critical engagement.

Our beloved Prophet was born as an orphan [lost his father 3 months before his birth]. He lost his beloved mother at the age of 6, when the bondage of son with mother becomes strong. Then his grandfather Abdul Muttalib took care of him, but he also died when the Prophet was 13. Then his uncle Abu Talib took charge of him. It was a very difficult time for the prophet, because in a tribal society, then, it was not easy to survive in the absence of parents. After a few years, his uncle Abu Talib also left him. Prophet [sas] also lost all of his three sons in infancy. Out of his four daughters, he lost three of them during his life time, only Fatema was alive at the time of his death. Brothers and sisters, just imagine what sort of difficult tests our beloved Prophet had to undergo. Our Prophet showed patience of highest order.

After the death of his protective uncle [Abu Talib] and his most beloved wife, supporter and confidant [Khadijah], and at a time when the disbelievers were trying to humiliate him for his belief in Allah ([swt], at the most difficult and trying time of the holy Prophet's life, Allah [swt] rewarded him [highest reward for his patience] by taking His beloved servant on a Journey by night, a journey that reached far beyond the parameters of human travel, beyond the perception that a human mind could ever imagine {Prophet [sas] over powered the time, space and speed that even the modern technology could not attain] by the will, mercy and favor of Allah [swt]. Even the archangel Jibreel who accompanied the Prophet on the journey reached a point beyond which he could not traverse. Prophet Muhammad [sas] ascended unto the highest manifestation of the Divine Presence till the summation at sidrat-ul-muntaha. Only Prophet Muhammad, the most beloved of Allah, the greatest of His creation, the finest specimen of the artwork of the Ultimate Artist could go to this Uppermost Limit, the limit of being before the Absolute. What a wonderful honor, attainment and reward from the creator?

In **Surah an-Najm (53:16)** Allah [swt] says:

$$إِذْ يَغْشَى السِّدْرَةَ مَا يَغْشَى$$

When there covered the Lote tree that which covered it [Then and there he saw Gabriel in angelic form].

Among the gifts that the holy Prophet descended with from that highest sphere is Salah, the gift of prayer [anywhere in the world]; a means of expiation for the self, purification for the soul, a mode for moral rejuvenation and spiritual elevation. No wonder the Prophet said; "Salah is the Miraj of the believer".

The truth is that the Prophet was taken on the Night Journey when he was awake [the Servant in ayah 17:1 means it was a physical not spiritual], not in a dream. Historically and religiously Jerusalem is, has always been, and will forever be significant to the Muslims. Let all be reminded that Muslims refer to Jerusalem as BAYT UL MUQADDAS [The Sacred Place]. On the night of the twenty-seventh Rajab, Muhammad [sas] was in a deep sleep in a house in Makkah when [Gabriel] woke him up. With the arch angel was Al-Buraq: an animal unique in creation. It resembled lightning in swiftness and luster, was of clear white color, medium in size, smaller than a mule and taller than an ass, and so quick in movement that it put its feet in the farthest limits of sight. When he reached the door of the sanctuary, he tied up his animal by the door and entered, where he prayed two Rak`ahs to 'greet the Masjid'.

Then the Mi`raj was brought to him, which is a ladder with steps which one climbs up. So he went up on it to the first heaven, then he went up to the rest of the seven heavens. In each heaven he was welcomed by the most pious of its inhabitants, and he greeted the Prophets who were in the various heavens according to their positions and status. He passed by Musa, the one who spoke with Allah, in the sixth heaven, and Ibrahim, the close friend [Khalil] of Allah in the seventh heaven. Then he surpassed them and all the Prophets in status and reached a level where he could hear the creaking of the pens, i.e., the pens of destiny which write down what is decreed to happen. Then he was carried to Sidrat-al- Muntaha [the remotest lote tree] covered by the command of Allah, and its greatness, its butterflies of gold and various colors, surrounded by the angels. There he saw Jibril in his real form, with six hundred wings. He saw green cushions blocking the horizon. He saw Al-Bayt Al-Ma`mur, and Ibrahim Al-Khalil, the builder of the earthly Ka`bah, leaning back against it, the heavenly Ka`bah; every day, seventy thousand angels enter and worship therein, then they do not return to it until the Day of Resurrection. He was then presented to the Divine Presence and experienced the thrill of witnessing the Divine Glory and Manifestation at the closest possible propinquity. There the Lord revealed unto His servant that which He revealed, and ordained the daily prayers for him.

Allah [swt] says in **Surah an-Najm (53:17):**

$$\text{مَازَا غَ الْبَصَرُ وَمَا طَغَى}$$

The sight [of the prophet (sas)] did not swerve, nor did it transgress [its limit].

Sight [Al-Basr] is a physical faculty, not a spiritual one, and he was carried on Al-Buraq, a shining white animal. This too indicates a physical journey, because the soul does not need a means of transportation of this nature. And Allah knows best.

Jerusalem is one of the oldest cities in the world, the birth place of many civilizations and a city central to the three "Abrahamic faiths", Judaism, Christianity and Islam. To Muslims, the sacredness of Jerusalem lies in the religious reality, it being an integral part of our sacred history and thus considered an important manifestation of our sacred geography. The significance of Jerusalem is further evidenced through reference to it and its precincts in (17:1) and numerous sayings of the holy Prophet [sas]. This is the area of the world where Prophet Dawood [David], Sulayman [Solomon] and 'Isa [Jesus] were born, grew up and carried out their missions; the place to which Prophets Ibrahim [Abraham] and Lut [Lot] migrated; where Yahya [John] preached and where Ibrahim [Abraham], Ishaq [Isaac], Ya'qub [Jacob], Yusuf [Joseph] and Musa [Moses] are buried. May Allah be pleased with all of them?

Narrated Ibn Abbas: Regarding: 'And We granted the vision (Ascension to the Heaven *"Miraj"* which We showed you [O Muhammad as an actual eye witness] but as a trial for mankind as mentioned by Allah (swt) in **Surah al-'Isra (17.60):**

وَإِذْ قُلْنَا لَكَ إِنَّ رَبَّكَ أَحَاطَ بِالنَّاسِ وَمَا جَعَلْنَا الرُّءْيَا الَّتِى أَرَيْنَاكَ إِلَّا فِتْنَةً لِّلنَّاسِ وَالشَّجَرَةَ الْمَلْعُونَةَ فِى الْقُرْءَانِ وَنُخَوِّفُهُمْ فَمَا يَزِيدُهُمْ إِلَّا طُغْيَانًا كَبِيرًا

And [remember, O Muhammad]) when We told you: "Indeed, your Lord has encompassed the people [Allah would protect him from their harm]". And We did not make the sight which We showed you except as a trial for the people, as was the accursed tree [mentioned] in the Qur'an. And We threaten [warn] them, but it increases them not except in great transgression.

It was an actual eye-witness which was shown to Allah's Apostle during the night he was taken on a journey [through the heavens]. And the cursed tree is the tree of Az-Zaqqum [a bitter pungent tree which grows at the bottom of Hell]. (Bukhari, book #60, hadith #240,)

Jerusalem was spiritually linked with Makkah when Masjid-ul-Aqsa became the destination of the Isra' [Night Journey of the Prophet Muhammad]. Only Muslims equally recognize all these Prophets, since Jews do not revere Prophet Jesus or Prophet Muhammad and the Christians do not accept Prophet Muhammad as a messenger of Allah.

Jerusalem was the first Qiblah for the Muslims and has throughout history been considered the third most holy city after Makkah and Madinah. The Prophet Muhammad is reported to have exhorted Believers to "undertake journeys to visit three mosques, Masjid ul Haraam [in Makkah], Masjid ul-Nabawi [in Madinah] and Masjid ul Aqsa [in Jerusalem]" (Muslim, book#007, hadith#3218).

Allah [swt] says in **Surah an-Najm (53:8-10):**

ثُمَّ دَنَا فَتَدَلَّى - فَكَانَ قَابَ قَوْسَيْنِ أَوْ أَدْنَى - فَأَوْحَى إِلَى عَبْدِهِ مَا أَوْحَى

Then he approached and descended and was at a distance of two bow lengths or nearer. And He [Allah] revealed to His servant what He revealed [conveyed].

While he [Gabriel] was in the highest part of the horizon, then he [Gabriel] approached and came closer, and was at a distance of two bows length or [even] nearer. So [Allah] revealed to His slave Muhammad [sas] through [Gabriel] whatever He revealed.

Some narrations mention that Prophet Muhammad [sas] saw Allah [swt] on Miraj is not correct. In Ayah (**53:18**),

Allah [swt] says:

$$لَقَدْ رَأَىٰ مِنْ آيَاتِ رَبِّهِ الْكُبْرَىٰ$$

He certainly saw of the greatest signs of his Lord.

In the above Ayah Allah [swt] clarifies that the prophet [sws] saw the greatest signs of His Rabb. If Prophet [sws] had seen Allah [swt] it would have been mentioned somewhere in the Qur'an. 'Aisha [ra] said, "If anyone tells you that Muhammad has seen his Lord, he is a liar, for Allah says in **Surah al-An'am (6:103):**

$$لَا تُدْرِكُهُ الْأَبْصَارُ وَهُوَ يُدْرِكُ الْأَبْصَارَ وَهُوَ اللَّطِيفُ الْخَبِيرُ$$

Vision perceives Him not [in the life of this world], but He perceives [all] vision; and He is the Subtle, the Acquainted [with all things]" (Bukhari, book #93, hadith #477).

May Allah [swt] give us the proper knowledge and guidance to understand His miracles in its true perspectives, and to perform salat as it were performed by the greatest prophet Muhammad [sas] in order that we may receive the mercy and forgiveness of Allah [swt]? **Amin!**

Moral Vaccination: Islamic Perspective

Islam has laid down some universal fundamental rights for humanity as a whole, which are to be observed and respected under all circumstances. To achieve these rights Islam provides not only legal safeguards but also a very effective moral system. Thus whatever leads to the welfare of the individual or the society is morally good in Islam and whatever injurious is morally bad. Islam attaches so much importance to the love of God and love of man that it warns against too much of formalism. We read in the Quran **Surah al-Baqarah (2:177):**

لَّيْسَ الْبِرَّ أَن تُوَلُّوا وُجُوهَكُمْ قِبَلَ الْمَشْرِقِ وَالْمَغْرِبِ وَلَكِنَّ الْبِرَّ مَنْ ءَامَنَ بِاللَّهِ وَالْيَوْمِ الْأَخِرِ وَالْمَلَـئِكَةِ وَالْكِتَبِ وَالنَّبِيِّينَ

وَءَاتَى الْمَالَ عَلَى حُبِّهِ ذَوِى الْقُرْبَى وَالْيَتَـمَى وَالْمَسَكِينَ وَابْنَ السَّبِيلِ وَالسَّآئِلِينَ وَفِى الرِّقَابِ وَأَقَامَ الصَّلَوةَ وَءَاتَى الزَّكَوةَ

وَالْمُوفُونَ بِعَهْدِهِمْ إِذَا عَـهَدُوا وَالصَّابِرِينَ فِى الْبَأْسَآءِ وَالضَّرَّاءِ وَحِينَ الْبَأْسِ أُوْلَـئِكَ الَّذِينَ صَدَقُوا وَأُوْلَـئِكَ هُمُ الْمُتَّقُونَ-

Righteousness is not that you turn your faces towards East or West; but [true] righteousness is [in] one who believes in Allah, the Last Day, the Angels, the Book, and the Messengers and give wealth, in spite of love for it, to relatives, orphans, the needy, the traveler, those who ask [for help], and for freeing slaves; [and who] establishes prayers and gives Zakah, [those who] fulfill their promise; and [those who] are patient in poverty and hardship and during battle. Those are the ones who have been true, and it is those who are righteous.

We are given a beautiful description of the righteous and Allah-conscious man in these verses. At a time when the abnormal is considered as the standard, where the immoral is not only becoming socially acceptable but is actually legislated; character, responsibility, accountability and rectitude are essential for maintaining what is left of human civility.

This is the standard by which a particular mode of conduct is judged and classified as good or bad. This standard of judgment provides the nucleus around which the whole moral conduct should revolve. Before laying down any moral injunctions Islam seeks to firmly implant in man's heart the conviction that his dealings are with Allah who sees him at all times and in all places; that he may hide himself from the whole world but not from Him; that he may deceive everyone but cannot deceive Allah; that he can flee from the clutches of anyone else but not from Allah [swt].

In short, no sphere of life is exempted from the universal and comprehensive application of the moral principles of Islam. It makes morality reign supreme and ensures that the affairs of life, instead of dominated by selfish desires and petty interests, should be regulated by norms of morality.

Humility, modesty, control of passions and desires, truthfulness, integrity, patience, steadfastness, and fulfilling one's promises are moral values which are emphasized again and again in the Quran. Allah [swt] says in **Surah Luqman (31:17-9):**

أَقِمِ الصَّلَوٰةَ وَأْمُرْ بِالْمَعْرُوفِ وَانْهَ عَنِ الْمُنْكَرِ وَاصْبِرْ عَلَى مَآ أَصَابَكَ إِنَّ ذَلِكَ مِنْ عَزْمِ الْأُمُورِ - وَلَا تُصَعِّرْ خَدَّكَ لِلنَّاسِ وَلَا تَمْشِ فِي الْأَرْضِ مَرَحاً إِنَّ اللَّهَ لَا يُحِبُّ كُلَّ مُخْتَالٍ فَخُورٍ - وَاقْصِدْ فِي مَشْيِكَ وَاغْضُضْ مِن صَوْتِكَ إِنَّ أَنْكَرَ الْأَصْوَاتِ لَصَوْتُ الْحَمِيرِ -

Establish prayer, enjoin what is right, forbid what is wrong, and be patient over what befalls you. Indeed, [all] that is of the matters [requiring] determination. And do not turn your cheek [with pride] toward people and do not walk through the earth exultantly. Indeed, Allah does not like everyone self-deluded and boastful. And be moderate in your pace and lower your voice; indeed, the harshest of sounds is the braying of the donkeys.

In a way which summarizes the moral behavior of a Muslim, the Prophet [sas] said: "Allah has forbidden you (1) to be undutiful to your mothers (2) to withhold (what you should give) or (3) demand (what you do not deserve), and (4) to bury your daughters alive. And Allah has disliked that (a) you talk too much about others (b), ask too many questions (in religion), or (c) waste your property." (Bukhari, book #73, hadith #6)

Thus, on the basic moral characteristics, Islam builds a higher system of morality by virtue of which mankind can realize its greatest potential. Islam purifies the soul from self-seeking egotism, tyranny, wantonness and indiscipline. It creates God-conscious men, devoted to their ideals, possessed of piety, abstinence and discipline and uncompromising with falsehood, It induces feelings of moral responsibility and fosters the capacity for self control. Islam generates kindness, generosity, mercy, sympathy, peace, sincere goodwill, scrupulous fairness and truthfulness towards all creation in all situations. It nourishes noble qualities from which only good may be expected.

There are some Muslims who seem to believe that morality and acts of worship are two different and separate things. We see Muslims who pray but they still cheat and lie. They fast but they do not abstain from what is wrong. They may give Zakat but they do not care how they earn their money whether form Halal or Haram, and they also make Hajj but they return with hearts full of wickedness and evil. Such acts of worship may be Islamic in form and appearance, but most certainly they are not Islamic in substance and spirit

Salat, Siyam Zakat, Hajj and other forms of worship are the stepping stones for real perfection, and are the means of purity and sanctity that makes the secure and magnificent. On account of high attributes and noble qualities that are the inalienable parts and the consequences of these forms of worship, they have been given a very high and important place in our religion.

We all know that when a new baby is born, the parents are advised to make sure that he or she gets the necessary vaccination shots, a vaccine against measles, against diphtheria, polio and German measles, etc. They do those because they care for the health of the new baby, because it is the right thing to do and, because such vaccines give the child immunity against those diseases.

So, in order to protect our bodies we take vaccines for immunizations, but we are not only made of a physical body. We also have a soul, and morality. There are moral ills and diseases and they are just as contagious as physical diseases and illnesses. The medical principle of early immunization also applies to the moral state of our soul. We need a moral vaccination to immunize the soul in order to resist these moral ailments. It is common knowledge that our society is full of moral ills. This is an undisputed fact that needs no proof. Modern society is infected with violence, pornography, greed, racism, homosexuality, drugs and alcohol. The list goes on.

This type of vaccination is a responsibility that we owe to our children. It is a responsibility to give them proper Islamic upbringing; responsibility which must be carried out with great amount of patience, love, dedication, knowledge, and wisdom. It is a tough responsibility but with great rewards for the children and their parents. The proper upbringing that we may provide our children today will be a good investment for the future, especially even after death.

This Islamic upbringing is a duty we owe to our children as Muslim parents. It is a noble duty that cannot not be left or assigned to others. It is the joint responsibility of the parents who will be asked about it on the Day of Judgment. Some parents fail to take their responsibility seriously. They are either too busy earning a living, making money, or are unaware of this responsibility at all, either because of ignorance or indifference. When things start to go wrong they suddenly remember their forgotten responsibility. When it is a bit too late, they are shocked and devastated, because their spoiled daughter has a boyfriend or that she ran away to marry a boy from other religion or when their son comes home drunk or when he is arrested for taking or selling drugs. I am sure we have heard many similar stories. Parents, who ignored their responsibility towards their children for twenty years or so, should not expect their children who are not children any more to be good Muslims in a day or two. Such an attitude is a sign of shortsightedness, because we do not prepare the soldier for the battle before the battle. He should be prepared for it a long time before it starts.

When the disease is caught, we are not looking for immunity; we are looking for treatment. But it is immunity that we would like to cultivate in our children so when a Muslim child is offered drugs or a beer he would say "No!" When his friends say, "Come on, you are not a child, be a man". He would have the courage to say, "No, we do not drink that, I am a Muslim." And when the girl is ridiculed for not having a boyfriend, or not going for a dance, she too would say: "we do not do that, I am a Muslim".

When invited to sex, drugs or such things, he/she would have the courage to say, "I am a Muslim, I do not do that." Only a Muslim, properly prepared, properly brought up, would say "No, I do not do that!" In this case the Muslim would be providing a role model for others to be followed.

Statistics shows that most of those children who fall into vice think that they have to do that because they were overwhelmed by peer pressure. They just cannot resist the pressure of their companions and their classmates. When things go wrong we should not despair. Even for those who have gone astray and committed the most heinous sins, the gates of repentance are always open. We are told in the Qur'an that even those who commit serious crimes such as murder or Zena [unlawful sexual intercourse] could be forgiven if they repent and return to Allah, to His right way with faith and righteous deeds.

For Allah will change the evil of such persons into good. And Allah is Often Forgiving. Most Merciful as Allah (swt) says in **Surah al-Furqan (25:70-1):**

إِلَّا مَن تَابَ وَءَامَنَ وَعَمِلَ عَمَلًا صَلِحًا فَأُوْلَٰٓئِكَ يُبَدِّلُ ٱللَّهُ سَيِّئَاتِهِمْ حَسَنَٰتٍ وَكَانَ ٱللَّهُ غَفُورًا رَّحِيمًا ۖ وَمَن تَابَ وَعَمِلَ صَلِحًا فَإِنَّهُۥ يَتُوبُ إِلَى ٱللَّهِ مَتَابًا ۖ

Except for those who repent, believe and do righteous deeds. For them Allah will replace their evil deeds with good. And ever is Allah Forgiving and Merciful. And he who repents and does righteous good deeds does indeed turn to Allah with [accepted] repentance.

And also in **Surah an-Nisa' (4:110)** Allah [swt] says:

وَمَن يَعْمَلْ سُوٓءًا أَوْ يَظْلِمْ نَفْسَهُۥ ثُمَّ يَسْتَغْفِرِ ٱللَّهَ يَجِدِ ٱللَّهَ غَفُورًا رَّحِيمًا ۖ

And whoever does a wrong or wrongs himself but then seeks forgiveness of Allah will find Allah Forgiving and Merciful.

May Allah [swt] provides us with the proper guidance so that we may ask Allah [swt] for forgiveness from sinful acts and also give us the courage to provide our children and family members with proper guidance at the proper time. **Amin!**

Mosque: The House of Allah

Mosque is the house of Allah [swt] built for praying and is the meeting place of the mumeen. Allah [swt] says in **Surah al-Jinn (72:18):**

$$وَأَنَّ الْمَسَاجِدَ لِلَّهِ فَلَا تَدْعُوا مَعَ اللَّهِ أَحَدًا$$

And [He revealed] that the masjids [every place of worship] are for Allah, So do not invoke with Allah anyone. It means no place of worship whatever should be used for the worship of any other but Allah [swt]. Worship should not be mixed up with vain objects, but must be reserved for the service of Allah [swt] alone.

The first Mosque [house] established for humanity was 'Masjidul Haram' as Allah [swt] says in **Surah al-'Imran (3:96):**

$$إِنَّ أَوَّلَ بَيْتٍ وُضِعَ لِلنَّاسِ لَلَّذِي بِبَكَّةَ مُبَارَكًا وَهُدًى لِلْعَالَمِينَ -$$

Indeed, the first House [of worship] established for mankind was that at Bakkah [Makkah] - blessed and guidance for the worlds [mankind and Jinn].

Allah [swt] also stresses the importance of the establishment of the first mosque in **Surah al-Mai'dah (5:97):**

$$جَعَلَ اللَّهُ الْكَعْبَةَ الْبَيْتَ الْحَرَامَ قِيَامًا لِلنَّاسِ وَالشَّهْرَ الْحَرَامَ وَالْهَدْىَ وَالْقَلَائِدَ ذَلِكَ لِتَعْلَمُوا أَنَّ اللَّهَ يَعْلَمُ مَا فِي السَّمَوَاتِ وَمَا فِي$$
$$الْأَرْضِ وَأَنَّ اللَّهَ بِكُلِّ شَيْءٍ عَلِيمٌ$$

Allah has made the Ka`bah, the Sacred House, standing for the people and [has sanctified] the sacred months and the sacrificial animals and the garlands [by which they are identified]. That is so you may know that Allah knows what is in the heavens and what is in the earth and that Allah is Knowing of all things.

As we know, the first act of the Prophet [sas] towards establishment of Islamic state after his migration to Madinah was the "Bond of Fraternity" and the building of the Mosque at Quba. This exemplifies the importance of the establishment of mosque in Islam. And it is the duty of the Muslims as a community to build a mosque and make its proper maintenance.

Allah [swt] directs us on how to dress up when going to Mosque in **Surah Al-Ar'af (7:31)** as:

$$يَبَنِي آدَمَ خُذُوا زِينَتَكُمْ عِندَ كُلِّ مَسْجِدٍ وَكُلُوا وَاشْرَبُوا وَلَا تُسْرِفُوا إِنَّهُ لَا يُحِبُّ الْمُسْرِفِينَ$$

O Children of Adam, take your adornment [wear your clothing] at every masjid, and eat and drink, but be not extravagant. Indeed, He [Allah] likes not those who commit excess.

Allah (swt) says in **Surah at-Tawbah (9:17-8):**

مَا كَانَ لِلْمُشْرِكِينَ أَن يَعْمُرُوا مَسَاجِدَ اللهِ شَهِدِينَ عَلَى أَنفُسِهِم بِالْكُفْرِ أُوْلَئِكَ حَبِطَتْ أَعْمَالُهُمْ وَفِي النَّارِ هُمْ خَالِدُونَ - إِنَّمَا يَعْمُرُ مَسَاجِدَ اللَّهِ مَنْ ءَامَنَ بِاللَّهِ وَالْيَوْمِ الأَخِرِ وَأَقَامَ الصَّلَوةَ وَءَاتَى الزَّكَوةَ وَلَمْ يَخْشَ إِلاَّ اللَّهَ فَعَسَى أُوْلَئِكَ أَن يَكُونُوا مِنَ الْمُهْتَدِينَ -

It is not for the polytheists, to maintain the mosques of Allah [while] witnessing against them with disbelief. [For] those, their deeds have become worthless, and in the Fire they will abide eternally. The mosques of Allah are only to be maintained by those who believe in Allah and the Last Day and establish prayer and give Zakah and fear none but Allah, for it is expected that those will be [rightly] guided. Therefore, Allah [swt] testifies to the faith of those who maintain the Mosques.

Allah [swt] says in **Surah al-'Imran (3:103):**

وَاعْتَصِمُوا بِحَبْلِ اللَّهِ جَمِيعا -

And hold firmly to the rope [the Quran] of Allah all together and do not become divided.

One-way of holding fast the rope of Allah is to perform salat in congregation whenever possible especially in the Mosque. Mumeen goes to the Mosque only for the sake of Allah [swt]. Moreover, when mumeen get together in the Mosque they greet one another with Salam for the pleasure of Allah [swt] and discuss problems facing the Muslim Ummah that puts them in achieving the mercy and blessings of Allah [swt].

During the time of Prophet Muhammad [sas], Mosque was the center point of all activities. At time of the Prophet [sas], the Masjid of Madinah was fully utilized as a place of Worship, Study, Discussion and Consultation, Congregation for Celebration, Center for Propagation, Treasury, Hosting of Guests, Administration, and Military Head Quarter etc.

Today as Muslims we have almost abandoned the Mosques. Rulers of Muslim Countries have deserted the importance of Mosques in building the Muslim community as part of the Muslim Ummah.

Building a mosque is of great Hasanah. Narrated 'Ubdaidullah Al-Khaulani: I heard 'Uthman bin 'Affan saying, when people argued too much about his intention to reconstruct the mosque of Allah's Apostle, "You have talked too much. I heard the Prophet saying, 'whoever built a mosque, [[Bukair thought that 'Asim, another sub narrator, added, "Intending Allah's Pleasure"], and Allah would build for him a similar place in Paradise." (Bukhari, book #8, hadith #441)

The importance of mosques has been emphasized in the following Hadiths: The Prophet [sas] said, "The prayer offered in congregation is twenty five times more superior [in reward] to the prayer offered alone in one's house or in a business center, because if one performs ablution and does it perfectly, and then proceeds to the Mosque with the sole intention of praying, then for each step which he takes towards the Mosque, Allah upgrades him a degree in reward and (forgives) crosses out one sin till he enters the Mosque. When he enters the Mosque he is considered in prayer as long as he is waiting for the prayer and the angels keep on asking for Allah's forgiveness for him and they keep on saying: 'O Allah! Be Merciful to him, O Allah! Forgive him, as long as he keeps on sitting at his praying place and does not pass wind." (Bukhari, book #8, hadith #466)

As mosques are place of worship, those within the mosque are required to remain respectful to those in prayer. Loud talking within the mosque, as well as discussion of topics deemed disrespectful, is forbidden in areas where people are praying. But now a day, we see brothers coming to the mosque talk among them loudly even when others are performing prayers in the mosque. We should refrain from such activities and even if we simply sit in the mosque silently, Allah [swt] will reward us.

The Prophet also said, "If anyone of you enters a mosque, he should not sit until he has offered a two-Rakat prayer." (Bukhari, book #8, hadith #435) As if it is a right of the house of Allah on His slave.

The raising of voices in the mosque is forbidden, and spitting therein is called a sin. In all those matters that related to the sanctity of the mosque, Muslims were, however, told to be lenient. Carrying on any kind of trade in the mosque is strictly prohibited, as is also the reciting of poems, and even sitting in circles and indulging in talk at the time of prayer. (Bukhari, book #8, hadith #459, 407)

Mosque is only the place of worshiping Allah [swt] and discussing religious affairs that benefits the Muslim Ummah. Allah's Apostle [sas] said, "When the Imam is delivering the Khutba, and you ask your companion to keep quiet and listen, then no doubt you have done an evil act." (Bukhari, book #13, hadith #56)

In order to establish and maintain the axis of the Muslim community, the symbol and manifestation of Islamic presence, we must make concerted efforts to establish, maintain, and visit Mosques whenever possible. May Allah [swt] give us the proper guidance so that we can help in building Mosques and maintain them and their sanctity use them in order to regain the past glory of the Ummah? **Amin!**

Muharram: First Month of the Hijri [Islamic] Calendar

The Muslim nation must have a distinct and independent identity [an Islamic Calendar] that is derived solely from the essence of Islam. It is incumbent on the Muslim Ummah that it be distinguished from other nations as far as morals; manners and entire way of life are concerned. This nation cannot be a subservient one that is always tending towards the blind imitation of others; this kind of blind imitation will not entail any goodness or prevent any evil.

Is there any indication by Allah [swt] in preparing the calendar for the Muslim ummah? In **Surah al-Baqarah (2:189)** Allah [swt] says:

$$يَسْـَٔلُونَكَ عَنِ الْأَهِلَّةِ قُلْ هِىَ مَوَاقِيتُ لِلنَّاسِ وَالْحَجِّ ۗ$$

They ask you [O Muhammad] about the new moon. Say: "These are measurements of time for the people and for hajj."

Also in **Surah Yunus (10:5)** Allah [swt] says:

$$هُوَ الَّذِى جَعَلَ الشَّمْسَ ضِيَآءً وَالْقَمَرَ نُورًا وَقَدَّرَهُ مَنَازِلَ لِتَعْلَمُوا عَدَدَ السِّنِينَ وَالْحِسَابَ ۗ$$

It is He who made the sun a shining light and the moon a derived light and determined for it stages - that you may know the number of years and account [of time]. The days are revealed by the action of the sun, and the months and the years by the moon.

Allah then stated in **Surah ar-Rahman (55:5):**

$$وَالشَّمْسُ وَالْقَمَرُ بِحُسْبَانٍ ۗ$$

The sun and the moon [move] by precise calculation.

It is thus clearly indicated by Allah [swt] that the Islamic calendar must be prepared by using the lunar periods.

The Islamic [Lunar] calendar was first introduced during the era of the Amir Al-Mu'mineen Umar ibn Al-Khattab [ra] on the sixteenth or seventeenth year after the Hijrah, or migration of the Prophet [sas] to Madinah. Umar [ra] sought the people's advice on when the Hijri calendar should start. Some held that it should be started from the birth of the Prophet [sas], whilst others thought that it should begin from the very first day that the Messenger of Allah [sas] began his mission. Another group believed that the calendar should be started from the emigration, and the last group held that the calendar should have begun from the death of the Prophet [sas].

'Umar' [ra] agreed with those who wished to start the Islamic Calendar with the Hijrah of the Prophet [sas] due to the fact that this marked the point in history when Allah [swt] differentiated between truth and falsehood by giving the Prophet [sas] real power and authority that was manifested in the form of the first Islamic State.

The companions were also consulted on which month should mark the beginning of the year; 'Umar ibn Al-Khattaab and 'Uthmaan ibn 'Affaan [ra] chose Al-Muharram due to it being a sacred month and because it follows the month of Dhu'l-Hijjah, which is when the Muslims perform Hajj, or the pilgrimage, which was the last pillar of Islam that Allah [swt] enjoined upon the Muslims. Al-Muharram also follows the month in which the Prophet [sas] pledged allegiance to the Ansars [His Madinan supporters] to emigrate to Madinah and this pledge of allegiance was one of the introductory acts of emigration. Due to all these reasons, Al-Muharram was deemed the most suitable month to begin the Islamic Calendar. It is a manifestation of the mercy of Allah [swt] towards His worshipers that He has made the sun and the moon follow exactly computed courses. By observing the sun, people can know the different seasons and by looking at the moon, people will be able to deduce the beginning and end of each month.

Moreover, it is also one of the four sacred months as Allah (swt) has divided the year into twelve months as He said in **Surah at-Tawbah (9:36):**

$$ إِنَّ عِدَّةَ الشُّهُورِ عِندَ اللَّهِ اثْنَا عَشَرَ شَهْرًا فِي كِتَابِ اللَّهِ يَوْمَ خَلَقَ السَّمَاوَاتِ وَالأَرْضَ مِنْهَا أَرْبَعَةٌ حُرُمٌ ذَلِكَ الدِّينُ الْقَيِّمُ فَلاَ تَظْلِمُواْ $$

$$ فِيهِنَّ ۚ $$

Indeed, the number of months with Allah is twelve [lunar] months in the register of Allah [from] the day He created the heavens and the earth; of these, four are sacred. That is the correct religion [way], so do not wrong yourselves during them. Of the four sanctified months, three of them are in sequence; Zul-qadah (11th), Zul-hijjah (12th), Muharram (1st), and the fourth Rajab (7th).

A reason for the easiness of Allah's religion is that the calculation of the beginning and end of each Islamic month is based on the sighting of the moon. Therefore, every person will be easily informed of each new month regardless of whether they are literate or not. The advent of a new month is known by the appearance of the crescent in the west after sunset; once the crescent is manifest, one month has come to an end and another has begun. Therefore, we also come to know that the day starts at the sunset and not at midnight, because the first day of the month is marked by the sunset of the last day of the previous month.

Another important aspect of the lunar calendar is that many of the important events: Ramadhan, Hajj, and others of the religion of Islam are related to the lunar months. The beauty of this is that wherever a Muslim lives in this world, by rotation he/she will have different seasons, different days of the year in performing these events and as such there will be equality among the mankind in observing the events.

The word Muharram means "forbidden", and even before the mission of Prophet Muhammad [sas], this month was always known as a scared month in which specific acts were considered forbidden/restricted; prominently warfare/the shedding of blood.

Among the virtues of this month is that it contains the day of 'Ashura'. The word "Ashura" is derived from the Arabic word Ashara that means ten falls on its tenth day. 'Aa'ishah [ra] narrated that: "Qura'ysh [the tribe of the Prophet] as well *as* the Prophet [sas] used to fast the day of 'Ashura' during the days of Jahiliyah [pre-Islamic ignorance]. When the Prophet [sas] migrated to Medina he continued to fast it and commanded the people to do so. However, when the revelations regarding fasting in the month of Ramadhan came, he gave it up and used to fast during Ramadhan instead. After this, some people continued to fast the day of 'Ashura' [optionally] whilst others gave up fasting it" (Bukhari, book #58, hadith #172).

Ibn 'Abbaas [ra] reported that: "When prophet [sas] arrived in Madinah, he observed that the Jews were fasting on the day of 'Ashura', so the Prophet [sas] asked them: "Why do you fast on this day?" They replied, "This is a great day. It is on this day that Allah (swt) saved Musa [as] and his followers while drowning Pharaoh and his people, so Musa [as] fasted this day out of gratitude to Allah [swt]. That is why we fast on this day" The Prophet [sas] said in response: "We have more right to Musa [as] than you [i.e. we love Musa] and follow what he came with [Islam] more than you do." and there upon the Prophet [sas] fasted this day and commanded the people to do likewise." (Bukhari, book #31, hadith #222)

The Sahaba [ra] asked him: "O Messenger of Allah [swt] this is the day the Jews, and Christians respect and honor... The Prophet [sas] promised them that next year Allah willing, we shall fast the ninth along with the tenth". (Muslim, book #006, hadith #2529)

As Muslims, we should be keen to fast the ninth along with the tenth of this month. Slaves of Allah [swt]! Know that this is the month in which Allah [swt] gave victory to Musa [as] and his followers, despite the fact that they were vastly outnumbered, over the tyrant Pharaoh and his people.

There are many pharaoh-like authorities who have appeared through history and there were those incorruptible standard-bearers of justice who opposed them. It is in that vein that another significant event occurred on Muharram 10th in 61 AH, an event that serves as a milestone in the history of the faithful; the martyrdom of the beloved grandson of the Prophet Muhammad [sas], Imam Husain at Karbala, Iraq. A martyrdom at the hands of those who claimed to act in the name of Islam yet unremorsefully and shamelessly were prepared to obliterate its true exponent; those who [like so many who proclaim faith] are prepared to kill for Islam yet are unable to live by it.

The memory of Husain excites the spirit; the very name of Husain evokes the tradition of resistance against tyranny and inequity. His colossal struggle and monumental martyrdom is so poignant that it continues to serve as a beacon of light to all the faithful who struggle for freedom and justice.

Any man, no matter how eloquent he is, cannot enumerate the evil and harm that they do to the Muslims. Some others - either those who oppose and have enmity towards al-Husain and his family or ignorant people who try to fight evil with evil, corruption with corruption, lies with lies and bid'ah with bid'ah - opposed them by fabricating reports in favor of making the day of 'Ashura' a day of celebration, by wearing kohl and hena, spending money on one's children, cooking special dishes and other things that are done on Eids and special occasions. These people took the day of 'Ashura' as a festival like Eid, whereas others took it as a day of mourning. Both are wrong, and both go against the Sunnah, even though the other groups [those who take it as a day of mourning] are worse in intention and more ignorant and more plainly wrong. Neither the Prophet [sas] nor his successors [the khulafa' al-rashidun] did any of these things on the day of 'Ashura', they neither made it a day of mourning nor a day of celebration.

Dear brothers and sisters in Islam, today we celebrate with great enthusiasm the English new years day, but many of us do not know the beginning of the Islamic calendar or the month of the calendar accept Ramadhan. What an irony of fate? Yet we claim ourselves to be Muslims.

Let us renew our faith, repent to Allah [swt] and purify our hearts in order to attain Paradise, as well as the pleasure of our creator in this life and the Hereafter. Allah loves those who respond to His call, He grants them victory, mercy, and strengthens their faith due to their reliance on Him.

We ask Allah to make us followers of the Sunnah of His Noble Prophet, to make us live in Islam and die in a state of faith. May He help us to do that which He loves and which pleases Him? We ask Him to help us to remember Him and be thankful to Him, to worship Him properly and to accept our good deeds. May He make us of those who are pious and fear Him? May Allah bless our Prophet Muhammad [sas] and all his family and companions? **Amin!**

Muslim Women and Western Media

During the European dark ages, philosophers culminated in declaring that a woman has a soul greatly inferior to that of a man. In the Roman law, the wife was the purchased property of her husband, who could also divorce her. The situation was even worse as they did not allow women to inherit. In India, there existed the practice of burning the widow along with her husband's corpse. A woman, in the Arab men's eyes, was a den of shame, a jinx and a source of poverty.

Refuting their claims, Allah [swt] says in **Surah at-Takweer (81:8-9):**

بِأَيِّ ذَنۢبٍ قُتِلَتْ ۞ وَإِذَا الصُّحُفُ نُشِرَتْ ۞ وَإِذَا السَّمَآءُ كُشِطَتْ

And when the girl [who was] buried alive is asked, for what sin she was killed? What has this innocent girl done to be treated in this way?

Upon examining Eve's legacy, all throughout the Judeo-Christian heritage, we find a negative image of women in general. This negativity is a result from the temptress image of Hawwa [peace be on her] portrayed in the Bible. She has been given the appearance of a seducer, temptress, as well as a deceiver. From the beginning, the Judeo-Christian religions placed total blame on Hawwa (peace be on her). According to their scriptures, Allah [swt] said to Hawwa [peace be on her]: "I will greatly increase your pain in childbearing."

Jewish rabbis list nine curses inflicted upon women as a result of Hawwa's [peace be on her] sin: "To the women He gave nine curses and death: the burden of the blood of menstruation and the blood of virginity; the burden of pregnancy; the burden of childbirth; the burden of bringing up children; her head is covered as one in mourning; she pierces her ear like a permanent slave or slave girl who serves her master; she is not to be believed after a witness; and after everything-death" (Leonard J. Swindler, Women in Judaism: The Status of women in formative Judaism Metuchen, N.J: Scarecrow Press, 1976 pg 155). This implies that Allah [swt] is punishing Hawwa [peace be on her] as well as the entire female population for Hawwa's [peace be on her] sin. Allah, according to the Holy Qur'an, punishes no one for another's faults.

Mother Hawwa [peace be on her] according to Qur'an is not blamed for Adam's first mistake. Both were jointly wrong in their disobedience to Allah, both repented, and both were forgiven as mentioned in **Surah al-Ar'af (7:23):**

قَالَا رَبَّنَا ظَلَمْنَآ أَنفُسَنَا وَإِن لَّمْ تَغْفِرْ لَنَا وَتَرْحَمْنَا لَنَكُونَنَّ مِنَ الْخَـٰسِرِينَ

They said, "Our Lord! We have wronged ourselves, and if You do not forgive and have mercy upon us, we will surely be among the losers."

In another verse, in fact, Adam [peace be on him] specifically, was blamed in **Surah Ta-Ha (20:121)**:

وَعَصَىٰ ءَادَمُ رَبَّهُ فَغَوَىٰ

And Adam disobeyed his Creator and erred.

When it comes to female or male gender, religious attitude is present as well. The Catholic Bible does say explicitly that, "The birth of a daughter is a loss." (Ecclesiastics: 22:3). In Leviticus (12: 2-5), we have "If a woman has conceived seed, and born a male child: then she shall be unclean seven days...but if she bears a female child, then she shall be unclean two weeks."

When it comes to education, there is also a great distinction between the three religions. In Judaism, the Torah is the Law. However, according to the Talmud, "women are exempt from the study of the Torah." Many Jewish rabbis declare, "Whoever teaches his daughter Torah is as though he taught her obscenity" (Denise L. Carmody, "Judaism, in Arvind Sharma", ed., op., ct., 197*). Church authorities convicted Galileo for advocating Copernicus's theory that the earth revolved round the sun and was punished. Socrates was charged on charges of impiety and of corrupting the youths of Athens. He was condemned, sentenced to death, and executed. These are some examples of how Church authorities during the Roman Empire and contemporary rulers were engaged in restricting the search for knowledge and scientific investigations.

According to the New Testament, "let your women keep silent in the churches for it is not permitted unto them to speak; but they are commanded to be under obedience, as also saith the law, and if they will learn anything, let them ask their husbands at home: FOR IT IS A SHAME FOR A WOMAN TO SPEAK IN THE CHURCH."(Corinthians, 14:34-35). But in Islam, education is made mandatory for all men and women.

Let us have a look at the activities of Pope and Priesthood during the 11th and 12th centuries. It is true that no civil government in Europe has been patterned directly on Plato's model of *"rule by aristocracy"*; nevertheless, there is a striking similarity between the position of the Catholic Church in mediaeval Europe and that of Plato's guardian class. Pope Urban II [original name Odo de Lagery] was born in France and was elected Pope in 1088. On November 27, 1095; the Pope instigated the politicians and Church officials to start *"Crusade"* or Holy war that lasted for about 200 year, in which millions of men, women, and children were killed and property destroyed. Although the *"Crusade"* started against the Muslims, but subsequently Christians and Jews of Non-European origin were also branded as infidels, and they were also killed and driven away from Europe.

Moreover, although St. Paul was the originator of the "Protestant Christians", Protestant theologian John Calvin, an intolerant man, and those whom he considered heretics received short shrift in Geneva. One of his most famous victims was Michael Servetus, a Spanish physician and theologian who did not believe in the *"doctrine of the Trinity"* was arrested, tried for heresy and burnt of the stake in 1553. That was how Christianity subjugated the voice of others.

Why women are excluded from priesthood? Is this not a violation of equal rights as the western societies advocate for?

Let us now look at the status of women in Islam that Allah [the Most Merciful] revealed 1431 years ago through Prophet Muhammad [peace be on him]. There is a Chapter named "An-Nisa" that means [the women]. There is no Chapter in the Qur'an that is named "The Men". Also, there is no chapter in the Bible called "The Women". Not only that, only woman mentioned by name in our holy book Quran is *Mariam*. There is a complete chapter after the name of *Mariam* in the holy Quran (Chapter # 19).

In Islam there is no distinction between boy and girl. In fact, a recent discovery made while studying the mathematical aspect of the Qur'an shows that the word "man" and "woman" both appear the same number of times in it. This is probably Allah's way of showing us that man and woman are equal. In the Qur'an, it was revealed that male and female off springs are both gifts from Allah. One should not forget that biologically speaking it is the male who determines the sex of the child. So if it is a boy or a girl, it is due to the man's X or Y chromosome.

In terms of religious obligations, such as the Daily Prayers, Fasting, and Pilgrimage, woman is no different from man. In some cases indeed, woman has certain advantages over man. For example, the woman is exempted from the daily prayers and from fasting during her menstrual periods and forty days after childbirth. She is also exempted from fasting during her pregnancy and when she is nursing her baby if there is any threat to her health or her baby's. If she missed fasting [during the month of Ramadan], she can make up for the missed days whenever she can. She does not have to make up for the prayers missed for any of the above reasons. Although women can and did go into the mosque during the days of the prophet and thereafter attendance at the Friday congregational prayers is optional for them while it is mandatory for men [on Friday].

This is clearly a tender touch of the Islamic teachings for they are considerate of the fact that a woman may be nursing her baby or caring for him, and thus may be unable to go out to the mosque at the time of the prayers. They also take into account the physiological and psychological changes associated with her natural female functions.

In the later part of 18th century (1780), there began a transition from manual labor and draft-animal-based economy towards machine- based manufacturing in Great Britain. The effects spread throughout Western Europe and North America during the 19th century (1850 onwards). They call it "*Industrial Revolution*". Thus Western civilization is of a very recent phenomenon (about 300 years old).

What did the women of these countries do before that? They were engaged in agriculture, so woman working outside home in western societies is a phenomenon of 150-200 years only. One will see the same situation in the predominant Muslim countries: men and women are working in agricultural fields side by side. Western media and those who hate Islam forget that "*Islam is a code of life for the Muslims. Muslims- men and women- believe and try to practice it.*" What is the harm in it? Moreover, they forget the distinction between the rights and responsibilities given by religion, vis-à-vis, the rights and responsibilities assigned by state. Are the Westerners following the instructions of the religions they belong to? Definitely not, by most of them.

What did modernization gave as gift to the western world? It has given speed, but took away love and affection. It forsook the teachings of religion; instituted unfaithfulness among married couples by engaging in extra-marital sex, and gave women the liberty of wearing half naked dress, and so on. Modernization took away modesty and honor from majority of the Western women; replaced by nudity and females as material for satisfying sexual lust of men. Brothers and Sisters of Christianity, how do you dress up mother "*Mary*" when you present her while observing the Christmas Day? Is it not the dress that the Christian Nuns wear? If you believe in Trinity, why you do not advise your women to wear the dress of Mary? If not, how can you expect Jesus to intercede on the day of Final Judgment for your mercy and going to Heaven?

Islamophobes, and specially a major part of the Western media are propagating that religion of Islam is subjugating women by asking them to wear "*Hijab*" [veil similar to the dress that their mother Mary used to wear], that according to them, reminds them of the uncivilized behavior and brand them as fundamentalist, and as assign of backwardness.

What does "*Hijab*" means? Allah (swt) explains in **Surah al-Ahzab (33:59)** as

يَـٰٓأَيُّهَا ٱلنَّبِيُّ قُل لِّأَزْوَٰجِكَ وَبَنَـٰتِكَ وَنِسَآءِ ٱلْمُؤْمِنِينَ يُدْنِينَ عَلَيْهِنَّ مِن جَلَـٰبِيبِهِنَّ ذَٰلِكَ أَدْنَىٰٓ أَن يُعْرَفْنَ فَلَا يُؤْذَيْنَ وَكَانَ ٱللَّهُ غَفُورًا رَّحِيمًا

O Prophet, tell your wives and your daughters and the women of the believers to bring down over themselves [part] of their outer garments hilbab [a cloak covering the head and reaching to the ground] over their bodies. That is more suitable that they will be known [as chaste believing women] and not to be annoyed. And ever Allah is Forgiving and Merciful.

And also in **Surah an-Nur (24:30)** Allah advises:

قُل لِّلْمُؤْمِنِينَ يَغُضُّوا۟ مِنْ أَبْصَـٰرِهِمْ وَيَحْفَظُوا۟ فُرُوجَهُمْ ذَٰلِكَ أَزْكَىٰ لَهُمْ إِنَّ ٱللَّهَ خَبِيرٌۢ بِمَا يَصْنَعُونَ

Tell the believing men to reduce some of their vision [averting their eyes from what is unlawful] and guard their private parts [from unlawful acts]. That is purer for them. Indeed, Allah is acquainted with what they do.

It is also to distinguish the believing women from the women of the Jahiliyyah and the deeds of the pagan women, who did not do that but would pass in front of men with their chests completely uncovered, and with their necks, forelocks, hair and earrings uncovered.

Since looking provokes the heart to evil, Allah commanded (the believers) to protect their private parts just as he commanded them to protect their gaze which can lead to that. Men are more tempted than women to go for illicit/illegal sexual encounter. They provoke women, the act of Shaytan, to come for illegal sexual activity.

When Allah commands women to observe Hijab in front of men to whom they are not related, He explains the relatives before whom they do not need to observe Hijab in Surah An-Nur (24:31):

وَقُل لِّلْمُؤْمِنَـٰتِ يَغْضُضْنَ مِنْ أَبْصَـٰرِهِنَّ وَيَحْفَظْنَ فُرُوجَهُنَّ وَلَا يُبْدِينَ زِينَتَهُنَّ إِلَّا مَا ظَهَرَ مِنْهَا وَلْيَضْرِبْنَ بِخُمُرِهِنَّ عَلَىٰ جُيُوبِهِنَّ

وَلَا يُبْدِينَ زِينَتَهُنَّ إِلَّا لِبُعُولَتِهِنَّ أَوْ ءَابَآئِهِنَّ أَوْ ءَابَآءِ بُعُولَتِهِنَّ أَوْ أَبْنَآئِهِنَّ أَوْ أَبْنَآءِ بُعُولَتِهِنَّ أَوْ إِخْوَٰنِهِنَّ أَوْ بَنِىٓ إِخْوَٰنِهِنَّ أَوْ بَنِىٓ

أَخَوَٰتِهِنَّ أَوْ نِسَآئِهِنَّ أَوْ مَا مَلَكَتْ أَيْمَـٰنُهُنَّ أَوِ التَّـٰبِعِينَ غَيْرِ أُو۟لِى الْإِرْبَةِ مِنَ الرِّجَالِ أَوِ الطِّفْلِ الَّذِينَ لَمْ يَظْهَرُوا۟ عَلَىٰ عَوْرَٰتِ

النِّسَآءِ وَلَا يَضْرِبْنَ بِأَرْجُلِهِنَّ لِيُعْلَمَ مَا يُخْفِينَ مِن زِينَتِهِنَّ وَتُوبُوٓا۟ إِلَى اللَّهِ جَمِيعًا أَيُّهَ الْمُؤْمِنُونَ لَعَلَّكُمْ تُفْلِحُونَ

And tell the believing women to reduce some of their vision [averting their eyes from what is unlawful], and guard their private parts and not to show off their adornment except that which is apparent, and to draw their head covers over their chests and not to display their adornment [i.e. beauty] except to their husbands, their fathers, their husband's fathers, their sons, their husband's sons, their brothers or their brother's sons, their sister's sons, their women, their right hand possess [female slaves], or those male attendants who having no physical desire [in which a man is devoid of sexual feeling], or children who are not yet aware of the private aspects of women. And let them not stamp their feet to make known that they conceal their adornment. And turn to Allah in repentance, all of you, O believers! That you might succeed.

Of course, Muslim women are proud to wear "*Hijab*" as a sign of modesty. But the same media do not consider the torture, rape, and killing of innocent children and women by invading forces in Palestine, Iraq, and Afghanistan as violation of human rights. Because, they consider themselves immune of all sins. The Western media does not want to know the real sufferings of Muslims, and that's it. They would buy a tiny piece of stuff such as "*woman stoned for sex adultery*", in a population of more than 1.5 billion Muslims, and start blames faming Islam. When anti-Muslims criticize Islam, they call it freedom of expression; but when Muslims defend and practice their religion, they brand it as fundamentalist and extremist!!

Muslims, especially Muslim women, become victim of racist comments and threats just because of holding their Muslim identity. Double standard of western media towards Muslims, especially women, is very naked and derogatory, and nothing but a real hypocrisy.

Islam emphasizes that man is the "*Head*" while woman is the "*Heart*" of the family. Both are necessary and complimentary to one another. In his farewell sermon our beloved Prophet Muhammad [peace be on him] said, "O people, to you a right belongs with respect to your women, and to your women a right with respect to you. Do treat your women well, and be kind to them, for they are your partners and committed helpers". What a beautiful sermon for the whole mankind, not only for the believers and the Muslims alone!!

Is it only the Western media who are spreading venoms against Islam? No, there are some who carry a Muslim name and brand them as ex-Muslim: Syed K. Mirza [original name Khurshed A. Chowdhury], Mohammad Asgar, Jafrullah , of Bangladeshi origin et.al., are running a web-site just to propagate falsehood through devious, deceitful bigotry writings to humiliate the religion of Islam, its Prophet, and its Holy Book. These are nothing but devils in the guise of human being. Be careful! They are more dangerous transgressors, *Munafiquns*, who are doing more harm to the religion of Islam than the Western media. For them Allah [the All Powerful] said in **Surah al-Fath (48:6):**

وَيُعَذِّبَ الْمُنَـٰفِقِينَ وَالْمُنَـٰفِقَـٰتِ وَالْمُشْرِكِينَ وَالْمُشْرِكَـٰتِ الظَّآنِّينَ بِاللَّهِ ظَنَّ السَّوْءِ عَلَيْهِمْ دَآئِرَةُ السَّوْءِ وَغَضِبَ اللَّهُ عَلَيْهِمْ وَلَعَنَهُمْ وَأَعَدَّ لَهُمْ جَهَنَّمَ وَسَآءَتْ مَصِيرًا

And that He may punish the hypocrite men and women, and also the polytheist men and women – those who assume about Allah an assumption of evil nature. Upon them is a misfortune of evil nature; and Allah has become angry with them and has cursed them and prepared for them Hell, and worst it is as a destination.

Those who consider ignorance is bliss, they can comment on anything without proper knowledge in the guise of freedom of speech. Of the Christians who believe in *"Trinity"* also believe that Prophet Jesus [peace be on him] died in the *"cross"* with their sins that they will commit in this worldly life. So they have, in their hand, an open cheque of doing things that they wish. I will advise them to practice their own religion before interfering on the religion of Islam. If they are atheists, they do not deserve the right of criticizing any religion, what so ever, in the name of right of speech.

O, brothers and sisters in Islam! Try to follow the instructions of Islam not only in private but also in public life. Sisters, please try to wear dresses and behave in the Islamic way that will burn the hearts of the disbelievers, pagans, and the Western media more and more. Allah will surely reward us all for that. **Amin!**

Mysteries of Human Creation

Allah [swt] is the creator of the Heavens and Earth and whatever in and in between them and also the mankind. In **Surah al-Mu'minun (23:12) -** Allah [swt] says how He has started the creation of man:

وَلَقَدْ خَلَقْنَا الْإِنْسَانَ مِن سُلَالَةٍ مِّن طِينٍ

And certainly did We create man from an extract of clay.

Allah [swt] tells us how He initially created man from an extract of Tin. This was Adam [as] whom Allah created from sounding clay of altered black smooth mud. This is the more apparent meaning and is closer to the context, for Adam [as] was created from a sticky Tin, which is sounding clay of altered black smooth mud, and that is created from dust, as Allah says in **Surah ar-Rum (30:20):**

وَمِنْ ءَايَتِهِ أَنْ خَلَقَكُم مِّن تُرَابٍ ثُمَّ إِذَا أَنتُم بَشَرٌ تَنتَشِرُونَ-

And of His signs is that He created you [Adam] from dust; then, suddenly you are human beings dispersing [throughout the earth]!

After creating Adam [as] when Allah [swt] ordered the angels to prostrate to him, all of them prostrated except Iblis. The reason Why Iblis denied prostrating to Adam (as) is described in **Surah Saad (38:75-6):**

قَالَ يَإِبْلِيسُ مَا مَنَعَكَ أَن تَسْجُدَ لِمَا خَلَقْتُ بِيَدَيَّ أَسْتَكْبَرْتَ أَمْ كُنتَ مِنَ الْعَلِينَ قَالَ أَنَا خَيْرٌ مِّنْهُ خَلَقْتَنِى مِن نَّارٍ وَخَلَقْتَهُ مِن طِينٍ-

[Allah] said, "O Iblees, What prevented you from prostrating to that I created with My Hands? Were you arrogant [then] or were you [already] among the haughty?" [Ibleess] said, "I am better than him. You created me from fire and created him from clay."

In the above verse (75) Allah [swt] described that He has created Adam [as] with His both hands.

Then Adam [as] fell asleep, as the People of the Book and other scholars such as Ibn `Abbas have stated, Allah took one of Adam's left ribs and made flesh grow in its place, while Adam was asleep and unaware. Allah then created Adam's wife, 'Hawwa', from his rib and made her a woman, so that she could be a comfort for him. When Adam woke up and saw Hawwa' next to him, it was claimed, he said, "My flesh and blood, my wife". Hence, Adam reclined with Hawwa'. When Allah married Adam to Hawwa' and gave him comfort.

He created you [all] from a single person; means, He created you, with all your varied races, types, languages and colors, from a single soul, who was Adam [as]:

ثُمَّ جَعَلَ مِنْهَا زَوْجَهَا

Then made from him his wife [Hawwa (ra)].

This is the ayah of **Surah an-Nisa (4:1)** in Which Allah (swt) said:

يَـٰٓأَيُّهَا ٱلنَّاسُ ٱتَّقُوا۟ رَبَّكُمُ ٱلَّذِى خَلَقَكُم مِّن نَّفْسٍ وَٰحِدَةٍ وَخَلَقَ مِنْهَا زَوْجَهَا وَبَثَّ مِنْهُمَا رِجَالًا كَثِيرًا وَنِسَآءً وَٱتَّقُوا۟ ٱللَّهَ ٱلَّذِى تَسَآءَلُونَ بِهِۦ وَٱلْأَرْحَامَ إِنَّ ٱللَّهَ كَانَ عَلَيْكُمْ رَقِيبًا ۔

O mankind, fear your Lord who created you from one soul and created from it its mate, and dispersed from both of them many men and women. And fear Allah through whom [whose name] you ask one another [request favors and demand rights], and the wombs [fear Allah in regards to relations of kinship]. Indeed, Allah is ever, over you, an Observer.

It is very clear from the above discussion that Adam [as] and Hawwa [ra] were created by special power of Allah [swt] without embryo. The question remains how the rest of the mankind was created by Allah [swt]? They were created through the development of embryo in the wombs of mothers.

Allah [swt] describes here that He has first created Adam [as] from clay and the rest are created from semen of dispersed water. In **Surah al-Insan (76:1-3):**

هَلْ أَتَىٰ عَلَى ٱلْإِنسَـٰنِ حِينٌ مِّنَ ٱلدَّهْرِ لَمْ يَكُن شَيْـًٔا مَّذْكُورًا ۔ إِنَّا خَلَقْنَا ٱلْإِنسَـٰنَ مِن نُّطْفَةٍ أَمْشَاجٍ نَّبْتَلِيهِ فَجَعَلْنَـٰهُ سَمِيعًۢا بَصِيرًا ۔ إِنَّا هَدَيْنَـٰهُ ٱلسَّبِيلَ إِمَّا شَاكِرًا وَإِمَّا كَفُورًا ۔

Has there [not] come upon man a period of time when he was not a thing [even] mentioned. Indeed, We created man from a sperm-drop mixture [a combination of the male and female substance] that We may try him, and We made him hearing and seeing. Indeed, We guided him to the way, be he grateful or ungrateful.

In **Surah al-Hajj (22:5),** Allah [swt] further explains the mechanism of the creation of the main stream of mankind as:

يَـٰٓأَيُّهَا ٱلنَّاسُ إِن كُنتُمْ فِى رَيْبٍ مِّنَ ٱلْبَعْثِ فَإِنَّا خَلَقْنَـٰكُم مِّن تُرَابٍ ثُمَّ مِن نُّطْفَةٍ ثُمَّ مِنْ عَلَقَةٍ ثُمَّ مِن مُّضْغَةٍ مُّخَلَّقَةٍ وَغَيْرِ مُخَلَّقَةٍ لِّنُبَيِّنَ لَكُمْ وَنُقِرُّ فِى ٱلْأَرْحَامِ مَا نَشَآءُ إِلَىٰٓ أَجَلٍ مُّسَمًّى ثُمَّ نُخْرِجُكُمْ طِفْلًا ثُمَّ لِتَبْلُغُوٓا۟ أَشُدَّكُمْ وَمِنكُم مَّن يُتَوَفَّىٰ وَمِنكُم مَّن يُرَدُّ إِلَىٰٓ أَرْذَلِ ٱلْعُمُرِ لِكَيْلَا يَعْلَمَ مِنۢ بَعْدِ عِلْمٍ شَيْـًٔا وَتَرَى ٱلْأَرْضَ هَامِدَةً فَإِذَآ أَنزَلْنَا عَلَيْهَا ٱلْمَآءَ ٱهْتَزَّتْ وَرَبَتْ وَأَنۢبَتَتْ مِن كُلِّ زَوْجٍۭ بَهِيجٍ

O People, If you should be in doubt about the Resurrection, then [consider that] indeed, We created you from dust, then from a sperm-drop, then from a clinging clot, and then from a little lump of flesh -- formed and unformed -- that We may make [it] clear to you [Our power and creative ability]. And We cause whom We will to remain in the wombs for an appointed term, We settle in the wombs whom We will for a specified term, then We bring you out as a child, and when [We develop you] that you may reach your [time of] maturity. And among you is he who return to the most decrepit [old] age so that he knows after [once having] knowledge, nothing. And you see the earth barren, but when We send down upon it rain, it quivers and swells and grows [something] of every beautiful kind.

If the nutfah establishes itself in the woman's womb, it stays like that for forty days, then more material is added to it and it changes into a red clot, by the leave of Allah, and it remains like that for forty days. Then it changes and becomes a lump of flesh, like a piece of meat with no form or shape in forty days. Then it starts to take on a form and shape, developing a head, arms, chest, stomach, thighs, legs, feet and all its members. Sometimes a woman miscarries before the fetus is formed and sometimes she miscarries after it has formed.

Mujahid said, "This means the miscarried fetus, formed or unformed. When forty days have passed of it being a lump of flesh, then Allah sends an angel to it who breathes the soul into it and forms it as Allah wills, handsome or ugly, male or female. He then writes its provision, its allotted length of life and whether it is to be one of the blessed or the wretched". It was recorded in the Two Sahihs that Ibn Mas`ud said, "The Messenger of Allah, who is the true and truly inspired one, told us: Every one of you is collected in the womb of his mother for the first forty days, and then he becomes a clot for another forty days, and then a lump of flesh for another forty days. Then Allah sends an angel to write four words: He writes his provision, his deeds, his life span, and whether he will be blessed or wretched. Then he blows the soul into him" (Bukhari, book #55, hadith #549).

"Then out of a piece of chewed flesh, partly formed and partly unformed," This part of Surah 22:5 seems to indicate that the embryo is composed of both differentiated and undifferentiated tissues. For example, when the cartilage bones are differentiated, the embryonic connective tissue or mesenchyme around them is undifferentiated. It later differentiates into the muscles and ligaments attached to the bones. "And We cause whom We will to rest in the wombs for an appointed term".

This next part of Surah 22:5 seems to imply that Allah [swt] determines which embryos will remain in the uterus until full term. It is well known that many embryos abort during the first month of development, and that only about 30% of zygotes that form, develop into fetuses that survive until birth. This verse has also been interpreted to mean that Allah [swt] determines whether the embryo will develop into a boy or girl (Moore).

In **Surah az-Zumar (39:6)** Allah [swt] says:

خَلَقَكُمْ مِّن نَّفْسٍ وَحِدَةٍ ثُمَّ جَعَلَ مِنْهَا زَوْجَهَا وَأَنزَلَ لَكُم مِّنَ الْأَنْعَمِ ثَمَنِيَةَ أَزْوَجٍ يَخْلُقُكُمْ فِى بُطُونِ أُمَّهَتِكُمْ خَلْقًا مِّن بَعْدِ خَلْقٍ فِى ظُلُمَتٍ ثَلَثٍ ذَلِكُمُ اللَّهُ رَبُّكُمْ لَهُ الْمُلْكُ لَا إِلَهَ إِلَّا هُوَ فَأَنَّى تُصْرَفُونَ-

He created you from one soul. Then He made it its mate and He produced for you from the grazing livestock eight pairs. He creates you in the wombs of your mothers, creation after creation, within three darkness [the belly, the womb, and the amniotic membrane]. That is Allah, your Lord; to Him belongs dominion. There is no deity except Him, so how are you averted.

Allah [swt] described again in **Surah al-Mu'minun (23:12-4):**

وَلَقَدْ خَلَقْنَا الْإِنسَنَ مِن سُلَـٰلَةٍ مِّن طِينٍ - ثُمَّ جَعَلْنَـٰهُ نُطْفَةً فِى قَرَارٍ مَّكِينٍ - ثُمَّ خَلَقْنَا النُّطْفَةَ عَلَقَةً فَخَلَقْنَا الْعَلَقَةَ مُضْغَةً فَخَلَقْنَا الْمُضْغَةَ

عِظَـٰمًا فَكَسَوْنَا الْعِظَـٰمَ لَحْمًا ثُمَّ أَنشَأْنَـٰهُ خَلْقًا ءَاخَرَ فَتَبَارَكَ اللَّهُ أَحْسَنُ الْخَـٰلِقِينَ -

And certainly We did create man out of an extract of clay. Then We placed him as a sperm-drop [as a zygote] in a firm lodging the womb]. Then We made the sperm-drop into a clinging clot, and We made the clot into a little lump [of flesh], and We made [from] the lump, bones, and We covered the bones with flesh; then We developed him into another creation. So blessed is Allah, the Best of creators [the most skillful and only true creator].

Allah says in the Qur'an about the stages of the creation of man: Man we did create from a quintessence [of clay]; Then we placed as [a drop of] sperm [*nutfah*] in a place firmly fixed; Then we made the sperm into a clot of congealed blood ['*alaqah*]; Then of that clot we made a [*fetus*] lump [*mudghah*]; then we made out of that lump bones and clothed the bones with flesh; then we developed out of it another creature.

In **Surah at-Tariq (86:5-7)** Allah [swt] explains:

فَلْيَنظُرِ الْإِنسَـٰنُ مِمَّ خُلِقَ - خُلِقَ مِن مَّآءٍ دَافِقٍ - يَخْرُجُ مِن بَيْنِ الصُّلْبِ وَالتَّرَآئِبِ

So let man observe from what he was created. He was created from a fluid, ejected, and emerging from between the back-bone and the ribs.

The Arabic word '*alaqah* has three meanings. The first meaning is "*leech*". The second is "*a suspended thing*". The third meaning is "*a blood clot*". The fresh-water leech to the embryo is the '*alaqah* stage the embryo during the '*alaqah* stage acquires an appearance very similar to that of leech.

The second meaning of the word '*alaqah* is "a suspended thing", and this is what we can see in the attachment of the embryo during the '*alaqah* stage to the uterus [womb] of the mother. The third meaning of the word '*alaqah*' is a blood clot. It is significant to note that the embryo during the '*alaqah* stage goes through well known internal events, such as the formation of blood in closed vessels, until the metabolic cycle is completed through placenta. During the '*alaqah* stage, the blood is caught within closed vessels and that is why the embryo acquires the appearance of a blood clot, in addition to the leech-like appearance. Both descriptions are miraculously given by a single Qur'anic word '*alaqah*'.

How could Muhammad [sas] have possibly known that by himself? Professor Moore* also studied the embryo at the mudghah [chewed-like substance] stage. He took a piece of raw clay and chewed it in his mouth, then compared it with a picture of the embryo at the mudghah stage. Professor Moore concluded that the embryo at the mudghah stage acquires the exact appearance of a chewed-like.

The developing embryo was considered to be human at 40 to 42 days and no longer resemble an animal embryo at this stage. [The human embryo begins to acquire human characteristics at this stage]. The Qur'an also states that the embryo develops with - three veils of darkness. This probably refers to (1) the maternal anterior abdominal wall, (2) the uterine wall, and (3) the amniochorionic membrane.

The Qur'an identifies the stages of pre-natal development as follows: Nutfah, which means "a drop" or "small amount of water"; 'alaqah' which means a "leech-like structure"; mudghah, which means a "chewed-like structure"; 'idhaam', which means "bones" or "skeleton"; kisaa ul idham bil-laham, which means the clothing of bones with flesh or muscle, and al-nash'a which means "the formation of distinct fetus". These Qur'anic divisions are actually based on the different phases of pre-natal development. These divisions provide elegant scientific descriptions that are comprehensible and practical.

Scientists in the 7th century A.D. likely knew that the human embryo developed in the uterus. The realization that the human embryo develops in stages was not discussed and illustrated until the 15th century.

"Then We placed him as a drop in a place of rest" This statement is from Sura 23:13. The drop or nutfah has been interpreted as the sperm or spermatozoon, but a more meaningful interpretation would be the zygote that divides to form a blastocyst which is implanted in the uterus "a place of rest". This interpretation is supported by another verse in the Qur'an which states that "a human being is created from a mixed drop". The zygote forms by the union of a mixture of the sperm and the ovum "The mixed drop".

"Then We made the drop into a leech-like structure".

This statement is from Sura 23:14. The word 'alaqah refers to a leech or bloodsucker. This is an appropriate description of the human embryo from days 7-24 when it clings to the endometrial of the uterus, in the same way that a leech clings to the skin. Just as the leech derives blood from the host, the human embryo derives blood from the deciduas or pregnant endometrial. It is remarkable how much the embryo of 23-24 days resembles a leech. As there were no microscopes or lenses available in the 7th century, doctors would not have known that the human embryo had this leech-like appearance. In the early part of the fourth week, the embryo is just visible to the unaided eye because it is smaller than a kernel of wheat.

"Then of that leech-like structure, We made a chewed lump." This statement is also from Surah 23:14. The Arabic word "mudghahh" means "chewed substance or chewed lump." Toward the end of the fourth week, the human embryo looks somewhat like a chewed lump of flesh. The chewed appearance results from the smites that resemble teeth marks. The smites represent the beginnings or primordial of the vertebrae.

"Then We made out of the chewed lump, bones, and clothed the bones in flesh." This continuation of Surah 23:14 indicate that out of the chewed lump stage, bones and muscles form. This is in accordance with embryological development. First the bones form as cartilage models and then the muscles [flesh] develop around them from the somatic mesoderm.

"Then We developed out of it another creature." This next part of Surah 23:14 imply that the bones and muscles result in the formation of another creature. This may refer to the human-like embryo that forms by the end of the eighth week. At this stage it has distinctive human characteristics and possesses the primordial of all the internal and external organs and parts. After the eighth week, the human embryo is called a fetus. This may be the new creature to which the verse refers, "And He gave you hearing and sight and feeling and understanding."

Allah (swt) says in **Surah as-Sajdah (32:7-9)**:

الَّذِى أَحْسَنَ كُلَّ شَىْءٍ خَلَقَهُ وَبَدَأَ خَلْقَ الإِنْسَـٰنِ مِن طِينٍ - ثُمَّ جَعَلَ نَسْلَهُ مِن سُلَالَةٍ مِّن مَّآءٍ مَّهِينٍ - ثُمَّ سَوَّاهُ وَنَفَخَ فِيهِ مِن رُّوحِهِ وَجَعَلَ لَكُمُ السَّمْعَ وَالأَبْصَـٰرَ وَالأَفْئِدَةَ قَلِيلاً مَّا تَشْكُرُونَ -

Who perfected everything which He created and He began the creation of man from clay. Then He made his reproduction out of the extract of a liquid disdained. Then He proportioned him and breathed into him from His [created] soul and made for you hearing and vision and hearts [intellect]; little are you grateful.

This part of Surah 32:9 indicates that the special senses of hearing, seeing, and feeling develop in this order, which is true. The primordial of the internal ears appear before the beginning of the eyes, and the brain [the site of understanding] differentiates last.

The question is how the Prophet Muhammad [sas], fourteen centuries ago, could describe the embryo and its development phase in such detail and accuracy, which scientists have come to know only in the last thirty years. It is clear that these statements must have come to Muhammad from Allah, because almost all of this knowledge was not discovered until many centuries later. This proves that Muhammad [sas] must have been a Messenger of Allah [swt].

Ibrahim [as] (Abraham) and his wife Sarah [ra] were very old when their son Ishaq [Isaac] was conceived. Not only was Sarah old, far beyond menopause, she also had been sterile all of her life. Allah [swt] says in **Surah Hud (11: 71-3)**:

وَامْرَأَتُهُ قَآئِمَةٌ فَضَحِكَتْ فَبَشَّرْنَـٰهَا بِإِسْحَـٰقَ وَمِن وَرَآءِ إِسْحَـٰقَ يَعْقُوبَ - قَالَتْ يَـٰوَيْلَتَىٰ ءَأَلِدُ وَأَنَاْ عَجُوزٌ وَهَـٰذَا بَعْلِى شَيْخًا إِنَّ هَـٰذَا لَشَىْءٌ عَجِيبٌ - قَالُوٓاْ أَتَعْجَبِينَ مِنْ أَمْرِ اللَّهِ رَحْمَتُ اللَّهِ وَبَرَكَـٰتُهُ عَلَيْكُمْ أَهْلَ الْبَيْتِ إِنَّهُ حَمِيدٌ مَّجِيدٌ -

And his wife was standing, and she smiled. Then We gave her good tidings of Ishaq, and after Ishaq, of Ya`qub. She said [in astonishment], "Woe to me [an expression of surprise and amazement]! Shall I bear a child while I am an old woman, and this, my husband is an old man? Indeed, this is an amazing thing!" They said, "Are you amazed at the decree of Allah? May the mercy of Allah and His blessings be upon you, people of the house? Indeed, He is praiseworthy and Honorable".

And also in **Surah adh-Dhariyat (51:28-30)** Allah [swt] says:

فَأَوْجَسَ مِنْهُمْ خِيفَةً قَالُوا لَا تَخَفْ وَبَشَّرُوهُ بِغُلَمٍ عَلِيمٍ - فَأَقْبَلَتِ امْرَأَتُهُ فِي صَرَّةٍ فَصَكَّتْ وَجْهَهَا وَقَالَتْ عَجُوزٌ عَقِيمٌ - قَالُوا كَذَلِكِ قَالَ رَبُّكِ إِنَّهُ هُوَ الْحَكِيمُ الْعَلِيمُ

And he felt from them apprehension. They said, "Fear not," and gave him good tidings of a son having knowledge. And his wife approached with a cry [of alarm] and struck her face and said: "[I am] a barren old woman!" They said, "Thus has said your Lord; indeed, He is the Wise, the Knowing."

The same was true with the birth of Yahya [John]; his father Zakariya [as] and mother Elizabeth [ra] were much too old to have a child, and his mother was sterile. In **Surah Al-'Imran (3:38-41)** Allah [swt] says:

هُنَالِكَ دَعَا زَكَرِيَّا رَبَّهُ قَالَ رَبِّ هَبْ لِي مِن لَّدُنْكَ ذُرِّيَّةً طَيِّبَةً إِنَّكَ سَمِيعُ الدُّعَاءِ - فَنَادَتْهُ الْمَلَئِكَةُ وَهُوَ قَائِمٌ يُصَلِّي فِي الْمِحْرَابِ أَنَّ اللَّهَ يُبَشِّرُكَ بِيَحْيَى مُصَدِّقًا بِكَلِمَةٍ مِّنَ اللَّهِ وَسَيِّدًا وَحَصُورًا وَنَبِيًّا مِّنَ الصَّالِحِينَ - قَالَ رَبِّ أَنَّى يَكُونُ لِي غُلَمٌ وَقَدْ بَلَغَنِيَ الْكِبَرُ وَامْرَأَتِي عَاقِرٌ قَالَ كَذَلِكَ اللَّهُ يَفْعَلُ مَا يَشَاءُ - قَالَ رَبِّ اجْعَل لِّي ءَايَةً قَالَ ءَايَتُكَ أَلَّا تُكَلِّمَ النَّاسَ ثَلَثَةَ أَيَّامٍ إِلَّا رَمْزًا وَاذْكُر رَّبَّكَ كَثِيرًا وَسَبِّحْ بِالْعَشِيِّ وَالْإِبْكَرِ -

At that Zakariya called upon his Lord, saying, "My Lord, Grant me from yourself, a good offspring. Indeed, You are the Hearer of supplication." So the angels called him while he was standing in prayer in the chamber, "Indeed, Allah gives you good tidings of Yahya, confirming a word from Allah and [who will be] honorable, and abstaining [from women], and a Prophet from among the righteous." He said, "My Lord, how will I have a boy when I have reached old age and my wife barren?" He [the angel] said, "Such is Allah; He does what He wills." He said, "My Lord, make for me a sign." He said: "Your sign is that you will not [be able to] speak to the people for three days except by gesture. And remember your Lord much and glorify (Him) in the evening and the morning". At that time, Zakariyah [as] had become an old man, his bones feeble and his head full of gray hair. His wife was an old woman who was barren. Yet, he still supplicated to Allah and called Him in secret,

رَبِّ هَبْ لِي مِن لَّدُنْكَ -

O my Lord! Grant me from you. And Allah [swt] granted his prayer.

What is about the creation of ['Isa' (as)] Jesus? Allah (swt) says in **Surah al-'Imran (3:45-7):**

$$\text{إِذْقَالَتِ الْمَلَـٰئِكَةُ يَـٰمَرْيَمُ إِنَّ اللَّهَ يُبَشِّرُكِ بِكَلِمَةٍ مِّنْهُ اسْمُهُ الْمَسِيحُ عِيسَى ابْنُ مَرْيَمَ وَجِيهًا فِي الدُّنْيَا وَالْآخِرَةِ وَمِنَ الْمُقَرَّبِينَ ۝ وَيُكَلِّمُ}$$

$$\text{النَّاسَ فِي الْمَهْدِ وَكَهْلًا وَمِنَ الصَّـٰلِحِينَ ۝ قَالَتْ رَبِّ أَنَّى يَكُونُ لِي وَلَدٌ وَلَمْ يَمْسَسْنِي بَشَرٌ قَالَ كَذَٰلِكِ اللَّهُ يَخْلُقُ مَا يَشَاءُ إِذَا قَضَى أَمْرًا}$$

$$\text{فَإِنَّمَا يَقُولُ لَهُ كُنْ فَيَكُونُ ۝}$$

[And mention] when the angels said, "O Maryam, indeed, Allah gives you good tidings of a word from Him, whose name will be the Messiah, `Isa, the son of Maryam – distinguished in this world and the Hereafter and among those brought near [to Allah]. He will speak to the people in the cradle and immaturity and will be of the righteous". She said, "O My Lord, how will I have a child when no man has touched me?" He said, "Such is Allah; He creates what He wills. When He decrees a matter, He only says to it 'Be' and it is".

The creation of Jesus, as far as Allah [swt] is concerned, is equal to the creation of Adam; Allah [swt] created Adam from clay, and then said to him, "Be," and he was. As Allah [swt] says in **Surah al-'Imran (3:59-60):**

$$\text{إِنَّ مَثَلَ عِيسَى عِنْدَ اللَّهِ كَمَثَلِ آدَمَ خَلَقَهُ مِنْ تُرَابٍ ثُمَّ قَالَ لَهُ كُنْ فَيَكُونُ ۝ الْحَقُّ مِنْ رَبِّكَ فَلَا تَكُنْ مِنَ الْمُمْتَرِينَ}$$

Indeed, the example of 'Isa' to Allah [regarding His creation of him] is like that of Adam. He created him from dust; then He said to him, 'Be' and he was. The truth is from your Lord, so do not be among the doubters.

Then Allah [swt] advised Prophet Muhammad [sas] to through challenge to those who believe in the creation of Isa [as] by some other means in **Surah al-'Imran (3:61):**

$$\text{فَمَنْ حَاجَّكَ فِيهِ مِنْ بَعْدِ مَا جَاءَكَ مِنَ الْعِلْمِ فَقُلْ تَعَالَوْا نَدْعُ أَبْنَاءَنَا وَأَبْنَاءَكُمْ وَنِسَاءَنَا وَنِسَاءَكُمْ وَأَنْفُسَنَا وَأَنْفُسَكُمْ ثُمَّ نَبْتَهِلْ}$$

$$\text{فَنَجْعَلْ لَعْنَتَ اللَّهِ عَلَى الْكَـٰذِبِينَ ۝}$$

Then whoever argues with you about it after [this] knowledge has come to you - say: "Come, let us call our sons and your sons, our women and your women, ourselves and yourselves, then supplicate earnestly [together] and invoke the curse of Allah upon the liars [among us]". But none took that challenge.

The creation of Ishaq [Isaac] in the womb of Sarah, and the creation of Yahya [John] in the womb of Elizabeth were just as miraculous as the creation of Isa [Jesus] inside Mary's womb.

In spite of this, the Christians still continue to argue even though Allah has sent them evidence after evidence and proof after proof. Then when they are asked why they persist in this controversy, they reply that they have never seen or heard of anybody being created without a father and a mother. But modern science now revealed that many animals and beings in this world are born and reproduced without fertilization from the male of the species. For example, a male bee is no more than an egg that has not been fertilized by the male, whereas the egg that has been fertilized by the male functions as a female. Moreover, a male creates male bees from the eggs of the queen but without fertilization. There are many other examples such as this in the animal world.

If Allah [swt] created Adam without a father, or a mother, why should it be strange that He created a man from a mother and no father? The birth of Isa [Jesus] without a father completes the picture of miraculous creations:

1. The creation of a man, Adam, with neither a father nor a mother;

2. The creation of a woman, Hawwa [Eve], from a `father' [Adam] and without a mother; and finally,

3. The creation of a man, Isa [Jesus], from a mother without a father.

4. The creation of Ishaq and Yahya from old and sterile mothers.

And Allah [swt] said in **Surah Fussilat (41:53):**

سَنُرِيهِمْ ءَايَـٰتِنَا فِى ٱلْءَافَاقِ وَفِىٓ أَنفُسِهِمْ حَتَّىٰ يَتَبَيَّنَ لَهُمْ أَنَّهُ ٱلْحَقُّ أَوَلَمْ يَكْفِ بِرَبِّكَ أَنَّهُۥ عَلَىٰ كُلِّ شَىْءٍ شَهِيدٌ -

We will show them Our signs in the horizons and within themselves until it becomes clear to them that it is the truth. But is it not sufficient concerning your Lord that He is, over all things, a witness? Amin!

*Keith L. Moore, Ph.D., F.I.A.C. "The Journal of the Islamic Medical Association", Vol.18, Jan-June 1986, pp.15-16.
 Professor of Anatomy and Associate Dean, Basic Sciences, Faculty of Medicine, Department of Anatomy, University of Toronto, Canada.

**www.quaranicstudies.com

Nafs: What Is It?

Along with *ruh* [the spirit)], Allah [swt] has placed within us something called the '*nafs*' [means soul, the psyche, the ego, self, life, person, heart, or mind], which encourages our evil passions, our relish for food and other sensual gratification. The nafs also keeps us occupied with the worldly affairs thus preventing us from following the orders of Allah [swt].

The *nafs* [(inner desire] was created along with the *ruh* so that it would serve as a transportation vehicle to the *ruh*. In other words, the *nafs* is like an engine of a car and *ruh* is like the driver of that car. Mechanical knowledge of the body is only given to the *nafs*. The *nafs* is not holy, divine or absolutely pure, it was created to acquire knowledge of the world's physical, chemical and biological mechanism so that they would serve their worldly purpose. Thus we should understand the connection between *Nafs* and *Ruh*; the *Ruh* is not called *Nafs* except when it joins the body and is affected by it. So in conclusion we may say: the *Ruh* is the origin and essence, and the *Nafs* consists of the *Ruh* and its connection to the body. So they are the same in one sense but not in another.

And once the *nafs* is no longer under the control of the *ruh*, the *ruh* will find itself in the control of the evil *nafs* or evil passions providing a destructive weapon for the devil against humans. These evil passions are implanted in the *nafs* at the time of birth and grow in magnitude over time. For example, the evil *nafs* will draw human beings towards idol worship and will inspire them to take part in corruptive dealings. In other words, it could be stated that evil *nafs* and passions represent the devil's workshop.

The *ruh* is given to human beings and contains intellect and power over planning and talking and reciting the holy words and gradually putting them into action, but the real meaning of the *ruh* is to obey Allah [swt] - the Quran says in **Surah al-Isra (17:85):**

وَيَسْـَٔلُونَكَ عَنِ الرُّوحِ قُلِ الرُّوحُ مِنْ أَمْرِ رَبِّى وَمَآ أُوتِيتُم مِّنَ الْعِلْمِ إِلَّا قَلِيلًا

And they ask you [O Muhammad], about the *ruh* [the spirit]. Say, "The *ruh* [the spirit] is one of the affairs [concern] of my Lord, the knowledge of which is only with my Lord. And of knowledge, you [mankind] have been given only a little."

The *ruh* is immortal that never dies, but all *nafs* will test death. In other words, *Ruh* is something, the presence of which indicates we are alive, and the absence of which indicate we are dead. The object of the *ruh* is to discover its original source i.e. Allah [swt] and obey His orders and receive His love and affections. The body of a man is a vehicle for the *ruh*. The *nafs* is not given the power to order the body, so in order to control the body; the *nafs* will have to take control of the *ruh* first.

For example, Hazrat Musa [as] [Moses] asked Allah [swt], "Can you show me where Satan lives in our body?" Allah [swt] showed him that the Satans' head is watching over our *qalb* [heart] as if a kingfisher is watching his prey on the seawater. Whenever Satan sees divine input, he tries to grab it before it can reach us. Satan's actions are extremely fast as he can enter and exit the body seventy times in a pulse circulating within our blood stream where he is in a position to draw a person towards his evil plans (Tafsir-Ibn-Kathir).

If the *nafs* is not pure, the Satan enters into the *nafs* and draws it towards his evil intentions and over time the *ruh* becomes weaker and weaker and eventually these passions and are unable to bring them under their control may find themselves the servants of *nafs* or evil passions and thus moving away from the righteous path since the greatest enemy of the *nafs* or passions is obedience to Allah [swt].

When death of the *nafs* comes, the body will return to earth [just as a body of a car damaged will go back to the scrap yard]. When the body returns to the earth, the *ruh* will return to Allah [swt], its origin.

Nafs is defined by three names in the process of evolution. In the first stage: **'nafs al-ammara'** .The Soul which Commands evil.

This is the *nafs* that brings punishment by itself. By its very nature it directs its owner towards every wrong action. No one can get rid of its evil without the help from Allâh. As Allâh refers to this *nafs* in the story of the wife of al-Azîz [Zulaikha] and Prophet Yûsuf in **Surah Yusuf (12:53):**

$$النَّفَسَ لأَمَّارَةٌ$$

Indeed, the [human] soul is a persistent enjoiner of evil.

The *nafs* of a disbeliever is of the type **'nafs- al- ammara'**. A disbeliever is pleased with this *nafs* and the nafs is pleased with him. This is because whatever the *nafs* wants in terms of all its worldly requirements such as wealth, food, pride, selfishness, and a disbeliever provides for satisfaction. This is the case even if these requirements are contrary to the laws of Allah, They are disobedient to Allah [swt], and they are outside of His law. So Allah [swt] has nothing to do with them. The nafs al-ammara has Saytân as its ally. He promises it great rewards and gains, but casts falsehood into it. He invites it and entices the soul to do evil. He leads it on with hope after hope and presents falsehood to the *ruh* in a form that it will accept and admire. This *nafs* resides in the world of the senses and is dominated by earthly desires (shahwat) and passions….Evil lies hidden in the *nafs* and it is this that leads it on to do wrong. If Allâh were to leave the servant alone with his self, the servant would be destroyed between its evil and the evil that it craves; but if Allâh grants him success and help, then he will survive. We seek refuge in Allâh [the Almighty], both from the evil in ourselves and from the evil of our actions.

2. Nafs al-Lawwama [The Soul that Blames]

This *nafs* is conscious of its own imperfections. Allâh [swt] refers to this nafs in **Surah al-Qyiamah (75:2):**

$$وَلاَ أُقْسِمُ بِالنَّفْسِ اللَّوَّامَة -$$

And I swear by the reproaching soul [which blames him when he falls into sin or error.

Hasan al-Basrî said, "You always see the believer blaming himself and saying things like 'did I want this'? Why did I do that? Was this better than that?" (Tafsir-Ibn-Kathir)

A mumins' *nafs* is able to distinguish between good and bad and cares for Allah [swt]'s order. Sometimes their *nafs* may be influenced by Satan but as soon as the realization takes place, it repents and asks for forgiveness from Allah [swt], and Allah [swt] forgives them. It has been said that the **nafs al-lawwâma** is the one, which cannot rest in any one state. It often changes, remembers and forgets, submits and evades, loves and hates, rejoices and become sad, accepts and rejects, obeys and rebels.

3. **Nafs al-Mutma'inaa** The Soul at Peace. This *nafs* is tranquil as it rests on the certitude of Allah [swt].

Allâh [swt] *refers to this* nafs *in* **Surah al- Fajr (89:27):**

$$ \text{يَٰأَيَّتُهَا النَّفْسُ الْمُطْمَئِنَّةُ} $$

[To the righteous it will be said], "O reassured soul,"

Al-qatâdah [ra] said, "It is the soul of the believer, made calm by what Allâh [swt] has promised. Its owner is at rest and content with his knowledge of Allâh's names and attributes, and with what He has said about Himself and His messenger. (Tafsir-Ibn-Kathir)

So he submits to the will of Allah [swt] and surrenders to Him contentedly, never dissatisfied or complaining, and with his faith never wavering. He does not rejoice at his gains, nor do his afflictions make him despair - for he knows that they were decreed long before they happened to him, even before he was created.

The *nafs* of a good mumin such as a wali Allah or Dervish, those who are ready to sacrifice themselves for Allah [swt] their *nafs* will never die. Their *nafs* is developed to such an extent that it becomes a watchdog for them. For such devout beings, even the worldly obligations become a part of Allah's orders. Whatever they do they are pleased with Allah [swt], and Allah [swt] is pleased with them.

There are ways to control the *nafs* as narrated by the sahaba ikram [companions of our Prophet [sas]]. One wali Allah [Allah's friend], for example has said, "Little food, little drink, little sleep and little talk is helpful to bring the nafs of passion into control easily". Another wali Allah said, "As it is obligatory to eat and sleep because this is also ibaadah, this is the reason I am sleeping and eating, otherwise I could have spent all my time in worshipping Allah [swt]". He stated that it is very difficult to control the *nafs* without the help of Allah [swt]. (Tafsir-Ibn-Kathir)

To engage oneself in the battle against the evil *nafs* for the sake of Allah [swt] is equated with **jihadul Akbar** [or the greatest battle one can ever fight]. Our Prophet [sas] said that *nafs* is our greatest enemy. When sahabas came back from physical Jihad the Prophet [sas] advised them that now their greatest jihad is against their *nafs*. The Quran reads in **Surah as-Shams (91:9-10):**

قَدْأَفْلَحَ مَن زَكَّهَا-وَقَدْخَابَ مَن دَسَّهَا

He has succeeded who purifies it, and he has failed who instills it [with corruption].

The *nafs* is a single entity, although its state may change: from the **nafs al-ammâra**, to the **nafs al-lawwâma**, to the **nafs al-mutma'inna**, which is the final aim of perfection.

One of the functions of the *nafs* is to prevent man from performing divine duties. One must not forget that Satan was a most pious and obedient servant of Allah [swt]. He was a leader of Angels and Jinn, before Adam [as] was created. But Satan was deceived by his *nafs*, which caused his jealousy and pride. Our Prophet Muhammad [sas]) said that your worst enemy is your *nafs*.

Unless the good influence predominates, and one gets rid of the evil self, which is the seat of passion, this evil self will gradually take over and present itself as the good self. Eventually it will reach a status whereby the *nafs* will dictate all our actions.

In order to become a good Muslim, one must get rid of his evil self [*nafs*], but one must also develop the *nafs* as a watchdog. Only then can we find Allah [swt]'s mercy and help. Once this stage is reached, Allah [swt] will come to us through His own grace, to provide us with the nourishment for the *ruh*. We will find Him everywhere and our negative passions will vanish.

Allâh [swt] also says in **Surah an-Nur (24:21):**

وَلَوْلَا فَضْلُ اللَّهِ عَلَيْكُمْ وَرَحْمَتُهُ مَا زَكَى مِنكُم مِّنْ أَحَدٍ أَبَداً وَلَـكِنَّ اللَّهَ يُزَكِّى مَن يَشَآءُ

وَاللَّهُ سَمِيعٌ عَلِيمٌ

And if not for the favor of Allâh upon you and His Mercy, not one of you would have been pure, ever, but Allâh purifies whom He wills, and Allâh is Hearing and Knowing. Amin!

Number 19: The Mathematical Miracle of the Qur'an

A miracle is defined as an act or event that does not follow the laws of nature and is believed to be caused by Allah (Wehmeier edt. 2000). In other words any known law of nature cannot explain a miracle. The miracle of the Qur'an resides in the very structure of its text, in its orthographic and numerical arrangements.

Allah (swt) says in **Surah al-Jinn (72:28):**

$$لِّيَعْلَمَ أَن قَدْ أَبْلَغُوا رِسَالَاتِ رَبِّهِمْ وَأَحَاطَ بِمَا لَدَيْهِمْ وَأَحْصَى كُلَّ شَيْءٍ عَدَدًا$$

That he [Muhammad (sas)] may know that they have conveyed the messages of their Lord; and He has encompassed whatever is with them and has enumerated all things in number.

And also in **Surah al-Muddathir (74:30 and 35):**

$$عَلَيْهَا تِسْعَةَ عَشَرَ -$$

Over it is nineteen [angels].

$$إِنَّهَا لَإِحْدَى الْكُبَرِ -$$

This is one of the great miracles.

Importantly, Surah al-Muddathir which was the second revelation after the first revelation of the few verses of Surah Al-Alaq contains the mention of the number 19. These verses indicate that Allah has used numbers in creating things and this application of the code 19 is a miracle.

Let us start our discussion by analyzing the opening verse of the Qur'an and also the first Surah of the Qur'an. The first verse of the first Surah [Al-Fatihah] in the Qur'an is "Bismillah Al-Rahman Al-Rahym" consists of nineteen Arabic alphabetic letters. The first word of the first Ayah is "Bism" –its root is "Ism"- and the word "Ism" occurs in the entire text of the Qur'an 19 times. The second word "Allah" occurs 2698 (19 x 42) times, the third word "Al-Rahman" occurs 57 times, and the fourth word "Al-Rahym" occurs 114 times (19 x 6) in the entire text of the Qur'an. Moreover, there are 1919 verses in the entire Qur'an which contains at least one of the four words of the "Bismillah".

The opening verse of the Qur'an as we call it "Bismillah", appears twice as a verse: verse 1 of Surah 1 and verse 30 of Surah 27. Except Surah 9, all the other Surahs start with "Bismillah" not as a verse of the Surah. Thus Surah 27 has two "Bismillah" one at the beginning [not as a part of the verse] and other as verse number 30. If "Bismillah" in Surah 27 were not put twice, the total number of "Bismillah" in the whole of the Qur'an would have been 113, which is not a multiple of 19. However, if we start counting from Surah 9, we find that the missing Bismillah is compensated for, exactly 19 Surahs later, in Surah 27. Moreover, not only the missing "Bismillah" was found after 19 Surah; the Surah number and verse number (27 + 30 =57) is also a multiple of 19. The number of Arabic words from the first "Bismillah" in Surah 27 to the second one in verse 30 of the same Surah is 342 (19 x18). This is also the same number to be obtained if we add all the Surah numbers from Surah 9 through Surah 27.

If we combine the Surah number with the verse number where the "Bismillah" appears, if there is no verse number against "Bismillah" it will be 0, for example the first verse of Surah 1 is "Bismillah", so the Surah number and the verse number of "Bismillah" will be 11, Similarly for Surah 2, "Bismillah" has no verse number so the Surah number and verse number for Surah 2 will be 20), for each of the 114 "Bismillah", the total will be 68,191 (19x3589). Moreover, between the first Qur'anic initialed Surah (Surah: 2) and the last initialed Surah (Surah: 68), there are 38 (19 x 2) uninitiated Surahs.

The sequence number of each word in the "Bismillah" followed by the number of letters in each word forms a 8-digit number 1 3 2 4 3 6 4 6 which is a multiple of 19. If the number of letters is replaced by the geometrical value (numerical value of each letter of the Arabic alphabets) of that word, we get a 15 digit number which is also a multiple of 19. In a similar way, If the geometrical value of each letter is followed by the total geometrical value, i.e. the sequence number of each word is followed by its geometrical value to form a 15-digit number which is also a multiple of 19: 1 102 2 66 3 329 4 289 = 19 x 5801401752331.

In the opening statement of Qur'an, the words: Bism, Allah, Al-Rahman, and Al-Rahym: have a total geometrical values of 102, 66, 329, and 289 (total 786) respectively. We know that "Bismillah" consists of 4 words, 19 letters with a total geometrical value of 786. If we put these numbers one after another, the result will be a 6-digit number which is a multiple of 19: 4 19 786 = 19 x 22094.

If we write down the geometrical value of each letter followed by its sequence number (1 through 19) followed by the total geometrical value of the word, the result will be a 73-digit number, which is also a multiple of 19:

2 1 60 2 40 3 102 1 4 30 5 30 6 5 7 66 1 8 30 9 200 10 8 11 40 12 50 13 329 1 14 30 15 200 16 8 17 10 18 40 19 289 = 19 x 113696858432...

What is the probability for the "Bismillah's" mathematical composition to occur by coincidence? Abdullah Arik showed that the probability of the mathematical phenomenon is very close to 1 in trillion quadrillion and it is clear that the probability will approach zero. Therefore, one would be illogical to even suggest that the mathematical composition of the "Bismillah" is nothing more than a mere coincidence. Thus it becomes evident that Allah has deliberately structured the "Bismillah" in a particular way to result in this remarkable mathematical system.

If we write the Surah number followed by the number of verses, followed by the number of every verse in the Surah, and finally the sum of the verse numbers (1 7 1 2 3 4 5 6 7 28..................................) the total consists of a 759 digit number and is also a multiple of 19).

The word Allah occurs in the Qur'an 2698 (19 x 142) times. The number of verses where the word Allah is mentioned adds up to 118,123 (19 x 6217). In the Qur'an 30 different numbers are mentioned and the sum of these numbers is 162,146 (19 x 8534). Of the 400 attributes of Allah mentioned in the Qur'an, only four attributes have a geometrical values divisible by 19: these are Waheed [One] 19 times, Zul Fad Al-' Azim [Possessor of Infinite Grace] 2698 (19 x 142) times, Majid [Glorious] 57 (19 x 3) times, and Jaami [Summoner, Gatherer, Editor 114 (19 x 6) times. The only attributes of Allah whose geometrical values are multiple of 19 correspond exactly to the frequency of occurrences of the "Bismillah's" four letters.

Surah 96 [the first Surah revealed to Prophet Muhammad (sas)] has 19 verses and the first five verses revealed first have 19 words [Qur'an, 96]. Surprisingly, the last revelation [Surah 110] also consists of 19 words.

Do all these evidences mere coincidence? The answer is no and never. The highly sophisticated mathematical system based on the prime number 19 embedded in the fabric of the Qur'an was first discovered by Khalifa (1973) by using computer. Now the question is why Allah has chosen the number 19 as a code in writing and preserving the Qur'an? The number 19 starts with the first numeral (1) and ends with the last numeral (9). 19 is also an unusual prime number as the sum of the first powers of 9 and 10 and the difference between the second powers of 9 and 10. As mentioned earlier, it is also the geometrical value of the word 'Waheed" which means "one" and what a better way of having a personal stamp that indicates the One number for One Allah, after all, Allah has created all the numbers and assigned their values.

Allah has reassured that it will be preserved and protected in an ingenious way. It is stated in **Surah al-Buruj (85:21-2):**

$$\text{بَلْ هُوَ قُرْءَانٌ مَّجِيدٌ - فِى لَوْ حٍ مَّحْفُوظٍ -}$$

But this is an honored Qur'an [inscribed] in a preserved Slate.

Allah thus preserves the hard copy of the Qur'an. Again the Qur'an says in **Surah al-Hijr (15:9):**

$$\text{إِنَّا نَحْنُ نَزَّلْنَا الذِّكْرَ وَ إِنَّا لَهُ لَحَفِظُونَ -}$$

Indeed, it is We who sent down the message [the Qur'an] and indeed We will guard it [from corruption].

It means that millions of believers will also preserve the Qur'an by memorizing it. No other book in the world is daily read by millions of people or keeps it in memory except the Qur'an.

The mathematical literary composition and the mathematical structure involving the number of Surahs and verses, while maintaining a poetic and stylistic literature that has not and will never are surpassed. Allah has also reaffirmed in **Surah Fussilat (41:42):**

$$\text{لاَّ يَأْتِيهِ الْبَطِلُ مِن بَيْنِ يَدَيْهِ وَلاَ مِنْ خَلْفِهِ تَنزِيلٌ مِّنْ حَكِيمٍ حَمِيد}$$

Falsehood cannot approach it from before it or behind it; [it is] a revelation from a [Lord who is] Wise and Praiseworthy.

The Qur'an's formidable mathematical composition guarantees that any addition, deletion, or distortion of a single letter, or any other element in the Qur'an, is exposed and utterly rejected [19 based codes] (Khalifa, 1989). Number 19 is thus can be attributed to be the password to open the dialogue with Allah and also the authentication signature of Allah.

Allah is the One, the Great, the Supreme, the Beneficent, the Merciful, and the Glorious.

References

1. Khalifa, Rashad (1973). "Miracle of the Qur'an": Significance of the Mysterious Alphabets, Islamic Productions, St. Louis, Missouri, USA.

2. Khalifa, Rashad (1989). "Qur'an: the Final Testament, Authorized English Version", Islamic Publications, Tuscon, Arizona, USA.

3. Wehmeier, Sally (etd.) (2000). "Oxford Learner's Dictionary of Current English", Sixth Edition, Oxford University Press.

4. www.submission.org.

Prophet [sas]: The Best of Creation

Approximately 1477 years ago, was born in Makkah that superbly dynamic personality whose life example serves as the exemplary epitome of the ideal human being. We have inherited his glorious mission and it is our duty to manifest his noble tradition. Allah [swt] sent him to perfect all moral values and to serve as the best example for mankind to follow as mentioned in **Surah al-Ahzâb (33:21):**

لَقَدْ كَانَ لَكُمْ فِي رَسُولِ اللَّهِ أُسْوَةٌ حَسَنَةٌ لِّمَن كَانَ يَرْجُو اللَّهَ وَالْيَوْمَ الْأَخِرَ وَذَكَرَ اللَّهَ كَثِيرًا-

Indeed in the Messenger of Allah you have a good example to follow for him who hopes in Allah and the Last Day, and remembers Allah much.

Muhammad [sas] should serve as a source of inspiration and a model for excellence, holistic personality. In **Surah al-Ahzâb (33:45-6)** Allah (swt) says:

يَا أَيُّهَا النَّبِيُّ إِنَّا أَرْسَلْنَاكَ شَاهِدًا وَمُبَشِّرًا وَنَذِيرًا-وَدَاعِيًا إِلَى اللَّهِ بِإِذْنِهِ وَسِرَاجًا مُّنِيرًا

O Prophet [Muhammad], indeed We have sent you as witness and a bringer of good tidings and a Warner. And one who invites to Allah, by His permission, and an illuminating lamp.

Allah [swt] tells us in **Surah ash-Sharh (94:4):**

وَرَفَعْنَا لَكَ ذِكْرَكَ-

And raised high for you your repute,

When we consider our situation today; over fourteen hundred years after the exemplary mission of the Final Messenger, we realize that we are more than ever in need of such inspiration and motivation; more in need of such a role model who represents the best legacy of our human heritage and whose life message was an embodiment of the universal values that we all can share.

The Pinnacle and Culmination of Prophet hood with Muhammad (sas) is mentioned in **Surah al-Ahzâb (33:40):**

مَّا كَانَ مُحَمَّدٌ أَبَا أَحَدٍ مِّن رِّجَالِكُمْ وَلَكِن رَّسُولَ اللَّهِ وَخَاتَمَ النَّبِيِّينَ وَكَانَ اللَّهُ بِكُلِّ شَيْءٍ عَلِيمًا

Muhammad is not the father of [any] of your men, but [he is] the Messenger of Allah and seal [last] of the prophets. And ever is Allah, of all things, knowing.

Universal and Abiding Mission of the Prophet [sas] is mentioned in **Surah Saba' (34:28):**

$$وَمَآ أَرْسَلْنَاكَ إِلاَّ كَآفَّةً لِّلنَّاسِ بَشِيراً وَنَذِيراً وَلَكِنَّ أَكْثَرَ النَّاسِ لاَ يَعْلَمُونَ$$

And We have not sent you except comprehensively to mankind as a bringer of good tidings and a warner. But most of the people do not know.

Allah [swt] instructs us to follow the prophet [sas] in **Surah al- A'râf (7:157)** as he is will teach us the best of everything:

$$الَّذِينَ يَتَّبِعُونَ الرَّسُولَ النَّبِيَّ الأُمِّيَّ الَّذِي يَجِدُونَهُ مَكْتُوباً عِندَهُمْ فِي التَّوْرَاةِ وَالإِنجِيلِ يَأْمُرُهُم بِالْمَعْرُوفِ وَيَنْهَاهُمْ عَنِ الْمُنْكَرِ$$

$$وَيُحِلُّ لَهُمُ الطَّيِّبَاتِ وَيُحَرِّمُ عَلَيْهِمُ الْخَبَائِثَ وَيَضَعُ عَنْهُمْ إِصْرَهُمْ وَالأَغْلاَلَ الَّتِي كَانَتْ عَلَيْهِمْ فَالَّذِينَ آمَنُواْ بِهِ وَعَزَّرُوهُ وَنَصَرُوهُ$$

$$وَاتَّبَعُواْ النُّورَ الَّذِي أُنزِلَ مَعَهُ أُوْلَـئِكَ هُمُ الْمُفْلِحُونَ-$$

Those who follow the Messenger, the unlettered Prophet, whom they find written [mentioned] in Torah and the Gospel, who enjoins upon what is right and forbids them what is wrong and makes lawful things and prohibits them the evil and relieves them of their [difficulties] in religious practice and the shackles which were upon them. So they, who have believed in him, honored him, supported him and followed the light which was sent down with him - it is those who will be the successful.

One of the names by which the Prophet Muhammad [sas] is known - is Khayru-l-Khalq or "Best of Creation." Other similar names of his with identical meaning are Khayru-l-Bariyya, Khayru Khalqillah, and Khayru-l-`Alamina Turra, Khayru-n-Nas, Khayru Hadhihi-l-Ummah, and Khîratullah. These titles refer to his high status over all human, Prophets and Messengers as well as over the Jinn and angels [peace be upon them].

In **Surah al-Qalam (68:4)** Allah [swt] certifies:

$$وَإِنَّكَ لَعَلى خُلُقٍ عَظِيمٍ-$$

Verily, you are an exalted standard of character

The reality of this compliment - khuluqin `azim - can be fathomed only by the Speaker Himself and whoever He wills as Allah [swt] says in **Surah al-Baqarah (2:253):**

$$تِلْكَ الرُّسُلُ فَضَّلْنَا بَعْضَهُمْ عَلَى بَعْضٍ مِّنْهُم مَّن كَلَّمَ اللّهُ وَرَفَعَ بَعْضَهُمْ دَرَجَاتٍ-$$

Those Messengers - Some of them We caused to exceed others. Among them were those to whom Allah spoke [directly] and He raised some of them in degree.

Allah [swt] says in **Surah al-Ahzâb (33:56):**

إِنَّ اللَّهَ وَمَلَٰئِكَتَهُ يُصَلُّونَ عَلَى النَّبِيِّ يَٰأَيُّهَا الَّذِينَ ءَامَنُواْ صَلُّواْ عَلَيْهِ وَسَلِّمُواْ تَسْلِيمًا

Indeed, Allah confers blessings upon the Prophet, and His angels. O you who have believed, ask [Allah to confer] blessings upon him and ask [Allah to grant him] peace.

The noble Qur'an in **Surah al-Anbiya (21:107)** Allah [swt] introduces Muhammad [sas] as a mercy not for the Muslim Ummah, the mankind, but for the whole creation of Allah [swt]:

وَمَآ أَرْسَلْنَٰكَ إِلَّا رَحْمَةً لِّلْعَٰلَمِين

And We have not sent you [O Muhammad], except as a mercy to the worlds.

All these and many more Quranic Verses testifies Proof of the Prophet's Status as 'Best of Creation'. Allah [swt)] assures in **Surah al-Ghâshiyah (88:21-2)** that Muhammad [sas] is not a dictator, but only a reminder:

فَذَكِّرْ إِنَّمَآ أَنتَ مُذَكِّرٌ ۟ لَّسْتَ عَلَيْهِم بِمُسَيْطِرٍ

So remind, O [Muhammad], you are only a reminder. You are not over them a controller.

The Message delivered by our Prophet changed injustice to equity, aggressiveness to kindness and brotherhood, cruel, ruthless inhumanity to mercy and forgiveness. Through the mercy of Allah [swt] his followers became the leaders of the then civilized world. They ruled with justice and called people to the true religion of Peace. Surely Allah honored the world with Muhammad [sas]. The true followers of Muhammad [sas] spread the teachings of this great religion throughout the world until the flag of Islam flew over the earth from east to west. The life of the Holy Prophet was one great example of how to build up, guide and strive in the way of Allah. He guided humanity and called them to the truth and to those things in which lie their success and happiness. He warned us against all things which are harmful to ourselves and reason.

The Prophet [sas] died, but he left humanity with everlasting teachings. His comprehensive and universal teachings will continue to guide mankind as long as there are people who seek for the truth. His teachings constitute the most comprehensive, practical, sensible and truthful guidance to all peoples in all walks of life and in all conditions of human endeavor. The universality of his mission therefore makes him the World's Great Prophet.

Allah [swt] honored the Ummah of Muhammad [sas] as the 'Best Ummah'; as such Muhammad [sas] who is the leader of this Ummah must be the 'Best of Creation'.

O Allah, give us the courage, the proper knowledge and guidance to marshal with the flag hoisted by our beloved Prophet [sas] for the benefit and guidance of the whole mankind. As members of 'Best Ummah,' give us the strength to carry on with his mission successfully till our death. **Amin!**

Qiyamah: The Day of Resurrection and Final Judgment

The true believers believe in the life after death and the final Day of Judgment because they made use of their faculties of mind and heart and realized the truth. Did they realize the truth through perceptual consciousness? Not so, as perceptual experience of life after death is impossible. Actually Allah [swt] has given men besides perceptual consciousness, rational, aesthetic and moral consciousness too. It is this consciousness that guides men regarding realities that cannot be verified through sensory data. That is why all the prophets of Allah [swt] while calling people to believe in Allah [swt] and life after death, appeal to the aesthetic, moral and rational consciousness of men. Allah [swt] reminds the disbelievers in **Surah Ya-Sin (36:78-81):**

وَضَرَبَ لَنَا مَثَلاً وَنَسِيَ خَلْقَهُ قَالَ مَن يُحي الْعِظَمَ وَهِيَ رَمِيمٌ۔ قُلْ يُحْيِيهَا الَّذِى أَنشَأَهَا أَوَّلَ مَرَّةٍ وَهُوَ بِكُلِّ خَلْقٍ عَلِيمٌ۔ الَّذِى جَعَلَ لَكُم مِّنَ الشَّجَرِ الأَخْضَرِ نَاراً فَإِذَا أَنتُم مِّنْهُ تُوقِدُونَ أَوَلَيْسَ الَّذِى خَلَقَ السَّمَوَتِ وَالأَرْضِ بِقَدِرٍ عَلَى أَن يَخْلُقَ مِثْلَهُم بَلَى وَهُوَ الْخَلَّقُ الْعَلِيمُ۔

And he presents for Us a parable and forgets his [own] creation. He says, "Who will give life to bones while they are disintegrated?" Say, "He will give them life who produced them for the first time; and He is, of all creation, Knowing". [It is] He who made for you from the green tree fire and then from it you ignite. Is not He who created the heavens and the earth able to create the likes of them? Yes, [it is so]; He is the Knowing creator.

On another occasion the Qur`an very clearly says that the disbelievers have no sound basis for their denial of life after death. It is based on pure conjecture as described in **Surah al-Jathiyah (45:24-5):**

وَقَالُوا مَا هِىَ إِلاَّ حَيَاتُنَا الدُّنْيَا نَمُوتُ وَنَحْيَا وَمَا يُهْلِكُنَا إِلاَّ الدَّهْرُ وَمَا لَهُم بِذَلِكَ مِنْ عِلْمٍ إِنْ هُمْ إِلاَّ يَظُنُّونَ۔ وَإِذَا تُتْلَى عَلَيْهِمْ ءَايَتُنَا بَيِّنَتٍ مَّا كَانَ حُجَّتَهُمْ إِلاَّ أَن قَالُوا ائْتُوا بِابَآئِنَا إِن كُنتُمْ صَدِقِينَ۔

And they say, "There is nothing but our worldly life; we die and live, and nothing destroys us except Ad-Dahr [time]". And they have no knowledge of it, they only presume. And when Our verses are recited to them as clear evidences, their argument is only that they say, "Bring [back] our [dead] forefathers, if you are truthful."

Surely Allah [swt] will raise all the dead. A day will come when the whole universe will be destroyed and then again the dead will be resurrected to stand before Allah [swt]. Allah's Messenger [May peace be upon him] as saying: The earth would consume every son of Adam except his spinal cord from which his body would be reconstituted [on the Day of Resurrection]. (Muslim, book #041, hadith #7056)

That day will be the beginning of the life that will never end, and that day every person will be rewarded by Allah [swt] according to his or her good or evil deeds. The explanation that the Qur'an gives about the necessity of life after death is what moral consciousness of man demands. Actually if there is no life after death, the very belief in Allah [swt] becomes irrelevant or even if one believes in Allah [swt], which would be an unjust and indifferent Allah: having once created men not concerned with his fate.

Surely, Allah [swt] is just; He will punish the tyrants whose crimes are beyond count: having killed hundreds of thousands of innocent persons, created great corruptions in the society, enslaved numerous persons to serve their whims etc. Men having a very short span of life in this world, and this physical world too being not eternal, punishments or rewards to the evil or noble deeds of persons are not possible here. The Qur'an very emphatically states that the Day of Judgment must come and Allah [swt] will decide about the fate of each soul according to his or her record of deeds. The Day of Resurrection will be the Day when Allah's [swt] attributes of Justice and Mercy will be in full manifestation.

The belief in life after death not only guarantees success in the Hereafter, but also makes this world place of peace and happiness by making individuals responsible and dutiful in their activities. The angel Israfil will blow into the Trumpet [Horn] and that will be the hour as said in **Surah Qaf (50:20)**:

وَنُفِخَ فِى الصُّورِ ذَلِكَ يَوْمُ الْوَعِيد-

And the Horn will be blown. That is the Day of [carrying out] the threat.

And what will happen is described in **Surah Ta-Ha (20:102-108)**:

يَوْمَ يُنْفَخُ فِى الصُّورِ وَنَحْشُرُ الْمُجْرِمِينَ يَوْمَئِذٍ زُرْقاً- يَتَخَافَتُونَ بَيْنَهُمْ إِن لَّبِثْتُمْ إِلاَّ عَشْراً- نَحْنُ أَعْلَمُ بِمَا يَقُولُونَ إِذْ يَقُولُ أَمْثَلُهُمْ طَرِيقَةً إِن لَّبِثْتُمْ إِلاَّ يَوْماً وَيَسْئَلُونَكَ عَنِ الْجِبَالِ فَقُلْ يَنسِفُهَا رَبِّى نَسْفاً- فَيَذَرُهَا قَاعاً صَفْصَفاً- لاَّ تَرَى فِيهَا عِوَجاً وَلا أَمْتاً- يَوْمَئِذٍ يَتَّبِعُونَ الدَّاعِىَ لاَ عِوَجَ لَهُ وَخَشَعَتِ الأَصْوَاتُ لِلرَّحْمَنِ فَلاَ تَسْمَعُ إِلاَّ هَمْساً-

The Day the Horn will be blown. We will gather the criminals that day, blue-eyed [from terror]. They will murmur among themselves, "You remained not but ten [days in the world]". We are most knowing of what they say when the best in manner [wisdom or speech] will say, "You remained not but one day". And they ask you about the mountains, so say, "My Lord will blow them away with a blast. And He will leave it [the earth] a level plain; you will not see therein a depression or elevation". That Day, they [everyone] will follow [the call] of the caller [with] no deviation there from, [all] voices will be stilled before the Most Merciful, so you will not hear except a faint sound [of footsteps].

Then, when the blast is sounded on the Trumpet. What will happen to mankind and the mountains is described in **Surah al-Qari'ah (101:4-5)**:

يَوْمَ يَكُونُ النَّاسُ كَالْفَرَاشِ الْمَبْثُوثِ ۔ وَتَكُونُ الْجِبَالُ كَالْعِهْنِ الْمَنفُوشِ

It is the Day when mankind will be like moths, dispersed, and the mountains will be like wool, fluffed up [beginning to disintegrate].

On that day everything will perish except the face of Allah as communicated in **Surah ar-Rahman (55:26-7):**

كُلُّ مَنْ عَلَيْهَا فَانٍ ۔ وَيَبْقَىٰ وَجْهُ رَبِّكَ ذُو الْجَلَٰلِ وَالْإِكْرَامِ

Everyone upon it [the earth] will perish, and there will remain the face of your Lord, owner of Majesty and Honor.

And also Allah [swt] says in **Surah az-Zumar (39:68):**

وَنُفِخَ فِي الصُّورِ فَصَعِقَ مَن فِي السَّمَٰوَٰتِ وَمَن فِي الْأَرْضِ إِلَّا مَن شَاءَ اللَّهُ ثُمَّ نُفِخَ فِيهِ أُخْرَىٰ فَإِذَا هُمْ قِيَامٌ يَنظُرُونَ ۔

And the Horn will be blown again, and whoever in the heavens and all who are on the earth will fall dead except whom Allah wills. Then it will be blown again, and at once they will be standing, looking on.

And also Allah [swt] says in **Surah Qaf (50:44)** how mankind will be gathered,

يَوْمَ تَشَقَّقُ الْأَرْضُ عَنْهُمْ سِرَاعًا ذَٰلِكَ حَشْرٌ عَلَيْنَا يَسِيرٌ

On the Day, the earth breaks away from them [and they emerge] rapidly; that is a gathering easy for Us.

What will happen to the Worldly bodies is mentioned in **Surah al-Qiyamah (75:7-10):**

فَإِذَا بَرِقَ الْبَصَرُ ۔ وَخَسَفَ الْقَمَرُ ۔ وَجُمِعَ الشَّمْسُ وَالْقَمَرُ ۔ يَقُولُ الْإِنسَٰنُ يَوْمَئِذٍ أَيْنَ الْمَفَرُّ

So when vision is dazzled, and the moon darkens, and the sun and moon are joined, man will say on that Day, "Where is the [place of] escape?"

And also in **Surah al-Haqqah (69:14-8):**

وَحُمِلَتِ الْأَرْضُ وَالْجِبَالُ فَدُكَّتَا دَكَّةً وَٰحِدَةً ۔ فَيَوْمَئِذٍ وَقَعَتِ الْوَاقِعَةُ ۔ وَانشَقَّتِ السَّمَاءُ فَهِيَ يَوْمَئِذٍ وَاهِيَةٌ ۔ وَالْمَلَكُ عَلَىٰ أَرْجَائِهَا

وَيَحْمِلُ عَرْشَ رَبِّكَ فَوْقَهُمْ يَوْمَئِذٍ ثَمَٰنِيَةٌ ۔ يَوْمَئِذٍ تُعْرَضُونَ لَا تَخْفَىٰ مِنكُمْ خَافِيَةٌ ۔

And the earth and the mountains are lifted and leveled with one blow [stroke] - then on that Day the event [Resurrection] will occur, and the heaven will split [open], for that Day it will infirm [weak and unstable]. And the angels are at its edges. And they will bear the Throne of your Lord above them, that Day, eight [of them]. That Day will be exhibited [for Judgment]; not hidden among you is anything concealed.

And also in **Surah az-Zumar (39:67):**

وَمَا قَدَرُوا اللَّهَ حَقَّ قَدْرِهِ وَالْأَرْضُ جَمِيعًا قَبْضَتُهُ يَوْمَ الْقِيَمَةِ وَالسَّمَوَتُ مَطْوِيَّتٌ بِيَمِينِهِ سُبْحَنَهُ وَتَعَالَى عَمَّا يُشْرِكُونَ-

They have not appraised Allah with true appraisal [appreciation of His attributes]. While the earth entirely will be [within] His grasp on the Day of Resurrection and the heavens will be folded in His right hand. Glorified is He, and high above what they associate with Him!

Allah [swt] says in **Surah al-Anbiya' (21:47)** that Justice will be done with each and every body:

وَنَضَعُ الْمَوَزِينَ الْقِسْطَ لِيَوْمِ الْقِيَمَةِ فَلَا تُظْلَمُ نَفْسٌ شَيْئًا وَإِن كَانَ مِثْقَالَ حَبَّةٍ مِّنْ خَرْدَلٍ أَتَيْنَا بِهَا وَكَفَى بِنَا حَسِبِينَ-

And We place the scales of justice for the Day of Resurrection, so no soul will be treated unjustly at all. And if there is [even] the weight of a mustard seed, We will bring it forth. And sufficient are We as accountant.

Allah [swt] assures all of us of justice and nothing but justice will be done on that day when He says in **Surah al-Nisa' (4:85):**

مَّن يَشْفَعْ شَفَعَةً حَسَنَةً يَكُن لَّهُ نَصِيبٌ مِّنْهَا وَمَن يَشْفَعْ شَفَعَةً سَيِّئَةً يَكُن لَّهُ كِفْلٌ مِّنْهَا وَكَانَ اللَّهُ عَلَى كُلِّ شَيْءٍ مُّقِيتًا

Whosoever intercedes for a good cause, will have a share [reward] there from; and whosoever intercedes for an evil cause will have a share [burden] there from. And ever is Allah, over all things, a Keeper.

Fellow Muslims, contemplate the Day of Resurrection with your hearts, think of the destination of the two kinds of people, either to paradise or to the Hellfire, and determine which of the two you want and ponder with your imagination.

Paradise will be the permanent abode of the true believers and good doers according to the Qur'an and Sunnah of the Prophet [sas]. Hellfire will be the eternal residence of the disbelievers, the hypocrites, and those who took partners with Allah [swt] in worship and reject to worship Allah with sincerity, and who oppose His religion.

Allah [swt] tells us about the blessed believers, who will be taken to Paradise in groups, one group after another, starting with the best of them: those who are closest to Allah, then the most righteous, then the next best and the next best. Each group will be with others like them, Prophets with Prophets, the true believers with their peers, the martyrs with their counterparts, the scholars with their colleagues, every group composed of people of the same kind. When they arrive at the gates of Paradise, after passing over the Sirat, where they will be detained on a bridge between Paradise and Hell, and any injustice that existed between them in this world will be settled until they have all been purified from sin through this trial. Then permission will be granted for them to enter Paradise.

The successful believers will be given eternal residence in Paradise where they will be provided with all the good things as promised by Allah [swt] in **Surah az-Zumar (39:73):**

وَسِيقَ الَّذِينَ اتَّقَوْا رَبَّهُمْ إِلَى الْجَنَّةِ زُمَرًا حَتَّى إِذَا جَاءُوهَا وَفُتِحَتْ أَبْوَابُهَا وَقَالَ لَهُمْ خَزَنَتُهَا سَلَامٌ عَلَيْكُمْ طِبْتُمْ فَادْخُلُوهَا خَالِدِينَ.

But those who feared their Lord will be led to Paradise in groups, until when they reach it, while its gates have been opened and its keepers say, "Salam `Alaykum [peace be upon you], You have become pure; so enter it to abide eternally therein".

What will be provided as food and drink, and other comforts in paradise are described in **Surah at-Tur (52:19-24):**

كُلُوا وَاشْرَبُوا هَنِيئًا بِمَا كُنتُمْ تَعْمَلُونَ. مُتَّكِئِينَ عَلَى سُرُرٍ مَّصْفُوفَةٍ وَزَوَّجْنَاهُم بِحُورٍ عِينٍ. وَالَّذِينَ آمَنُوا وَاتَّبَعَتْهُمْ ذُرِّيَّتُهُم بِإِيمَانٍ أَلْحَقْنَا بِهِمْ ذُرِّيَّتَهُمْ وَمَا أَلَتْنَاهُم مِّنْ عَمَلِهِم مِّن شَيْءٍ كُلُّ امْرِئٍ بِمَا كَسَبَ رَهِينٌ. وَأَمْدَدْنَاهُم بِفَاكِهَةٍ وَلَحْمٍ مِّمَّا يَشْتَهُونَ. يَتَنَازَعُونَ فِيهَا كَأْسًا لَّا لَغْوٌ فِيهَا وَلَا تَأْثِيمٌ. وَيَطُوفُ عَلَيْهِمْ غِلْمَانٌ لَّهُمْ كَأَنَّهُمْ لُؤْلُؤٌ مَّكْنُونٌ.

[They will be told], "Eat and drink in satisfaction for what you used to do". They will be reclining on thrones lined up, and will marry them to [fair women] with large, [beautiful] eyes. And those who believed and whose descendents followed them in faith -- We will join with them their descendents, and We will not deprive them of anything of their deeds [the reward thereof]. Every person, for what he earned, is retained. And We will provide them with fruit and meat from whatever they desire. There they shall pass from hand to hand a cup, free from any idle talk, and free from sin. And there will go round boy-servants of theirs, to serve them as if they were preserved pearls.

Of Course some of the believers will also be in the Hellfire for a specific period to be determined by Allah [swt] as their amount of wrong doings will overweigh the good deeds and after the period of punishment, they will be allowed to enter paradise. The Prophet said, "Some people who will be scorched by Hell [Fire] as a punishment for sins they have committed, and then Allah will admit them into Paradise by the grant of His Mercy. These people will be called, 'Al-JahannamiyyLin' [the people of Hell]." (Bukhari, book #93, hadith #542) How the wrong doers will be treated is described in **Surah az-Zumur (39:71-2):**

وَسِيقَ الَّذِينَ كَفَرُوٓا إِلَى جَهَنَّمَ زُمَرًا حَتَّىٰٓ إِذَا جَآءُوهَا فُتِحَتْ أَبْوَٰبُهَا وَقَالَ لَهُمْ خَزَنَتُهَآ أَلَمْ يَأْتِكُمْ رُسُلٌ مِّنكُمْ يَتْلُونَ

عَلَيْكُمْ ءَايَٰتِ رَبِّكُمْ وَيُنذِرُونَكُمْ لِقَآءَ يَوْمِكُمْ هَٰذَا قَالُوا بَلَىٰ وَلَٰكِنْ حَقَّتْ كَلِمَةُ الْعَذَابِ عَلَى الْكَٰفِرِينَ - قِيلَ

ادْخُلُوٓا أَبْوَٰبَ جَهَنَّمَ خَٰلِدِينَ فِيهَا فَبِئْسَ مَثْوَى الْمُتَكَبِّرِينَ-

And those who disbelieved will be driven to Hell in groups until, when they reach it, its gates are opened and its keepers will say, "Did there not come to you messengers from yourselves, reciting to you the verses of your Lord and warning you of the meeting of this Day of yours?" They will say, "Yes, but the word [decree] of punishment has come into effect upon the disbelievers." [To them], it will be said: "Enter you the gates of Hell to abide eternally therein, and wretched is the residence of the arrogant!"

Allah tells us how the doomed disbeliever will be driven to Hell by force, with threats and warnings as reported in **Surah at-Tur (52:13-14):**

يَوْمَ يُدَعُّونَ إِلَىٰ نَارِ جَهَنَّمَ دَعًّا - هَٰذِهِ النَّارُ الَّتِى كُنتُم بِهَا تُكَذِّبُونَ

The Day they are thrust toward the fire of Hell with a [violent] thrust, [its angels will say], "This is the Fire which you used to deny".

And also in **Surah al-Isra' (17:97):**

وَنَحْشُرُهُمْ يَوْمَ الْقِيَٰمَةِ عَلَىٰ وُجُوهِهِمْ عُمْيًا وَبُكْمًا وَصُمًّا مَّأْوَاهُمْ جَهَنَّمُ كُلَّمَا خَبَتْ زِدْنَاهُمْ سَعِيرًا

And We will gather them on the Day of Resurrection [fallen] to their faces, - blind, dumb and deaf. Their refuge is Hell; every time it subsides, We increase them in blazing fire.

The kinds of food and drink, and other entertainment in the Hellfire are described in **Surah al-Waqi'ya (56:51-6):**

ثُمَّ إِنَّكُمْ أَيُّهَا الضَّآلُّونَ الْمُكَذِّبُونَ - لَءَاكِلُونَ مِن شَجَرٍ مِّن زَقُّومٍ - فَمَالِئُونَ مِنْهَا الْبُطُونَ - فَشَٰرِبُونَ عَلَيْهِ مِنَ الْحَمِيمِ - فَشَٰرِبُونَ

شُرْبَ الْهِيمِ - هَٰذَا نُزُلُهُمْ يَوْمَ الدِّينِ

Then indeed you, O those astray [who are] deniers, will be eating from trees of Zaqqum – and filling with it your bellies and drinking on top of it from scalding water and will drink as the drinking of thirsty camels. That is their hospitality on the Day of Recompense.

Allah [swt] says in **Surah ad-Dukhan (44:43-50):**

إِنَّ شَجَرَةَ الزَّقُّومِ - طَعَامُ الْأَثِيمِ - كَالْمُهْلِ يَغْلِي فِي الْبُطُونِ - كَغَلْيِ الْحَمِيمِ - خُذُوهُ فَاعْتِلُوهُ إِلَى سَوَاءِ الْجَحِيمِ - ثُمَّ صُبُّوا فَوْقَ رَأْسِهِ مِنْ

عَذَابِ الْحَمِيمِ - ذُقْ إِنَّكَ أَنتَ الْعَزِيزُ الْكَرِيمُ - إِنَّ هَذَا مَا كُنتُم بِهِ تَمْتَرُونَ

Indeed, the tree of Zaqqum is food of the sinful. Like murky oil, it boils within bellies like the boiling of scalding water. [It will be commanded], "Seize him and drag him into the midst of blazing Fire, then pour over his head from the torment of scalding water". [It will be said], "Taste! Indeed, you are the honored, the noble [as he claimed upon the earth]! Indeed, this is what you used to dispute" .

What will be given to the residents of the hell fire when they will ask for help is described in **Surah al-Haqqa (69:36-7):**

وَلَا طَعَامٌ إِلَّا مِنْ غِسْلِينٍ - لَا يَأْكُلُهُ إِلَّا الْخَاطِئُونَ

Nor any food except from the discharge of wounds; none will eat it except the sinners.

When their thirst reaches its ultimate, they would be given water from a boiling spring with extremely high temperature, which would split up their stomachs, damage their sinful bodies, and burn their disobedient faces.

The question remains whether it will be a onetime punishment? Let us see what Allah [swt] says in **Surah an-Nisa' (4:56):**

إِنَّ الَّذِينَ كَفَرُوا بِآيَاتِنَا سَوْفَ نُصْلِيهِمْ نَارًا كُلَّمَا نَضِجَتْ جُلُودُهُم بَدَّلْنَاهُمْ جُلُودًا غَيْرَهَا لِيَذُوقُوا الْعَذَابَ إِنَّ اللَّهَ كَانَ عَزِيزًا

حَكِيمًا

Indeed, those who disbelieve in Our verses - We will drive them into a fire. Every time their skins are roasted through, We will replace them with other skins so they may taste the punishment. Indeed, Allah is ever exalted in Might and Wise. So the punishment in Hell will be everlasting and they will never die.

Those who will have equal amounts of good and wrong deeds will be placed in a neutral place between Paradise and Hell known as Al-A'raf as Allah [swt] says in **Surah al-A'raf (7:46-7):**

وَبَيْنَهُمَا حِجَابٌ وَعَلَى الْأَعْرَافِ رِجَالٌ يَعْرِفُونَ كُلًّا بِسِيمَاهُمْ وَنَادَوْا أَصْحَابَ الْجَنَّةِ أَن سَلَامٌ عَلَيْكُمْ لَمْ يَدْخُلُوهَا وَهُمْ يَطْمَعُونَ -

وَإِذَا صُرِفَتْ أَبْصَارُهُمْ تِلْقَاءَ أَصْحَابِ النَّارِ قَالُوا رَبَّنَا لَا تَجْعَلْنَا مَعَ الْقَوْمِ الظَّالِمِينَ -

And between them will be a partition [wall] and on [its] elevations are men [those whose scales are balanced between good and evil deeds] who will recognize them by their mark. And they call out to the companions of Paradise, "Peace be upon you". They have not [yet] entered it [Paradise], but they hope to enter [it]. And when their eyes are turned toward the companions of the Fire, they say, "Our Lord, do not place us with the people who are wrongdoers."

Of course the day of Qiyammah will come surely nobody knows when it will happen. But the exact time and moment is known only to Allah [swt]. But there will be some signs before the Qiyammah. As Allah [swt] says in **Surah al-Naml (27:82):**

$$ \text{وَإِذَا وَقَعَ الْقَوْلُ عَلَيْهِم أَخْرَجْنَا لَهُم دَآبَّةً مِّنَ الأَرْضِ تُكَلِّمُهُمْ أَنَّ النَّاسَ كَانُوا بِآيَاتِنَا لاَ يُوقِنُونَ } $$

And when the Word [decree] befalls them [at the approach of the Hour], We will bring forth for them a creature from the earth speaking to them.

The Messenger of Allah said: "The Hour will not be established (1) till two big groups fight each other whereupon there will be a great number of casualties on both sides and they will be following one and the same religious doctrine, (2) till about thirty Dajjals [liars] appear, and each one of them will claim that he is Allah's Apostle, (3) till the religious knowledge is taken away [by the death of Religious scholars], (4) earthquakes will increase in number, (5) time will pass quickly, (6) afflictions will appear, (7) Al-Harj [i.e., killing] will increase, (8) till wealth will be in abundance ---- so abundant that a wealthy person will worry lest nobody should accept his Zakat, and whenever he will present it to someone, that person [to whom it will be offered] will say, 'I am not in need of it', (9) till the people compete with one another in constructing high buildings, (10) till a man when passing by a grave of someone will say, 'Would that I were in his place', (11) and till the sun rises from the West. So when the sun will rise and the people will see it [rising from the West] they will all believe [embrace Islam] but that will be the time when: [As Allah said], 'No good will it do to a soul to believe then, if it believed not before, nor earned good [by deeds of righteousness] through its Faith.' (6.158) And the Hour will be established while two men spreading a garment in front of them but they will not be able to sell it, nor fold it up; and the Hour will be established when a man has milked his she-camel and has taken away the milk but he will not be able to drink it; and the Hour will be established before a man repairing a tank [for his livestock] is able to water [his animals] in it; and the Hour will be established when a person has raised a morsel [of food] to his mouth but will not be able to eat it" (Bukhari, book #88, hadith #237).

Dawud At-Tayalisi recorded from Jabir that messenger of Allah said, Jibril said "O Muhammad, live how you wish, for verily you will die; love what you wish, for Verily you will part with it; and do whatever you wish, for verily you will meet it."

Umar Ibn Alkhattab said, "Judge yourself before you are judged and weigh your actions before they are weighed against you".

Brothers and sisters in Islam, Just ponder on the two statements above and think what we should do.

Brothers and Sisters in Islam, Allah [swt] said in **Surah al-A'raf (7:179):**

وَلَقَدْ ذَرَأْنَا لِجَهَنَّمَ كَثِيرًا مِّنَ الْجِنِّ وَالْإِنسِ لَهُمْ قُلُوبٌ لَّا يَفْقَهُونَ بِهَا وَلَهُمْ أَعْيُنٌ لَّا يُبْصِرُونَ بِهَا وَلَهُمْ ءَاذَانٌ لَّا يَسْمَعُونَ بِهَا أُوْلَـٰئِكَ كَالْأَنْعَـٰمِ بَلْ هُمْ أَضَلُّ أُوْلَـٰئِكَ هُمُ الْغَـٰفِلُونَ

And We have certainly created for Hell many of the Jinn and mankind. They have hearts with which they do not understand, they have eyes with which they do not see, and they have ears with which they do not hear [the truth]. Those are like livestock; rather, they are more astray. It is they who are the heedless.

Look at the warning of Allah [swt]. May Allah [swt] guide us so that we will not be in the group of people described above?

Slaves of Allah! These are some of the descriptions of the Fire and its people, so we ask Allah [swt] to protect us from Hell Fire. Ask Allah [swt] to keep us away from any words or deeds that would bring us closer to Hell Fire. We live in a time during which evil and trials are successive; trials of doubts and fast busy life, which lead anyone who falls in its trap to turn away from his faith, manners and behavior. Make our hearts and our bodies sense the heat of the Hellfire, its fetters, its depths, its fuel, its rocks, its chains and shackles, its boiling fluid, its dark murky fluid. Think of the blazing fire and its severely intolerable heat. Cry and call on one another to cry. Visualize in our hearts the image of the wrongdoers being tormented in the flames of the Hellfire.

So, fear Allah so that He may have mercy on us. O Allah! We seek refuge with You from Hellfire, and from words or deeds that may bring us near to it. Save us from the blazing fire that has been reserved for the disbelievers. **Amin!**

Qur'an: The Guide Book of the Muslims

Allah [swt] describes the "greatness" of Quran in **Surah al-Hashr (59:21)** as:

لَوْ أَنزَلْنَا هَـٰذَا ٱلْقُرْءَانَ عَلَىٰ جَبَلٍ لَّرَأَيْتَهُ خَـٰشِعًا مُّتَصَدِّعًا مِّنْ خَشْيَةِ ٱللَّهِ ۚ وَتِلْكَ ٱلْأَمْثَـٰلُ نَضْرِبُهَا لِلنَّاسِ لَعَلَّهُمْ يَتَفَكَّرُونَ

If We had sent down this Qur'an upon a mountain, you would have seen it humbled and coming apart from fear of Allah. And these examples We represent to the people that perhaps they will give thought.

If this is the case with a mountain which is hard and huge, that if it was made able to comprehend and understand this Qur'an, will feel humble and crumble from fear of Allah the Exalted, then what about you -- O mankind! Why do your hearts not feel softness and humbleness from the fear of Allah, even though you understand Allah's command and comprehend His Book. Allah [swt] says in **Surah al-Baqarah (2:23-4):**

وَإِن كُنتُمْ فِى رَيْبٍ مِّمَّا نَزَّلْنَا عَلَىٰ عَبْدِنَا فَأْتُوا بِسُورَةٍ مِّن مِّثْلِهِ وَٱدْعُوا شُهَدَآءَكُم مِّن دُونِ ٱللَّهِ إِن كُنتُمْ صَـٰدِقِينَ ۝ فَإِن لَّمْ تَفْعَلُوا وَلَن تَفْعَلُوا فَٱتَّقُوا ٱلنَّارَ ٱلَّتِى وَقُودُهَا ٱلنَّاسُ وَٱلْحِجَارَةُ ۖ أُعِدَّتْ لِلْكَـٰفِرِينَ

And if you [Arab pagans, Jews, and Christians] are in doubt about what We have sent down [i.e. the Qur'an] upon Our servant [Muhammad (sas)], then produce a Surah [chapter] the like thereof and call your witnesses [supporters and helpers] other than Allah, if you are truthful. But if you do not - you will never be able to - then fear the Fire [Hell], whose fuel is men and stones, prepared for the disbelievers.

Allah (swt) is explaining to us the reason for the revelation of this Holy book in **Surah al-Baqarah (2:185)** as:

شَهْرُ رَمَضَانَ ٱلَّذِىٓ أُنزِلَ فِيهِ ٱلْقُرْءَانُ هُدًى لِّلنَّاسِ وَبَيِّنَـٰتٍ مِّنَ ٱلْهُدَىٰ وَٱلْفُرْقَانِ

The month of Ramadan in which was revealed the Qur'an, a guidance for mankind and clear proofs for the guidance and the criterion (between right and wrong).

In this way, the proof of Islam is complete for all time to come, for it lies in the Book itself. The challenge has been made clear, that if anyone denies the Qur'an as true, all they have to do is produce one Surah [chapter] which is comparable in style [the shortest sized of which being Surah al-Kawthar, 3 lines long]. For 1400 years, no-one or a group has ever done this or will be able to do.

In this way, we see that the proof of the Qur'an, which is the foundation of the religion of Islam, stands as a challenge for the whole mankind.

On the basis of three reports from Abdullah Ibn Abbas, in Hakim, Baihaqi and Nasai, the Qura'n descended in two stages:

1. From the *lauhal-mahfuz,* the 'well-preserved tablet' to the lowest of the heavens *bait al-'izza* of the world, all together, in the *laila al-qadr.*

2. From the heavens to earth in stages throughout the twenty-three years of Muhammad's prophet hood, and first in the *laila tul-qadr* of Ramadan, through the Angel Gabriel; while the earlier scriptures were revealed to the prophets at one time.

Narrated by Abu Hurairah: The Prophet said "Every Prophet was given miracles because of which people believed but what I have been given is divine inspiration which Allah has revealed to me so I hope that my followers will outnumber the followers of the other Prophets on the Day of Resurrection" (Bukhari, volume # 6, hadith #504).

Al-Harith bin Hisham asked Allah's Apostle, "O Allah's Apostle! How is the divine inspiration revealed to you?" Allah's Apostle replied, "Sometimes it is [revealed] like the ringing of a bell, this form of inspiration is the hardest of all and then this state passes off after I have grasped what is inspired. Sometimes the Angel comes in the form of a man and talks to me and I grasp whatever he says." 'Aisha [ra] added: verily I saw the prophet being inspired divinely on a very cold day and noticed the sweat dropping from his forehead [as the inspiration is over] (Bukhari, book #1, hadith #2).

The miracles of all the Prophets ended with their departure, but the miracle of our beloved Prophet will [the Holy Quran] will continue to exist, , even after his departure, till the Final Day, Alhamdu-lillah.

Allah [swt] has sent the final revelation - the Qur'an - for the guidance of mankind. Hence, the Qur'an is the guidance [*Huda*] for us. As Allah [swt] says in **Surah al-Baqarah (2:2):**

$$ ذَلِكَ الْكِتَابُ لاَ رَيْبَ فِيهِ هُدًى لِّلْمُتَّقِينَ $$

This is the book about which there is no doubt, guidance for those conscious of Allah.

Therefore, the Qur'an is not merely for accumulating bits of rewards, but for using as comprehensive guidance for human life and for solving the problems in our Aakhirah-bound life in this world. But to make use of the Qur'an as guidance, one needs some basic capital, and that capital is Taqwa [Allah-consciousness]. That is why the Qur'an is the guidance but effectively only for those who are Muttoqun [Allah-conscious].

Allah (swt) has assured that He will protect the Qura`n in **Surah Al-Hijr (15:9)** as:

$$ إِنَّا نَحْنُ نَزَّلْنَا الذِّكْرَ وَ إِنَّا لَهُ لَحَفِظُونَ $$

Verily, We, it is We Who revealed the Dhikr (i.e. the Qur'an) and surely We will guard it (from corruption).

Also in **Surah Al-Fussilat (41:41-2),** Allah (swt) has reiterated its safeguard from any falsehood:

$$\text{إِنَّ الَّذِينَ كَفَرُوا بِالذِّكْرِ لَمَّا جَاءَهُمْ وَإِنَّهُ لَكِتَابٌ عَزِيزٌ ۝ لَا يَأْتِيهِ الْبَاطِلُ مِن بَيْنِ يَدَيْهِ وَلَا مِنْ خَلْفِهِ تَنزِيلٌ مِّنْ حَكِيمٍ حَمِيدٍ}$$

Verily, those who disbelieved in the Reminder when it came to them. And verily, it is an honorable well-fortified respected Book. Falsehood cannot come to it from before it or behind it, (it is) sent down by the All-Wise, Worthy of all praise.

Unlike the reading of a reference book, reading and reciting the Qur'an is an act in which our whole being: our soul, our heart, our tongue, our mind and body participate. When we recite Qur'an in your salâh [daily prayers], we try to think of every word that we are reciting. Reading or reciting Qur'an should never become mechanical. As the tongue recites, the words flow from the lips, the mind ponders, the heart reflects, the soul absorbs, tears well up in our eyes, our heart quakes and trembles. Allâh [swt] describes what the Qur'an does to us in **Surah az-Zumar (39:23):**

$$\text{اللَّهُ نَزَّلَ أَحْسَنَ الْحَدِيثِ كِتَابًا مُّتَشَابِهًا مَّثَانِيَ تَقْشَعِرُّ مِنْهُ جُلُودُ الَّذِينَ يَخْشَوْنَ رَبَّهُمْ ثُمَّ تَلِينُ جُلُودُهُمْ وَقُلُوبُهُمْ إِلَىٰ ذِكْرِ اللَّهِ ذَٰلِكَ هُدَى}$$

$$\text{اللَّهِ يَهْدِي بِهِ مَن يَشَاءُ وَمَن يُضْلِلِ اللَّهُ فَمَا لَهُ مِنْ هَادٍ}$$

Allâh has sent down the best statement: a consistent book wherein is reiteration. The skins shiver there from of those who fear their Lord; then their skins and their hearts relax at the remembrance [mention] of Allah. That is the guidance of Allah by which He guides whom He wills. And one whom Allah leaves astray, for him there is no guide.

Only with this deep faith and conviction, we will open our hearts to let the words soak in, awaken us, heal and transform us. When we listen to the words of the Qur'ân, it is not the voice but the words that enchant us — it is Allâh speaking! When the Qur'ân enters our hearts, we are filled with a tenderness, with such qualities as humility, sincerity, love and compassion, truthfulness and gratitude, and an eagerness to accept and respond to Allâh's Message. Yes, how do we get this faith and how can we keep it alive? The easiest and most effective way is to read or recite the Qur'ân. The more we recite it, the more will we recognize it is the Word of Allâh and the more will our faith increase in intensity and depth if we are convinced and have faith that the Qur'ân is the Word of Allâh, then we must consider carefully our intention of purpose: Why do we want to read the Qur'ân? It is not enough to read it to improve our knowledge or for pleasure. We become so thankful that Allâh has blessed us and guided us to read and study the Qur'ân. Al-Hamdulillah, praise be to Allâh, and in the words of the Qur'ân in **Surah al-A'raf (7:43):**

$$\text{وَنَزَعْنَا مَا فِي صُدُورِهِم مِّنْ غِلٍّ تَجْرِي مِن تَحْتِهِمُ الْأَنْهَارُ وَقَالُوا الْحَمْدُ لِلَّهِ الَّذِي هَدَانَا لِهَٰذَا وَمَا كُنَّا لِنَهْتَدِيَ لَوْلَا أَنْ هَدَانَا اللَّهُ لَقَدْ}$$

$$\text{جَاءَتْ رُسُلُ رَبِّنَا بِالْحَقِّ وَنُودُوا أَن تِلْكُمُ الْجَنَّةُ أُورِثْتُمُوهَا بِمَا كُنتُمْ تَعْمَلُونَ}$$

And We will have removed whatever is within their breasts of resentment, [while] flowing beneath them are rivers. And they will say, "Praise be to Allah, who has guided us to this; and we would never have been guided if Allah had not guided us. Certainly the messengers of our Lord had come with the truth." And they will be called, "This is Paradise, which you have been made to inherit for what you used to do."

Allah [swt] says in **Surah al-Isra' (17:9):**

$$إِنَّ هَـٰذَا الْقُرْءَانَ يَهْدِى لِلَّتِى هِىَ أَقْوَمُ وَيُبَشِّرُ الْمُؤْمِنِينَ الَّذِينَ يَعْمَلُونَ الصَّـٰلِحَاتِ أَنَّ لَهُمْ أَجْرًا كَبِيرًا$$

Indeed, this Qur'an guides to that which is most suitable and gives good tidings to the believers who do righteous deeds that they will have a great reward [Paradise].

The Qur'an is also a light as expressed in **Surah at-Taghâbun (64:8):**

$$فَـٔامِنُوا بِاللَّهِ وَرَسُولِهِ وَالنُّورِ الَّذِى أَنزَلْنَا وَاللَّهُ بِمَا تَعْمَلُونَ خَبِيرٌ$$

So believe in Allah and His Messenger and the Light [the Quran] which We have sent down. And Allah is acquainted with what you do.

And also Qur'an separates good from evil as enunciated in **Surah at-Târiq (86:13):**

$$إِنَّهُ لَقَوْلٌ فَصْلٌ$$

Indeed, it [the Quran] is a decisive statement.

Muslims do view 'The Book' as much greater than the sum of ink on paper. It is the musical score of Muslim spirituality, a Book whose mere recitation is considered an act of worship. Encyclopedia Britannica attests to the Qur'ans linguistic excellence," The best of Arab witness have never succeeded in producing anything equal to the merits in the Qur'an. To compose such revelations at will was beyond the power of the most expert literary artist.

It is the scripture Muslims turn to for guidance, calm, and perspective. Muslims view the book as much greater than the sum of ink on paper. It is the musical score of Muslim spirituality, a book whose mere recitation is considered an act of worship. The Qur'an is a source of guidance for the whole mankind as asserted in **Surah al-Qalam (68:52):**

$$وَمَا هُوَ إِلَّا ذِكْرٌ لِّلْعَالَمِينَ$$

But it is not except a reminder to the worlds.

Qur'an is the most often read, the most memorized and perhaps the most quoted book in the world. It is the only book that has a science [*tajweed*] that evolved to facilitate its rhythm and musicality. It is the last of Allah's revelation conveyed to humanity through the final Messenger Muhammad [sas]. Muslims consider the commands and wisdom found in the Qur'an to be a constant guide in all principle matters of daily life.

If we ask people of the books [accept Islam] to demonstrate the miracles of their Prophets, none of them will be able to demonstrate. But for those in Islam, the Qur'an was, is, and will be the living miracle of our beloved Prophet Muhammad [sas] till the last day of this world. Subhan Allah!

In order to truly benefit from the Qur'an we have to be able to relate the Qur'an in a practical way every day of our lives. Great scholars of Islam have advised us to keep our relationship with the Qur'an effective by maintaining the following five responsibilities:

Belief and Honor: We regard the Qur'an as the words of Allah and believe it to be the best book of guidance for those who want to live righteous lives. We respect its message and honor it above all other books. Allah's Apostle said, "Do not wish to be like anyone, except in two cases: (1) A man whom Allah has given wealth and he spends it righteously, (2) A man whom Allah has given wisdom (knowledge of the Quran and the Hadith) and he acts according to it and teaches it to others." (Bukhari, book #89, hadith #255)

Another virtue of the Holy Book is that it works as a cure and mercy described in **Surah Al-`Isra (17:82):**

$$ وَنُنَزِّلُ مِنَ الْقُرْءَانِ مَا هُوَ شِفَآءٌ وَرَحْمَةٌ لِّلْمُؤْمِنِينَ وَلاَ يَزِيدُ الظَّـٰلِمِينَ إِلاَّ خَسَارًا $$

And We send down of the Qur'an that which is a cure and a mercy to the believers and it increases the wrongdoers in nothing but loss.

Quran is a cure and a mercy for the believers, meaning that it takes away whatever is in their hearts of doubt, hypocrisy, Shirk, confusion and inclination towards falsehood. The Qur'an cures all of that. It is also a mercy through which one attains faith and wisdom and seeks goodness. This is only for those who believe in it and accept it as truthful; it is a cure and a mercy only for such people.

Reading and Recitation: Since the Qur'an was communicated to the Prophet (sws) through Gabriel orally and the Prophet in turn conveyed it to his companions orally we should learn to read the Qur'an properly and recite it correctly. There are great blessings [*barakah*] in reading the Qur'an in the correct manner.

Understanding and Reflecting: Many Muslims learn to read the Qur'an but few strive to understand its meaning. Since the Qur'an is mainly a book of guidance, we have a responsibility to understand its message and reflect on what it says.

Implementing the Guidelines:

One of the greatest duties we have is to perform and live by the commands of Allah. The primary reason why Allah sent revelation was to guide human beings to be good and to be of benefit to the world, not to do wrong, nor to harm the world.

Conveying and Clarifying: Each Muslim has the responsibility of conveying the message of Islam to others. If we believe in the Qur'an, respect the Qur'an, read it how it is supposed to be read, recite it properly, understand its message and live by its commands then our behavior will reflect the Qur'an. The Prophet lived his life according to the message of the Qur'an. The best way to attract people to Islam is to live as good Muslims, to live like the Prophets, to live according to the Qur'an.

The Prophet [sas] said, "The best among you [Muslims] are those who learn the Qur'an and teach it (Bukhari, book#6, hadith 545).

The holy book Qura'n was finally compiled during the khilafat of Hazrat Usman. Through this great service Hazrat Usman [ra] is famous as [*Jamiul-Qura'n*] compiler of the Qura'n, in fact united the entire Ummah on the single script. Thus the Qura'n is authenticated, compiled and spread throughout the Muslim world within twenty years after the death of Prophet (sas). But the diacritical [vowel] signs were introduced in the Quranic script during the time of the fifth "Umayyad Caliph Malik-ar-Marwan (66-86 Hijri/685-705 A.D.) and during the governorship of Al-Hajaj in Iraq. That made the recitation of the Holy Qura'n more uniform throughout the non-Arab Muslims.

The Qur'an as scripture forms the bedrock of Islamic ideology and teachings. The commands of Allah, the criterion for truth, the standard for justice, the balance between right and wrong ... all of these are taken by Muslims directly from the Qur'an. The authenticity of the Qur'an is thus synonymous with the veracity of the Islamic faith.

Allah (swt) is reminding us that the revelation of the Holy Quran in Surah **Al-Qamar (55:17)** for admonition:

وَلَقَدْ يَسَّرْنَا الْقُرْءَانَ لِلذِّكْرِ فَهَلْ مِن مُّدَّكِرٍ

We have made this Qur'an an easy means of admonition. Then, is there any who would take admonition?

Rasulullah (sas) said:

"Saum and the Qur'an will intercede on behalf of the servant (of Allah). Saum will say, 'My Rabb! I forbade him from food and desires during the day, therefore, accept my intercession on his behalf.' The Qur'an will say: I forbade him from sleep at night, therefore accept my intercession on his behalf'. Thus, their intercession will be accepted".

O Allah! Increase our Iman in intensity and depth. Strengthen our niyyah [intention] to read the Qur'ân. Grant us, through the barakah of the Qur'ân, true guidance and pleasure. O, Allâh! Help us become thankful and increase our eagerness to uncover the richness of the Qur'ân. **Amin!**

Ramadhan: Month of Blessings and Forgiveness

We are approaching the month of Ramadhân and in this preparatory phase - the last few days, we evaluate our beliefs and our actions…a process, which we may consider as our spiritual stocktaking. Yes, we do not sit and wait passively for this special month to arrive to fill the atmosphere with a spirit of piety and virtue and hope that it will inspire us and set us alight! How can our saum and 'aml or good deeds, be effective? So effective that they help transform and direct our lives towards Allâh permanently? This is our prayer and our hopes for the Ramadhân and, inshâ-Allâh [Allâh-willing], there is no reason why it cannot be attained!

Allâh states in **Surah al–Baqarah (2: 183):**

يَٰٓأَيُّهَا ٱلَّذِينَ ءَامَنُوا۟ كُتِبَ عَلَيْكُمُ ٱلصِّيَامُ كَمَا كُتِبَ عَلَى ٱلَّذِينَ مِن قَبْلِكُمْ لَعَلَّكُمْ تَتَّقُونَ-

O you who have believed, Fasting is decreed upon you as it was decreed upon those before you that you may become righteous.

In this often quoted verse, we are reminded that saum was observed by people long before is one of the fundamental pillars of Faith and has always been integral part of religious traditions throughout history … Prophets Musa [Moses], 'Isa [Jesus], Dawood [David], Ilyaas [Elijah] [peace be upon them], all fasted [according to the Bible] the advent of our Prophet Muhammad [sas] -- the rules or method differed but the goals remained the same.

Allah's Apostle said, "Saum is a shield [or a screen or a shelter]. So, the person observing saum should avoid sexual relation with his wife and should not behave foolishly and impudently, and if somebody fights with him or abuses him, he should tell him twice, 'I am in saum. "He has left his food, drink and desires for My sake. The fast is for Me. So I will reward [the fasting person] for it and the reward of good deeds is multiplied ten times." (Bukhari, book #31, hadith #118)

But in the course of time, that shield grows onto us and becomes part of our inner armor, our personalities. We are then able to withstand any onslaught or temptation, any attempt to disrupt our values and our beliefs as Muslims

Imam Ahmad recorded from Abu Huraiyrah "When Ramadhan would come, the Messenger of Allah would say, verily, the month of Ramadhan has come to you all. It is a blessed month, which Allah has obligated you all to fast. During it the gates of Paradise are opened, the gates of Hell are closed and the devils are shackled. In it there is a night that is better than one thousand months. Whoever is deprived of its good, he has truly been deprived".

Benefits of fasting include:

*Fasting instills patience, teaches self control and discipline.

*Fasting increases compassion for the less fortunate.

*Fasting builds focus on spirituality and diminishes focus on materialism.

*Fasting has many health benefits.

*Fasting can be atonement for sin and can earn great reward.

*Fasting is part of a strong spiritual and physical renewal plan.

*Fasting commemorates important sacred religious events.

Allah (swt) said:

عَنْ أَبِي هُرَيْرَةَ رَضِيَ اللهُ عَنْهُ، عَنِ النَّبِيِّ صَلَّى اللهُ عَلَيْهِ وَسَلَّمَ قَالَ

"يَقُولُ اللهُ عَزَّ وَجَلَّ: الصَّوْمُ لِي، وَأَنَا أَجْزِي بِهِ، يَدَعُ شَهْوَتَهُ وَأَكْلَهُ وَشُرْبَهُ مِنْ أَجْلِي (1)، وَالصَّوْمُ جُنَّةٌ، وَلِلصَّائِمِ فَرْحَتَانِ: فَرْحَةٌ

حِينَ يُفْطِرُ، وَفَرْحَةٌ حِينَ يَلْقَى رَبَّهُ، وَلَخُلُوفُ (2) فَمِ الصَّائِمِ عِنْدَ اللهِ مِنْ رِيحِ الْمِسْكِ".

On the authority of Abu Hurayrah (ra) from the Prophet (sas), who said:

Allah (mighty and sublime be He) says: 'Fasting is Mine and it is I Who give reward for it. [A man] gives up his sexual passion, his food and his drink for My sake.' Fasting is like a shield, and he who fasts has two joys: a joy when he breaks his fast and a joy when he meets his Lord. The change in the breath of the mouth of him who fasts is better in Allah's sight the smell of mask (Hadith Qudsi: 10).

Allah praised the month of Ramadhan out of the other months by choosing it to send down the Glorious Qur'an, just as He did for all of the Divine Books He revealed to the Prophets. Imam Ahmad reported Wathilah bin Al-Asqa` that Allah's Messenger said: The Suhuf [Pages] on Ibrahim, the Torah on Musa, the Injil on Isa [as] were also sent in the month of Ramadhan.

For one short month we will be able to pick up the fruit of saum, enjoy it and strengthen our faith [Imân] and our piety [taqwa] in the process. The tree remains and the fruit is there for the picking! Let us not allow our saum to degenerate into starving. Then it is surely not for Allâh [swt] and not worthy of Allâh's blessings. Hence our Nabi Muhammad [sas] warns us like a true father concerned for the wellbeing of his children. Saum in Islam involves abstinence from three primal physical needs of human beings; food, drink, and intimate relationships from dawn to dusk during the entire month of Ramadhan.

Imam Abu Hamid al-Ghazali made reference to 3 Levels of saum:

Ordinary: saum-ul-'umoom: means abstaining from food, drink and sexual satisfaction.

Special: saum-ul-khusoos: means keeping one's ears, eyes, tongue, hands and feet -- and all other organs -- free from sin.

Extra-special: saum-ul-khusoos al-khusoos: means fasting of the heart by abstaining completely from unworthy concerns and unnecessary material matters; focusing more on one's relationship with Allah and one's duties to the creation of Allah,

The Messenger of Allah stated that every act has a charity and the charity of our health is the fast. The saum mobilizes the body's fuel and energy stores and increases the excretion of waste products, this has a purifying effect. The Islamic principles of moderation, self-restraint and avoidance of harm can go a long way in overcoming these pitfalls.

Ramadhan is the best time to recite the Qur'an for it is a food for the soul and because of the fact that the authority of a mind that tells man to do evil weakens during the month. The soul will then prevail and get strength by the Qur'an and the man, as a result, will derive the highest possible benefit from it. The nights of Ramadhan should be spent with the Qur'án – reading it, listening to it, understanding it and allowing it to shine its light into our souls to guide us to the straight path,

Qur'an is like a beneficial rain, the soul is like the earth and Ramadhan is like the good season for rainfall that enables the hearts to produce the pairs of blooming crops.

The Prophet [sas] said, "Whoever established prayers on the night of Qadr out of sincere faith and hoping for a reward from Allah, then all his previous sins will be forgiven, and whoever fasts in the month of Ramadhan out of sincere faith, and hoping for a reward from Allah, then all his previous sins will be forgiven." (Bukhari, book #31, hadith #125)

There are lessons in the changing of the times as there are reminders in the pages of history. Whenever a month of Ramadhan passes by us, the memories of the great Battle of Badr and its victory is rekindled in us. Yes, Ramadhan reminds us of the victories of Muslims like those battles of Yarmuk and Al-Qadisiyah. We should bear in mind that those glory and victory nor achieve happiness and power except through their strict adherence to Islam in all spheres of their lives. They dedicated all their acts of worship to Allah alone and earned as a result glory and exaltation for this religion. May Allah [swt] give us the spiritual guidance so that we may perform our saum with full devotion in the way as directed by Allah [swt] and advised by Prophet [sas]?

Let this month be an opportunity that we take full advantage of. Let us get used to these customs - the customs of the Prophet [sas]. Let us get rid of the habit of overeating like animals. Let this month be a chance to purify ourselves and become elevated from lusts, desires, and trivialities that are of no real value. Let us elevate our souls to the heavens with faith – we can elevate them from the pleasures of this world to the pleasures of the world to come.

Brothers and sisters, If we cannot review our activities, forsake at least one of our bad habits; and develop the habit of doing at least a good deed during this blessed month, then our purpose of fasting deserve to be incomplete.

We pray to Alláh [swt] to make this Ramadhán a means for us to attain Taqwa, to earn forgiveness for our sins and mercy, to gain access to Al-Jannah where we can meet our Lord and enjoy His good pleasure. **Amin!**

Rights of Children on Parents

Saying of Azaan in the ear of a new-born child is the right of the child on parents just after birth. Prophet [sas] said: "Every child is pledged in exchange for the animal of its Aqeeqah". Umm Kurz said I heard the Messenger of Allāh say: "In the case of a boy, two goats, and in the case of a girl, one goat [should be sacrificed]."(Tirmidhi-Mishkat, 19:3.) The animal should be sacrificed on the seventh day and the child's head should be shaved, and a name given. (Abu Dawud, book #15, hadith #2831)

It, too, is a right of the child that he/she is given a good name. Clear directions are found in this regard in the sayings of the holy Prophet [sas]. Apostle of Allah said: On the Day of Resurrection you will be called by your names and by your father's names, so give yourselves good names. (Abu Dawud, book #41, hadith #4930)

The child begins to receive the impression of what it sees or hears from the time of its birth. The chanting of Azaan and Iqamat in the ears of a newly born infant, also, gives a clear indication of it. Abū Rāfi' said, I saw the Messenger of Allāh calling out adhān for prayer in the ear of Hasan ibn 'Alī, when Fātimah gave birth to him (Tirmidhi-Mishkat. 19:1). Showing respect to one's children denotes that they should be treated not as a burden, but a blessing and a trust of Allah, and brought up with care and affection.

The parents are supposed to teach their children the recitation of the Holy Qur'an and basic principles of Islam. Prophet [sas] said: "Command your children to pray when they become seven years old, and beat them for it [prayer] when they become ten years old; and arrange their beds [to sleep] separately". (Abu Dawud, book #2, hadith #0495) The command of the Prophet [sas] to separate between children at the time of sleep comes as a deterrent to prevent corruption and to bring the attention of the Muslim Nation of their obligations to safe guard and preserve the religion.

Even now daughters are considered an unwanted burden in some societies and instead of rejoicing, an atmosphere of grief and disappointment is produced in the family at their birth. This is the position, today, but, in the pre-islamic times, the daughters were positively considered a shame and disgrace among the Arabs, so much so that even the right to live was denied to them. Many a hard-hearted parent used to strangle his daughter to death, with his own hands, when she was born, or bury her alive.

The Qur'an in **Surah an-Nahl (16:58-9)** states:

$$وَإِذَا بُشِّرَ أَحَدُهُم بِالْأُنثَى ظَلَّ وَجْهُهُ مُسْوَدًّا وَهُوَ كَظِيمٌ ۔ يَتَوَارَىٰ مِنَ الْقَوْمِ مِن سُوءِ مَا بُشِّرَ بِهِ أَيُمْسِكُهُ عَلَىٰ هُونٍ أَمْ يَدُسُّهُ فِي التُّرَابِ$$

$$أَلَا سَاءَ مَا يَحْكُمُونَ$$

And when one of them informed of [the birth of] a female - his face becomes dark, and he suppresses grief. He hides himself from the people because of the ill of which he has been informed. Should he keep it in humiliation or bury it in the ground? Unquestionably, evil is what they decide?

The holy Prophet [sas] again has emphasized that parents should be just and fair to the children particularly in matters of liberality and beneficence and it must not be that while one gets more, the other gets less or nothing. Besides being desirable in itself, it also meets the demands of justice and equity that is pleasing to the Almighty. Apart from it, if discrimination is made among children and one is favored more than the other, it will lead to ill-will and jealousy, and nothing but evil can come out of it. The child who is discriminated against, will, again bear a grudge against parents, the painful consequences of which are easy to imagine.

The marriage of the children, too, on their attaining the age of marriage, has been made a responsibility of the father. But, alas! We are growing increasingly indifferent to it mainly because we have made marriage a most tedious and expensive affair by following the example of others and adopting their customs.

A righteous child is one of the greatest bounties and favors from Allah. Why would it not be when the Prophet [sas] says: "When the son of Adam dies, he loses benefit from his deeds except from three? A charity that is continuous in benefit, beneficial knowledge and a righteous son that supplicates for him". (Muslim, book #013, hadith #4005)

Servants of Allah! Adhering to the command and advice of Allah concerning children and family is to be sincere in supplicating for them to have all well. Not to curse them even at the time of anger, that is because the supplications for or against the child is normally accepted

Fathers and mothers, take care of your children, raise them righteously to be grateful and they will be helpful and heavier on your scale on the Day of Judgment; even though they seem to be a burden at young age, because teaching and raising properly from a young age is like someone engraving on rocks, it stays and its effect is lasting.

O Muslims, it is the right of our children upon us to be just between them when giving gifts. Our children are a special gift from Allah...but this special gift comes with a special responsibility... to offer them constant care and guidance. Little children are great imitators. Just watch any child, how they imitate their parents. Alláh has programmed them to learn from us. We are their role models. We must be ever mindful of the personal example we set for our children. It is this example that they emulate and which will form the basis of their own adult life in years to come

Brothers and Sisters in Islam! Fear Allah concerning the children of the Muslims. Do not push them towards destruction; rather, be an honest advisor and a pious close friend. O sons Daughters! Heed to the advice of your parents. Fulfill their commands and avoid what they forbid you to do! If your father, out of his care for you, forbids you to indulge in your clothing and your appearance, you should comply. You should lead a middle course in all your affairs.

Supposing that mercy towards a child is removed from the heart of his father, mother or relatives. Can education avail that child who is deprived of this mercy? Will he accept advice or admonition? Can advice avail someone who has gone astray or about to go astray?

Brother Muslims! Fear Allah the Almighty and know that instructions given to children by the Prophet [sas] and his worthy Companions reveal the great responsibility that lies on the shoulders of parents and teachers in educating and bringing up their sons and daughters. If we look at our society today, we find our children in strange conditions that we have never experienced before. We observe, among other things, unsteadiness of character, exaggerated interest in the different types of clothes and luxuries cars. Our daughters, on the other hand, have become much interested in browsing in shops and following every update of the fashions of clothes and hairs, as well as fashion magazines.

The mass media, including satellite channels, compete with parents and teachers in the process of bringing up children. Thus, the roles of parents and teachers have lost their effectiveness, not to mention the role of religion, due to the many hours spent daily in watching the programs released by these channels.

The evil company, moreover, is the cause of all problems faced by our children. If it is not the duty of the father to monitor the conduct of his children and to bring them up, whose responsibility is it then? Shall we rely on distant relatives and acquaintances to carry out this duty? Should we leave such children to be victims of misleading ideologies, biased tendencies, and destructive moralities, thus bringing up a corrupt generation that does not observe the rights of Allah and the rights of people? Such a generation will be an anarchic, reckless generation that can hardly distinguish between good and bad. Such will be a liberal generation that is loyal to none but the devil, breaking all constraints, except those of lusts and desires. Such will be the inevitable result, except if Allah wills something else.

What we teach our children at home we must believe in and do ourselves. We cannot tell our children to be honest and trustworthy while we tell lies, behave dishonorably or underpay our employees. We cannot insist that our children perform their salah regularly while we are seldom home to lead them in the salah. We cannot teach them the meaning of peace and human dignity, while we allow them to watch movies that degrade and deprave human beings in the name of entertainment. We cannot have two sets of values: one that is pure and good for our children and the other that we think is good enough for us. Such values our children will not accept, and rightly so. They are our children; they love us and want to be like us. And is that asking too much? So, let us not fool ourselves into believing that we can produce good Muslim children while we ourselves remain less than good Muslim parents. We must realize that, good, Islamic values do not flow from our mouths but from our deeds.

Some parents give their children unlimited freedom to do what they want, without over viewing their affairs, counseling them, having meals with them, etc. Thus, strange relationship prevails in the relations between parents and their children and each feels averse to the other. How can parents, then, expect that their children will obey them or abide by their directions? To whom will children resort to when they face a problem or are in a dilemma?

Brothers and sisters, when our children grew up in an alien culture, we should teach them, without hesitation, how to refuse politely offer for "dating" and "alcoholic drinks" as these acts are prohibited in Islam. If from the beginning parents fear Allah and rear their children in a way that pleases Allah, Allah would improve their conditions in this worldly life and in the Hereafter.

O, Allah [swt]! Help us to remember that we care for the most precious of all your creation, the innocent children. Help us always to remember that we are leaving our marks on them which time will never erase. Give us patience with those who are slow to learn, and tolerance with those who don't want to learn. When we have to discipline our children, help us to do so with firmness, and yet, with Love. Help us to let the children not only store things in their memories, but create things with their minds. And amidst all the worrying and irritation of our task, help us to remember that the future of our community and our 'Ummah' is with our children.

May Allah [swt] give us proper knowledge and guidance to discharge our responsibilities in guiding our children in the right path and forgive us from any mistake we may commit in upbringing them properly. O Allah! Give us the ability and courage to bring up our children in a way so that they will be helpful and heavier on your scale on the Day of Judgment, rather than a burden. **Amin!**

Rights of Parents on Children

We come into the world through the agency of parents; parents who are our nurturers, our caretakers, our protectors and our supporters. When Allah commands us with duties, he puts a priority on parents' above all social relations.

Abu Hurayrah [ra] narrates that [once] a person enquired from the Apostle of Allah "Who has the greatest claim on me with regard to service and kind treatment?" The Prophet [sas] replied: "Your mother; and again, your mother; and once again, your mother. After her, there is the claim of your father, and, after it, of your near kinsmen, and then, of the kinsmen who are next to them." (Muslim, book #032, hadith #6181)

Luqmân (as) reminds his son of the rights of his parents on him in **Surah Luqman (31:14):**

وَوَصَّيْنَا الْإِنْسَانَ بِوَالِدَيْهِ حَمَلَتْهُ أُمُّهُ وَهْنًا عَلَى وَهْنٍ وَفِصَالُهُ فِي عَامَيْنِ أَنِ اشْكُرْ لِي وَلِوَالِدَيْكَ إِلَيَّ الْمَصِيرُ

And we have enjoined upon man [care] for his parents. His mother carried him, [increasing her] in weakness upon weakness [hardships mothers face bearing children] and his weaning is in two years. Be grateful to Me and to your parents; To Me is the [final] destination.

Of all the bonds of relationships, the mother holds a unique position. We are asked to reflect on and appreciate the selfless nature of the mother. Abu Hurairah reported Allah's Apostle [sas] as saying: Let him be humbled into dust; let him be humbled into dust. It was said: Allah's Messenger, who is he? He said: He who sees either of his parents during their old age or he sees both of them, but he does not enter Paradise. (Muslim, book #32, hadith #6189)

Concerning care and kind treatment, the claim of mother is greater than that of father. From the Qur'an, too, it appears that, the pain and suffering of the mother during pregnancy and at childbirth and in fostering and bringing up the children has been mentioned, in particular, along with the exhortation of showing kindness to parents.

In **Surah al-Ahqaf (46:15)** Allah [swt] says:

وَوَصَّيْنَا الْإِنْسَانَ بِوَالِدَيْهِ إِحْسَانًا حَمَلَتْهُ أُمُّهُ كُرْهًا وَوَضَعَتْهُ كُرْهًا وَحَمْلُهُ وَفِصَالُهُ ثَلَاثُونَ شَهْرًا حَتَّى إِذَا بَلَغَ أَشُدَّهُ وَبَلَغَ أَرْبَعِينَ

سَنَةً قَالَ رَبِّ أَوْزِعْنِي أَنْ أَشْكُرَ نِعْمَتَكَ الَّتِي أَنْعَمْتَ عَلَيَّ وَعَلَى وَالِدَيَّ وَأَنْ أَعْمَلَ صَالِحًا تَرْضَاهُ وَأَصْلِحْ لِي فِي ذُرِّيَّتِي إِنِّي تُبْتُ إِلَيْكَ

وَإِنِّي مِنَ الْمُسْلِمِينَ

And We have enjoined upon man, to his parents: good treatment. His mother carried him with hardship and gave birth to him with hardship, and his gestation and weaning [period] is thirty months. [He grows] until, when he reaches maturity and reaches [the age of] forty years, he says, "My Lord, enable me to be grateful for Your favor which You has bestowed upon me and upon my parents and to work righteousness

of which You will approve and make righteous for me my offspring. Indeed, I have repented to You, and indeed, I am of the Muslims".

Indeed, a man should seek the pleasure of his mother, even if he displeases all the other people for her sake. O Muslim brothers and sisters! Forbid our children to hurt our mothers with words or deeds, and strictly reject the complaints made by our wives about our mothers. We should rather exhort our wives to respect our mothers and to be more patient with her occasional mistakes. This is better for us.

How true is this anecdote not? Can we ever repay even one moment of the time and effort our mother gave to us? Has she not sacrificed her health and her wealth to bear us? What great pains did she not endure during childbirth? For two years we were helpless and she sacrificed her strength, her personal comfort to breast-feed and carry us around. How many times did we not cause her embarrassment and humiliation? Did she ever complain when she had to feed, clean and clothe us? No, she served us with love! How young and beautiful was she then? How healthy and energetic? Today she may be grey and wrinkled not so much with age, but endless hours, days and years of sacrifice as mother.

When we were ill, she suffered with us, fearful that some misfortune might befall us. In her worry and anxiety she would cry and beseech Allah to restore us to good health and grant us a long and prosperous life. In the same way, too, a good deed from us brings joy to her heart, but when we do something wrong, it fills her heart with disappointment and tears stream down her cheeks. Love deserves love!

Besides our mother no one deserves our mercy, our respect, our kindness and our bounty more than our father. It is he who struggled in the rain, the cold, and the heat of the day to earn enough to feed, clothe and educate us. He was responsible for teaching us what was of beneficent to us materially and spiritually. Let us take care not to display any animosity or unkindness towards him, for then our children will treat us in like manner.

Allah [swt] directs us in **Surah al-Isra' (17:23):**

وَقَضَىٰ رَبُّكَ أَلَّا تَعْبُدُوٓا۟ إِلَّآ إِيَّاهُ وَبِالْوَٰلِدَيْنِ إِحْسَـٰنًا إِمَّا يَبْلُغَنَّ عِندَكَ الْكِبَرَ أَحَدُهُمَآ أَوْ كِلَاهُمَا فَلَا تَقُل لَّهُمَآ أُفٍّ وَلَا تَنْهَرْهُمَا وَقُل لَّهُمَا قَوْلًا كَرِيمًا

And your Lord has decreed that you not worship except Him, and to parents, good treatment. Whether one or both of them reach old age [while] with you, say not to them [so much as], "uff," [an expression of disapproval or irritation] and do not repel them but speak to them a noble word.

We should address our parents gently and politely and consult them in our affairs, and make many supplications for them and ask Allah to forgive their sins. We should not raise our voice in their presence, nor look at them angrily or with contempt. We should not wave our hands when we talk to them, nor interrupt them when they speak. We should not argue with them, tell those lies, nor travel except after taking their permission. All of these are some aspects of being kind and dutiful to parents.

Many children think that kindness to parents is only practiced when it coincides with their own desires. However, kindness to parents cannot be achieved except by doing what pleases them, even if it is against the tendencies of the children.

The Prophet was asked about the great sins. He said, "They are: (1) to join others in worship with Allah, (2) To be undutiful to one's parents, (3) To kill a person [which Allah has forbidden to kill i.e. to commit the crime of murdering], (4) and to give a false witness." (Bukhari, book #48, hadith #821)

O Muslims! Fear Allah! Be aware that kindness or unkindness to our parents is an act that will be repaid likewise. If a Muslim obeys his parents, his children will obey him. If he honors his parents, his children will honor him, and vice versa. It was narrated in a hadith: "As you are kind to your parents, so will your children be kind to you." The rights of parents do not come to an end with their death. Some rights, actually, take effect after the parents have died and it is a religious obligation of good and dutiful children to fulfill them.

In the Qur'an, the Muslims have been exhorted, particularly, to pray for the salvation of their parents. It says in **Surah al-Isra (17:24):**

وَاخْفِضْ لَهُمَا جَنَاحَ الذُّلِّ مِنَ الرَّحْمَةِ وَقُل رَّبِّ ارْحَمْهُمَا كَمَا رَبَّيَانِي صَغِيرً

And lower to them the wing of humility out of mercy and say, "My Lord, have mercy upon them as they brought me up [when I was] small".

Let us pray to Alláh [swt], that he should grant our mothers and fathers, a very special place in Jannah. They cared for us and nurtured us with love and Imán, when we were helpless little children. And they continued to pray for us, when we became adults with children of our own. May Alláh help our own children, to continue this cycle of loving care and respect for their parents, so that the cycle may repeat from one generation to the next? May Alláh grant all of us His Love, His Mercy, and Forgiveness for our sins and for our human frailties? May Alláh allow us all to move ever closer to him in our thoughts, our words and our actions?

We ask Allah [swt] to guide us to be kind to our parents and to bestow His Mercy upon them and forgive them. **Amin!**

Riyya: The Hidden Shirk

Narrated 'Umar bin Al-Khattab: I heard Allah's Apostle saying, "The reward of deeds depends upon the intentions and every person will get the reward according to what he has intended. So whoever emigrated for worldly benefits or for a woman to marry, his emigration was for what he emigrated for." (Bukhari, book #1, hadith #1)

So it is clear that intension plays the pivotal role in getting the benefit from Allah [swt] for any of our actions. If the intension is solely to please Allah [swt], He will give us the full reward and in addition may be something more. If we pray or do good deeds as prescribed by Allah [swt] and His messenger, even then if the intension is to achieve glory and/or fame only for the individual, the good deeds will not be accepted by Allah [swt] and will not be rewarded.

Narrated Abu Musa: A man came to the Prophet and asked, "A man fights for war booty; another fights for fame and a third fights for showing off; which of them fights in Allah's Cause?" The Prophet said, "He who fights that Allah's Word [i.e. Islam] should be superior, fights in Allah's Cause." (Bukhari, book #52, hadith #65)

Narrated Al-Mustawrid: The Prophet [sas] said: "If anyone eats once at the cost of a Muslim's honor, Allah will give him a like amount of Jahannam to eat; if anyone clothes himself with a garment at the cost of a Muslim's honor, Allah will clothe him with like amount of Jahannam; and if anyone puts himself in a position of reputation and show Allah will disgrace him with a place of reputation and show on the Day of Resurrection". (Abu Dawud, Book #41, hadith #4863)

The primary cause of Riya is the weakness in Iman. When a person does not have strong faith in Allah [swt], he will love and intend the admiration of people over the pleasure of Allah.

Riyya comes from three sources: (1) The love of Praise; (2) Fear of Criticism; (3) Greed for wealth, rank, position.

The scholar [who acquired knowledge for fame], the martyr [who fought for fame], and the person who gave his money in charity [so people would say he is generous], all these three types of people desired the pleasure of people over the pleasure of Allah. The person who desires the praise of people must feel some pride in him, for he feels himself worthy of being praised. There is a danger, therefore, of him becoming arrogant and boastful.

Allah also warned against falling into the category of those Christians and Jews whom the Quran mentions in **Surah al-'Imran (3:188):**

لَا تَحْسَبَنَّ الَّذِينَ يَفْرَحُونَ بِمَا أَتَوا وَّيُحِبُّونَ أَن يُحْمَدُوا بِمَا لَمْ يَفْعَلُوا فَلَا تَحْسَبَنَّهُم بِمَفَازَةٍ مِّنَ الْعَذَابِ وَلَهُمْ عَذَابٌ أَلِيمٌ

And never think that those who rejoice in what they have perpetrated and like to be praised for what they did not do – never think them [to be] in safety from the punishment, and for them is a painful punishment.

No one likes to be criticized. A person may neglect a commandment of Allah in order to avoid the criticism of his peers. But for the faithful and true believers Allah [swt] says in **Surah al-Mai'dah (5:54):**

وَلاَ يَخَـٰفُونَ لَوۡمَةَ لاَبِمِ ذَٰلِكَ فَضۡلُ اللّهِ يُؤۡتِيهِ مَن يَشَآءُۚ وَاللّهُ وَسِـعٌ عَلِيمٌ

And do not fear the blame of a critic. That is the favor of Allah; He bestows it upon whom He wills. And Allah is all-Encompassing and Knowing.

A person who obeys certain commandments of Islam, not for the sake of Allah, but because he fears people will look down on him and criticize him if he does not do it. For example, a man may make his formal prayers in the mosque because he does not want people to criticize him for praying at home, or to think that he is not praying at all.

If a person is jealous of what other people possess, whether it is rank, money or power, then he will wish to have them. For example, if he is jealous of a position of a certain person in society, he will try by every possible means to attain the same position. Such desires lead people to spend their lives putting on a show so that people will admire their rank, money, or power.

Prophet [sas] said, "He who lets the people hear of his good deeds intentionally, to win their praise, Allah will let the people know his real intention [on the Day of Resurrection], and he who does good things in public to show off and win the praise of the people, Allah will disclose his real intention [and humiliate him]. (Bukhari, book #76, hadith #506)

In order to Avoid Riya, we should: Increase our knowledge of Islam, knowledge of Riya, always remembering one's shortcomings, remembering the day of Final Judgment and Heaven and Hell, always trying to accompany the pious people, and trying to not show off the good deeds.

Remove the causes of Riya` from ourselves by considering the opinion of people as important to us as animals and small children. Do not differentiate in our worship between the presence of people and their absence, or between their knowledge of our actions and their ignorance. Rather be conscious of the infinite knowledge of Allah alone.

O Allah! Save us from Riya [the hidden Shirk]. May Allah [swt] guide and help us in performing prayer and other good deeds for the sake of Allah [swt] only, and not for glory or fame or pride? **Amin!**

Sabr: Noble Quality of a Believer

As we travel though life we find ourselves in one of two situations: either something good is happening in our lives and in which case - as Muslims- our role is to thank Allah [swt] for the blessing, or something bad is happening to us, something we dislike and our role here is to wait with *Sabr*. This is the formula for a happy life, a life cruising towards the pleasure of Allah [swt].

The Believers are tested so that it may be known who is sincere and who is lying. In the Qur'an, Allah [swt] says in **Surah al-'Ankabut (29:2):**

أَحَسِبَ النَّاسُ أَن يُتْرَكُوا أَن يَقُولُوا ءَامَنَّا وَهُمْ لاَ يُفْتَنُونَ

Do the people think that they will be left to say, "we believe" and they will not be tested?

This is a rebuke in the form of a question, meaning that Allah will inevitably test His believing servants according to their level of faith. How we will be tested? Allah [swt] will test us by things that are very favorites to us – our wealth, our lives and lives of our near and dear ones, and the things that we dislike - fear and hunger as well, in this world. Allah [swt] says in **Surah al-Baqarah (2:155):**

وَلَنَبْلُوَنَّكُم بِشَيْءٍ مِّنَ الْخَوْفِ وَالْجُوعِ وَنَقْصٍ مِّنَ الأَمْوَالِ وَالأَنفُسِ وَالثَّمَرَتِ

And We will surely test you with something of fear and hunger and a loss of wealth and lives and fruits.

Hence, He tests us sometimes with the bounty and sometimes with the afflictions of fear and hunger, with something of [fear, hunger] meaning, a little of each; [loss of wealth] meaning, some of the wealth will be destroyed; [lives] meaning, losing friends, relatives and loved ones to death, [and fruits] meaning, the gardens and the farms will not produce the usual or expected amounts.

Much of what befalls us - the hard times - is the direct result of our own sins. Allah [swt] says in **Surah ash-Shuara (42:30):**

وَمَا أَصَبَكُم مِّن مُّصِيبَةٍ فَبِمَا كَسَبَتْ أَيْدِيكُمْ وَيَعْفُوا عَنكَثِيرٍ

And whatever strikes you of disaster - it is for what your hands have earned; but He pardons much.

The trials of this life are not words that can be written or statements made. These trials are the pains and the suffering that overwhelms man's soul and confront him with hardship and frustration. These trials are real situations that a man faces on the path of life, which shows his real character and what he is made off. We do not know when we will be tested, how we will be tested, how severe the test will be or how long the test will last. We do know on what we will be tested.

The question is what we should do when we are tested? The answer is given by Allah [swt] in **Surah al-Baqarah (2:155-156)**:

$$وَبَشِّرِ الصَّابِرِينَ - الَّذِينَ إِذَآ أَصَابَتْهُم مُّصِيبَةٌ قَالُوٓاْ إِنَّا لِلّهِ وَإِنَّآ إِلَيْهِ رَاجِعونَ - أُوْلَـٰئِكَ عَلَيْهِمْ صَلَوَاتٌ مِّن رَّبِّهِمْ وَرَحْمَةٌ وَأُوْلَـٰئِكَ هُمُ الْمُهْتَدُونَ$$

But give good tidings to the patient, who, when disaster strikes them, says, "Indeed we belong to Allah, and indeed to Him we will return." Those are the ones upon who are blessings from their Lord and mercy. And it is those who are the [rightly] guided.

Meaning, those who recite: إِنَّا لِلّهِ وَإِنَّآ إِلَيْهِ رَاجِعونَ to comfort themselves in the face of their loss and affliction, Allah [swt] assure them of three great rewards: His blessings and forgiveness, mercy, and guidance in the right path.

Brothers and sisters, what a great reward for being patient! What can we expect more than that?

But Allah [swt] reminds us in **Surah al-`Imran (3:186)** that to have patience and taqwa is an act of bravery:

$$لَتُبْلَوُنَّ فِىٓ أَمْوَٰلِكُمْ وَأَنفُسِكُمْ وَلَتَسْمَعُنَّ مِنَ الَّذِينَ أُوتُواْ الْكِتَـٰبَ مِن قَبْلِكُمْ وَمِنَ الَّذِينَ أَشْرَكُوٓاْ أَذًى كَثِيرًا وَإِن تَصْبِرُواْ وَتَتَّقُواْ فَإِنَّ ذَٰلِكَ مِنْ عَزْمِ الْأُمُورِ$$

You will surely be tested in your possessions and in yourselves. And you will surely hear from those who were given the Scripture before you [Jews and Christians] and from those who associate others with Allah much abuse. But if you are patient and fear Allah – indeed, that is of the matters [worthy] of determination.

There are several types of *Sabr*: one for avoiding the prohibitions and sins, one for acts of worship and obedience even if it is hard on the heart and the body. The second type carries more rewards than the first type. There is a third type of **sabr** required in the face of the afflictions and hardship, which is mandatory, likes repentance. Those who acquire these qualities will be among the *as - sabirin* whom Allah shall greet in the life Hereafter.

In an instantaneous world: a world of microwave dinners, instant coffee, live global television and worldwide Internet, we have become accustomed to immediacy and quick results. We have come to regard waiting as accidental in life rather than occupying a place at the core and center of human life. In the world of "want", the operative word becomes "now" This is where the Satan whispers 'shortcuts', 'loopholes', 'temptations' and 'quick band-aid fixes' to problems – the chief deceiver is at his best, and he lures people away from the straight path. It is during our times of difficulty and weakness that Shaytan is most active and tries very hard to influence us to his evil ways, as stated in the following verses of the Qur'an.

How Shaytan will mislead us during our hard times, are mentioned in the following verses of **Surah an–Nisa'** **(4:119):**

وَلَأُضِلَّنَّهُمْ وَلَأُمَنِّيَنَّهُمْ وَلَآمُرَنَّهُمْ فَلَيُبَتِّكُنَّ ءَاذَانَ الْأَنْعَمِ وَلَآمُرَنَّهُمْ فَلَيُغَيِّرُنَّ خَلْقَ اللَّهِ وَمَن يَتَّخِذِ الشَّيْطَنَ وَلِيًّا مِّن دُونِ اللَّهِ فَقَدْ خَسِرَ خُسْرَانًا مُّبِينًا

And I will mislead them, and I will arouse in them [sinful] desires, and I will command them so they will slit the ears of cattle, and I will command them so they will change the creation of Allah. And whoever takes Satan as an ally instead of Allah has certainly sustained a clear loss.

And in **Surah al-A'raf (7:17):**

ثُمَّ لَآتِيَنَّهُم مِّن بَيْنِ أَيْدِيهِمْ وَمِنْ خَلْفِهِمْ وَعَنْ أَيْمَنِهِمْ وَعَن شَمَآئِلِهِمْ وَلَا تَجِدُ أَكْثَرَهُمْ شَكِرِينَ

Then I will come to them from before them and on their right and on their left, and You will not find most of them grateful [to You].

Instructing the Prophet to have Patience, Allah [swt] commands in **Surah al-Ma`arij (70:5):**

فَاصْبِرْ صَبْرًا جَمِيلًا

So be patient with gracious patience.

Holy Prophet Mohammad [sas] said: "He who remains patient, Allah will bestow patience upon him, and he who is satisfied with what he has, Allah will make him self – sufficient. And there is no gift better and vast than sabr." (Bukhari, book #76, hadith #477)

Prophet [sas] said: "Strange are the ways of a believer for there is good in every affair of his and this is not the case with anyone else except in the case of a believer for if he has an occasion to feel delight, he thanks [Allah], thus there is a good for him in it, and if he gets into trouble and shows resignation [and endures it patiently], there is a good for him in it. (Muslim, book #042, hadith #7138)

There are several verses in the Holy Qur'an, which make reference to the value of applying the tools of sabr and perseverance in order to attain success in this world and in the hereafter. For example:

In **Surah Hud (11: 115)** Allah [swt] says:

وَاصْبِرْ فَإِنَّ اللَّهَ لَا يُضِيعُ أَجْرَ الْمُحْسِنِينَ-

And be patient, for indeed, Allah does not allow to be lost the reward of those who do good.

May Allah [swt] give us the strength and courage to bear the trials of this world with patience and perseverance? May He not place on us a burden greater than we can bear? May Allah [swt] forgive our shortcomings and may He be merciful on us on the Day of Reckoning, which is sure to come, sooner than we think. **Amin!**

Safety Net for the Disadvantaged in Islam

Allah [swt] created mankind and divided them into groups such as color of the body, language, region of residence, rich or poor etc. It is permissible in Islam to acquire wealth in an honest and righteous way. Everyone will be asked on the Day of Judgment how the wealth was acquired and how it was spent.

Allah [swt] has allocated a share of the wealth of the rich for the needy and disadvantaged groups of the society. Thus zakat is the share of the disadvantaged and poor groups in the society. Allah [swt] also prescribed in the Holy Quran how to behave with the orphans (according to Wikipedia, the free encyclopedia: Any child that has lost one parent is an orphan), the poor and the other disadvantaged groups. In **Surah al-Maun (107: 1-3)**, Allah [swt] sternly warns us regarding our behavior towards the orphans and the poor. When He says:

أَرَءَيْتَ الَّذِى يُكَذِّبُ بِالدِّينِ ـ فَذَلِكَ الَّذِى يَعَلَى طَعَامِ الْمِسْكِيدُ عُّ الْيَتِيمِ وَلاَ يَحُضُّ

Have you seen him who the Recompense? For, that is the one who drives away the orphan, and does not encourage the feeding of the poor.

In **Surah Adh-Dhuha (93: 9-10)**, Allah [swt] even taught our Prophet [sas] the way of treating the orphans and the poor as:

فَأَمَّا الْيَتِيمَ فَلَا تَقْهَر ـ وَأَمَّا السَّائِلَ فَلَا تَنْهَرْ

So as for the orphan, do not oppress [him]. And as for the petitioner [anyone who seeks aid or knowledge], do not repel [him].

In **Surah al-Baqarah (2:220)**, Allah [swt] teaches us how to behave with the orphans and take care of their property [wealth, they inherit] as:

وَيَسْئَلُونَكَ عَنِ الْيَتَـمَى قُلْ إِصْلاَ حُّ لَّهُمْ خَيْرٌ وَإِن تُخَالِطُوهُمْ فَإِخْوَنُـكُمْ وَاللَّهُ يَعْلَمُ الْمُفْسِدَ مِنَ الْمُصْلِحِ وَلَوْ شَآءَ اللَّهُ لَاعْنَتَـكُمْ إِنَّ اللَّهَ عَزِيزٌ حَكِيم

And they ask you about orphans. Say, "Improvement for them is the best. And if you associate with them - they are your brothers. And Allah knows the corruptor from the amender. And if Allah had wished, He could have put you in difficulty. Indeed, Allah is Exalted in Might and Wise".

 And also in **Surah al-An'am (6:152)**, Allah [swt] warns:

وَلاَتَقْرَبُواْ مَالَ الْيَتِيمِ إِلاَّ بِالَّتِي هِيَ أَحْسَنُ حَتَّى يَبْلُغَ أَشُدَّهُ وَأَوْفُواْ الْكَيْلَ وَالْمِيزَانَ بِالْقِسْطِ لاَ نُكَلِّفُ نَفْسًا إِلاَّ وُسْعَهَا وَإِذَا

قُلْتُمْ فَاعْدِلُواْ وَلَوْ كَانَ ذَا قُرْبَى وَبِعَهْدِ اللّهِ أَوْفُواْ ذَلِكُمْ وَصَّاكُم بِهِ لَعَلَّكُمْ تَذَكَّرُونَ

And do not approach the orphan's property except in a way that is best [intending improvement] until he reaches maturity. And give all measure and weight in justice. We do not charge any soul except [with that within] its capacity. And when you speak [testify], be just, even if [it concerns] a near relative. And fulfill [every] covenant of Allah. This has He instructed you that you may remember.

And also in **Surah al-Isra' (17:34):**

وَلاَتَقْرَبُواْ مَالَ الْيَتِيمِ إِلاَّ بِالَّتِي هِيَ أَحْسَنُ حَتَّى يَبْلُغَ أَشُدَّهُ وَأَوْفُواْ بِالْعَهْدِ إِنَّ الْعَهْدَ كَانَ مَسْؤُولاً

And do not approach the orphan's property except to improve it, until he reaches maturity. And fulfill [every] commitment. Indeed, the commitment is ever a [that about which one will be] questioned.

Similar warning is also given by Allah [swt] regarding handling the orphans' property in **Surah an-Nisa' (4:2):**

وَآتُواْ الْيَتَامَى أَمْوَالَهُمْ وَلاَ تَتَبَدَّلُواْ الْخَبِيثَ بِالطَّيِّبِ وَلاَ تَأْكُلُواْ أَمْوَالَهُمْ إِلَى أَمْوَالِكُمْ إِنَّهُ كَانَ حُوبًا كَبِيرًا

And give to the orphans their properties and do not substitute the defectives [of your own] for the good of [theirs]. And do not consume their properties into your own. Indeed, this is a great sin.

And also in **Surah an-Nisa' (4:10)** as:

إِنَّ الَّذِينَ يَأْكُلُونَ أَمْوَالَ الْيَتَامَى ظُلْمًا إِنَّمَا يَأْكُلُونَ فِي بُطُونِهِمْ نَارًا وَسَيَصْلَوْنَ سَعِيرًا

Indeed, those who eat up the property of orphans unjustly are only consuming into their bellies fire. And they will be burnt in a blazing Hellfire.

Allah [swt] directs us to financially help the poor and also describes the characteristic of the poor in **Surah al-Baqarah (2:273):**

لِلْفُقَرَاء الَّذِينَ أُحصِرُواْ فِي سَبِيلِ اللّهِ لاَ يَسْتَطِيعُونَ ضَرْبًا فِي الأَرْضِ يَحْسَبُهُمُ الْجَاهِلُ أَغْنِيَاء مِنَ التَّعَفُّفِ تَعْرِفُهُم بِسِيمَاهُمْ لاَ يَسْأَلُونَ

النَّاسَ إِلْحَافًا وَمَا تُنفِقُواْ مِنْ خَيْرٍ فَإِنَّ اللّهَ بِهِ عَلِيمٌ

[Charity is] for the poor who have been restricted from the cause of Allah, unable to move about the land [for trade or work]. An ignorant [person] would think them self-sufficient because of their modesty, but you will know them by their sign. They do not beg of people persistently [or at all]. And whatever you spend of good, Allah knows it well.

Characteristic of those who are to be considered for help and financial consideration is also mentioned **in Surah al-Baqarah (2:215):**

يَسْـَلُونَكَ مَاذَا يُنفِقُونَ قُلْ مَآ أَنفَقْتُم مِّنْ خَيْرٍ فَلِلْوَالِدَيْنِ وَالأَقْرَبِينَ وَالْيَتَـٰمَىٰ وَالْمَسَـٰكِينِ وَابْنِ السَّبِيلِ وَمَا تَفْعَلُوا مِنْ خَيْرٍ فَإِنَّ اللَّهَ

بِهِ عَلِيمٌ

They ask you [O Muhammad], what they should spend. Say, "Whatever you spend of good is [to be] for parents and relatives and orphans and the needy and the traveler. And whatever you do of good - indeed, Allah is Knowing of it."

A person asked Allah's Apostle. "What (sort of) deeds in or (what qualities of) Islam are good?" He replied, 'To feed (the poor) and greet those whom you know and those whom you don't know." (Bukhari, Book #2, Hadith #27)

What type of charity is accepted as righteousness is described in **Surah al- `Imran (2:92)** as:

لَن تَنَالُوا الْبِرَّ حَتَّىٰ تُنفِقُوا مِمَّا تُحِبُّونَ

By no means shall you attain Al-Birr unless You spend of that which you love.

And also in Surah Al-`Imarn (2:134), Allah (swt) said:

الَّذِينَ يُنفِقُونَ فِي السَّرَّآءِ وَالضَّرَّآءِ وَالْكَـٰظِمِينَ الْغَيْظَ وَالْعَافِينَ عَنِ النَّاسِ وَاللَّهُ يُحِبُّ الْمُحْسِنِينَ

Those who spend (in Allah's cause) in prosperity and in adversity, who repress anger, and who pardon men; verily, Allah loves the Muhsinin (the good-doers).

Allah's Apostle said, "The poor person is not the one who goes round the people and ask them for a mouthful or two (of meals) or a date or two but the poor is that who has not enough [money] to satisfy his needs and whose condition is not known to others, that others may give him something in charity, and who does not beg of people." (Bukhari, Book #24, Hadith #557)

Allah's Messenger [sas] also said: "Miskin is not he who is dismissed with one or two dates, and with one morsel or two morsels. [In fact] A miskin is he who abstains [from begging]. Read if you so desire [the verse]: "They beg not of men importunately" (ii. 273). This hadith has been narrated through another chain of transmitters (Muslim, book #005, hadith #2262)"

Allah (swt) has mentioned those who are to be preferred for receiving the zakat in **Surah at-Tawba (9:60):**

$$\text{إِنَّمَا الصَّدَقَاتُ لِلْفُقَرَاءِ وَالْمَسَاكِينِ وَالْعَامِلِينَ عَلَيْهَا وَالْمُؤَلَّفَةِ قُلُوبُهُمْ وَفِي الرِّقَابِ وَالْغَارِمِينَ وَفِي سَبِيلِ اللَّهِ وَابْنِ السَّبِيلِ}$$

$$\text{فَرِيضَةً مِّنَ اللَّهِ ۗ وَاللَّهُ عَلِيمٌ حَكِيمٌ}$$

Zakat expenditure is only for the needy and for those employed to collect [the funds]; and for bringing hearts together [for Islam] and for freeing the captives [or slaves] and for those in debt and for the cause of Allah and for the stranded traveler - an obligation [imposed] by Allah. And Allah is Knowing and Wise.

We must take into consideration the commands of Allah [swt] and the sayings of our beloved prophet [sas] in treating the orphans, the poor, and the disadvantaged groups. Care must be taken in identifying the needy and the poor while giving help [financial or otherwise] in the light of the instructions of Allah [swt] and the prophet [sas].

May Allah [swt] provide us the proper guidance so that we may spend our wealth and extend our help to the proper needy and moderate our behavior to them as prescribed by Allah [swt]? **Amin!**

Salat: Second Pillar of Islam

Prophet Muhammad [sas] said: "Prayer is the backbone of the religion, he who establishes it has established his religion and he who does not establish has abandoned faith."

Salat [contact or link prayer] is the obligatory prayers that are performed five times a day, and are a direct contact or link between the worshipper and Allah [swt] with no earthly intermediaries. Allah has mentioned this aspect of the prayer when He has said in **Surah al-Ankabut (29:45):**

اتْلُ مَآ أُوحِىَ إِلَيْكَ مِنَ الْكِتَبِ وَأَقِمِ الصَّلَوٰةَ إِنَّ الصَّلَوٰةَ تَنْهَى عَنِ الْفَحْشَآءِ وَالْمُنكَرِ وَلَذِكْرُ اللَّهِ أَكْبَرُ وَاللَّهُ يَعْلَمُ مَاتَصْنَعُونَ-

Recite, [O Muhammad], what has been revealed to you of the Book, and establish prayer. Indeed, prayer prohibits from immorality and evil deeds, and the remembrance of Allah is greater. And Allah knows that what you do.

Abu Al-`Aliyah commented on the Ayah:

إِنَّ الصَّلَوٰةَ تَنْهَى عَنِ الْفَحْشَآءِ وَالْمُنْكَرِ

Verily, the Salah prevents from immoral sins and evil wicked deeds. Prayer has three attributes, and any prayer that contains none of these attributes is not truly prayer: Being done purely and sincerely for Allah alone [*Ikhlas*], fear of Allah, and remembrance of Allah. Ikhlas makes a person do good deeds, fear prevents him from doing evil deeds, and the remembrance of Allah is the Qur'an which contains commands and prohibitions." (Tafsir-Ibn-Kathir)

The overall affect that the properly performed prayers should have upon humans is described in verses in the Qur'an in **Surah al-Marij (70:19-23):**

إِنَّ الإِنسَنَ خُلِقَ هَلُوعاً- إِذَا مَسَّهُ الشَّرُّ جَزُوعاً- وَ إِذَا مَسَّهُ الْخَيْرُ مَنُوعاً- إِلاَّ الْمُصَلِّينَ الَّذِينَ هُمْ عَلَى صَلاَتِهِمْ دَآئِمُونَ-

Indeed, mankind was created as impatient; when evil touches him, impatient, and when good touches him withholding [of it], except those who are devoted to prayer and those who are constant in their prayer.

The five-time prayers become obligatory from the moment a person embraces Islam. This is an extremely important tenet of Islam and has been enjoined with great emphasis in the Holy Qur'an. It is a form of worship that establishes the link between man and his Creator and Benefactor Allah. Through 'Salah' a person communes with his Rabb, the Creator and the Sustainer of the Universe.

Praying to the Creator on a daily basis is the best way to cultivate in a man a sound personality and to actualize his aspiration. Allah [swt] does not need man's prayer because He is free of all needs. Prayer is for our immeasurable benefit, and the blessings are beyond imagination. The importance of the prayer in Islam cannot be understated. It is the second pillar of Islam that the Prophet [sas] mentioned after mentioning the testimony of faith, by which one becomes a Muslim. It was made obligatory upon all the prophets and for all people.

Allah has declared its obligatory status under majestic circumstances. For example, when Allah spoke directly to Moses, He said in **Surah Ta-Ha (20:13-4):**

وَأَنَا اخْتَرْتُكَ فَاسْتَمِعْ لِمَا يُوحَى - إِنَّنِى أَنَا اللَّهُ لَا إِلَهَ إِلَّا أَنَا فَاعْبُدْنِى وَأَقِمِ الصَّلَوةَ لِذِكْرِى

And I have chosen you, so listen to what is revealed [to you]. Indeed, I am Allah. There is no deity except Me, so worship Me and establish prayer for My remembrance. Similarly, the prayers were made obligatory upon the Prophet Muhammad [sas] during his ascension to heaven. Furthermore, when Allah praises the believers, such as in the beginning of **Surah al-Muminun (23:2, 9):**

الَّذِينَ هُمْ فِى صَلَاتِهِمْ خَشِعُون -

Those who are during their prayer humbly submissive,

وَالَّذِينَ هُمْ عَلَى صَلَوَتِهِمْ يُحَفِظُون -

And those who strictly maintain their prayer.

One of the first descriptions [about the believers] that Allah states is their adherence to the prayers. Khasiu`n means a state where we can feel the presence of Allah [swt] while praying. If it is not possible to achieve that state, we will feel that Allah [swt] is seeing us.

Brothers and sisters in Islam, when we think of somebody, our dear and near ones [dead or alive] we dearly love, we can feel their presence. Now, while we are praying, we should feel the presence of Allah [swt] who created us and loves us dearly in our *"Ruku"* and *"Sujud"*. We should sincerely try to achieve that state in the course of our salah.

And *"hafizone"* means guarding the salah, which basically means performing salah in the appointed times regularly.

Allah (swt) also says in **Surah al-Baiyyinah (98:5):**

وَمَا أُمِرُوا إِلَّا لِيَعْبُدُوا اللَّهَ مُخْلِصِينَ لَهُ الدِّينَ حُنَفَآءَ وَيُقِيمُوا الصَّلَوةَ وَيُؤْتُوا الزَّكَوةَ وَذَلِكَ دِينُ القَيِّمَةِ -

And they were not commanded except to worship Allah, [being] sincere tin religion, inclining to truth, and to establish regular prayer and to give zakah. And that is the correct religion.

The importance of the prayers lies in the fact that no matter what actions one performs in his life, the most important aspect is one's relationship to Allah, that is, one's faith [*Iman*], God-consciousness [*taqwa*], sincerity [*ikhlas*] and worship of Allah [`*ibadah*]. This relationship with Allah is demonstrated and put into practice, as well as improved and increased, by the prayer. Worship cannot be complete or perfect unless it is accompanied by both fear and hope. Fear stops one from doing things that are forbidden, and hope makes one do more good deeds

Contact prayer [Salah] is a distinct entity from worship in its wider sense that is communicating our feelings to Allah [swt] at any time in any place and asking for His guidance, help and forgiveness, an ingredient of life which is highly commendable. Salah takes a special form and content, where both body and soul are harmoniously involved. As for the Hereafter, Allah's forgiveness and pleasure is closely related to the prayers.

In Salah every muscle of the body joins the soul and the mind in the worship and glory of Allah. Prayer is an act of worship. It is a matchless and unprecedented formula of intellectual meditation and spiritual devotion, of moral elevation and physical exercise, all combined.

By speaking certain words in Salah, we, in turn, are opening a gateway to our Rabb. Interestingly, Al-Fateha, the surah that we recite during our Salah means "the opening or the key". It is like making "contact [Salah]" with Allah [swt] through a "key (*Al-Fateha*)" or an "opening". Also these words have been so numerically structured that brings about that "opening" to "contact" our creator. For example, when we recite [*Al-Fateha*] our lips will touch each other exactly "19" times.

In fact Allah [swt] tells us in **Surah an-Nisa' (4:103):**

فَإِذَا قَضَيْتُمُ الصَّلَوٰةَ فَاذْكُرُوا اللَّهَ قِيَـٰمًا وَقُعُودًا وَعَلَىٰ جُنُوبِكُمْ فَإِذَا اطْمَأْنَنتُمْ فَأَقِيمُوا الصَّلَوٰةَ إِنَّ الصَّلَوٰةَ كَانَتْ عَلَى الْمُؤْمِنِينَ كِتَـٰبًا مَّوْقُوتًا-

Just as performing 'Salah' is obligatory, learning to perform it in the prescribed way is also obligatory. So that one should know what he/she is saying to his/her Rabb, and enjoy the full blessings and benefits of praying. And when you have completed the prayer, remember Allah standing, sitting, or [lying] on your sides. But when you become secure, re-establish [regular] prayer. Indeed, prayer has been decreed upon the believers at fixed hours.

Further information is necessary to perform 'Salah ' under abnormal conditions i.e. sickness, war, etc. Almighty Allah has granted some concessions in these conditions in the Holy Qur'an. Allah [swt] says in **Surah an-Nisa' (4:101):**

وَإِذَا ضَرَبْتُمْ فِي الْأَرْضِ فَلَيْسَ عَلَيْكُمْ جُنَاحٌ أَن تَقْصُرُوا مِنَ الصَّلَوٰةِ إِنْ خِفْتُمْ أَن يَفْتِنَكُمُ الَّذِينَ كَفَرُوا إِنَّ الْكَـٰفِرِينَ كَانُوا لَكُمْ عَدُوًّا مُّبِينًا-

And when you travel throughout the land, there is no blame upon you for shortening the prayer, [especially] if you fear that those who disbelieve may disrupt [or attack] you. Indeed, the disbelievers are ever to you a clear open enemy.

Allah [swt] also says in **Surah al-Muzammil (73:20):**

عَلِمَ أَن سَيَكُونُ مِنكُم مَّرْضَى وَءَاخَرُونَ يَضْرِبُونَ فِي الْأَرْضِ يَبْتَغُونَ مِن فَضْلِ اللَّهِ وَءَاخَرُونَ يُقَـٰتِلُونَ فِي سَبِيلِ-

He has known that there will be among you those who are ill and others traveling throughout the land seeking [something] of the bounty of Allah and others fighting for the cause of Allah.

Prayer, obligatory and spontaneous, is an immense spiritual treasure to be tapped. It inspires peace, purity and tranquility and instills companionship with Allah [swt]. It amazingly reduces the hustle and bustle of life to tame proportions. By their spacing to five times a day, including its beginning, prayers tend to maintain a therapeutic level and practically leave no room for mischievous thought or deed.

Requirements of prayer: performing of ablution [*wudu*], purity of the whole body, clothes [basically these will be impure and cannot be purified at all if our sustenance is based on unlawful (*haram*) income] by using water, but special permission is allowed in special circumstances, as Allah [swt] says in **Surah an-Nisa' (4:43):**

يَـٰٓأَيُّهَا الَّذِينَ ءَامَنُوا لَا تَقْرَبُوا الصَّلَوٰةَ وَأَنتُمْ سُكَـٰرَىٰ حَتَّىٰ تَعْلَمُوا مَا تَقُولُونَ وَلَا جُنُبًا إِلَّا عَابِرِى سَبِيلٍ حَتَّىٰ تَغْتَسِلُوا وَإِن كُنتُم مَّرْضَىٰ أَوْ

عَلَىٰ سَفَرٍ أَوْ جَآءَ أَحَدٌ مِّنكُم مِّنَ الْغَآئِطِ أَوْ لَـٰمَسْتُمُ النِّسَآءَ فَلَمْ تَجِدُوا مَآءً فَتَيَمَّمُوا صَعِيدًا طَيِّبًا فَامْسَحُوا بِوُجُوهِكُمْ

وَأَيْدِيكُمْ إِنَّ اللَّهَ كَانَ عَفُوًّا غَفُورًا-

O you who have believed, do not approach prayer while you are in a druken state until you know what you are saying or in a state of [sexually impure], except those passing through [a place of prayer], until you have washed [your entire body]. And if you are ill or on a journey or one of you comes from the place of relieving himself [toilet] or you have contacted women [had sexual intercourse] and find no water, then seek clean earth and wipe over your faces and hands [with it]. Indeed, Allah is ever Pardoning and Forgiving.

And ground used for prayer, dressing properly, having the intention, concentrating fully the body and mind in such a way as if we see Allah [swt] or at least Allah [swt] is seeing us, and facing the Qiblah [the direction of the Ka'ba at Mecca]. Only around the Ka'ba mosque in Makkah do Muslims stand in circles for their prayers [quite an impressive scene].

When we stand up for salat our attention must be concentrated to the fact that we are standing before our creator Allah (swt) and as if we see Him or at least He sees us. Allah [swt] says in **Surah ash-Shua'ra' (26:218-9):**

الَّذِى يَرَاكَ حِينَ تَقُومُ -- وَتَقَلُّبَكَ فِى السَّاجِدِينَ -

Who sees you when you stand up and your movements among those who prostrate? When you pray - He sees you - when you pray alone and when you pray in congregation. This was the view of `Ikrimah, `Ata' Al-Khurasani and Al-Hasan Al-Basri. We must try to perform Salat as if this will be the last Salat of our life because we don't know whether we will be alive up to the time of the next Salat. (Tafsir-Ibn-Kathir)

Stealing is an offense. One of the worst forms of theft or cheating is cheating in prayer. The Messenger of Allah [swt] said: "The worst type of thief is the one who steals from his prayer." The people asked, "O Messenger of Allah, how can a person steal from his prayer?" He said: "By not doing rukoo' and sujood properly." (Ahmad, 5/310)

But stealing in salat [not praying properly] is a great offense. Narrated Abu Hurairah: Allah's Apostle entered the mosque and a person followed him. The man prayed and went to the Prophet and greeted him. The Prophet returned the greeting and said to him, "Go back and pray, for you have not prayed." The man went back prayed in the same way as before, returned and greeted the Prophet who said, "Go back and pray, for you have not prayed." This happened thrice. The man said, "By Him Who sent you with the Truth, I cannot offer the Prayer in a better way than this. Please, teach me how to pray." The Prophet said, "When you stand for Prayer say Takbir and then recite from the Holy Qur'an [of what you know by heart] and then bow till you feel at ease. Then raise your head and stand up straight, then prostrate till you feel at ease during your prostration, then sit with calmness till you feel at ease [do not hurry] and do the same in all your Prayers (Bukhari, book #12, hadith #759).

Bowing down and prostrating oneself [to Allah] interjecting "Glory to my Lord the Great", "Glory to my Lord the Highest", Allah [swt] listens to those who thank Him, the prayer is concluded in the sitting position by reiterating the affirmation of the faith, the Shahada.

Salat [Contact Prayers] are obligatory at dawn, noon, mid-afternoon, sunset and nightfall, and thus determine the rhythm of the entire day. Although it is preferable to worship together in a mosque, a Muslim may pray almost anywhere, such as in fields, offices, factories and universities. Visitors to the Muslim world are struck by the centrality of prayers in daily life.

Ziyād said that He delivered the adhān, and Bilāl desired to call out the iqāmah but the Prophet [sas] said:"O, brother of *Sudā'*! The one who calls out the adhān shall call out the iqāmah."(Ahmad, book #4, hadith# 169)

Many Muslims do not know that all the five prayers are clearly mentioned in several verses of the Holy Qur'an and that all the steps we do are found also in the Quran. Allah [swt] gave us the times for the Salat [contact Prayers] in the Quran. In **Surah Hud (11:114)** Allah [swt] says:

وَأَقِمِ الصَّلَوةَ طَرَفِى النَّهَارِ وَزُلَفاً مِّنَ الَّيْلِ إِنَّ الْحَسَنَتِ يُذْهِبْنَ السَّيِّئَتِ ذَلِكَ ذِكْرَى لِلذَّكِرِينَ -

And establish prayer at the two ends of the day and at the approach of the night. Indeed, good deeds remove the evil deeds. That is a reminder for those who remember.

In **Surah al-Isra' (17:78)** Allah [swt] says:

أَقِمِ الصَّلَوٰةَ لِدُلُوكِ الشَّمْسِ إِلَىٰ غَسَقِ الَّيْلِ وَقُرْءَانَ الْفَجْرِ إِنَّ قُرْءَانَ الْفَجْرِ كَانَ مَشْهُودًا

Establish prayer at the decline of the sun [from its meridian] until the darkness of the night and [also] the Qur'an [recitation] at dawn. Indeed, the recitation of dawn is ever witnessed.

In **Surah al-Baqarah (2:238)** Allah [swt] says:

حَٰفِظُواْ عَلَى الصَّلَوَٰتِ وَالصَّلَوٰةِ الْوُسْطَىٰ وَقُومُواْ لِلَّهِ قَٰنِتِين

Guard strictly [five obligatory] prayers and in particular the middle ['asr] prayer and stand before Allah devoutly obedient.

In **Surah al-Isra' (17:110)** Allah [swt] tell us how to recite from the Quran in prayers:

وَلَا تَجْهَرْ بِصَلَاتِكَ وَلَا تُخَافِتْ بِهَا وَابْتَغِ بَيْنَ ذَلِكَ سَبِيلًا

And do not recite [too] loudly in your prayer or [too] quietly but seek between that an [intermediate] way.

In **Surah al-Hajj (22:77)** Allah [swt] says:

يَٰٓأَيُّهَا الَّذِينَ ءَامَنُواْ ارْكَعُواْ وَاسْجُدُواْ وَاعْبُدُواْ رَبَّكُمْ وَافْعَلُواْ الْخَيْرَ لَعَلَّكُمْ تُفْلِحُون

O you, who have believed, bow and prostrate and worship your Rabb and do good - that you may be succeed.

What we say when we bow down: "*Subhana Rabbiya Al-Azeem*", can be found in **Surah al-Waqi'ah (56:74):**

فَسَبِّحْ بِاسْمِ رَبِّكَ الْعَظِيم

So exalt the name of your Lord, the Most Great.

What we say when we fall prostrate: "*Subhana Rabbiya Al-A'ala*" can be found in **Surah al-A'la (87:1):**

سَبِّحِ اسْمَ رَبِّكَ الْأَعْلَى

Exalt the name of your Lord, the Most High.

The noon congregational prayer of Friday afternoon is mandated to be a collective and must be said in a Mosque whenever possible, and is preceded by a sermon [*Khutbah*]. The importance of Friday has been narrated in authentic collection of hadiths as: It was during Friday when Allah finished the creation, the sixth day, during which Allah created the heavens and earth. During Friday, Allah created Adam, and he was placed in Paradise, and ironically, it was a Friday when he was taken out of Paradise. It will be on a Friday when the Last Hour will commence. There is a time on Friday at which no Muslim would stand and pray and beg Allah for what is good but He would give it to him; and he pointed with his hand that [this time] is short and narrow. (Muslim, book #004, hadith #1850)

In **Surah al-Jumu'ah (62:9)** Allah [swt] says:

يَٰٓأَيُّهَا ٱلَّذِينَ ءَامَنُوٓا۟ إِذَا نُودِىَ لِلصَّلَوٰةِ مِن يَوْمِ ٱلْجُمُعَةِ فَٱسْعَوْا۟ إِلَىٰ ذِكْرِ ٱللَّهِ وَذَرُوا۟ ٱلْبَيْعَ ذَٰلِكُمْ خَيْرٌ لَّكُمْ إِن كُنتُمْ تَعْلَمُونَ

O you who have believed, when the [the adhan] is called for the prayer on the day of Jumu`ah [Friday], then proceed to the remembrance of Allah and leave off business. That is better for you, if you only knew.

The Imam [*prayer leader*] is not a priest nor need be the same person every time, but considerations of scholarship and knowledge of the Qur'an and the religion is exercised in choosing him.

Brothers and sisters in faith! We perform salat but yet we do things prohibited by Allah (swt). Why we do this? What is wrong with our salat? The reason is – we do not offer salat as we are supposed to do. Look at the advice of the Pophet (sas):

Once Allah's Apostle entered the mosque and a person followed him. The man prayed and went to the Prophet and greeted him. The Prophet returned the greeting and said to him, "Go back and pray, for you have not prayed." The man went back prayed in the same way as before, returned and greeted the Prophet who said, "Go back and pray, for you have not prayed." This happened thrice. The man said, "By Him Who sent you with the Truth, I cannot offer the prayer in a better way than this. Please, teach me how to pray." The Prophet said, "When you stand for Prayer say Takbir and then recite from the Holy Qur'an (of what you know by heart) and then bow till you feel at ease. Then raise your head and stand up straight, then prostrate till you feel at ease during your prostration, then sit with calmness till you feel at ease (do not hurry) and do the same in all your prayers (Bukhari, Book 12, hadith 759).

Brothers and sisters in Islam, let us make attempts to learn and obey how our beloved Prophet used to perform salat and we must follow him in performing salat and then let us hope to be benefitted from salat.

The prayers are a type of purification for a human being. He turns and meets with his Rabb five times a day. As alluded to above, this repeated standing in front of Allah should keep the person from performing sins during the day. May Allah [swt] gives us the strength, Proper guidance and help to perform Salat with full concentration so that we may derive full benefits and Allah's forgiveness. **Amin!**

Shall We be Resurrected [Given Life Again]?

It is obligatory for the Muslims to believe on the Day of Resurrection. But still we, many a time in our lives, have hesitation or doubt creep in our mind about life hereafter. In **Surah Ya-Sin (36:77-9)**, Allah (swt) reminds us,

أَوَلَمْ يَرَ الإِنسَانُ أَنَّا خَلَقْنَاهُ مِن نُّطْفَةٍ فَإِذَا هُوَ خَصِيمٌ مُّبِينٌ ۔ وَضَرَبَ لَنَا مَثَلاً وَنَسِيَ خَلْقَهُ قَالَ مَن يُحِي الْعِظَمَ وَهِيَ رَمِيمٌ ۔ قُلْ يُحْيِيهَا الَّذِى أَنشَأَهَا أَوَّلَ مَرَّةٍ وَهُوَ بِكُلِّ خَلْقٍ عَلِيمٌ ۔

Does man not consider that We created him from a [mere] sperm-drop - then at once [as soon as he becomes self-sufficient] he is clear adversary? And he presents for Us an example [attempting to establish the finality of death] and forgets his own creation. He says: "Who will give life to bones while they are rotten and have become dust"? Say, "He will give them life who created them for the first time; and He is, of all creation, knowing."

Allah [swt] reminds us in these all creation, yet how we were created initially. Allah [swt] reassures us that He will give us life again as He did earlier. Let us think, is not the initial creation difficult? If our own creation, let it be in art, writing, somehow get lost, it becomes easy to recreate it with much less effort than the initial one. Then why doubt will cast our mind about our recreation by the Almighty creator Allah [swt]?

Allah [swt] cites an example from the parable of Musa [as], how eighty of his followers who insisted to see Allah [swt] in their own eyes were dead from the sight of light of Allah [swt] and later given back their life again on the request of Allah [swt] in **Surah al-Baqarah (2:55-56)**:

وَإِذْ قُلْتُمْ يَمُوسَى لَن نُّؤْمِنَ لَكَ حَتَّى نَرَى اللَّهَ جَهْرَةً فَأَخَذَتْكُمُ الصَّعِقَةُ وَأَنتُمْ تَنظُرُونَ ۔ ثُمَّ بَعَثْنَاكُم مِّن بَعْدِ مَوْتِكُمْ لَعَلَّكُمْ تَشْكُرُونَ

And [recall] when you said, "O Musa, We shall never believe you until we see Allah outright"; so the thunderbolt took you while you were looking on. Then We revived you after your death that perhaps you will be grateful.

And [remember] when you said: "O Musa! We shall never believe in you until we see Allah plainly.'" - Means, "Publicly'", "So that we gaze at Allah." Also, `Urwah bin Ruwaym said that Allah's statement,

[وَأَنتُمْ تَنظُرُونَ]

[While you were looking] means, "Some of them were struck with lightning while others were watching" Allah resurrected those, and struck the others with lightning. As-Suddi commented on,

$$[\text{فَأَخَذَتْكُمُ الصَّاعِقَةُ}]$$

[But you were seized with a bolt of lightning] saying; "They died, and Musa stood up crying and supplicating to Allah, `O Lord! What should I say to the Children of Israel when I go back to them after You destroyed the best of them?

$$[\text{لَوْ شِئْتَ أَهْلَكْتَهُم مِّن قَبْلُ وَإِيَّـىَ أَتُهْلِكُنَا بِمَا فَعَلَ السُّفَهَاءُ مِنَّآ}]$$

[If it had been Your will, You could have destroyed them and me before; would You destroy us for the deeds of the foolish ones among us] Allah revealed to Musa [as] that these seventy men were among those who worshipped the calf. Afterwards, Allah brought them back to life one man at a time, while the rest of them were watching how Allah was bringing them back to life. That is why Allah's said,

$$[\text{ثُمَّ بَعَثْنَاكُم مِّن بَعْدِ مَوْتِكُمْ لَعَلَّكُمْ تَشْكُرُونَ}]$$

Then We raised you up after your death, so that you might be grateful. (Tafsir-Ibn-Kathir).

Allah [swt] also referring to another incident from the parable of Musa [as] where a dead man was turned alive by Allah [swt] for a short period of time in **Surah al-Baqarah (2:72-73):**

$$\text{وَإِذْ قَتَلْتُمْ نَفْسًا فَادَّارَأْتُمْ فِيهَا وَاللَّهُ مُخْرِجٌ مَّا كُنتُمْ تَكْتُمُونَ - فَقُلْنَا اضْرِبُوهُ بِبَعْضِهَا كَذَلِكَ يُحْيِ اللَّهُ الْمَوْتَى وَيُرِيكُمْ آيَتِهِ لَعَلَّكُمْ تَعْقِلُونَ}$$

And [recall] when you killed a man and disputed [exchanged accusations and denials] over it, but Allah was to bring out that which you were concealing. **So We said, "Strike him [the slain man] with a part of it [the cow]." Thus does Allah bring the dead to life, and He shows you His signs [proofs, evidences, etc.] that you might understand."**

This Ayah demonstrates Allah's ability in bringing the dead back to life. Allah made this incident proof against the Jews that the Resurrection shall occur, and ended their disputing and stubbornness over the dead person.

Again Allah [swt] informs Prophet Muhammad [sas] how a group of people restored the life of a group of people after their death in **Surah al-Baqarah (2:243):**

$$\text{أَلَمْ تَرَ إِلَى الَّذِينَ خَرَجُوا مِن دِيَارِهِمْ وَهُمْ أُلُوفٌ حَذَرَ الْمَوْتِ فَقَالَ لَهُمُ اللَّهُ مُوتُوا ثُمَّ أَحْيَـهُمْ إِنَّ اللَّهَ لَذُو فَضْلٍ عَلَى النَّاسِ وَلَـكِنَّ أَكْثَرَ النَّاسِ لاَ يَشْكُرُونَ}$$

Have you [O Muhammad] not considered those who went left their homes in the thousands, fearing death? Allah said to them, "Die"; then He restored them to life. And Allah is full of bounty to the people, but most of the people do not show gratitude.

Furthermore, several scholars among the Salaf said that these people were the residents of a city during the time of the Children of Israel. The weather in their land did not suit them and an epidemic broke out. They fled their land fearing death and took refuge in the wilderness. They later arrived at a fertile valley and they filled what is between its two sides. Then Allah sent two angels to them, one from the lower side and the other from the upper side of the valley. The angels screamed once and all the people died instantly, just as the death of one man. They were later moved to a different place, where walls and graves were built around them.

They all perished, and their bodies rotted and disintegrated. Long afterwards, one of the Prophets of the Children of Israel, whose name was Hizqil [Ezekiel], passed by them and asked Allah to bring them back to life by his hand. Allah accepted his supplication and commanded him to say, "O rotted bones, Allah commands you to come together." The bones of everybody were brought together. Allah then commanded him to say, "O bones, Allah commands you to be covered with flesh, nerves and skin." That also happened while Hizqil was watching. Allah then commanded him to say, "O souls, Allah commands you to return, each to the body that it used to inhabit." They all came back to life, looked around and proclaimed, "All praise is due to You [O Allah!]. And there is no deity worthy of worship except You." Allah brought them back to life after they had perished long ago (Tafsir-Ibn-Kathir).

Allah [swt] is putting illustration of a man [Uzair (as)] who saw a ruined town and asked himself how Allah [swt] will ever bring to life again. The man was kept dead for one hundred years and then raised him again; the story is described in **Surah al-Baqarah (2:259):**

وَ كَالَّذِى مَرَّ عَلَى قَرْيَةٍ وَهِىَ خَاوِيَةٌ عَلَى عُرُوشِهَا قَالَ أَنَّى يُحْيِ هَـذِهِ اللَّهُ بَعْدَ مَوْتِهَا فَأَمَاتَهُ اللَّهُ مِائَةَ عَامٍ ثُمَّ بَعَثَهُ قَالَ كَمْ لَبِثْتَ قَالَ لَبِثْتُ يَوْمًا أَوْ بَعْضَ يَوْمٍ قَالَ بَل لَّبِثْتَ مِائَةَ عَامٍ فَانظُرْ إِلَى طَعَامِكَ وَشَرَابِكَ لَمْ يَتَسَنَّهْ وَانظُرْ إِلَى حِمَارِكَ وَلِنَجْعَلَكَ ءَايَةً لِّلنَّاسِ وَانظُرْ إِلَى الْعِظَامِ كَيْفَ نُنشِزُهَا ثُمَّ نَكْسُوهَا لَحْمًا فَلَمَّا تَبَيَّنَ لَهُ قَالَ أَعْلَمُ أَنَّ اللَّهَ عَلَى كُلِّ شَيْءٍ قَدِيرٌ

[Such an example] as the one who passed by a town which has had fallen into ruin. He said, "How will Allah bring this to life after its death?" So Allah caused him to die for a hundred years; then He revived him. He said, "How long have you remained?" He [the man] said, "I have remained [dead] a day or part of a day." He said, "Rather, [you have remained (dead] one hundred years. Look at your food and your drink; it has not changed with time. And look at your donkey; and We will make you a sign for the people. And look at the bones [of this donkey] - how We raise them together and them We clothe them with flesh." And when it became clear to him, he said, "I know that Allah is over all things competent."

Allah [swt] demonstrated His power by showing how He can give life to dead to Ibrahim [as] known as Khalil Ullah in **Surah al-Baqarah (2:260):**

وَإِذْ قَالَ إِبْرَٰهِيمُ رَبِّ أَرِنِي كَيْفَ تُحْيِ الْمَوْتَىٰ قَالَ أَوَلَمْ تُؤْمِن قَالَ بَلَىٰ وَلَٰكِن لِّيَطْمَئِنَّ قَلْبِي قَالَ فَخُذْ أَرْبَعَةً مِّنَ الطَّيْرِ فَصُرْهُنَّ إِلَيْكَ ثُمَّ اجْعَلْ عَلَىٰ كُلِّ جَبَلٍ مِّنْهُنَّ جُزْءًا ثُمَّ ادْعُهُنَّ يَأْتِينَكَ سَعْيًا وَاعْلَمْ أَنَّ اللَّهَ عَزِيزٌ حَكِيمٌ

And [mention] when Ibrahim said, "My Lord, Show me how You give life to the dead." [Allah] said, "Have you not believed?" He [Ibrahim] said, "Yes, but [I ask] only that my heart may be satisfied." [Allah] said, "Take four birds and commit them to yourself [train them to come to you on command]. Then [after slaughtering them] put on each hill a portion of them; then call them - they will come [flying] to you in haste". And know that Allah is Exalted in Mighty, Wise.

Ibrahim [as] wanted to solidify his knowledge about resurrection by actually witnessing it with his eyes.

The Messenger of Allah [swt] said,

«نَحْنُ أَحَقُّ بِالشَّكِّ مِنْ إِبْرَاهِيمَ إِذْ قَالَ رَبِّ أَرِنِي كَيْفَ تُحْيِ الْمَوْتَىٰ قَالَ أَوَلَمْ تُؤْمِن قَالَ بَلَىٰ وَلَٰكِن لِّيَطْمَئِنَّ قَلْبِي»

We are more liable to be in doubt than Ibrahim when he said, "My Lord! Show me how You give life to the dead.'" Allah said, "Don't you believe'?" Ibrahim said, "Yes [I believe], but [I ask] in order to be stronger in faith.'" (Bukhari, book # 55, hadith # 591)

The Prophet's statement in the Hadith means, "We are more liable to seek certainty."

Allah [swt] narrated the story of the men of the cave showing His power of giving life to the dead in **Surah al-Kahf (18:25):**

وَلَبِثُوا فِي كَهْفِهِمْ ثَلَاثَ مِائَةٍ سِنِينَ وَازْدَادُوا تِسْعًا

And they remained in their cave for three hundred years and exceeding nine.

Here Allah tells His Messenger the length of time the people of the Cave spent in their cave, from the time when He caused them to sleep until the time when He resurrected them and caused the people of that era to find them. The length of time was three hundred plus nine years in lunar years, which is three hundred years in solar years.

Brothers and sisters in Islam, the above stories elucidated in the Holy Qur`an bears testimony to His power of resurrecting the dead. O Allah! Provide us with your help and bestow on us Your mercy so that our faith in bringing the dead to life again increases, and no doubt about it ever creep in our mind. **Amin!**

Should We not be Grateful to Allah [swt]?

Of all the creations of Allah [swt], human beings are designated as the best of creation. Allah [swt] has given human beings not only a structure like other creations, but also spiritual faculties that were not given to any other creature including the angels. Allah [swt] tells us how He has honored the sons of Adam and made them noble by creating them in the best and most perfect of forms, as in **Surah at-Tin (95:4):**

$$\text{لَقَدْ خَلَقْنَا الْإِنسَـٰنَ فِى أَحْسَنِ تَقْوِيمٍ}$$

We have certainly created man in the best of stature [balanced in form and nature].

Brothers and sisters in Islam! If we ponder on the above ayah why we should not be grateful to Allah [swt]? Allah [swt] created us in the best of form, which means nothing is lacking in the creation of human beings. Allah [swt] admittedly made our physical structure, colors, language, possession of worldly goodies like- wealth, children, siblings, status, power, ways of livings different in order to test us whether we remain grateful to Him.

Let us try to understand when Allah [swt] proclaimed in **Surah Ibrahim (14:7):**

$$\text{وَإِذْ تَأَذَّنَ رَبُّكُمْ لَئِن شَكَرْتُمْ لَأَزِيدَنَّكُمْ وَلَئِن كَفَرْتُمْ إِنَّ عَذَابِى لَشَدِيدٌ}$$

And [remember] when your Lord proclaimed, "If you are grateful, I will surely increase you [in favor]; but if you deny, indeed, My punishment is severe."

Thus if we are thankful to Allah [swt] and accept what Allah [swt] has provided us with gratitude, He is promising to increase His favors on us. We always try to look at the worldly things given to others and consider ourselves deprived, but we do not at all try to console ourselves by looking at those who are not given the prosperities as ours. For example, if a man has one eye, he should be grateful to Allah [swt] as he has at least one eye when his brother is blind and cannot see any beauty of the creation of Allah [swt]. We may be dissatisfied with the wealth and children we have when others are seen to be in a better position than us, but we may still thank Allah (swt) if we look at our brothers who are not given the favors that we enjoy.

Allah [swt] reminds us of favors bestowed upon us in **Surah al-`Isra (17:70):**

$$\text{وَلَقَدْ كَرَّمْنَا بَنِى ءَادَمَ وَحَمَلْنَـٰهُمْ فِى الْبَرِّ وَالْبَحْرِ وَرَزَقْنَـٰهُم مِّنَ الطَّيِّبَـٰتِ وَفَضَّلْنَـٰهُمْ عَلَىٰ كَثِيرٍ مِّمَّنْ خَلَقْنَا تَفْضِيلاً}$$

And We have certainly honored the children of Adam and carried them on the land and sea and provided for them of the good things and preferred them over much of what We have created, with [definite] preference.

Allah [swt] has given us the ability and put His other creations under our control and for the use of human beings. He has created the lands [we cultivate the lands for food, vegetables, fruits] and for our unhindered movement;

and the seas [for water, journey from one place to another, sea foods for our living etc.] for the benefit of mankind.

Allah [swt] reminds us that He has provided us with At-Tayyibat [sustenance things good and pure] meaning agricultural produce, fruits, meat, and milk with all kinds of delicious and desirable flavors and colors and beautiful appearance, and fine clothes of all kinds of shapes, colors and sizes, which we make for ourselves or are brought to us by others from other regions and areas.

Allah [swt] also preferred the human beings over all living beings and other kinds of creation. This Ayah indicates that human are also preferred even over the angels. Allah [swt] encourages us to enjoy things of His creation and advised us to be grateful for His unending favors in **Surah al-Baqarah (2:172)** as:

يَـٰٓأَيُّهَا ٱلَّذِينَ ءَامَنُوٓا۟ كُلُوا۟ مِن طَيِّبَـٰتِ مَا رَزَقْنَـٰكُمْ وَٱشْكُرُوا۟ لِلَّهِ إِن كُنتُمْ إِيَّاهُ تَعْبُدُونَ

O, you who have believed, eat from the good [lawful] things We have provided for you and be grateful to Allah if it is [indeed] Him that you worship.

Man's gratitude to Allah [swt] is not a thing that benefits Allah [swt], for Allah is high above all needs; it benefits a man's own soul and gives him higher rank in the eternal life to come. There is no pleasure or advantage to Allah [swt] in punishing His own creatures, over whom He watches with loving care. On the contrary, He recognizes any good- however little – which He finds in us and delights to give us a reward beyond all measures. His recognition of us compared a bold metaphor to our gratitude to Him for His favors. Allah [swt] describes in **Surah an-Nisa' (4:147)**:

مَّا يَفْعَلُ ٱللَّهُ بِعَذَابِكُمْ إِن شَكَرْتُمْ وَءَامَنتُمْ وَكَانَ ٱللَّهُ شَاكِرًا عَلِيمًا

What would Allah do with [gain from] your punishment if you are grateful and believe? And ever is Allah appreciative [of good] and Knowing.

Sulayman [as] was blessed with complete authority and power whereby mankind, the Jinn and the birds were subjugated to him. He also knew the language of the birds and animals, which is something that had never been given to any other human being -- as far as we know from what Allah and His Messenger told us. All of Sulayman's troops of Jinn, men and birds were gathered together, and he rode with them in a display of might and glory, with people marching behind him, followed by the Jinn, and the birds flying above his head. When it was hot, they would shade him with their wings. Allah [swt] describes how Sulayman [as] has yet expressed his gratefulness in **Surah an-Naml (27:19)**:

فَتَبَسَّمَ ضَاحِكًا مِّن قَوْلِهَا وَقَالَ رَبِّ أَوْزِعْنِىٓ أَنْ أَشْكُرَ نِعْمَتَكَ ٱلَّتِىٓ أَنْعَمْتَ عَلَىَّ وَعَلَىٰ وَٰلِدَىَّ وَأَنْ أَعْمَلَ صَـٰلِحًا تَرْضَىٰهُ وَأَدْخِلْنِى بِرَحْمَتِكَ فِى عِبَادِكَ ٱلصَّـٰلِحِينَ

So [Sulayman] smiled, amused at her speech, and said, "My Lord, enable me [gather within me the utmost strength and ability] to be grateful for Your favor which You have bestowed upon me and my parents and to do righteousness of which You approve. And admit me by Your mercy into [the ranks of] Your righteous servants."

Here Sulayman [as] asked Allah [swt] to inspire him to give thanks for the blessings that He bestowed upon him by teaching him to understand what the birds and animals say, and the blessings that Allah [swt] has bestowed upon his parents by making them Muslims who believe in You.

In **Surah an-Naml (27:40),** once again Sulayman [as] expressed his deep sense of gratitude to Allah [swt] as:

قَالَ الَّذِى عِندَهُ عِلْمٌ مِّنَ الْكِتَبِ أَنَا ءَاتِيكَ بِهِ قَبْلَ أَن يَرْتَدَّ إِلَيْكَ طَرْفُكَ فَلَمَّا رَءَاهُ مُسْتَقِرًّا عِندَهُ قَالَ هَـذَا مِن فَضْلِ رَبِّى لِيَبْلُوَنِى أَءَشْكُرُ أَمْ أَكْفُرُ وَمَن شَكَرَ فَإِنَّمَا يَشْكُرُ لِنَفْسِهِ وَمَن كَفَرَ فَإِنَّ رَبِّى غَنِىٌّ كَرِيمٌ

Said one who had knowledge from the Scripture, "I will bring it to you before your glance return to you." And when he saw it placed before him, he said, "This is from the favor of my Lord to test me whether I will be grateful or ungrateful. And whoever is grateful - his gratitude is only for [the benefit of] himself. And whoever is ungrateful – then indeed, my Lord is free of need and Generous."

Sulayman [as] having almost all the powers such as had never been given to anyone else, before or since, did not show any pride or proud of the absolute power bestowed on him. Instead, considered the favors of the greatness of the power and authority that Allah had bestowed upon him and the troops that He had subjugated to him as a test whether he is grateful or not. If we are thankful to Allah [swt], He increases His favor on us.

Let us admire how our prophet Muhammad [sas] expressed his gratitude to Allah [swt]. Allah's Apostle worshipped so much that his feet were swollen. It was said to him: "Why do you undergo so much hardship despite the fact that Allah has pardoned for you your earlier and later sins?" Thereupon he said: "May I not [prove myself] to be a grateful servant [of Allah]?" (Muslim, book #039, hadith #6772)

وَسَيَجْزِى اللَّهُ الشَّـكِرِينَ

Gratitude for Allah's gifts is one form of worship.

Allah appreciates those who appreciate Him, and has knowledge of those whose hearts believe in Him, and He will give them perfect reward.

Allah's Apostle said, "There is a compulsory Sadaqa [charity] to be given for every joint of the human body [as a sign of gratitude to Allah] every day the sun rises (Bukhari, book #52, hadith #232).

Brothers and sisters in Islam, Allah [may He be exalted] says: "O My servants, if the first of you and the last of you, mankind and Jinn alike, were all to be as pious as the most pious among you, that would not add to My dominion in the slightest. O My servants, if the first of you and the last of you, mankind and Jinn alike, were all to be as evil as the most evil one among you, that would not detract from My dominion in the slightest."

Set aside all other things, should we not be grateful to Allah [swt] for creating us as human beings designated as the best of His creation? So if we are grateful to Allah [swt] for favors bestowed upon us that will in no way benefit Allah [swt], which will surely benefit us in deriving more of His favors and mercies. Let us ask ourselves, should we not be ungrateful for mercies and favors received? Should we not realize his noble destiny and prepare for real life in the Hereafter? May Allah [swt] inspire us and grant us power and ability to be grateful to Him for His favors, kindness, and mercy; so that we may derive more rewards from Him? **Amin!!**

Sources of Spiritual Ailment

We are familiar with the concept of physical and mental ailment. If the sources or causes of these ailments can be identified by medical experts, then appropriate treatment can be applied for their prevention or cure. Many of us may not be familiar with the concept of spiritual ailment. For its preventive or curative remedies, we must first of all know the sources and causes of spiritual ailment

There are mainly three sources of spiritual ailment. These are: *Hirs* [greed], *Hasad* [envy, jealousy], and *Kibr* [pride].

HIRS [greed]:

Allah [swt] says in **Surah al-Hijr (15:88):**

لاَتَمُدَّنَّ عَيْنَيْكَ إِلَى مَا مَتَّعْنَا بِهِ أَزْوَاجًا مِنْهُمْ وَلاَتَحْزَنْ عَلَيْهِمْ وَاخْفِضْ جَنَاحَكَ لِلْمُؤْمِنِينَ

Do not extend your eyes toward that by which We have given enjoyment to [certain] categories of them [the disbelievers], and do not grieve over them. And lower your wing [show kindness] to the believers.

The engrossment of the heart with wealth, etc. is Hirs. Hirs is the root of all spiritual ailments. It is, therefore, proper to describe it as the mother of all maladies. All mischief and strife are the consequences of this lowly attribute. It is because of *Hirs* that people plunder and usurp the rights of others. The basis of immorality is the lust for bestial pleasure.

Allah (swt) says in **Surah at-Taghabun (64:15):**

إِنَّمَا أَمْوَالُكُمْ وَأَوْلَادُكُمْ فِتْنَةٌ وَاللَّهُ عِنْدَهُ أَجْرٌ عَظِيمٌ

Your wealth and your children are but a trial, and Allah has with Him a great reward.

And also in **Surah al-Fajr (89:19, 20):**

وَتَأْكُلُونَ التُّرَاثَ أَكْلاً لَّمًّا ۙ وَتُحِبُّونَ الْمَالَ حُبًّا جَمًّا

And you consume inheritance devouring [it] altogether [not caring whether it is lawful or unlawful]. And you love wealth with immense love.

If man possesses two valleys filled with gold and silver, by nature he will desire a third. The more the demands of greed are satisfied, the greater will be its demands. Greed is like one afflicted with rash. The more he scratches, the worse the rash becomes. Allah [swt] says in **Surah al-'Aadiyat (100:8):**

$$وَإِنَّهُ لِحُبِّ الْخَيْرِ لَشَدِيدٌ$$

And indeed, he is in love of wealth, intense.

In other words, it is not possible for man to fulfill all his desires. It is for this reason that the Harees [the one who has greed] have no peace of mind. Nothing besides soil [i.e. the grave] can satiate his greed. Before a wish can attain fulfillment, another develops. When one is not contented with Taqdeer, one is smitten by a multitude of desires and hopes, the fulfillment of which is most difficult. The result of non-fulfillment of desire is frustration and worry. The Harees, in spite of, perhaps possessing wealth in abundance and enjoying luxury is perpetually afflicted with frustration.

We should always keep in mind that the more wealth one has in this world, the more difficult will be his trial on the day of judgment [because one shall have to answer how the wealth was accrued and how it was spent in this world].

Reducing expenditure will diminish concern and yearning for more earnings. Moreover do not compare our position with those who are above us, but look into the condition of those who are at worse position. Forget about the future and bear in mind that the Harres always is contemptible.

HASAD (jealousy, envy)

Allah [swt] says in **Surah al-Falaq (113:5):**

$$وَمِن شَرِّ حَاسِدٍ إِذَا حَسَدَ$$

And from the evil of an envier when he envies.

Prophet [sas] said: "Do not be jealous among you." (Muslim, book #032, hadith #6218) To be displeased with other's good position and to wish for its elimination is Hasad. Generally the basis of Hasad is takabbur [pride] and ghuroor [falsehood]. Without any valid reason man seeks to withhold the bounties of Allah [swt]. He desires [consciously or subconsciously] that like himself Allah too should restrict His bounties. Hasad is a malady of the heart. It is harmful to both one's spiritual life and worldly life. The harm to man's *Deen* [spiritual life] is the illumination of his good deeds and he becomes the victim of Allah's Wrath.

The harm to worldly life [*duniya*] is the frustration and worry that perpetually afflicts the envious person. He is consumed by frustration caused by Hasad for others whose disgrace and fall he always anticipates. In this way Hasid destroys his/her good deeds in addition to eliminating his worldly comfort and peace of mind. Allah's

Messenger [sas] said: "In the worshipper's heart, faith and envy cannot dwell together." [Sunan al-Nasâ'î (3109)]

The disease of *Hasad* is remedied by praising much the person against whom jealousy is directed. Praise him no matter how difficult this may seem. Honor him and meet him with respect and humility.

In **Surah Ta-Ha (20:131)** Allah (swt) says:

$$وَلاَ تَمُدَّنَّ عَيْنَيْكَ إِلَى مَا مَتَّعْنَا بِهِ أَزْوَاجًا مِّنْهُمْ زَهْرَةَ الْحَيَوةِ الدُّنْيَا لِنَفْتِنَهُمْ فِيهِ وَرِزْقُ رَبِّكَ خَيْرٌ وَأَبْقَى$$

And do not extend your eyes toward that by which We have given enjoyment to [some] categories of them, [its being but] the splendor of worldly life by which We test them. And the provision of your Lord is better and more lasting.

Meaning be content with the Grand Qur'an that Allah has given to you, and do not long for the luxuries and transient delights that they have in this world. He [in this Ayah] forbade a man to wish for what his companion has.

KIBR (pride)

Allah [swt] says in **Surah an-Nisa' (4:36)**;

$$إِنَّ اللَّهَ لاَ يُحِبُّ مَن كَانَ مُخْتَالاً فَخُوراً$$

Indeed, Allah does not like those who are self-deluding and boastful.

Proud man means one who is arrogant, insolent and boasts to others. He thinks that he is better than other people, thus thinking high of him even though he is insignificant to Allah and hated by people.

Allah's Messenger [sas] said: "Allah, Most Great and Glorious said: Pride is my cloak and majesty is my lower garment, and I shall throw him who views with me regarding one of them into Hell". (Muslim, book #032, hadith #6349; Abu Dawud, book #32, hadith #4079)

Takabbur [Pride] is the feeling of superiority--considering one to be great or oneself superior to others in attributes of excellence. In a nutshell takabbur is to voluntarily and consciously regard oneself superior to others in religious or mundane [may be in education, wealth, and or children] excellence in a way that engenders contempt in the heart for others. This is the reality of takabbur and this is haram.

In **Surah al-Hadeed (57:20)** Allah [swt] says:

$$اعْلَمُوا أَنَّمَا الْحَيَوةُ الدُّنْيَا لَعِبٌ وَهُوَ وَزِينَةٌ وَتَفَاخُرٌ بَيْنَكُمْ وَتَكَاثُرٌ فِي الأَمْوَلِ وَالأَوْلَدِ$$

Know that the life of this world is but amusement and diversion and adornment and boasting to one another and competition in increase of wealth and children.

The Prophet [sas] said: "He who has in his heart the weight of a mustard seed of pride shall not enter Paradise". A person [amongst his hearers] said: "Verily a person loves that his dress should be fine, and his shoes should be fine". He [the Holy Prophet] remarked: "Verily, Allah is Graceful and He loves Grace. Pride disdains the truth [out of self-conceit] and contempt for the people". (Muslim, book #001, hadith #0164)

All the A'rifin [Auliya of Allah] maintains that the foundation of Akhlaq-e-Razeelah is *Kibr* [pride] and *Kibr* is synonymous with the desire for fame. Thus, the basis of Kibr too is Hirs.

Allah [swt] says in **Surah an-Nahl (16:23):**

لَاجَرَمَ أَنَّ ٱللَّهَ يَعْلَمُ مَا يُسِرُّونَ وَمَا يُعْلِنُونَ إِنَّهُ لَا يُحِبُّ الْمُسْتَكْبِرِينَ

Certainly, Allah knows what they conceal and what they reveal. Indeed, He does not like the arrogant.

Allah [swt] also warns those who are proud in **Surah an-Nahl (16:29):**

فَٱدْخُلُوٓاْ أَبْوَابَ جَهَنَّمَ خَـٰلِدِينَ فِيهَا فَلَبِئْسَ مَثْوَى الْمُتَكَبِّرِينَ

So enter the gates of Hell to abide certainly therein, and how wretched is the residence of the arrogant.

One who intentionally considers himself better than others becomes arrogant. His nafs swells up with pride, the consequences of which then manifest them. Examples of pride are: to regard others with contempt; to take offence when others do not greet one first; to be offended if others do not offer you respect; to be annoyed when someone admonishes you; refusal to concede the truth even after having realized it. Where the condition of contempt for others is non-existent, takabbur-- will not be applicable. Proud one will not accept any kind of criticism from anybody else, and this is *kibr*.

In **Surah al-'Araf (7:146)** Allah [swt] threatens:

سَأَصْرِفُ عَنْ ءَايَـٰتِيَ الَّذِينَ يَتَكَبَّرُونَ فِي الْأَرْضِ

I will turn away from My signs those who are arrogant upon the earth without right.

It was takabbur that made shaytan a deviate. Prophet [sas] said that the *mutakabbireen* [the proud ones] will be encased in trunks of fire of Jahannam. Allah [swt] has warned that the abode of the proud ones will indeed be vile. Pride is the exclusive prerogative of Allah [swt]. Allah [swt] will destroy all those who desire to participate in this exclusive attribute of greatness.

On the authority of Abu Huraiyrah (may Allah be pleased with him), who said that the Messenger of Allah (sas) said: Allah (mighty and sublime be He) said:

Pride is my cloak and greatness My robe, and he who competes with Me in respect of either of them I shall cast into Hell-fire (Hadith Qudsi # 19).

To get rid of pride, humble ourselves in the presence of those whom we regard as our inferior by giving them Salam first when we meet them. Be respectful to them so that we become imbued with humility.

May Allah [swt] keep us under His Protection and save us from greed, jealousy, and pride, for indeed, these are the severest of maladies? These are the roots of all spiritual ailments. **Amin**

Specialty of Hajj as an Ibadah

Islamic tradition holds that the Mosque was first built by the angels before the creation of mankind, when Allah ordained a place of worship on Earth to reflect the house in heaven called *al-Bayt l-Ma'mur* (البيت المعمور, "The Worship Place of Angels"). From time to time, the Mosque was damaged by a storm (flood) and was rebuilt anew. According to Islamic belief it was built by Ibrahim (Abraham), with the help of his son Ismail (Ishmael). They were ordered by Allah to build the mosque, and the Kaba. The Black Stone is situated near the eastern corner of the Kaba, believed to be the only remnant of the original structure made by Ibrahim (as).

Allah (swt) says in **Surah Al-Baqarah (2: 125):**

وَإِذْ جَعَلْنَا الْبَيْتَ مَثَابَةً لِّلنَّاسِ وَأَمْناً وَاتَّخِذُوا مِن مَّقَامِ إِبْرَهِيمَ مُصَلًّى وَعَهِدْنَا إِلَى إِبْرَهِيمَ وَإِسْمَعِيلَ أَن طَهِّرَا بَيْتِيَ لِلطَّائِفِينَ وَالْعَكِفِينَ وَالرُّكَّعِ السُّجُودِ

And We commanded Ibrahim (Abraham) and Isma`il (Ishmael) that they should purify My House (the Ka`bah at Makkah) for those who are circumambulating it, or staying (Etikaf), or bowing or prostrating themselves (there, in prayer).

It is a demonstration of submission to Allah and solidarity of the Ummah's journey of the hearts. The Hajj pilgrimage is one of the Five Pillars of Islam, required of all able-bodied Muslims who can afford the trip.

1. For salat and saum, we don't need to travel or spend any money. Because, the whole world has been allowed to be used for salat, although it is better to perform in the mosque in which case only we are required to travel. For saum, we don't need to travel or spend money. For paying Zakat, we don't need to travel. But for Hajj we must travel and spend money.

2. It is not necessary to wear same type of clothes by everyone in performing salat, but in Hajj, it is mandatory to wear the simple, white Ihram clothing, which is intended to make everyone appear the same, as Muslims believe that in the eyes of Allah there is no difference between a prince and a pauper. So even the king will have leave his king's dress and wear a dress that all other people wear to express solidarity.

3. The tawaf of the first built mosque on this earth is another specialty of hajj as an Ibadah.

4. According to Islamic tradition, it was on Mount Arafah that Adam and Eve, separated for 200 years following their expulsion from the Garden of Eden, met and recognized each other and were reunited. Here too they were forgiven by Allah for their transgression after offering their repentance. A main reason of the ritual of pilgrimage is the renewal of that Prayer of repentance every year standing on the hill of mercy, the climax of Hajj. The pilgrims will spend the whole day in Arafah supplicating to Allah to forgive their sins and praying for personal strength in the future.

5. In all ibadah, we will have to do something. But in hajj, just attendance in Arafah (in the designated area) is enough for the hajj.

6. Millions of Muslims each year go for performing hajj and there will be dashing, pushing, and a lot of other physical obstruction in performing hajj, but in no other ibadah such actions are allowed. This is a test for patience.

7. In Islamic tradition, Ibrahim (Abraham) was commanded by Allah to leave his wife Hajera and their infant son Ismael alone in the desert, with only basic provisions, to test their faith. The place was between Al-Safa and Al-Marwah. When their provisions were exhausted, she went in search of help or water. To make her search easier and faster, she went alone, leaving the infant Ismael on the ground. She first climbed the nearest hill, Al-Safa, to look over the surrounding area. When she saw nothing, she then went to the other hill, Al-Marwah, to look around. While Hajera was on either hillside, she was able to see Ismael and know he was safe. However, when she was in the valley between the hills she was unable to see her son. Thus Hazrat Hajra would run while in the valley between the hills and walk at a normal pace while on the hillsides.

Hajera travelled back and forth between the hills seven times in the scorching heat before she returned to Ismael. When she arrived, she found that a spring had sprouted forth from the crying baby kicking at the sand with his feet. This spring is now known as the Zamzam Well. This Zamzam well was granted from the angels of Allah to reward Hajera. Allah (swt) was so happy with the act of Hajera (ra) that it was given a part of the status of ibadah. Performing the **Sa'i**, also known as **Sa'ee**, serves to commemorate Hajera's search for water and Allah's mercy in answering prayers. Sa'i is a search. It is a movement with an aim. It is depicted by running and hurrying. In Ibrahim's position you acted as Ibrahim and Ismael. Once you begin "trying" (Sa'i) you are acting as Hajera.

Allah (swt) says in **Surah Al-Baqarah (2: 158):**

[إِنَّ الصَّفَا وَالْمَرْوَةَ مِن شَعَآئِرِ اللَّهِ فَمَنْ حَجَّ الْبَيْتَ أَوِ اعْتَمَرَ فَلاَ جُنَاحَ عَلَيْهِ أَن يَطَّوَّفَ بِهِمَا وَمَن تَطَوَّعَ خَيْرًا فَإِنَّ اللَّهَ شَاكِرٌ عَلِيمٌ]

Verily, As-Safa and Al-Marwah are of the symbols of Allah. So it is not a sin on him who performs Hajj or `Umrah (pilgrimage) of the House to perform Tawaf between them. And whoever does good voluntarily, then verily, Allah is All-Recognizer, All-Knower.

8. All those who come for Hajj and Umrah, come by using all sorts of vehicles (traditional and modern). As Allah (swt) says in **Surah Al-Hajj (22: 26-7):**

[وَإِذْ بَوَّأْنَا لِإِبْرَهِيمَ مَكَانَ الْبَيْتِ أَن لاَّ تُشْرِكْ بِي شَيْئًا وَطَهِّرْ بَيْتِيَ لِلطَّآئِفِينَ وَالْقَآئِمِينَ وَالرُّكَّعِ السُّجُودِ - وَأَذِّن فِي النَّاسِ بِالْحَجِّ يَأْتُوكَ رِجَالاً وَعَلَى كُلِّ ضَامِرٍ يَأْتِينَ مِن كُلِّ فَجٍّ عَمِيقٍ]

And (remember) when We showed Ibrahim the site of the House (saying): "Associate not anything with Me, and sanctify My House for those who circumambulate it, and those who stand up (for prayer), and those who bow and make prostration (in prayer). And proclaim to mankind the Hajj (pilgrimage). They will come to you on foot and on every lean camel; they will come from every Fajj `Amiq.

9. We sacrifice animals in the name of Allah in Meena in remembrance of the preparation for the sacrifice of Ismae`l (as) by Ibrahim (as).

Finally, Allah (swt) tells us in **Surah Hajj (22:37):**

لَن يَنَالَ اللَّهَ لُحُومُهَا وَلَا دِمَاؤُهَا وَلَـكِن يَنَالُهُ التَّقْوَى مِنكُمْ

It is neither their meat nor their blood that reaches Allah, but it is Taqwa from you that reach Him.

Brothers and sisters in Islam, in performing Hajj, we enjoy and remember the reunion of the father and mother of mankind Adam (as) and their grant of forgiveness by Allah (swt), we remember this act while in Arafah and ask for Allah's forgiveness. The work of Ibrahim and Ismae`l (as) in rebuilding the house of Kaba, we remember this act during Tawaf. The Saee of Hajera (as), we remember the act of Hajera (as) during our Saee; and the devotion of Ibrahim (as) in his preparation for sacrificing his son Ismae`l (as), we remember while making sacrifice of animals in Mina.. Is there be any better ibadah than Hajj on whom it becomes obligatory and perform it at the earliest opportunity?

Finally, brothers and sisters in Islam, if we cannot slaughter our ego, pride of wealth, honor, and power; then just slaughtering an animal (which is symbolic) will not be able to take us to Allah (swt). **Amin!!**

Status of Isa [as] Jesus and Mariyam [ra] Mary in Islam

Muslims and Christians do have differing perspectives on Jesus' life and teachings, but his spiritual legacy, as a righteous and principle guide, his mission as a Prince of Peace offers an alternative opportunity for people of faith to recognize their shared religious heritage. Christians and Muslims would do well to reflect on **Surah al-Baqarah (2:136)** in the Qur'an reaffirming Allah's eternal message of spiritual unity:

$$قُولُوٓاْ ءَامَنَّا بِاللَّهِ وَمَآ أُنزِلَ إِلَيۡنَا وَمَآ أُنزِلَ إِلَىٰٓ إِبۡرَٰهِـۧمَ وَإِسۡمَٰعِيلَ وَإِسۡحَٰقَ وَيَعۡقُوبَ وَالۡأَسۡبَاطِ وَمَآ أُوتِيَ مُوسَىٰ وَعِيسَىٰ وَمَآ أُوتِيَ النَّبِيُّونَ مِن رَّبِّهِمۡ لَا نُفَرِّقُ بَيۡنَ أَحَدٍ مِّنۡهُمۡ وَنَحۡنُ لَهُۥ مُسۡلِمُونَ$$

Say, [O Believers], "We have believed in Allah and what has been revealed to us and what has been revealed to Ibrahim [Abraham], Isma`il [Ishmael], Ishaq [Isaac], Ya`qub [Jacob], and the descendants [the twelve tribes of Israel descended from Ya`qub] and what was given to Musa [Moses] and `Isa [Jesus], and what was given to the Prophets from their Lord. We make no distinction between any of them, and we are Muslims [in submission] to Him."

Islam as a religion is a divine system based on reason, truth, culminating in practical faith, expressed via beneficial action, emanating from sincere intention and manifesting goodwill for all humanity.

Good deeds, therefore, include every worthy, pure action that contributes towards individual or social welfare; that can be applied in the way towards soul-perfection, moral improvement; affirmation of justice and alleviation of evil, impurity and oppression.

Although the Christians give a very high status to Maryam [ra] because she gave birth to Isa [as] Jesus, in Islam Maryam [ra] was given a very high status by Allah [swt] since her birth and in her upbringing by Zakariya [as]. In the Holy Qur`an, Allah [swt] mentioned Maryam [Mary] by name several times. Entire chapter 19 in the Qur'an is titled as Maryam/Mary. Allah [swt] expressed in **Surah al-'Imran (3:35-7)** as:

$$إِذۡ قَالَتِ امۡرَأَتُ عِمۡرَٰنَ رَبِّ إِنِّي نَذَرۡتُ لَكَ مَا فِي بَطۡنِي مُحَرَّرًا فَتَقَبَّلۡ مِنِّي إِنَّكَ أَنتَ السَّمِيعُ الۡعَلِيمُ فَلَمَّا وَضَعَتۡهَا قَالَتۡ رَبِّ إِنِّي وَضَعۡتُهَآ أُنثَىٰ وَاللَّهُ أَعۡلَمُ بِمَا وَضَعَتۡ وَلَيۡسَ الذَّكَرُ كَالۡأُنثَىٰ وَإِنِّي سَمَّيۡتُهَا مَرۡيَمَ وَإِنِّي أُعِيذُهَا بِكَ وَذُرِّيَّتَهَا مِنَ الشَّيۡطَٰنِ الرَّجِيمِ فَتَقَبَّلَهَا رَبُّهَا بِقَبُولٍ حَسَنٍ وَأَنۢبَتَهَا نَبَاتًا حَسَنًا وَكَفَّلَهَا زَكَرِيَّا كُلَّمَا دَخَلَ عَلَيۡهَا زَكَرِيَّا الۡمِحۡرَابَ وَجَدَ عِندَهَا رِزۡقًا قَالَ يَٰمَرۡيَمُ أَنَّىٰ لَكِ هَٰذَا قَالَتۡ هُوَ مِنۡ عِندِ اللَّهِ إِنَّ اللَّهَ يَرۡزُقُ مَن يَشَآءُ بِغَيۡرِ حِسَابٍ$$

[Mention, O Muhammad], when the wife of `Imran said, "My Rabb, indeed I have pledged to You what is in my womb, dedicated for [Your service], so accept this from me. Indeed, you are the Hearing, the Knowing." But when she delivered her, she said, "My Rabb, I have delivered a female." And Allah was most knowing of what she delivered, and the male is not like the female. And I have named her Maryam,

and I seek refuge for her in You and [for] her descendants from Satan, the expelled [from the mercy of Allah]. So her Rabb [Allah] accepted her with good acceptance and caused her to grow in a good manner and put her in the care of Zakariya. Every time he entered upon her in the prayer chamber, he found with her provision. He said, "O Maryam, from where is this [coming] to you?" She said, "It is from Allah. Indeed, Allah provides for whom He wills without limit."

The birth of Isa [Jesus] is described in two places of the Quran – Surah 3 and Surah 19. Reading from the beginning of his birth, we come across the story of Maryam, and the esteemed position that she occupies in the House of Islam, before the actual annunciation of the birth of Jesus is given.

It is generally accepted by Christians that Mary was married to Joseph [Yusuf] prior to the birth of Jesus. This understanding is derived from verses in the Gospels of Matthew and Luke. Jacob [Yakub] was the father of Joseph [Yusuf] the husband of Mary. It was of her that Jesus who is called the Messiah was born. Jesus was the Messiah for whom the Jews waited.

Allah [swt] has chosen Mariyam [ra] for creating Isa [as] through her as described in **Surah al-'Imran (3:42-4):**

وَإِذْ قَالَتِ الْمَلَٰئِكَةُ يَٰمَرْيَمُ إِنَّ اللَّهَ اصْطَفَاكِ وَطَهَّرَكِ وَاصْطَفَاكِ عَلَىٰ نِسَآءِ الْعَٰلَمِينَ - يَٰمَرْيَمُ اقْنُتِى لِرَبِّكِ وَاسْجُدِى وَارْكَعِى مَعَ الرَّٰكِعِينَ - ذَٰلِكَ مِنْ أَنۢبَآءِ الْغَيْبِ نُوحِيهِ إِلَيْكَ وَمَا كُنتَ لَدَيْهِمْ إِذْ يُلْقُونَ أَقْلَٰمَهُمْ أَيُّهُمْ يَكْفُلُ مَرْيَمَ وَمَا كُنتَ لَدَيْهِمْ إِذْ يَخْتَصِمُونَ - إِذْ قَالَتِ الْمَلَٰئِكَةُ يَٰمَرْيَمُ إِنَّ اللَّهَ يُبَشِّرُكِ بِكَلِمَةٍ مِّنْهُ اسْمُهُ الْمَسِيحُ عِيسَى ابْنُ مَرْيَمَ وَجِيهًا فِى الدُّنْيَا وَالْآخِرَةِ وَمِنَ الْمُقَرَّبِينَ - وَيُكَلِّمُ النَّاسَ فِى الْمَهْدِ وَكَهْلًا وَمِنَ الصَّٰلِحِينَ - قَالَتْ رَبِّ أَنَّىٰ يَكُونُ لِى وَلَدٌ وَلَمْ يَمْسَسْنِى بَشَرٌ قَالَ كَذَٰلِكِ اللَّهُ يَخْلُقُ مَا يَشَآءُ إِذَا قَضَىٰ أَمْرًا فَإِنَّمَا يَقُولُ لَهُ كُن فَيَكُونُ

And [mention] when the angels said, "O Maryam, indeed Allah has chosen you and purified you and chosen you above the women of the worlds. O Maryam, be devoutly obedient to your Rabb and prostrate and bow with those who bow [in prayer]." This is from the news of the unseen which We reveal to you [O Muhammad]. And you were not with them when they cast their pens [threw lots] as to which of them should be responsible for Maryam. Nor were you with them when they disputed.

In **Surah Maryam (19:19-21)**, Allah [swt] again says:

قَالَ إِنَّمَا أَنَا رَسُولُ رَبِّكِ لِأَهَبَ لَكِ غُلَٰمًا زَكِيًّا - قَالَتْ أَنَّىٰ يَكُونُ لِى غُلَٰمٌ وَلَمْ يَمْسَسْنِى بَشَرٌ وَلَمْ أَكُ بَغِيًّا - قَالَ كَذَٰلِكِ قَالَ رَبُّكِ هُوَ عَلَىَّ هَيِّنٌ وَلِنَجْعَلَهُ آيَةً لِّلنَّاسِ وَرَحْمَةً مِّنَّا وَكَانَ أَمْرًا مَّقْضِيًّا

He [the angel] said, "I am only the messenger of your Rabb to give you [news of] a pure boy [son]." She said, "How can I have a boy while no man touched me and I have not been unchaste?" He said, "Thus [it

will be]; your Rabb says, `It is easy for Me [Allah] and We will make him a sign to the people and a mercy from Us. And it is a matter [already] decreed [by Allah]."

Though the unique birth of Isa [as] with one parent is no indication of divinity [as the Christians think] just as Adam's creation was without any parentage, Allah [swt] tells us in **Surah al-'Imran (3:59):**

$$ إِنَّ مَثَلَ عِيسَىٰ عِندَ اللَّهِ كَمَثَلِ ءَادَمَ خَلَقَهُ مِن تُرَابٍ ثُمَّ قَالَ لَهُ كُن فَيَكُونُ $$

Indeed, the example of Isa [as] to Allah [regarding His creation of him] is like that of Adam [as]. He created him from dust; then He said to him: `Be` and he was.

Jesus ['Isa] is referred 25 times in the Qur'an 9 times as 'Isa and 16 times as "Isa ibn Maryam" [Jesus, son of Mary]; He is also addressed with respect as: Ibn Maryam, meaning "The son of Mary"; and as the Maseeh [the Messiah], as Abdullah, "The servant of Allah"; and as Rasul-ul-Allah, the messenger of Allah. He is spoken of as Ruhullah "The Spirit of Allah", as an Ayatullah "Sign of Allah", and numerous other epithets of honor spread over fifteen different chapters. Allah bears testimony to his truthfulness, mission, character, and his status in **Surah Mariyam (19:29-36):**

$$ فَأَشَارَتْ إِلَيْهِ قَالُوا۟ كَيْفَ نُكَلِّمُ مَن كَانَ فِى الْمَهْدِ صَبِيًّا ۞ قَالَ إِنِّى عَبْدُ اللَّهِ ءَاتَانِىَ الْكِتَبَ وَ جَعَلَنِى نَبِيًّا ۞ وَ جَعَلَنِى مُبَارَكًا أَيْنَ مَا $$

$$ كُنتُ وَ أَوْصَنِى بِالصَّلَوٰةِ وَ الزَّكَوٰةِ مَا دُمْتُ حَيًّا ۞ وَ بَرًّۢا بِوَ الِدَتِى وَ لَمْ يَجْعَلْنِى جَبَّارًا شَقِيًّا ۞ وَ السَّلَمُ عَلَىَّ يَوْمَ وُلِدتُّ وَ يَوْمَ أَمُوتُ $$

$$ وَ يَوْمَ أُبْعَثُ حَيًّا ذَلِكَ عِيسَى ابْنُ مَرْيَمَ قَوْلَ الْحَقِّ الَّذِى فِيهِ يَمْتَرُونَ ۞ مَا كَانَ لِلَّهِ أَن يَتَّخِذَ مِن وَلَدٍ سُبْحَنَهُ إِذَا قَضَى أَمْرًا فَإِنَّمَا يَقُولُ لَهُ $$

$$ كُن فَيَكُونُ ۞ وَ إِنَّ اللَّهَ رَبِّى وَ رَبُّكُمْ فَاعْبُدُوهُ هَذَا صِرَطٌ مُّسْتَقِيمٌ $$

So she pointed to him. They said, "How can we speak to one who is in the cradle a child?" He [Isa] said, "Indeed, I am the servant of Allah. He has given me the Scripture and made me a Prophet. And He has made me blessed wherever I am and has enjoined upon me prayer and Zakah as long as I remain alive. And [made me] dutiful to my mother, and He has not made me a wretched tyrant. And peace is on me the day I was born and the day I will die and the day I am raised alive." That is `Isa, son of Maryam - the word of truth about which they are in dispute. It is not [befitting] for Allah to take a son; exalted is He! When He decrees an affair, He only says to it, 'Be,' and it is. ['Isa said], "And indeed, Allah is my Rabb and your Rabb, so worship Him. That is the straight path".

Immediately following this, Isa [as] is given special attention as described in **Surah al-Mai'dah (5:110):**

إِذْ قَالَ اللَّهُ يَعِيسَى ابْنَ مَرْيَمَ اذْكُرْ نِعْمَتِى عَلَيْكَ وَ عَلَى وَلِدَتِكَ إِذْ أَيَّدتُّكَ بِرُوحِ الْقُدُسِ تُكَلِّمُ النَّاسَ فِى الْمَهْدِ وَ كَهْلاً وَ إِذْ عَلَّمْتُكَ

الْكِتَبَ وَ الْحِكْمَةَ وَ التَّوْرَاةَ وَ الإِنجِيلَ وَ إِذْ تَخْلُقُ مِنَ الطِّينِ كَهَيْئَةِ الطَّيْرِ بِإِذْنِى فَتَنفُخُ فِيهَا فَتَكُونُ طَيْرًا بِإِذْنِى وَ تُبْرِىءُ الأَكْمَهَ

وَ الأُبْرَصَ بِإِذْنِى وَ إِذْ تُخْرِجُ الْمَوتَى بِإِذْنِى وَ إِذْ كَفَفْتُ بَنِى إِسْرَءِيلَ عَنكَ إِذْ جِئْتَهُم بِالْبَيِّنَتِ فَقَالَ الَّذِينَ كَفَرُوا مِنْهُمْ إِنْ هَذَا إِلاَّ سِحْرٌ

مُّبِينٌ-

[The Day] when Allah will say, "O `Isa, Son of Maryam, remember My favor upon you and upon your mother when I supported you with the Pure Spirit [the angel Jibril] and you spoke to the people in the cradle and in maturity; and [remember] when I taught you writing and wisdom and the Tawrah and the Injil; and when you designed from clay [what was] like the form of a bird with My permission; then you breathed into it, and it became a bird with My permission; and you healed the blind [from birth] and the leper with My permission; and when you brought forth the dead with My permission; and when I restrained the Children of Israel from [killing] you when you came to them with clear proofs." And those who disbelieved among them said, "This is not but obvious magic."

The recognition of the Trinity as an innovation started very early in Christian history. Back in the seventh century, the Eastern theologian John of Damascus, in defending his icons, stated that icons were as unscriptural as the Trinity. Thus the doctrine of the Trinity does not originate in the gospels, or in the teachings of Jesus. It demonstrates the human tendency to exalt the object of our love and admiration. Division suggests that the one is not an Absolute One, but a compound of some variants and that which is a composed being can never be really one in the true meaning of oneness. And certainly the one dependent in its existence upon its different components can never be independent in its action, whereas Allah is the Absolute One, Independently Omnipotent in His Will and His Action. About their belief in 'Trinity,' Allah [swt] does not only refute and rejected their claim, but also warns them against great torments in the life hereafter. You shall not say, "Trinity." You shall refrain from this for your own good. Allah is only one. Be He glorified; He is much too glorious to have a son. To Him belongs everything in the heavens and everything on earth. Allah suffices as Creator and Master.

In **Surah al-Mai'dah (5:116-7)** Allah [swt] says:

وَ إِذْ قَالَ اللَّهُ يَعِيسَى ابْنَ مَرْيَمَ أَأَنتَ قُلْتَ لِلنَّاسِ اتَّخِذُونِى وَ أُمِّىَ إِلَهَيْنِ مِن دُونِ اللَّهِ قَالَ سُبْحَنَكَ مَا يَكُونُ لِى أَنْ أَقُولَ مَا لَيْسَ لِى بِحَقٍّ إِن

كُنتُ قُلْتُهُ فَقَدْ عَلِمْتَهُ تَعْلَمُ مَا فِى نَفْسِى وَ لاَ أَعْلَمُ مَا فِى نَفْسِكَ إِنَّكَ أَنتَ عَلَّمُ الْغُيُوبِ- مَا قُلْتُ لَهُمْ إِلاَّ مَا أَمَرْتَنِى بِهِ أَنِ اعْبُدُوا اللَّهَ

رَبِّى وَ رَبَّكُمْ وَ كُنتُ عَلَيْهِمْ شَهِيداً مَّا دُمْتُ فِيهِمْ فَلَمَّا تَوَفَّيْتَنِى كُنتَ أَنتَ الرَّقِيبَ عَلَيْهِمْ وَ أَنتَ عَلَى كُلِّ شَىءٍ شَهِيد

And [beware of the Day] when Allah will say, "O `Isa, son of Maryam, did you say to the people, `worship me and my mother as two gods besides Allah?" He will say, "Exalted are You! It was not for me to say that

to which I have no right. If I have said it, You would have known it. You know what is within me, and I do not know that is within yourself. Indeed, it is You who is Knower of the unseen. I said not to them except what You commanded me - to `worship Allah, my Rabb and your Rabb. And I was a witness over them as long as I was among them; but when You took me up, You were the observer over them, and You are, over all things, a witness."

Also in **Surah al-Mai'dah (5:72-3)** Allah [swt] says:

لَقَدْ كَفَرَ الَّذِينَ قَالُوٓا۟ إِنَّ ٱللَّهَ هُوَ ٱلْمَسِيحُ ٱبْنُ مَرْيَمَ وَقَالَ ٱلْمَسِيحُ يَٰبَنِىٓ إِسْرَٰٓءِيلَ ٱعْبُدُوا۟ ٱللَّهَ رَبِّى وَرَبَّكُمْ إِنَّهُۥ مَن يُشْرِكْ بِٱللَّهِ فَقَدْ

حَرَّمَ ٱللَّهُ عَلَيْهِ ٱلْجَنَّةَ وَمَأْوَىٰهُ ٱلنَّارُ وَمَا لِلظَّٰلِمِينَ مِنْ أَنصَارٍ ۖ لَّقَدْ كَفَرَ ٱلَّذِينَ قَالُوٓا۟ إِنَّ ٱللَّهَ ثَٰلِثُ ثَلَٰثَةٍ وَمَا مِنْ إِلَٰهٍ إِلَّا إِلَٰهٌ وَٰحِدٌ وَإِن لَّمْ

يَنتَهُوا۟ عَمَّا يَقُولُونَ لَيَمَسَّنَّ ٱلَّذِينَ كَفَرُوا۟ مِنْهُمْ عَذَابٌ أَلِيمٌ

They have certainly disbelieved who say, "Allah is the Messiah [`Isa], the son of Maryam" while the Messiah has said, "O Children of Israel worship Allah, my Rabb and your Rabb. Indeed, he who associates others with Allah - Allah has forbidden him Paradise, and his refuge is the Fire. And there are not for the wrongdoers any helpers." They have certainly disbelieved who say, "Allah is the third of three." And there is no god except One God. And if they do not desist from what they are saying, there will surely afflict the disbelievers among them a painful punishment.

They said, "Allah most gracious has begotten a son!" You have committed a gross blasphemy. The heavens are about to explode from such a blasphemy, the earth is about to tear as under, and the mountains are about to crumble, because they claim that the Most High has begotten a son. Everyone in the heavens and the earth, before the Most High, is no more than a servant. He has numbered each and every one of them. Each and every one of them will come before Him on the Day of Resurrection as a single [helpless] individual. As for those who believe and lead a righteous life the Most High will shower them with love. In **Surah Mariyam (19:88-92)**, Allah [swt] angrily said:

وَقَالُوا۟ ٱتَّخَذَ ٱلرَّحْمَٰنُ وَلَدًا ۗ لَّقَدْ جِئْتُمْ شَيْئًا إِدًّا ۚ تَكَادُ ٱلسَّمَٰوَٰتُ يَتَفَطَّرْنَ مِنْهُ وَتَنشَقُّ ٱلْأَرْضُ وَتَخِرُّ ٱلْجِبَالُ هَدًّا ۚ أَن دَعَوْا۟ لِلرَّحْمَٰنِ

وَلَدًا ۚ وَمَا يَنۢبَغِى لِلرَّحْمَٰنِ أَن يَتَّخِذَ وَلَدًا

And they say, "The Most Merciful has taken [for Himself] a son." you have done an atrocious thing. The heavens almost rupture there from and the earth split open and the mountains collapse in devastation - That they attribute the Most Merciful a son. And it is not appropriate for the Most Merciful that He should take a son.

In fact, much of what we recognize today as the basic teachings of Christianity came to us through Paul, originally known as Paul of Tarsus. Though he never met Jesus, he was the major missionary to the gentiles in the years immediately following the crucifixion.

In any serious study of the Gospels, we have always to keep in mind that Jesus himself left nothing in writing, and that the earliest records of his career which have come down to us were not put into writing until about forty years after his death. All our knowledge of him is drawn from the deposit of a tradition that was transmitted for several decades by word of mouth. We are, therefore, obliged to raise the question of the relationship between the documents as we have them and the events and sayings which they report. For it must be realized that in a generation or more of oral transmission, sayings and stories do not remain unchanged. Once they have been committed to writing, they are to some degree stabilized, as it were; though even at this stage, we have to observe that Luke and Matthew do not shrink from altering the Marcan record which they are both using.

Allah states that the Children of Israel tried to kill `Isa [as] by conspiring to defame him and crucify him. As for the last 12 hours portrayed in 'The Passion of the Christ' and the issue of the crucifixion in particular, the Qur'an says in **Surah an-Nisa' (4:156-8):**

وَبِكُفْرِهِمْ وَقَوْلِهِمْ عَلَى مَرْيَمَ بُهْتَاناً عَظِيماً- وَقَوْلِهِمْ إِنَّا قَتَلْنَا الْمَسِيحَ عِيسَى ابْنَ مَرْيَمَ رَسُولَ اللَّهِ وَمَا قَتَلُوهُ وَمَا صَلَبُوهُ وَلَـكِن شُبِّهَ لَهُمْ وَإِنَّ الَّذِينَ اخْتَلَفُواْ فِيهِ لَفِى شَكٍّ مِّنْهُ مَا لَهُم بِهِ مِنْ عِلْمٍ إِلاَّ اتِّبَاعَ الظَّنِّ وَمَا قَتَلُوهُ يَقِيناً- بَل رَّفَعَهُ اللَّهُ إِلَيْهِ وَكَانَ اللَّهُ عَزِيزاً أَحَكِيماً-

And [We cursed them] for their disbelief and their saying against Maryam a great slander [when they accused her of fornication]. And for their saying, "Indeed, We have killed the Masih, `Isa, the son of Maryam, the messenger of Allah." And they did not kill him, nor did they crucify him; but [another] was made to resemble him to them. And indeed, those who differ over it are in doubt about it. They have no knowledge of it except the following of assumption. And they did not kill him, for certain. Rather, Allah raised him to Himself. And ever is Allah Exalted in Might and Wise.

According to all four [John, Luke, Mathew, Mark] gospels, Jesus was crucified on Friday, and resurrected Sunday morning. This amounts to less than two days, and two nights. The discrepancy is obvious; Jesus was not in the grave "for three days and three nights."

There is also some confusion about how early the resurrection could have taken place. In John's narration, it was still dark when Mary Magdalene first went to the tomb. In other narrations, it was after sunrise. In any case, it seems clear that the common Christian idea of the resurrection at sunrise is impossible.

It is narrated from Abu Huraira that Allah's Apostle said, "By Him in Whose Hands my soul is, surely [Jesus], the son of Mary will soon descend amongst you and will judge mankind justly [as a Just Ruler]; he will break the Cross and kill the pigs and there will be no Jiziya [i.e. taxation taken from non Muslims]" (Muslim, book #001, hadith #0287). Money will be in abundance so that nobody will accept it, and a single prostration to Allah [in prayer] will be better than the whole world and whatever is in it. Abu Huraira added, If you wish, you can recite [this verse of the Holy Book] of **Surah an-Nisa' (4:159)** in which Allah [swt] says:

وَإِن مِّنْ أَهْلِ الْكِتَبِ إِلَّا لَيُؤْمِنَنَّ بِهِ قَبْلَ مَوْتِهِ وَيَوْمَ الْقِيَمَةِ يَكُونُ عَلَيْهِمْ شَهِيداً

And there is none from the People of the Scripture but that he will surely believe in him [Isa] before his death. And on the Day of Resurrection he will be against them a witness.

Allah [swt] says that among all the faith traditions, those who are Christians will be closest to Muslims in **Surah al-Ma'idah (5:82):**

لَتَجِدَنَّ أَشَدَّ النَّاسِ عَدَاوَةً لِّلَّذِينَ ءَامَنُوا الْيَهُودَ وَالَّذِينَ أَشْرَكُوا وَلَتَجِدَنَّ أَقْرَبَهُم مَّوَدَّةً لِّلَّذِينَ ءَامَنُوا الَّذِينَ قَالُوا إِنَّا نَصَارَى ذلِكَ بِأَنَّ مِنْهُمْ قِسِّيسِينَ وَرُهْبَاناً وَأَنَّهُمْ لاَ يَسْتَكْبِرُونَ-

You will surely find the most intense of the people in animosity toward the believers [to be] the Jews and those who associate others with Allah; and you will find the nearest of them in affection to the believers those who say, "We are Christians." That is because among them are priests and monks and because they are not arrogant.

After years of Hollywood portraying Middle-Easterners and Muslims as demons and devils, we can imagine how upset these image-makers might feel to see their investment going to waste now that Christ himself walks and dresses like an Arab, speaks a dialect of Arabic and has a beard; not to mention that his mother and female companions are seen wearing a piece of cloth over their heads which many Western politicians would like to see banned. And what language does Christ speak? Is it American English? Is it modern Europeanized Israeli Hebrew? No. It is Aramaic, a cognate language of Arabic [and ancient Hebrew] still spoken in parts of Iraq and Syria by the Assyrians.

May Allah [swt] give us the courage to speak the truth, reveal the truth for the benefit of the mankind, and especially for those who believe in one and only creator Allah (swt)? **Amin!**

Status of Women in Islam

After creating Adam [as], how and why Allah has created Hawwa [ra] is described in **Surah al-A'râf (7:189):**

$$\text{هُوَ الَّذِى خَلَقَكُم مِّن نَّفْسٍ وَحِدَةٍ وَجَعَلَ مِنْهَا زَوْجَهَا لِيَسْكُنَ إِلَيْهَا فَلَمَّا تَغَشَّاهَا حَمَلَتْ حَمْلاً خَفِيفًا فَمَرَّتْ بِهِ فَلَمَّا أَثْقَلَت دَّعَوَا}$$

$$\text{اللَّهَ رَبَّهُمَا لَئِنْ ءَاتَيْتَنَا صَلِحًا لَّنَكُونَنَّ مِنَ الشَّكِرِينَ}$$

It is He Who has created you from one soul, and created from it its mate that he might dwell in security with her. And when he covers [had sexual relation with] her, she becomes pregnant and continues therein. And when it becomes heavy, they both invoke Allah, their creator [saying], "If You give us a good [physically sound and righteous] child, we will surely among the grateful."

Allah [swt] also says in **Surah ar-Rum (30:21):**

$$\text{وَمِنْ ءَايَتِهِ أَنْ خَلَقَ لَكُم مِّنْ أَنفُسِكُمْ أَزْوَجًا لِّتَسْكُنُوا إِلَيْهَا وَجَعَلَ بَيْنَكُم مَّوَدَّةً وَرَحْمَةً إِنَّ فِي ذَلِكَ لَأَيَتٍ لِّقَوْمٍ يَتَفَكَّرُونَ}$$

And of His Signs is that He created for you mates from yourselves that you may find tranquility in them; and He placed between you affection and mercy. Indeed, in that are Signs for the people who give thought?

In the above two verses Allah [swt] clearly described women's need for men is just like his need for her. Being with each other, they gain rest and peace of mind as vicegerents on the earth. What was the condition of women and what was their status before Islam? How has Islam elevated their status? What are the differences between men and women from the perspective of Islam? What are the responsibilities of women in our present society?

During the European dark ages, philosophers used to hold meetings to discuss the matter of a woman having a soul like that of man. Does a woman have a human or bestial soul? Their discussions culminated in declaring that a woman has a soul greatly inferior to that of a man. In the Roman law, the wife was the purchased property of her husband, who could also divorce her. The situation was even worse as they did not allow women to inherit. In India, there existed the practice of burning the widow along with her husband's corpse.

A woman, in the Arab men's eyes, was a den of shame, a jinx and a source of poverty. Refuting their claims, Allah [swt] says in **Surah at-Takweer (81:8-9):**

$$\text{وَ إِذَا الْمَوْءُودَةُ سُئِلَتْ - بِأَيِّ ذَنبٍ قُتِلَتْ}$$

And when the girl [who was] buried alive is asked for what crime she was killed.

In Judaism, a menstruating woman is considered impure. The Jewish worshippers used to isolate menstruating women to remote tents and avoid talking or sitting with them for, according to their distorted Torah, when such a woman touches anything it becomes impure. In Judaism, women were also deprived of inheritance, for males alone were to inherit. Christianity, in its distorted Gospel, considered women the devil's gateway. King Henry VIII decreed that a woman should not touch the Gospel for she is impure. In Hammurabi's law [king of Babylon], a woman was one of her husband's animals. This was the status of woman before Islam. However, what did Islam do for women? Every Muslims should know that it was Islam that brought honor and dignity to women in many respects.

Upon examining Eve's legacy, all throughout the Judeo-Christian heritage, we find a negative image of women in general. This negativity is a result from the temptress image of Hawwa [ra] portrayed in the Bible. She has been given the appearance of a seducer, temptress, as well as a deceiver. From the beginning, the Judeo-Christian religions placed total blame on Hawwa [ra]. According to their scriptures, Allah [swt] said to Hawwa [ra]: "I will greatly increase your pain in childbearing." Jewish rabbis list nine curses inflicted upon women as a result of Hawwa's [ra] sin: "To the women He gave nine curses and death: the burden of the blood of menstruation and the blood of virginity; the burden of pregnancy; the burden of childbirth; the burden of bringing up children; her head is covered as one in mourning; she pierces her ear like a permanent slave or slave girl who serves her master; she is not to be believed after a witness; and after everything-death" (Leonard J. Swindler, Women in Judaism: The Status of women in formative Judaism Metuchen, N.J: Scarecrow Press, 1976 pg 155). This implies that Allah [swt] is punishing Hawwa [ra] as well as the entire female population for Hawwa's [ra] sin. Allah, according to the Holy Qur'an, punishes no one for another's faults.

When it comes to female or male gender, religious attitude is present as well. The Catholic Bible does say explicitly that, "The birth of a daughter is a loss." (Ecclesiasticus: 22:3). In Leviticus (12: 2-5), we have "If a woman has conceived seed, and born a male child: then she shall be unclean seven days...but if she bears a female child, then she shall be unclean two weeks."

When it comes to education, there is also a great distinction between the three religions. In Judaism, the Torah is the Law. However, according to the Talmud, "women are exempt from the study of the Torah." Many Jewish rabbis declare, "Whoever teaches his daughter Torah is as though he taught her obscenity." (Denise L. Carmody, "Judaism, in Arvind Sharma" (ed.,op.,ct.,197*).

According to the New Testament, "let your women keep silent in the churches for it is not permitted unto them to speak; but they are commanded to be under obedience, as also saith the law, and if they will learn anything, let them ask their husbands at home: FOR IT IS A SHAME FOR A WOMAN TO SPEAK IN THE CHURCH." (Corinthians, 14:34-35). But in Islam, education is made mandatory for all men and women.

A very significant difference between the three religions is the question of female inheritance. Upon viewing the Holy Bible, Numbers 27:1-11, a wife is given no share in her husband's estate, while he is her first heir, even before her sons. If a male heir exists then the female cannot inherit.

Polygamy did not originate from either the Muslims or the Arabs. It was practiced and accepted by other religions and cultures way before Islam. Because Islam is a universal religion, polygamy is considered a remedy. It can solve many of societies' problems with unbalanced sex ratios, orphans, and widows. We ask the world," Which is more dignified to a woman in a civilized society, to be an accepted and respected second wife or to have adultery, fornication, and a thousand illegitimate children running around? And performing paternity [DNA] tests to decide the biological father of a child?"

Because of these moral reasons, Islam accepted polygamy, but with a restriction described in **Surah an-Nisa' (4:3):**

وَإِنْ خِفْتُمْ أَلَّا تُقْسِطُوا فِي الْيَتَـٰمَىٰ فَانكِحُوا مَا طَابَ لَكُم مِّنَ النِّسَاءِ مَثْنَىٰ وَثُلَـٰثَ وَرُبَـٰعَ فَإِنْ خِفْتُمْ أَلَّا تَعْدِلُوا فَوَ حِدَةً أَوْ مَا مَلَكَتْ أَيْمَـٰنُكُمْ ذَٰلِكَ أَدْنَىٰ أَلَّا تَعُولُوا

And if you fear that you will not deal justly with the orphan girls, then marry those that please you of [other] women, two or three or four. But if you fear that you will not be able to deal justly [with them], then [marry only] one or those right hands possess. That is more suitable that you may not incline [to injustice].

One should know that taking care of a girl makes a man enter paradise for the Prophet [sas] said: "Anyone who is given a female child and avoids harming, insulting or even giving his son priority over her, she'll be his ticket to enter Paradise." (Abu Dawud, book #41, hadith #5127)

In inheritance, for example, Allah [swt] says in **Surah an-Nisa' (4:11):**

يُوصِيكُمُ اللَّهُ فِي أَوْلَـٰدِكُمْ لِلذَّكَرِ مِثْلُ حَظِّ الْأُنثَيَيْنِ

Allah directs you concerning your children's their portions of inheritance: for the male, what is equal to the share of two females.

Moreover, Muslim women, whether she is a wife, mother, sister, or daughter receive a certain share upon the death of her father or kin. In **Surah an-Nisa' (4:7)** Allah [swt] says:

لِّلرِّجَالِ نَصِيبٌ مِّمَّا تَرَكَ الْوَٰلِدَانِ وَالْأَقْرَبُونَ وَلِلنِّسَاءِ نَصِيبٌ مِّمَّا تَرَكَ الْوَٰلِدَانِ وَالْأَقْرَبُونَ مِمَّا قَلَّ مِنْهُ أَوْ كَثُرَ نَصِيبًا مَّفْرُوضًا

For men is a share of what the parents and close relatives leave, and for women is a share of what the parents and close relatives leave, be it little or much - an obligatory share.

However, why do we not give woman a share equal to that of man? Since a woman in maintained either by her father, her husband or her brother, she is not وَلَهُنَّ مِثْلُ الَّذِى عَلَيْهِنَّ بِالْمَعْرُوفِ asked to spend even a penny from her own money. For example, if a man and his sister inherit three thousand dollars, the man takes two thousand and the woman takes one thousand in which case he is obliged to maintain her until she marries. She, on the contrary, is not asked to spend any money from her share. He is required to provide for his own family and if he is single, has the debt of preparing himself for marriage and, at the same time maintaining his sister. It is clear that man's financial duties are greater than that of a woman. Moreover, the woman is allowed to have Mehr that will be exclusively of her own and she also inherits the property of her husband.

In divorce, why do we not shift the authority of divorce to women? Scholars responded to this focusing on two aspects, the material aspect, and the emotional one. As for the material aspect, every Muslim man knows that by uttering the pronouncement of divorce he will be asked to pay the deferred dower, to pay maintenance which includes wife's food, and lodging during the waiting period, to provide for his children until they become old enough, to maintain himself and, on trying to marry a new wife to secure a dower for this new wife. All these financial responsibilities will be taken into consideration before uttering a declaration of divorce.

If he utters it, he does so out of conviction that he cannot tolerate living with his wife and thus wants to terminate this marriage at any cost. As for the emotional aspect, Allah created woman sensitive and emotional, qualities that are required in her duty of bringing up the children and fulfilling their needs. It is a good quality of a woman to be sensitive but if she is given authority of divorce, she may, at any moment of a dispute, utter a declaration of divorce especially as she will have no financial responsibilities to fulfill. In our everyday life, we see that as soon as a woman gets angry she demands a divorce. Family bondage would then be easily destroyed.

Finally a woman as a witness is mentioned in **Surah al-Baqarah (2:282):**

$$\text{وَاسْتَشْهِدُواْ شَهِيدَيْنِ مِن رِّجَالِكُمْ فَإِن لَّمْ يَكُونَا رَجُلَيْنِ فَرَجُلٌ وَامْرَأَتَانِ مِمَّن تَرْضَوْنَ مِنَ الشُّهَدَاءِ أَن تَضِلَّ إِحْدَاهُمَا فَتُذَكِّرَ إِحْدَاهُمَا الأُخْرَى}$$

And bring to witness two witnesses from among your men. And if there are not two men, then a man and two women from those whom you accept as witnesses, so that if one of them [the women] errs, the other can remind her.

Why is one male witness equated to two female witnesses? The scholars say: Witnessing may relate to matters pertaining to women or may relate to Allah's limits. If the matter concerned relates to women such as suckling or proving virginity or otherwise, then only one woman will be sufficient as witness. Umm al-Fadl reported: A Bedouin came to Allah's Apostle [sas] when he was in my house and said: Allah's Apostle, I have had a wife and I married another besides her, and my first wife claimed that she had suckled once or twice my newly married wife, thereupon Allah's Apostle [sas] said: "One suckling or two do not make the (marriage) unlawful". (Muslim, book #008, hadith #3415)

In Islam, it is required to ask another woman to support her as her witness, thus, the verse in **Surah al-Baqarah (2:282)** states:

$$\text{أَن تَضِلَّ إِحْدَاهُمَا فَتُذَكِّرَ إِحْدَاهُمَا الأُخْرَى}$$

If one of them errs, the other can remind her.

By establishing this rule, Islam seeks more perfect investigation. It does not mean belittling woman or debasing her as is claimed. Thus, the requirement that one man verses two women are needed assures an honest transaction from a lack of experience that the female may not have. It is a precautionary step to guarantee proper dealings between people.

In Islam there is absolutely no difference between men and women as far as their relationship to Allah is concerned, as both are promised the same reward for good conduct and the same punishment for evil conduct. The Qur'an says in **Surah an-Nahl (16:97)** that women have souls in exactly the same way as men and will enter Paradise if they do well:

مَنْ عَمِلَ صَـٰلِحًا مِّن ذَكَرٍ أَوْ أُنثَىٰ وَهُوَ مُؤْمِنٌ فَلَنُحْيِيَنَّهُ حَيَوٰةً طَيِّبَةً وَلَنَجْزِيَنَّهُمْ أَجْرَهُم بِأَحْسَنِ مَا كَانُوا يَعْمَلُونَ

Whoever does righteousness, whether male or female, while he is a believer - We will surely cause him to live a good life, and We will surely give them their reward [in the Hereafter] according to the best of what they used to do.

The Qur'an says in **Surah al-Baqarah (2:228):**

وَلَهُنَّ مِثْلُ الَّذِى عَلَيْهِنَّ بِالْمَعْرُوفِ وَلِلرِّجَالِ عَلَيْهِنَّ دَرَجَةٌ وَاللَّهُ عَزِيزٌ حَكِيمٌ

………..And due to them [the wives] is similar to what is expected of them, according to what is reasonable [the wife has specific rights upon her husband, just as the husband has rights upon her]. But the men have a degree over them [in responsibility and authority]." And Allah is Exalted in Might and Wise.

The Holy Prophet [sas] said, "O Muslims! I command you to behave well with your wives because woman has been created from the left rib of man. If you try to make it straight it will break, and if you allow letting it remain in its original condition, it will remain crooked. Obey my order and live a good life by treating your wives well." (Bukhari, book #55, hadith #548)

In Islam a woman is a completely independent personality. She can make any contract or bequest in her own name. She is entitled to inherit in her position as mother, as wife, as sister and as daughter. She has perfect liberty to choose her husband. The pagan society of pre-Islamic Arabia had an irrational prejudice against their female children whom they used to bury alive. The Messenger of Allah [swt] was totally opposed to this practice. He showed them that supporting their female children would act as a screen for them against the fire of Hell.

Islam says that both male and female were created from a single source as in **Surah an-Nisa' (4:1):**

يَـٰٓأَيُّهَا النَّاسُ اتَّقُوا رَبَّكُمُ الَّذِى خَلَقَكُم مِّن نَّفْسٍ وَٰحِدَةٍ وَخَلَقَ مِنْهَا زَوْجَهَا

O mankind, fear your Rabb, who created you from one soul and created from it its mate,

Also, notice the name of the surah that contains the verse above is named "An-Nisa' There is no surah in the Qur'an that is named "The Men". Also, there is no chapter in the Bible called "The Women".

In Islam there is no distinction between boy and girl. In fact, a recent discovery made while studying the mathematical aspect of the Qur'an shows that the word "man" and "woman" both appear the same number of times in it. This is probably Allah's way of showing us that man and woman are equal. In the Qur'an, it was revealed that male and female off springs are both gifts from Allah. One should not forget that biologically speaking it is the male who determines the sex of the child. So if it is a boy or a girl, it is due to the man's X or Y chromosome.

Woman according to Qur'an is not blamed for Adam's first mistake. Both were jointly wrong in their disobedience to Allah, both repented, and both were forgiven as mentioned in **Surah al-A'râf (7:23):**

قَالَا رَبَّنَا ظَلَمْنَا أَنفُسَنَا وَإِن لَّمْ تَغْفِرْ لَنَا وَتَرْحَمْنَا لَنَكُونَنَّ مِنَ الْخَاسِرِينَ

They said: "Our Lord, We have wronged ourselves, and if you do not forgive us and have mercy upon us, we will surely be among the losers."

In one verse, in fact, in **Surah Tâ Hâ (20:121)**, Adam (as) specifically, was blamed:

وَعَصَى ءَادَمُ رَبَّهُ فَغَوَى

And Adam disobeyed his Creator and erred.

In terms of religious obligations, such as the Daily Prayers, Fasting, and Pilgrimage, woman is no different from man. In some cases indeed, woman has certain advantages over man. For example, the woman is exempted from the daily prayers and from fasting during her menstrual periods and forty days after childbirth. She is also exempted from fasting during her pregnancy and when she is nursing her baby if there is any threat to her health or her baby's. If the missed fasting is obligatory [during the month of Ramadan], she can make up for the missed days whenever she can. She does not have to make up for the prayers missed for any of the above reasons. Although women can and did go into the mosque during the days of the prophet and thereafter attendance at the Friday congregational prayers is optional for them while it is mandatory for men [on Friday].

This is clearly a tender touch of the Islamic teachings for they are considerate of the fact that a woman may be nursing her baby or caring for him, and thus may be unable to go out to the mosque at the time of the prayers. They also take into account the physiological and psychological changes associated with her natural female functions.

If we look at the prayer of the wife of Fir`awn [whose name was Asiyah bint Muzahim (ra)] mentioned in **Surah at-Tahreem (66:11) :**

إِذْ قَالَتْ رَبِّ ابْنِ لِي عِندَكَ بَيْتاً فِي الْجَنَّةِ وَنَجِّنِي مِن فِرْعَوْنَ وَعَمَلِهِ وَنَجِّنِي مِنَ الْقَوْمِ الظَّالِمِينَ

My Creator, build for me near You a house in Paradise and save me from Fir`awn and his deeds and save me from the wrong doing people.

Allah [swt] granted her prayer, though a woman and wife of a disbeliever. Moreover there is a Surah, after the name of a virgin mother Maryam [ra] the daughter of 'Imran and mother of Jesus [as] as Surah **Maryam** (19), although she was a woman. Moreover, maximum number of hadith was reported by A'isha [ra], the wife of the Prophet [sas]. Moreover Allah [swt] has made Sa'i [Tawaf] between As-Safa and Al-Marwah obligatory comes from the Tawaf of Hajara [Prophet Ibrahim's wife], between As-Safa and Al-Marwah seeking water for her son [Isma`il]. Ibrahim had left them in Makkah, where there was no habitation for her. When Hajara feared that her son would die, she stood up and begged Allah for His help and kept going back and forth in that blessed area between As-Safa and Al-Marwah. She was humble, fearful, frightened and week before Allah and Allah [swt] liked the Sa'i of Hajara (ra) as mentioned in **Surah al-Baqarah (2:158):**

إِنَّ الصَّفَا وَالْمَرْوَةَ مِن شَعَآئِرِ اللَّهِ فَمَنْ حَجَّ الْبَيْتَ أَوِ اعْتَمَرَ فَلاَ جُنَاحَ عَلَيْهِ أَن يَطَّوَّفَ بِهِمَا وَمَن تَطَوَّعَ خَيْراً فَإِنَّ اللَّهَ شَاكِرٌ عَلِيمٌ

Indeed, as-Safa and al-Marwah are among the symbols [places designated for the rites of] *hajj and'umrah* **of Allah. So whoever performs hajj [pilgrimage] to the House or performs `umrah –there is no blame upon him for walking between them. And whoever volunteers good – then indeed, Allah is Appreciative and Knowing.**

These four specific instances testify clearly that the status of women is no lower than that of men in the religion of Islam.

Mahmud Shaltut says about the status of women in Islam, "It is a status that the woman had not enjoyed in any divine law, nor in any society that people set up for themselves." He adds, "Islam has granted women all that is good, and protected her from all that is evil". The only thing it denied her was the liberty that false culture [namely, the western culture] has pushed her into. That liberty causes the western woman, whenever she retreats to her human conscience, to weep tears of blood over her forfeited respect, misused honor, and lost happiness.

On the contrary, the woman in Islam is a "precious jewel" not to be viewed by all and sundry. She is far too precious then to be viewed and exhibited to any lecherous man. Her beauty and charms are reserved for the only person that truly appreciates and loves her - her husband. Thus, she is highly protected and covered at all times, unlike the cheap, shameless woman of the West, who is the playmate of thousands but loved by none for what she really is.

The treatment expected from the husband, whether or not he is on good terms with his wife, is clearly laid down in **Surah an-Nisa' (4:19):**

وَعَاشِرُوهُنَّ بِالْمَعْرُوفِ فَإِن كَرِهْتُمُوهُنَّ فَعَسَى أَن تَكْرَهُواْ شَيْئاً وَيَجْعَلَ اللَّهُ فِيهِ خَيْراً كَثِيراً

And live with them in kindness. For if you disliked them – perhaps you dislike a thing and Allah brings therein much good.

Even if divorce is decided upon, the good treatment is still required for the divorcee as described in a full surah on divorce called **Surah At-Talâq (65).**

As a mother, a woman is given respect and preference over the father because the Prophet [sas] said as reported by Abu Hurairah that a man came to the Messenger of Allah [swt] and asked: "Who has the greatest claim on me with regard to service and kind treatment?" The Prophet [sas] replied: "Your mother; and again, your mother; and once again, your mother. After her, there is the claim of your father, and, after it, of your near kinsmen, and then, of the kinsmen who are next to them." (Muslim, book #032, hadith #6181)

Muslim women have been enjoying equal status and respectful position in the family and society, at large since the advent of Islam about fourteen hundred years ago. But the status that women now enjoy in non-Muslim societies and in the west is a very recent phenomenon [of about sixty to seventy years] not on the basis of religion but on the basis of worldly laws only.

Allah hasn't given equality to man and woman as the west perceive it to be, but has given equality according to the difference in the creation of man and woman. If a bat cannot see during the day, one cannot blame the brightness of the sun. So if one cannot understand the Hikmat and Wisdom of Allah [swt] blame you, not.

May Allah [swt] provide all men and women in Islam, the proper guidance to carry on with the responsibilities entrusted on them by the Qur'an and the Sunnah of Prophet Muhammad [sas] to show respect and guard the rights of one over the other? **Amin!**

Taqwah: Most Lovable Act in Allah's Sight

Taqwa is an invaluable treasure, the matchless jewel in a priceless treasure of precious stones, a mysterious key to all doors of Allah, and a mount on the way to Paradise. Its value is so high that, among other life-giving expressions, the Qur'an mentions it 151 times, each mention resembling a ray of light penetrating our minds and spirits.

The origin of the word taqwa is from the Arabic root letters و ق ي [meaning shield] and its verb is from the word

انقى which means to be careful or to be protected or to be cautious. Taqwa is unique to the Qur'an and the religious system of Islam. .

Possessors of tawqa are called al-muttaqun or muttaqeen. Though taqwa is a state of the heart, we cannot judge the taqwa of others, but many aspects of taqwa will have a reflection in their character and behavior.

The four verses in **Surah al-Baqarah (2:2-5)** summarize the guiding principle in the noble Qur'an for the people of taqwa:

ذَلِكَ الْكِتَابُ لاَ رَيْبَ فِيهِ هُدًى لِّلْمُتَّقِينَ الَّذِينَ يُؤْمِنُونَ بِالْغَيْبِ وَ يُقِيمُونَ الصَّلوةَ وَ مِمَّا رَزَقْنَهُمْ يُنفِقُونَ وَ الَّذِينَ يُؤْمِنُونَ بِمَآ

أُنزِلَ إِلَيْكَ وَ مَآ أُنزِلَ مِن قَبْلِكَ وَ بِالأَخِرَةِ هُمْ يُوقِنُونَ أُوْلَـئِكَ عَلَى هُدًى مِّن رَّبِّهِمْ وَ أُوْلَـئِكَ هُمُ الْمُفْلِحُونَ-

This is the book [this Qur'an] about which there is no doubt, a guidance for those conscious of Allah - who believe in the unseen, establish prayer, and spend out of what We have provided for them. And who believe in what has been revealed to you [O Muhammad], and what was revealed before you, and of the Hereafter they are certain [in faith]. Those are upon [right] guidance from their Lord, and it is those who are the successful.

Since the Holy Qur'an is the one and only sacred book for the Muslims, Allah [swt] has categorically mentioned that this Qur'an is the guidebook for the muttaqeen only.

Some more meanings for the word taqwa may be mentioned here directly from Qur'an. Allah says in **Surah al-Baqarah (2:177):**

لَّيْسَ الْبِرَّ أَن تُوَلُّواْ وُجُوهَكُمْ قِبَلَ الْمَشْرِقِ وَ الْمَغْرِبِ وَ لَكِنَّ الْبِرَّ مَنْ ءَامَنَ بِاللهِ وَ الْيَوْمِ الأَخِرِ وَ الْمَلَـئِكَةِ وَ الْكِتَبِ

وَ النَّبِيِّنَ وَ ءَاتَى الْمَالَ عَلَى حُبِّهِ ذَوِى الْقُرْبَى وَ الْيَتَمَى وَ الْمَسَكِينَ وَ ابْنَ السَّبِيلِ وَ السَّآئِلِينَ وَ فِي الرِّقَابِ وَ أَقَامَ الصَّلوةَ وَ ءَاتَى

الزَّكوةَ وَ الْمُوفُونَ بِعَهْدِهِمْ إِذَا عَهَدُواْ وَ الصَّابِرِينَ فِي الْبَأْسَآءِ وَ الضَّرَّاءِ وَ حِينَ الْبَأْسِ أُوْلَـئِكَ الَّذِينَ صَدَقُواْ وَ أُوْلَـئِكَ هُمُ الْمُتَّقُونَ

Righteousness is not that you turn your faces toward the east or the west, but [true] righteousness is [in] one who believes in Allah, the Last Day, the Angels, the Books and the Prophets and gives wealth, in spite of love for it, to relatives, orphans, the needy, and the traveler, those who ask [for help], and freeing slaves; [and who] establishes prayer and gives zakah; [those who] fulfill their promise when they make it; and [those who] are patient in poverty and hardship and during battle. Those are the ones who have been true, and it is those who are the righteous.

The most honored in the sight of Allah is the believer with the most taqwa. The Glorious Qur'an mentioned this in **Surah al-Hujurat (49:13):**

$$إِنَّ أَكْرَمَكُمْ عِندَ اللَّهِ أَتْقَاكُمْ إِنَّ اللَّهَ عَلِيمٌ خَبِيرٌ$$

Indeed, the most honorable of you in the sight of Allah is the most righteous [consciousness and fear of Allah, piety]. Indeed, Allah is Knowing and Acquainted.

Allah [swt] warns us that it is neither wealth, nor social status, nor power in this world that will make us honorable in the eyes of Allah [swt], but it is only taqwa that will make us honorable.

The Qur'anic descriptions of taqwa are so precise and distinct that it is an indication of the importance of the involvement of this concept in the life of Muslims. These numerous verses elaborate the different dynamics and dimensions of inner meanings of taqwa that enables Muslims to be an ideal and a living example as a vicegerent of Allah.

In **Surah an-Najm (53:32)** Allah [swt] reminds us that:

$$فَلَا تُزَكُّوا أَنفُسَكُمْ هُوَ أَعْلَمُ بِمَنِ اتَّقَى$$

So do not claim yourselves to be pure; He is most knowing of who fears Him.

Hence, for the moral development and correct behavior of a good Muslim, it is necessary that he strictly analyze and establish his taqwa, but never claims to be a possessor of it. One may ask for the types of rewards that the muttaqeen will receive from Allah Almighty. Since taqwa includes beliefs, practices and good deeds in one's own life, the rewards from Allah are plenty. Among the many worldly and heavenly rewards are the following:

1. Love of Allah to the muttaqeen. In this regard Allah says in **Surah al-'Imran (15:45):**

$$إِنَّ الْمُتَّقِينَ فِي جَنَّاتٍ وَعُيُونٍ$$

Indeed, the righteous will be within gardens and springs.

2. Allah is with the muttaqeen. In this regard Allah says in **Surah al-Baqarah (2:194):**

وَاتَّقُوا اللَّهَ وَاعْلَمُوا أَنَّ اللَّهَ مَعَ الْمُتَّقِينَ۔

And fear Allah and know that Allah is with those who fear Him.

3. Allah is the supporter, the friend and the helper to the muttaqeen. In **Surah al-Jathiyah (45:19)** Allah says:

وَاللَّهُ وَلِيُّ الْمُتَّقِينَ۔

Allah is the Protector of the righteous.

4. The muttaqeen during the Day of Judgment will continue to be friends to one another, while others will be foes to one another. In this regard, Allah says in **Surah az-Zukhruff (43:67):**

الْأَخِلَّاءُ يَوْمَئِذٍ بَعْضُهُمْ لِبَعْضٍ عَدُوٌّ إِلَّا الْمُتَّقِينَ۔

Close friends, that Day, will be enemies to each other, except for the righteous.

5. The muttaqeen will go to paradise with all the good life they are to enjoy there. There are many verses in the Qur'an about this reward. Allah says in **Surah al-Hijr (15: 45-46):**

إِنَّ الْمُتَّقِينَ فِي جَنَّاتٍ وَعُيُونٍ۔ ادْخُلُوهَا بِسَلَامٍ آمِنِينَ۔

Indeed, the righteous will be within gardens and springs. [Having been told], "Enter it in peace and safe [and secure]."

Can we ask for a better reward than Allah [swt] has promised for the muttaqeen?

The following verse of the Qur'an of **Surah al-Baqarah (2:183)** confirms that taqwa is for everyone and not for a select group:

يَا أَيُّهَا الَّذِينَ آمَنُوا كُتِبَ عَلَيْكُمُ الصِّيَامُ كَمَا كُتِبَ عَلَى الَّذِينَ مِن قَبْلِكُمْ لَعَلَّكُمْ تَتَّقُونَ

O you who have believed, decreed upon you is fasting as it was decreed upon those before you that you may become righteous.

Allah [swt] reminds us that fasting is a process by which we can attain and increase our taqwa, because in the month of Ramadhan. Muslims are prohibited from eating and drinking even halal food and drink and refrain from some other activities not prohibited at other times, for a particular time of a day during fasting.

Taqwa is not such that we reach a certain level and we are there 100% all the time. Taqwa increases and decreases as well. We increase taqwa by our righteous deeds, and decrease it with our sins and evil deeds. The simple and only formula to increase taqwa is to increase our righteous deeds.

In conclusion, taqwa is the heavenly water of life, and a muttaquee is the fortunate one who has found it. Only a few individuals have achieved the blessing of this attainment. Every one of us should put our all out and sincere effort to become muttaqee.

O Allah, Include us among your pious servants who were sincere in all their religious acts and provide us proper guidance so that we can be included among the muttaqun. **Amin!**

Tawbah [Repentance]: Allah [swt] Loves Forgiveness

Seek nearness to Allah [swt] through performing good deeds and plentiful repentance for Allah is the Most Kind, All Aware. He is well aware that people's weaknesses and deficiencies make them commit sins; it is because of this that He opened the door of hope and forgiveness and enjoined them to resort to His favors and grace. He is Merciful to those who seek Him and near to those who call unto Him. Mistakes and negligence are part of man's nature. The Messenger of Allah [sas] said, "By He in whose hand is my soul, if you did not sin, Allah would wipe you out and bring into existence people who did sin, ask Allah for forgiveness - and He would forgive them." (Muslim, book #037, hadith #6622)

Allah [swt] says in **Surah ar-Ra'd (13:29):**

$$ الَّذِينَ آمَنُوا وَعَمِلُوا الصَّـٰلِحَاتِ طُوبَىٰ لَهُمْ وَحُسْنُ مَـَٔابٍ $$

Those who have believed and done righteous deeds – a good state is theirs, them and a good return. Tawbah is an Arabic word that means, `you have earned a good thing.'

The situation of the best amongst the pious and guided people is that when they sin they seek Allah's forgiveness and when they commit errors, they repent. The Prophet (sas) said, "All the sons of Adam are sinners and the best among the sinners are those who repent." (Ahmad)

Allah [swt] says in **Surah an-Nahl (16:119):**

$$ ثُمَّ إِنَّ رَبَّكَ لِلَّذِينَ عَمِلُوا السُّوءَ بِجَهَـٰلَةٍ ثُمَّ تَابُوا مِن بَعْدِ ذَٰلِكَ وَأَصْلَحُوا إِنَّ رَبَّكَ مِن بَعْدِهَا لَغَفُورٌ رَّحِيمٌ $$

Then, indeed your Lord, to those who have done wrong out of ignorance and then repent after that and correct themselves -indeed, your Lord, thereafter, is Forgiving and Merciful.

It is a manifestation of the mercy of Allah upon his slaves that He stretches out His Hand during the night so that those who do sin during the day may repent and stretches His Hand out during the day in order for those who sinned during the night to repent. He forgives all sins. People should therefore not despair of the mercy of their Rabb however great and serious their sins may be. Allah says in **Surah al-Hijr (15:56):**

$$ قَالَ وَمَن يَقْنَطُ مِن رَّحْمَةِ رَبِّهِ إِلَّا الضَّآلُّونَ $$

He said, "And who despairs of the mercy of his Lord except for those astray."

Allah [swt] also says in **Surah ash-Shura (42:25):**

$$ وَهُوَ الَّذِي يَقْبَلُ التَّوْبَةَ عَنْ عِبَادِهِ وَيَعْفُوا عَنِ السَّيِّئَاتِ وَيَعْلَمُ مَا تَفْعَلُونَ $$

And it is He who accepts repentance from His servants and pardons misdeeds, and He knows what you do.

Tirmidhi and others reported on the authority of Anas ibn Malik who said, I heard the Messenger of Allah [sas] saying: "Allah says, 'O son of Adam! As long as you call unto me and seek forgiveness from me, I will forgive you for all of the sins that you may commit and I do not care [how many they amount to]. O son of Adam! If you come to me with what is almost as much as the earth [in volume] in sins, but you meets me without having associated any partner with Me in worship, I will give you the same amount of forgiveness." Allah commanded His Messenger (sas) – even though he is the most pious of mankind - to be sincere in religion and frequently seek for forgiveness when He said in **Surah Muhammad (47:19):**

$$\text{فَاعْلَمْ أَنَّهُ لاَ إِلَهَ إِلاَّ اللَّهُ وَاسْتَغْفِرْ لِذَنبِكَ وَلِلْمُؤْمِنِينَ وَالْمُؤْمِنَتِ وَاللَّهُ يَعْلَمُ مُتَقَلَّبَكُمْ وَمَثْوَاكُمْ}$$

So know, [O Muhammad], that there is no deity except Allah and ask forgiveness for your sin and for the believing men and women. And Allah knows of your movement and your resting place.

The Messenger of Allah [sas] therefore used to seek Allah's forgiveness frequently during the day and night and said of himself, "I swear by Allah, I seek Allah's forgiveness and repent to Him seventy times a day." (Bukhari, book #75, hadith #319)

This is characteristic of the resolute and faithful Muslims; they often turn to Allah with a great deal of Istighfar and repent sincerely without despair or impatience. Their hearts are filled with the fear of Allah and their feet are firmly placed doing good deeds.

Allah [swt] says in **Surah al-'Imran (3:17):**

$$\text{الصَّبِرِينَ وَالصَّدِقِينَ وَالْقَنِتِينَ وَالْمُنفِقِينَ وَالْمُسْتَغْفِرِينَ بِالأَسْحَارِ}$$

The patient, the true, the obedient, those who spend [in the way of Allah], and those who seek forgiveness before dawn.

These are the pious people, those who observe their obligations, perform acts of obedience and seek Allah's forgiveness. Allah also commanded his Prophet [sas] to remember Him and seek His forgiveness after he finally finished the conveyance of his Rabb's Message. He says in **Surah an-Nasr (110):**

$$\text{إِذَا جَاءَ نَصْرُ اللَّهِ وَالْفَتْحُ - وَرَأَيْتَ النَّاسَ يَدْخُلُونَ فِي دِينِ اللَّهِ أَفْوَاجًا - فَسَبِّحْ بِحَمْدِ رَبِّكَ وَاسْتَغْفِرْهُ إِنَّهُ كَانَ تَوَّابًا}$$

When the victory of Allah has come and the Conquest [the conquest of Mecca], and you see the people entering into the religion of Allah in multitude, then exalt [Him] with praise of your Lord and ask forgiveness of Him. Indeed, He is ever accepting of repentance.

Brothers in faith! It is a manifestation of Allah's Mercy that He promises a generous reward for Al-Istighfar. Plentiful Istighfar and repentance brings forth divine mercy and success in this life and also in the Hereafter. Allah says in **Surah an-Nur (24:31):**

وَتُوبُوٓاْ إِلَى ٱللَّهِ جَمِيعًا أَيُّهَ ٱلْمُؤْمِنُونَ لَعَلَّكُمْ تُفْلِحُونَ

And turn to Allah in repentance, all of you, O believers, so that you might succeed.

Making much Istighfar also removes sorrow and distress, saves one from awkward situations and brings provision from unexpected sources. The Prophet [sas] said: "Whoever makes Istighfar frequently, Allah will provide a way for him out of every distress and provide for him from sources he could never expect." Allah revealed in **Surah al-Anfal (8:33):**

وَمَا كَانَ ٱللَّهُ لِيُعَذِّبَهُمْ وَأَنتَ فِيهِمْ وَمَا كَانَ ٱللَّهُ مُعَذِّبَهُمْ وَهُمْ يَسْتَغْفِرُونَ

And Allah would not punish them while you, [O Muhammad], are among them, and Allah would not punish them while they seek forgiveness. (Bukhari)

These are some of the virtues of Istighfar and their benefits that Allah and His Prophet [sas] have explained to us. The people of Iman and piety make a lot of Istighfar and repentance, for Istighfar is not merely empty words that are uttered, but rather these words must be rooted in the heart. One has have regret for the sins that they have committed and be determined never to commit them again. These are the conditions of sincere repentance that Allah enjoins on His slaves and for which He promises forgiveness and Paradise. He says in **Surah at-Tahrim (66:8):**

يَٰٓأَيُّهَا ٱلَّذِينَ ءَامَنُوا تُوبُوٓاْ إِلَى ٱللَّهِ تَوْبَةً نَّصُوحًا عَسَىٰ رَبُّكُمْ أَن يُكَفِّرَ عَنكُمْ سَيِّئَاتِكُمْ وَيُدْخِلَكُمْ جَنَّٰتٍ تَجْرِى مِن تَحْتِهَا ٱلْأَنْهَٰرُ

O you who have believed, repent to Allah with sincere repentance. Perhaps [it is expected or promised] your Lord will remove from you your misdeeds and admit you into gardens beneath which rivers flow.

Allah [swt] promises to change sins into good deeds through repentance in **Surah al-Furqan (25:70):**

إِلَّا مَن تَابَ وَءَامَنَ وَعَمِلَ عَمَلًا صَٰلِحًا فَأُوْلَٰٓئِكَ يُبَدِّلُ ٱللَّهُ سَيِّئَاتِهِمْ حَسَنَٰتٍ وَكَانَ ٱللَّهُ غَفُورًا رَّحِيمًا

Except for those who repent, believe and do righteous work; for them, Allah will replace their evil deeds with good, and ever is Allah Forgiving and Merciful.

Obey Allah and seek His forgiveness for He says in **Surah az-Zumar (39: 53-54):**

قُلْ يَـٰعِبَادِىَ الَّذِينَ أَسْرَفُوا عَلَىٰ أَنفُسِهِمْ لَا تَقْنَطُوا مِن رَّحْمَةِ اللَّهِ إِنَّ اللَّهَ يَغْفِرُ الذُّنُوبَ جَمِيعًا إِنَّهُ هُوَ الْغَفُورُ الرَّحِيمُ وَأَنِيبُوا إِلَىٰ رَبِّكُمْ وَأَسْلِمُوا لَهُ مِن قَبْلِ أَن يَأْتِيَكُمُ الْعَذَابُ ثُمَّ لَا تُنصَرُونَ

Say, "O My servants who have transgressed against themselves [by sinning], do not despair of the mercy of Allah. Indeed, it is He who is the forgiving, the Merciful. And return [in repentance] to your Lord and submit to Him before the punishment comes upon you, then you will not be helped."

Beware of postponing repentance and good deeds as death may come to us suddenly. Do not be deceived by the forbearance of Allah, for He only grants people respite and He does not forget. That is from the guidance of the Prophet [sas] – despite the fact that all his sins had been forgiven. Even Allah [swt] asked Prophet [sas] to ask for forgiveness in **Surah an- Nasr (110:3):**

فَسَبِّحْ بِحَمْدِ رَبِّكَ وَاسْتَغْفِرْهُ إِنَّهُ كَانَ تَوَّابًا

Then exalt [Him] with praises of your Lord, and ask forgiveness of Him. Indeed, He is ever accepting of repentance."

The Prophet Muhammad [sas] taught us that the individual, who pardons his enemy even while having the power to extract revenge, would be nearest to Allah in the Hereafter. May Allah [swt] provide us the guidance to make proper repentance in the true sense of the word so that we may be granted forgiveness of Allah [swt] in this world and the life hereafter? **Amin!**

Trade and Investment with Allah [swt]

In **Surah as-Saaf (61:10-3)** Allah [swt] proposes trade with His believing servants: its conditions, investments, and profits as:

يَا أَيُّهَا الَّذِينَ آمَنُوا هَلْ أَدُلُّكُمْ عَلَى تِجَارَةٍ تُنجِيكُم مِّنْ عَذَابٍ أَلِيمٍ - تُؤْمِنُونَ بِاللَّهِ وَرَسُولِهِ وَتُجَاهِدُونَ فِي سَبِيلِ اللَّهِ بِأَمْوَالِكُمْ وَأَنفُسِكُمْ ذَلِكُمْ خَيْرٌ لَّكُمْ إِن كُنتُمْ تَعْلَمُونَ - يَغْفِرْ لَكُمْ ذُنُوبَكُمْ وَيُدْخِلْكُمْ جَنَّاتٍ تَجْرِي مِن تَحْتِهَا الْأَنْهَارُ وَمَسَاكِنَ طَيِّبَةً فِي جَنَّاتِ عَدْنٍ ذَلِكَ الْفَوْزُ الْعَظِيمُ - وَأُخْرَى تُحِبُّونَهَا نَصْرٌ مِّنَ اللَّهِ وَفَتْحٌ قَرِيبٌ وَبَشِّرِ الْمُؤْمِنِينَ -

O you who have believed, Shall I guide you to a transaction that will save you from a painful punishment? [It is that] you believe in Allah and His Messenger and strive in the cause of Allah with your wealth and your lives. That is best for you, if you should know. He will forgive you your sins and admit you to gardens beneath which rivers flow and pleasant dwellings in gardens of perpetual residence. That is the great attainment. And [you will obtain] another [favor] that you will love - victory from Allah and an imminent conquest; and give good tidings to the believers.

There are four components in a trade deal. In the deal where Allah [swt] wants to guide us, Allah [swt] is the seller. Allah [swt] put the condition that says:

يَا أَيُّهَا الَّذِينَ آمَنُوا هَلْ أَدُلُّكُمْ عَلَى تِجَارَةٍ تُنجِيكُم مِّنْ عَذَابٍ أَلِيمٍ

O you who have believed, Shall I guide you to a transaction that will save you from a painful punishment?

It means the participant must be of the People of Iman, as advertised by, "O you who have believed...." in the afore-mentioned verse. The people of disbelief or hypocrisy are not allowed to participate [are not considered for the reward], because their acts are rotten and corrupt, and their capital is fraudulent.

Allah [swt] then explained this great trade that will never fail. The trade that will earn one what he wishes and saves him from what he dislikes. Allah the Exalted said,

تُؤْمِنُونَ بِاللَّهِ وَرَسُولِهِ وَتُجَاهِدُونَ فِي سَبِيلِ اللَّهِ بِأَمْوَالِكُمْ وَأَنفُسِكُمْ ذَلِكُمْ خَيْرٌ لَّكُمْ إِن كُنتُمْ تَعْلَمُونَ -

[It is that] you believe in Allah and His Messenger, and strive in the cause of Allah with your wealth and your lives. That is best for you, if you should know. This is better than the trade in this life and striving hard for it and amassing it.

The capital of investment for the participating believer is, of two forms as implied in the above verse as follows: "That you believe in Allah and His Messenger Muhammad [sws], and that you strive hard and fight in the cause of Allah [swt] with your wealth and your lives. Firstly - belief in Allah and His Prophet is the absolute assurance in the heart and the declaration by words, and performing deeds of righteousness, which are obligatory or recommended and abstaining from all kinds of sins and evil deeds that He has forbidden. Secondly - strive hard and fight in the cause of Allah [swt] and His Prophet [sas] with your tongue and hands, and sacrificing your wealth and lives for the cause of Allah [swt] only.

We have heard how to participate in capital investment, so what are the profits? As for its profits, Allah [swt] has revealed in His Words: "That [He] will save you from a painful Torment." This means that He will save and rescue the investor from a severe and painful punishment that no one will be saved from except him who takes precautions and fulfills the conditions for salvation.

And also Allah the Exalted said,

$$يَغْفِرْ لَكُمْ ذُنُوبَكُمْ ۔$$

He will forgive for you your sins, meaning, if the investor fulfills what I commanded and guided you to, then I will forgive your sins and admit you into the gardens of Paradise. In them, you will have exalted residences and high positions. This is why Allah [swt] said,

$$وَيُدْخِلْكُمْ جَنَّاتٍ تَجْرِى مِن تَحْتِهَا الأَنْهَرُ وَمَسَاكِنَ طَيِّبَةً فِى جَنَّاتِ عَدْنٍ ذَلِكَ الْفَوْزُ الْعَظِيمُ$$

And admit you to gardens beneath which rivers flow and pleasant dwellings in gardens of perpetual residence.

And also Allah [swt] said,

$$وَأُخْرَى تُحِبُّونَهَا ۔$$

And [you will obtain] another [favor] that you love. Meaning, `I will grant you more favors that you like,

$$نَصْرُ مِّنَ اللَّهِ وَفَتْحُ قَرِيبٌ ۔$$

Victory from Allah and an imminent conquest.- meaning, if you fight in Allah's cause and support His religion, He will grant you victory.

Victory from Allah means it will come sooner, and this is the increased favor that is earned in this life and continues, becoming the delight of the Hereafter. It is for those who obey Allah and His Messenger and support Allah and His religion. Allah said;

$$وَبَشِّرِ الْمُؤْمِنِينَ ۔$$

And give good tidings to the believers.

In the afore-mentioned Ayahs Allah Almighty sends the call to all believers of every time and place, by advertising the profitable investment for whosoever wants to contribute and gain the ultimate benefit. Allah explains the conditions to be fulfilled by the participants, its capital and its profit so that people may enter and be assured of his share and reward. He, who has opened the door for participation in this investment, is Allah the All-Knowing.

Brothers and Sisters in Islam! Have no fear that you will lose your share with Allah's investment, but rest assured that Allah will multiply your reward. These are the profits of the investments in the Hereafter, which are continuous and everlasting. There are additional, immediate profits in the life of this world namely; Allah will help and grant you victory against your enemies in conquering their lands by making use of its fruits, and becoming rulers with honor. This is reflected in the verse as: "And also He will give you another blessing which you love, - help from Allah against your enemies and a near victory." This blessing in this world is connected with the Grace of the Hereafter for the believer who answers this divine invitation and contributes in this investment.

Today people rush when they hear about and see advertisement for investments in property, land or other types and take the risk in investing their money to obtain profit without any assurance in many cases, nor do they certify the honesty and trust. After all, the advertiser is human and liable to make mistakes by having insufficient experience. However, people still take risks blindly, because greed overpowers their desires, with the result that they invest their money blindly for the sake of a return that might never materialize, and if it did, they would not know the consequences and the effect of the return. Why then, do many people not respond to the divine advertisement of the greatest investment, assured profit with the best outcome, knowing that the advertiser in this investment is He who is All Knowing, the Omniscient and the Most Merciful upon His Slaves?

Again Allah (swt) advertises for loans from the believers as in **Surah al-Baqarah (2:245):**

$$\text{مَّن ذَا الَّذِى يُقْرِضُ اللّهَ قَرْضًا حَسَنًا فَيُضَاعِفَهُ لَهُ أَضْعَافًا كَثِيرَةً وَاللّهُ يَقْبِضُ وَيَبْسُطُ وَإِلَيْهِ تُرْجَعُونَ-}$$

Who is it that will lend Allah a goodly loan so He may multiply it to him many times over? And it is Allah who withholds and grants abundance, and to Him you will return.

In this Ayah, Allah [swt] encourages His servants to spend in His cause. Allah [swt] repeats almost in the same language as in **Surah al-Hadid (57:11):**

$$\text{مَّن ذَا الَّذِى يُقْرِضُ اللّهَ قَرْضًا حَسَنًا فَيُضَاعِفَهُ لَهُ وَلَهُ أَجْرٌ كَرِيمٌ-}$$

Who is it that will lend Allah a goodly loan so He will multiply it for him and he will have an honorable reward?

Allah [swt] does not waste the good deeds of the believers, but instead increases the profit [reward] from ten to seven hundredfold. In **Surah al –Baqarah (2:261)** Allah [swt] says:

مَّثَلُ الَّذِينَ يُنفِقُونَ أَمْوَالَهُمْ فِي سَبِيلِ اللَّهِ كَمَثَلِ حَبَّةٍ أَنبَتَتْ سَبْعَ سَنَابِلَ فِي كُلِّ سُنبُلَةٍ مِّائَةُ حَبَّةٍ وَاللَّهُ يُضَاعِفُ لِمَن يَشَاءُ وَاللَّهُ وَاسِعٌ عَلِيمٌ-

The example of those who spend their wealth in the way of Allah is like a seed [of a grain] which grows seven spikes; and in each spike is a hundred grains. Allah multiplies [His reward] for whom He wills. And Allah is all-Encompassing and Knowing.

Allah [swt] reassures in **Surah Fatir (35:29)** that there will be no loss in investment with Him:

إِنَّ الَّذِينَ يَتْلُونَ كِتَابَ اللَّهِ وَأَقَامُوا الصَّلَاةَ وَأَنفَقُوا مِمَّا رَزَقْنَاهُمْ سِرًّا وَعَلَانِيَةً يَرْجُونَ تِجَارَةً لَّن تَبُورَ-

Indeed, those who recite the Book of Allah and establish prayer and spend [in His cause] out of what We have provided them, secretly and publicly, [can] expect a transaction [profit] that will never perish.

Brothers and Sisters in Islam! The reason why we retrieve from this investment that Allah has publicized and explained in the Glorious Qur'an is our weak Iman and our preferring the life of this world over our religion.

Man with human nature likes investments that will produce quick profits, or a deferred but permanent profit. Each of these has its clients, the people of Iman who are few in numbers; prefer the last type of investment, while others prefer the first type. Allah Almighty says in **Surah al- A'la (87:16-17)**:

بَلْ تُؤْثِرُونَ الْحَيَاةَ الدُّنْيَا-وَالْآخِرَةُ خَيْرٌ وَأَبْقَى-

Rather you prefer the worldly life, while the Hereafter is better and more lasting.

However, if he who prefers the permanent investment in the Hereafter, Allah will grant him reward in this world and in the Hereafter. On the other hand, he who prefers the investment for this world only, Allah grants him what he has decreed for him in this world, but he incurs a permanent loss in the Hereafter. Allah Almighty says in **Surah ash-Shuara (42:20)**:

مَن كَانَ يُرِيدُ حَرْثَ الْآخِرَةِ نَزِدْ لَهُ فِي حَرْثِهِ وَمَن كَانَ يُرِيدُ حَرْثَ الدُّنْيَا نُؤْتِهِ مِنْهَا وَمَا لَهُ فِي الْآخِرَةِ مِن نَّصِيبٍ-

Whoever desires the harvest of the Hereafter – We increase for him in his harvest [reward]. And whoever desires the harvest of this world - We give him thereof, but there is not for him in the Hereafter any share.

Brothers and Sister in Islam! Investing with Allah Almighty is very simple, its doors are always open for the interested believers and it is publicized in the Holy Qur'an. Allah [swt] increases the provisions with His hand at night /day, so that He can forgive the offender who committed a sin during the day/night time.

We are the servant, Hé is the Master. Prayers come from us answers come from Him. Abstinence comes from us protection comes from Him. Repentance comes from us acceptance comes from Him. Go towards him walking. He will come to us running.

Make our deeds pure for His sake alone, and He will extend His mercy to us. uphold His religion, and He will extend His bounty. Follow the Sunnah of His beloved, and He will extend His love to us. O Allah! Guide us properly so that we can make proper investment for your sake only and get the reward in the life hereafter promised by you. **Amin!**

Ummah of Muhammad [sas] is the Best Ummah

Allah [swt] mentions in **Surah al-'Imran (3:110):**

كُنتُمْ خَيْرَ أُمَّةٍ أُخْرِجَتْ لِلنَّاسِ تَأْمُرُونَ بِالْمَعْرُوفِ وَتَنْهَوْنَ عَنِ الْمُنكَرِ وَتُؤْمِنُونَ بِاللَّهِ وَلَوْ ءَامَنَ أَهْلُ الْكِتَبِ لَكَانَ خَيْرًا لَّهُمْ مِّنْهُمُ الْمُؤْمِنُونَ وَأَكْثَرُهُمُ الْفَسِقُونَ

You are the best of nation produced [as an example] for mankind. You enjoin what is right [all that Islam has ordained] and forbid what is wrong [all that Islam has forbidden] and believe in Allah. If only the People of Scripture [Jews and Christians] had believed, it would have been better for them. Among them are believers, but most of them defiantly disobedient.

The meaning of the Ayah is that the Ummah of Muhammad [sas] is the most righteous and beneficial nation for mankind, hence Allah's description of them. Allah [swt] granted this honor to Muslims – the honor of being the best of nations, the best of the community, and the best group of people.

It is the Ummah when practiced as the Prophet [sas] exemplified guarantees happiness, comfort, and peace of mind in this Duniya and the eternal joy in the Hereafter. History teaches us that in less than 50 years from the start of the final divine revelation – Al-Qur'an- this Ummah dominated the majority of world with justice, mercy and humility.

This Ummah is the owner of the best thoughts and achievement in the world and the hereafter. This Ummah promotes goodness, justice and truth. It is in concordance with every human nature. In this Ayah there is no ambiguity, nothing vagueness, but rather a clear simple statement that Muslims are the best of people who do good and forbid evil and believe in Allah. No exceptions here, there is no time frame here- just Muslims, you and I included.

Allah [swt] again says in **Surah al-Baqarah (2:143)** that this "Best Ummah" will also be witness over the mankind:

وَكَذَلِكَ جَعَلْنَكُمْ أُمَّةً وَسَطًا لِّتَكُونُوا شُهَدَآءَ عَلَى النَّاسِ وَيَكُونَ الرَّسُولُ عَلَيْكُمْ شَهِيدًا

And thus We have made you a median [just] community that you will be witnesses over the people and the messenger [Muhammad] will be a witness over you.

Can we internalize this statement that we are the best of nations? Are we carrying this responsibility of being witnesses to mankind as the best of people? Many of us have forgotten ourselves, our purpose in life and our entity. We have forgotten ourselves not only at an individual level but also collectively as an Ummah. Allah [swt]

The Qur'an reminds that the human being worships whoever or whatever occupies his mind most of the time. Today many of us can be identified by the professional degrees we hold, the work we do, the race, culture and the nationality that we belong to and somewhere at the bottom of the list, are that we are Muslims. In Islam we are Muslims first. And as Muslims we not only carry the highest standards of morals and values but we have a sense of responsibility – a responsibility towards all mankind as the best of nations and people. The question is how are we implementing Islam in our lives? How much Aqidah do we have? The standards to be honored as the Khayra Ummatin have been laid out and we need to determine and reflect on our actions in order to see how we meet those criteria. Hence our nationality is Islam and our loyalty should always remain with Islam regardless of where we are physically located.

The Qur'an reminds us in **Surah al-An'am (6: 162):**

قُلْ إِنَّ صَلَاتِي وَنُسُكِي وَمَحْيَايَ وَمَمَاتِي لِلَّهِ رَبِّ الْعَالَمِينَ

Say, "Indeed, my prayer, my rites of sacrifice, my living and my dying are [all] for Allah, Lord of the worlds."

Can we say this and internalize this statement deep within our heart and soul. Search within ourselves to know how and where we stand in terms of our faith, our purpose and our sacrifices?

A Muslim represents a good person, a person of truth, of sincerity and of virtue. And as Muslim our life should be an open invitation through which people see the beauty of Islam and find it an interesting code of ethics and teachings to follow. This light of Islam needs to be shared.

A most important criterion of the best is truthfulness. Truthfulness, justice, sincerity and honesty all flow from the same fountain. We cannot be trustworthy and sincere unless we are truthful. We cannot love and practice justice unless we love truth.

Fellow Muslims! Be aware that the prevention of evil through a good word or deed and the spreading of the truth with tact and understanding are praiseworthy and commendable acts. Conversely, cowardly acts of flattery and sycophancy, such as the refusal to speak out for the truth, or turning a blind eye to, or even expressly approving sinful acts are acts of grave misconduct.

The fulfillment of these three conditions: doing what is right, forbidding what is wrong and having faith in Allah. Therefore, any Muslim community, regardless of its race or ethnic origin, wherever it exists and whatever its standard of development, belongs to this noble group whom Allah (swt) describes as "the best community ever raised for mankind", provided that it fulfills these three conditions

We need to shoulder this responsibility at an individual level, at a leadership level and at a community level. Enjoining what is good; forbidding what is evil, it represents the responsibility in promoting and maintaining the true guidance of Allah in all dimensions of our life. Let every one of us ask him or her; am I practicing that at my personal level, at the community level, at the leadership level? Are we really, as Muslims adopting the true and pure beliefs that Rasul Allah [sas] taught us? Each person here, each leader here and all of us need to answer for ourselves, and take account of our deeds and actions.

Hence we should do what Allah [swt] stated first in the noble Qur'an – Iqra. Read. Read with the first Hadith of Bukhari in mind, "action is by intention". Then cultivate this as Sahabah did - understand and implement the message with inward conviction and outward action.

Today, we are still trapped by the worthless pleasures of this world; we are amused in the world of entertainment, consumed by consumerism and lost in foolish desires. We are more concerned about worldly pleasures rather than the world of Islam. We are more concerned about the dirt in our houses! But, neglect the dirt created by our nafs and desires? We are more concerned in the cleanliness of our homes! But we neglect the purity of our Iman. We love to decorate our houses. But, abandon decorating our minds with knowledge and wisdom?

No matter how big or small a contribution we need to act, we need to contribute with time, effort, knowledge, money and our lives. Then and then only can we claim the honor of Khayra Ummatin, Allah willing.

Our leaders here and everywhere need to understand that leadership is an Amanah. It is a trust that people place to do good – politically, spiritually and religiously. It is a trust to hold the reins and direct the community towards higher educational and social excellence. It carries the responsibility of bringing religious duties into action. Question yourselves as leaders about your actions, your sincerity and your integrity.

We have a responsibility to shoulder my brothers and sisters as parents, as relatives, as neighbors and as Muslims. Allah [swt] mentions in **Surah al –'Imran (3:104):**

وَلْتَكُن مِّنكُمْ أُمَّةٌ يَدْعُونَ إِلَى الْخَيْرِ وَيَأْمُرُونَ بِالْمَعْرُوفِ وَيَنْهَوْنَ عَنِ الْمُنكَرِ وَأُوْلَـئِكَ هُمُ الْمُفْلِحُونَ-

Let there be [arising] from you a nation inviting to [all that is] good, enjoining what is right and forbidding what is wrong [according to the laws of Allah], and those will be successful.

That is why Allah states in **Surah al -Ahzâb (33:70):**

يَأَيُّهَا الَّذِينَ ءَامَنُوا اتَّقُوا اللَّهَ وَقُولُوا قَوْلاً سَدِيدا-

O, you who have believed, fear Allah and speak words of appropriate justice.

O Allah, forgive us that which we did secretly and what we did publicly. What we did inadvertently and what we did deliberately; what we did knowingly and what we did out of ignorance. Give us the power and guidance to prepare ourselves as a worthy member of the Khayra Ummatin. **Amin!**

Victory Comes from Allah [swt] only

Prophet of Allah [swt] said: "If they break the covenant of Allah and His Messenger, Allah will send an external enemy against them who will seize some of their possessions; if they do not rule by the Book of Allah, or attempt to implement everything in it, Allah will spread enmity among them" (Bukhari, book #2, hadith #33). Allah [swt] says in **Surah al-Imran (3:160):**

إِن يَنصُرْكُمُ اللهُ فَلَا غَالِبَ لَكُمْ وَإِن يَخْذُلْكُمْ فَمَن ذَا الَّذِي يَنصُرُكُم مِّنْ بَعْدِهِ وَعَلَى اللهِ فَلْيَتَوَكَّلِ الْمُؤْمِنُونَ

If Allah helps you, none can overcome you; but if He forsakes you, who is there that can help you after Him? And upon Allah let believers put their trust.

This is a comprehensive clarification of the conditions for victory and the causes of defeat for the Muslim nations. Breaking the covenant of Allah and His messenger, or in other words, disobeying Allah and His messenger, is one of the reasons for its defeat and being subjugated by its enemies. Likewise, ruling by other than the rulings of Allah is the reason for the poverty, disunity and conflict which is occurring among the Muslims.

Conversely, obeying Allah and His Messenger [sas] is the source of victory. Allah says in **Surah Muhammad (47:7):**

يَا أَيُّهَا الَّذِينَ ءَامَنُوا إِن تَنصُرُوا اللَّهَ يَنصُرْكُمْ وَيُثَبِّتْ أَقْدَامَكُمْ

O who have believed, If you support Allah, He will support you, and plant firmly your feet.

Allah [swt] also says in **Surah As-Saaf (61:13):**

نَصْرٌ مِّنَ اللَّهِ وَفَتْحٌ قَرِيبٌ

Victory from Allah and an imminent conquest.

Let us look at the battle of Badr and how Allah [swt] gave a small group of 313 Muslims victory over more than thousand disbelievers. Allah [swt] says in **Surah al-Anfal (8:9-12):**

إِذْ تَسْتَغِيثُونَ رَبَّكُمْ فَاسْتَجَابَ لَكُمْ أَنِّي مُمِدُّكُم بِأَلْفٍ مِّنَ الْمَلَائِكَةِ مُرْدِفِينَ - وَمَا جَعَلَهُ اللَّهُ إِلَّا بُشْرَى وَلِتَطْمَئِنَّ بِهِ قُلُوبُكُمْ

وَمَا النَّصْرُ إِلَّا مِنْ عِندِ اللَّهِ إِنَّ اللَّهَ عَزِيزٌ حَكِيمٌ إِذْ يُغَشِّيكُمُ النُّعَاسَ أَمَنَةً مِّنْهُ وَيُنَزِّلُ عَلَيْكُم مِّنَ السَّمَاءِ مَاءً لِّيُطَهِّرَكُم بِهِ

وَيُذْهِبَ عَنكُمْ رِجْزَ الشَّيْطَنِ وَلِيَرْبِطَ عَلَى قُلُوبِكُمْ وَيُثَبِّتَ بِهِ الْأَقْدَامَ - إِذْ يُوحِى رَبُّكَ إِلَى الْمَلَٰئِكَةِ أَنِّي مَعَكُمْ فَثَبِّتُوا۟

الَّذِينَ ءَامَنُوا۟ سَأُلْقِى فِى قُلُوبِ الَّذِينَ كَفَرُوا۟ الرُّعْبَ فَاضْرِبُوا۟ فَوْقَ الْأَعْنَاقِ وَاضْرِبُوا۟ مِنْهُمْ كُلَّ بَنَانٍ

[Remember] when you asked help of your Rabb and He answered you [saying], "Indeed, I will reinforce you with a thousand from the angels, following one another." And Allah made it not but good tidings and so that your hearts would be assured thereby. And victory is not but from Allah. Indeed, Allah is Exalted in Might and Wise. [Remember] when He overwhelmed you with drowsiness [giving] security from Him and sent down upon you from the sky, rain by which to purify you and remove from you the evil [suggestions] of Satan, and to make steadfast your hearts and plant firmly thereby your feet. [Remember] when your Rabb inspired to the angels, "I am with you, so strengthen those who have believed. I will cast terror into the hearts of those who have disbelieved so strike [them] over the necks and strike from them every fingertip."

And also in **Surah al-Anfal (8:42-45):**

إِذْ أَنتُم بِالْعُدْوَةِ الدُّنْيَا وَهُم بِالْعُدْوَةِ الْقُصْوَى وَالرَّكْبُ أَسْفَلَ مِنكُمْ وَلَوْ تَوَاعَدتُّمْ لَاخْتَلَفْتُمْ فِى الْمِيعَادِ وَلَٰكِن لِّيَقْضِيَ اللَّهُ أَمْرًا

كَانَ مَفْعُولًا لِّيَهْلِكَ مَنْ هَلَكَ عَن بَيِّنَةٍ وَيَحْيَىٰ مَنْ حَىَّ عَن بَيِّنَةٍ وَإِنَّ اللَّهَ لَسَمِيعٌ عَلِيمٌ إِذْ يُرِيكَهُمُ اللَّهُ فِى مَنَامِكَ قَلِيلًا وَلَوْ أَرَاكَهُمْ كَثِيرًا

لَّفَشِلْتُمْ وَلَتَنَٰزَعْتُمْ فِى الْأَمْرِ وَلَٰكِنَّ اللَّهَ سَلَّمَ إِنَّهُ عَلِيمٌۢ بِذَاتِ الصُّدُورِ - وَإِذْ يُرِيكُمُوهُمْ إِذِ الْتَقَيْتُمْ فِى أَعْيُنِكُمْ قَلِيلًا وَيُقَلِّلُكُمْ فِى

يَٰٓأَيُّهَا الَّذِينَ ءَامَنُوٓا۟ إِذَا لَقِيتُمْ فِئَةً فَاثْبُتُوا۟ وَاذْكُرُوا۟ اللَّهَ كَثِيرًا لَّعَلَّكُمْ تُفْلِحُونَ - أَعْيُنِهِمْ لِيَقْضِيَ اللَّهُ أَمْرًا كَانَ مَفْعُولًا وَإِلَى اللَّهِ تُرْجَعُ

[Remember] when you [the Muslim army] were on the near side of the valley, and they on the farther side, and the caravan was lower [in position] than you. If you had made an appointment [to meet], you would have missed the appointment. But [it was] so that Allah might accomplish a matter already distained - that those who perished [through disbelief] would perish upon evidence and those who lived [in faith] would live upon evidence; and indeed, Allah is Hearing and Knowing. [And remember, O Muhammad], when Allah showed them to you in your dreams few; and if He had shown them to you as many, you [believers] would have lost courage and would have disputed in the matter [of whether to fight], but Allah saved [you from that]. Indeed, He knows of that within the breasts. And [remember] when He showed them to you, when you met, as few in your eyes so that Allah might accomplish a matter already destined. And to Allah are [all] matters [for decision] returned. O you who have believed, when you encounter a company [from the enemy forces], stand firm and remember Allah much that you may be successful.

Allah [swt)] explained how He helped the Muslims and why? How can we expect Allah to grant us victory while we are discarding prayers, refusing to pay Zakat and dealing with interest? What can we expect when alcoholic drinks and nightclubs become prevalent in our lands? What happens when evil becomes widespread?

Allah says in **Surah al-Anfal (8:25):**

وَٱتَّقُوا۟ فِتْنَةًۭ لَّا تُصِيبَنَّ ٱلَّذِينَ ظَلَمُوا۟ مِنكُمْ خَآصَّةًۭ وَٱعْلَمُوٓا۟ أَنَّ ٱللَّهَ شَدِيدُ ٱلْعِقَابِ

And fear a trial [an affliction] which will not strike those who have wronged among you exclusively, and know that Allah is severe in penalty.

Therefore, if Muslims truly wish for victory, then they must change what is in themselves as Allah says in **Surah ar-Ra'd (13:11):**

إِنَّ ٱللَّهَ لَا يُغَيِّرُ مَا بِقَوْمٍ حَتَّىٰ يُغَيِّرُوا۟ مَا بِأَنفُسِهِمْ

Indeed, Allah will not change the condition of a people until they change what is in themselves.

The Messenger prepared his forces for battle, and his army had seven hundred men. He appointed `Abdullah bin Jubayr, from Bani `Amr bin `Awf, to lead the archers who were of fifty men. The Prophet said to them: "Keep the horsemen away from us, and be aware that we might be attacked from your direction. If victory was for or against us, remain in your positions. And even if you see us being picked up by birds, do not abandon your positions."(Tafsir-Ibn-Kathir)

In **Surah al-'Imran (3:124-6)** Allah [swt] says:

إِذْ تَقُولُ لِلْمُؤْمِنِينَ أَلَن يَكْفِيَكُمْ أَن يُمِدَّكُمْ رَبُّكُم بِثَلَٰثَةِ ءَالَٰفٍۢ مِّنَ ٱلْمَلَٰٓئِكَةِ مُنزَلِينَ ۰ بَلَىٰٓ إِن تَصْبِرُوا۟ وَتَتَّقُوا۟ وَيَأْتُوكُم مِّن فَوْرِهِمْ هَٰذَا يُمْدِدْكُمْ رَبُّكُم بِخَمْسَةِ ءَالَٰفٍۢ مِّنَ ٱلْمَلَٰٓئِكَةِ مُسَوِّمِينَ ۰ وَمَا جَعَلَهُ ٱللَّهُ إِلَّا بُشْرَىٰ لَكُمْ وَلِتَطْمَئِنَّ قُلُوبُكُم بِهِۦ ۗ وَمَا ٱلنَّصْرُ إِلَّا مِنْ عِندِ ٱللَّهِ ٱلْعَزِيزِ ٱلْحَكِيمِ

[Remember] when you said to the believers, "Is it not sufficient for you that your Rabb should reinforce you with three thousand angels sent down? Yes, if you remain patient and conscious of Allah and they [the enemy] come upon you [attacking] in rage, your Lord will reinforce you with five thousand angels having marks [of distinction]." And Allah made it not except as [a sign of] good tiding for you and reassures your hearts thereby. And victory is not except from Allah, the Exalted in Might and the Wise.

And also in **Surah al-'Imran (3:152-5)** Allah [swt] says:

وَلَقَدْ صَدَقَكُمُ ٱللَّهُ وَعْدَهُۥٓ إِذْ تَحُسُّونَهُم بِإِذْنِهِۦ ۖ حَتَّىٰٓ إِذَا فَشِلْتُمْ وَتَنَٰزَعْتُمْ فِى ٱلْأَمْرِ وَعَصَيْتُم مِّنۢ بَعْدِ مَآ أَرَىٰكُم مَّا تُحِبُّونَ ۚ مِنكُم مَّن يُرِيدُ ٱلدُّنْيَا وَمِنكُم مَّن يُرِيدُ ٱلْءَاخِرَةَ ۚ ثُمَّ صَرَفَكُمْ عَنْهُمْ لِيَبْتَلِيَكُمْ ۖ وَلَقَدْ عَفَا عَنكُمْ ۗ وَٱللَّهُ ذُو فَضْلٍ عَلَى ٱلْمُؤْمِنِينَ ۰ إِذْ

تُصْعِدُونَ وَلَا تَلْوُونَ عَلَىٰ أَحَدٍ وَالرَّسُولُ يَدْعُوكُمْ فِي أُخْرَاكُمْ فَأَثَابَكُمْ غَمًّا بِغَمٍّ لِّكَيْلَا تَحْزَنُوا عَلَىٰ مَا فَاتَكُمْ وَلَا مَا

أَصَابَكُمْ وَاللَّهُ خَبِيرٌ بِمَا تَعْمَلُونَ ثُمَّ أَنزَلَ عَلَيْكُم مِّن بَعْدِ الْغَمِّ أَمَنَةً نُّعَاسًا يَغْشَىٰ طَائِفَةً مِّنكُمْ وَطَائِفَةٌ قَدْ أَهَمَّتْهُمْ أَنفُسُهُمْ

يَظُنُّونَ بِاللَّهِ غَيْرَ الْحَقِّ ظَنَّ الْجَاهِلِيَّةِ يَقُولُونَ هَل لَّنَا مِنَ الْأَمْرِ مِن شَيْءٍ قُلْ إِنَّ الْأَمْرَ كُلَّهُ لِلَّهِ يُخْفُونَ فِي أَنفُسِهِم مَّا لَا يُبْدُونَ لَكَ يَقُولُونَ

لَوْ كَانَ لَنَا مِنَ الْأَمْرِ شَيْءٌ مَّا قُتِلْنَا هَاهُنَا قُل لَّوْ كُنتُمْ فِي بُيُوتِكُمْ لَبَرَزَ الَّذِينَ كُتِبَ عَلَيْهِمُ الْقَتْلُ إِلَىٰ مَضَاجِعِهِمْ وَلِيَبْتَلِيَ اللَّهُ مَا فِي

صُدُورِكُمْ وَلِيُمَحِّصَ مَا فِي قُلُوبِكُمْ وَاللَّهُ عَلِيمٌ بِذَاتِ الصُّدُورِ - إِنَّ الَّذِينَ تَوَلَّوْا مِنكُمْ يَوْمَ الْتَقَى الْجَمْعَانِ إِنَّمَا اسْتَزَلَّهُمُ

الشَّيْطَانُ بِبَعْضِ مَا كَسَبُوا وَلَقَدْ عَفَا اللَّهُ عَنْهُمْ إِنَّ اللَّهَ غَفُورٌ حَلِيمٌ

And Allah had certainly fulfilled His promise to you when you were killing them [your enemy] by His permission until [the time] when you lost courage and fell to disputing about the order [Fashiltum] and fell to disputing about the order [given by the Prophet] and disobeyed after He had shown you that which you love. Among you are some who desire this world, and among you are some who desire the Hereafter. Then He turned you back from them [defeated] that He might test you. And He has already forgiven you, and Allah is the possessor of bounty for the believers. [Remember] when you [fled and] climbed the [the mountain] without looking aside at anyone while the the Messenger was calling you from behind. So Allah repaid you with distress so you would not grieve for that which had escaped you [of victory and spoils of war] or [for] that which had befallen you [of injury and death]. And Allah is fully acquainted with what you do. Then after distress, He sent down upon you security [in the form of] drowsiness, overcoming a faction of you, while another faction worried about themselves, thinking of Allah other than the truth -- the thought of ignorance, saying, "Is there anything for us [to have done] in this matter?" Say, "Indeed the matter belongs completely to Allah." They conceal within themselves what they will not reveal to you. They say, "If there was anything we could have done in the matter, we [some of us] would not have been killed right here." Say, "Even if you had been inside your houses, those decreed to be killed would have come out to their death beds." [It was] so that Allah might test what is in your hearts. And Allah knows of that within the breasts. Indeed, those of you who turned back on the day the two armies met [at Uhud] – it was Satan only caused them to slip because of some [blame] they had earned. But Allah has already forgiven them. Indeed, Allah is –Forgiving and forbearing.

Allah [swt] also says in **Surah al-'Imran (3:166)** what affliction was caused upon the Muslims where the desire of Allah to teach them a lesson:

وَمَا أَصَابَكُمْ يَوْمَ الْتَقَى الْجَمْعَانِ فَبِإِذْنِ اللَّهِ وَلِيَعْلَمَ الْمُؤْمِنِينَ

And what struck you on the day the two armies met [at Uhud] was by permission of Allah that He might **make evident the [true] believers.**

A Muslim must not feel despair and lose hope in Allah, as He may grant Muslims victory due to some of the oppressed or weak righteous people amongst them who cannot defend themselves. It is a fact that the leaders and rulers of the Muslims will be as unjust and oppressive as the Muslims are amongst themselves and their leaders will be dealt with as they deal with their subjects. Imam Ibn Al-Qayim said: "Reflect on the wisdom of Allah when the Muslims are subjugated by their enemies as a result of the powerful amongst them [Muslims)] oppressing the weak and denying the rights of the oppressed. Due to this, Allah will send those who will dominate these Muslim leaders and deal with them exactly as they dealt with the weak, an eye for an eye. This is the way of Allah from the time history began to when it will end"

Look how Allah has given the Muslims exactly the types of rulers that their own deeds and actions deserve. It is as though their actions are manifested in the form of their leaders and rulers. Therefore, whenever people are just among themselves, their rulers will be just to them; whenever people defraud and cheat each other, their rulers will do likewise to them; and if the people fail to fulfil the rights of Allah, then their rulers will fail to give them their rights.

Allah reminds the believers how He favored and blessed them by giving them victory in many battles with His Messenger. Allah mentioned that victory comes from Him, by His aid and decree, not because of their numbers or adequate supplies, whether the triumphs are few or many. Allah [swt] says in **Surah al-'Imran (3:126):**

وَمَا جَعَلَهُ اللهُ إِلاَّ بُشْرَى لَكُمْ وَلِتَطْمَئِنَّ قُلُوبُكُم بِهِ وَمَا النَّصْرُ إِلاَّ مِنْ عِندِ اللهِ الْعَزِيزِ الْحَكِيمِ

Allah made it not except as [a sign of] good tidings for you and to reassure your hearts thereby. And victory is not except from Allah, the Exalted in Might, the Wise.

On the day of Hunayn, the Muslims were proud because of their large number, which did not avail them in the least; they retreated and fled from battle. Only a few of them remained with the Messenger of Allah. Allah then sent down His aid and support to His Messenger and the believers who remained with him, so that they were aware that victory is from Allah alone and through His aid, even if the victorious were few. Many a small group overcame a larger opposition by Allah's leave, and Allah is ever with those who are patient. We will explain this subject in detail below, Allah willing.

Allah [swt] explains how the Muslims had a victory in the battle of Hunayn in **Surah at-Tawbah (9:25-6):**

لَقَدْ نَصَرَكُمُ اللهُ فِي مَوَاطِنَ كَثِيرَةٍ وَيَوْمَ حُنَيْنٍ إِذْ أَعْجَبَتْكُمْ كَثْرَتُكُمْ فَلَمْ تُغْنِ عَنكُمْ شَيْئاً وَضَاقَتْ عَلَيْكُمُ الْأَرْضُ بِمَا

رَحُبَتْ ثُمَّ وَلَّيْتُم مُّدْبِرِينَ۔ ثُمَّ أَنزَلَ اللهُ سَكِينَتَهُ عَلَى رَسُولِهِ وَعَلَى الْمُؤْمِنِينَ وَأَنزَلَ جُنُوداً لَّمْ تَرَوْهَا وَعَذَّبَ الَّذِينَ كَفَرُوا وَذلِكَ

جَزَاءُ الْكَافِرِينَ

Allah has already given you victory in many regions and [even] on the day of Hunayn, when your great number pleased you, but it did not avail you at all, and the earth was confining for you with [in spite of] its

vastness; then you turned back, fleeing. Then Allah sent down His tranquility upon His Messenger and upon the believers and sent down forces [angels] whom you did not see and punished those who disbelieved. And that is the recompense of the disbelievers.

Brothers and Sisters in faith, from the descriptions of Allah [swt] about the victory of the Muslims in the three important battles of Badr, Uhud, and Hunayn, we should take lessons how and why Allah [swt] helped the Muslims and let us try to acquire those qualities for our victory in this world and the life hereafter. Praise Allah and seek His forgiveness when He helps us and gives us victory. **Amin!**

Which "Bible" is the Word of God?

The 'gospel' is a frequently used word, but what Gospel did Jesus preach? Of the 27 books of the New Testament, only a small fraction can be accepted as the words of Jesus. The Christians boast about the Gospels according to St. Matthew, St. Mark, St. Luke and St. John, but there is not a single Gospel 'according' to (St.) Jesus himself! We sincerely believe that everything Christ [Isa (as)] preached was from God. That was the 'Injeel', the good news and the guidance of God for the Children of Israel. In his lifetime Jesus never wrote a single word, nor did he instruct anyone to do so. Although the language of Jesus was not Latin [Allah did send the revelation in the language of the Prophet], the first Bible was written in Latin.

According to Michael H. Hart* (1992), Christianity, unlike Islam, was not founded by a single person but by two people- Jesus and St. Paul- and the principal credit for its development must therefore be apportioned between these two figures. Jesus formulated the basic ethical ideas of Christianity, as well as its basic spiritual outlook and its main ideas concerning human conduct. Christian theology, however, was shaped principally by the work of St. Paul. Jesus presented the spiritual message; Paul added to that the worship of Christ. Furthermore, St. Paul was the author of a considerable portion of the New Testament, and was the main proselytizing force of Christianity during the first century. For these reasons, some people even contend that it is Paul, rather than Jesus, who should really be considered the founder of Christianity.

Hart also recorded that St. Paul who was the main architect of the New Testament was a Jew by birth born in (now) Turkey. Then he moved to Jerusalem to enrich his knowledge of 'Towrah'. Though Paul was in Jerusalem at the same time as Jesus, it is doubtful whether the two men ever met. Paul joined those who opposed the religion of Christianity and participated in crucifying the followers of Jesus [Isa (as)]. In his later life, Paul accepted the religion of Christianity and became the most vigorous and influential proponent of the new religion.

The question before us is: 'Do we accept that the Bible as God's Word?' The question is really in the form of a challenge. The questioner is not simply seeking enlightenment. The question is posed in the spirit of a debate. We may ask— 'Which Bible are you talking about?' The answer is: 'Why, there is only one Bible!' It depends on whom you are asking: ACatholic? A Protestant or ACult?

The Catholic Bible

Holding the Roman Catholic Version of the Bible aloft in our hand, we ask, 'Do you accept this Bible as the Word of God?' For reasons best known to them, the Catholic Truth Society has published their Version of the Bible in a very short, stumpy form. This Version is a very odd proportion of the numerous Versions in the market today. The Christian questioner is taken aback. "What Bible is that?" he asks. "Why, I thought you said that there was only one Bible!" we remind him. "Y-e-s," he murmurs hesitantly, "but what Version is that?" We enquire. "Why, would that make any difference?" Of course it does, and the professional preacher knows that it does. He is only bluffing with his 'One Bible' claim.

The Roman Catholic Bible was published at Rheims in 1582, from Jerome's Latin Vulgate and reproduced at Douay in 1609. As such the RCV [Roman Catholic Version] is the oldest Version that one can still buy today.

Despite its antiquity, the whole of the Protestant world, including the 'cults' condemn the RCV because it contains seven extra "books" which they contemptuously refer to as the 'apocrypha' i.e. of doubtful authority. Notwithstanding the dire warning contained in the Apocalypse, which is the last book in the RCV [renamed as 'Revelation' by the Protestants], it is 'revealed': ". . . If any man shall add to these things (or delete) God shall add unto him the plagues written in this Book (Revelation-22:18-19).

Protestant Bible

The Authorized Version (AV) of the Protestant Bible, which is also widely known as the 'King James Version (KJV)'. The authorized version of the Bible was published in 1611 by the will and commands of His Majesty king James the 1st whose name it bears till today.

The Roman Catholics, believing as they do that the Protestants have mutilated the Book of God, are yet aiding and abetting the Protestant crime by forcing their native converts to purchase the Authorized Version (AV) of the Bible, which is the only Bible available in some 1500 languages of the less developed nations of the world. The Roman Catholics milk their cows, but the feeding is left to the Protestants! The overwhelming majority of Christians — both Catholics and Protestant — use the Authorized (AV) or the King James Version (KJV) as it is alternatively called.

Glowing Tributes and now re-revised and brought up to date as the Revised Standard Version (RSV) 1952, and now again re-re-revised in 1971 (still RSV for short). Let us see what opinion Christendom has of this most revised Bible, the RSV

1."The finest version that has been produced in the present Century." — (Church of England Newspaper)

2. "A completely fresh translation by Scholars of the Highest Eminence." — (Times literary Supplement)

3. "The well-loved characteristics of the authorized version combined with a new accuracy of translation."—(Life and Work)

4."The most accurate and close rendering of the original"—(TheTimes).

The publishers [Collins] they, in their notes on the Bible at the end of their production, say on page 10: "This Bible [RSV] is the product of thirty-two scholars, assisted by an Advisory Committee representing fifty co-operating First published, as Sir Winston says, in 1611, and then revised in 1881 [RV], denominations." Why all this boasting? To inspire the public buy their product? All these testimonies convince the purchaser that he is backing the right horse; with the purchaser little suspecting that he is being taken for a ride.

The World's Best Seller

What about the Authorized Version of the Bible (AV), the 'World's Best Seller?' These Revisers, all good salesmen, have some very pretty things to say about it. However, their page iii, paragraph six of the PREFACE of the RSV reads;

The King James Version (alternative description of AV) has with good reason been termed 'The noblest monument of English prose.' Its verses in 1881 expressed admiration for 'its simplicity, its dignity, its power, its happy turns of expression ...the music of its cadences, and the felicities of its rhythm.' It entered, as no other book has, into the making of the personal character and the public institutions of the English-speaking peoples. We owe to it an incalculable debt.

Can we, dear reader, imagine a more magnificent tribute being paid to the 'Book of Books' than the above? I, for one, cannot. Let the believing Christian, now steel himself for the un-kindest blow of all from his own beloved Lawyers of Religion; for in the very same breath they say: 'Yet the King James Version has grave defects. And, "that these defects are so many and as serious as to call for revision.' This is straight from the horse's mouth, i.e. the orthodox Christian scholars of 'the highest eminence.' Another galaxy of Doctors of Divinity is now required to produce an encyclopedia explaining the cause of those grave and serious defects in their Holy Writ and their reasons for eliminating them.

Let us pose another question: if a 'Holy' book contains conflicting verses would you still consider it to be Holy? It is worth noting, and well known throughout the religious world, that the choice of the present four "gospels" of the New Testament (Matthew, Mark, Luke and John) were imposed in the Council of Nicea 325 CE for political purposes under the auspices of the pagan Emperor Constantine, and not by Jesus. Constantine's mind had not been enlightened either by study or by inspiration. He was a pagan, a tyrant and criminal who murdered his son, his wife and thousands of innocent individuals because of his lust for political power. Constantine ratified other decisions in the Nicene Creed such as the decision to call Christ 'the Son of God, only begotten of the father.'

The Nicea Council decided to destroy all gospels written in Hebrew, the Gospel of Barnabas, until now, is the only eyewitness account of the life and mission of Jesus. Even today, the whole of the Protestant word, Jehovah's Witnesses, Seventh Day Adventists and other sects and denominations condemn the Roman Catholic version of the Bible because it contains seven "extra" books. The Protestant have bravely expunged seven whole books from their word of God. A few of the outcasts are the Books of Judith, Tobias, Baruch and Esther.

The question is: what Gospel did Jesus preach? Of the 27 books of the New Testament, only a small fraction can be accepted as the words of Jesus, and only of the 27 books 4 are known to be attributed as the Gospel of Jesus. Paul supposedly wrote the remaining 23. Muslims do believe that Jesus was given God's "Good News." However, they do not recognize the present four Gospels as the utterances of Jesus. The earliest Gospel is that of Mark's which was written about 60-75 AD. Mark was the son of Barnabas's sister. Matthew was a tax collector, a minor official who did not travel around with Jesus. Luke's Gospel was written much later, and in fact, drawn from the same sources as Mark's and Matthew's. Luke was Paul's physician, and like Paul, never met Jesus. By the way, do you know that the names Marks and Luke were not included in the 12 appointed disciples of Jesus as mentioned in Matthew 10:2-4? Who is mentioned in Hebrews 7:3 as like unto the Son of God?

It is Melchisedec, King of Salem, as mentioned in Hebrews 7:1. He (Melchisedec) is more unique than Jesus or Adam. Why he is not preferred to be the Son of God? Moreover, Adam did not have a mother or father, but was the first human being created by God and in the likeness of God to exist in the Garden of Eden and on earth. Wouldn't this give more rights to Adam to be called the Son of God in its truest meaning? The teachings of Jesus as the Son of God was neither preached by Jesus nor accepted by Jesus, but was taught by Paul as supported in Acts 9:20: "And straightway he preached Christ in the synagogues that he is the Son of God."

Jesus' prayer not to die on the cross was accepted by God according to Luke 22:43 and Hebrews 5:7. Therefore, if God, including not dying on the cross, accepted all of Jesus' prayer how could he have died on the cross? Nestle-Aland agrees in the wording of 62.9% of the verses of the New Testament. The proportion ranges from 45.1% in Mark to 81.4% in 2 Timothy. Let us take an example the analysis of the four Gospels.

The percentage agreement of the verses when all the four Gospels are considered is 54.5%. This is very close to the probability that a tail (or head) appears when a coin is tossed once (i.e., the probability that a tail or head appears when a coin is tossed is 50 %!). For the Christian critic, it would have been better not to talk about the critical editions. This actually show that the New Testament is in a real bad shape and inspires the confidence that the Bible is not preserved, leave alone it being the 'inerrant' and 'unchangeable' word of God.

The suffix "IM" of the word "ELOHIM" is a plural of respect in Hebrew. In Arabic and Hebrew there are two types of plurals: One of numbers, and the other of honor as in Royal proclamations. Since the plural of honor is uncommon in the language of the European, he has confused these plurals to connote a plurality in the "god head," hence his justification for his Doctrine of the Holy Trinity-the Father, Son and Holy Ghost.

The Torah consists of the first five books of the Old Testament. They are believed by the Jews to have been written by Moses Musa (as). These five books are: "Genesis", "Exodus", "Leviticus", "Numbers", and "Deuteronomy". After the Christians decided to incorporate the Old Testament into their Bible, they began to study these books in great detail. It was noticed that in the beginning verses of the OT manuscripts, Deuteronomy says: "These are the words that Moses spoke to the children of Israel across the Jordan...". They noticed that the words "across the Jordan" refer to people who are on the opposite side of the Jordan River to the author. But the alleged author, Moses himself, was never supposed to have been in Israel in his life. [Gen 9:21]

"CHRIST" not a name

We must admit that the word CHRIST is not a name. It is a title. It is a translation of the Hebrew word Messiah, meaning "anointed". The Greek word for "anointed" is Christos from which we get the word Christ. Priests and kings were "anointed" when being consecrated to their office. The Holy Bible confers this title even on a heathen king CYRUS (Isaiah45:1).

We are reminded in the Gospel of St. Luke "When eight days were accomplished for the circumcising of the child, his name was called Jesus, which was so named of the angel before he was conceived in the womb." (Luke2: 21). The name that was given to Mary for her yet unborn son was Jesus and not Christ. It was only after his baptism at the hands of John the Baptist that he, Jesus, claimed to be the Christ. The Jews were not the ones to accept his claim on its face value. They wanted proof!

Matthew records that the learned men among the Jews -- the Scribes and Pharisees -- came to Jesus and asked, "Master we would see a sign from thee." (Matthew 12:38) The Jews mistook him for a sorcerer, a wizard, a charlatan.

With righteous indignation Jesus replies: "An evil and adulterous generation seeketh after a sign; and there shall be no sign (no miracle) be given to it, but the sign (miracle)of the Prophet Jonah: for as Jonah was three days and three nights in the whale's belly; so shall the son of man be three days and three nights in the heart of the Earth (Matthew, 12:39-40). Jesus says, "No Sign". He does not refer the Jews to blind whose sight he had restored. He does not speak about the 'woman with issues' who was healed by merely touching him; or about the 2000 pigs he had destroyed to heal 'a man possessed'; or the 5000 and the 3000 people he had fed and satiated with a few pieces of bread. "No sign", says Jesus, but one! -- "The sign of the Prophet Jonah"! He is putting all his "eggs" in one basket. His claim to being the Messiah (Christ) stands or falls by the only "sign" he was prepared to give. Did Jesus fulfill the only sign he gave? Christendom answers with a unanimous Y-E-S! Without heeding the Biblical advice -- 'not to take things for granted' -- but "prove all things"! (1 Thessalonians 5:21)

What was the sign (miracle) of (Jonah) Yunus as? We have to go to the "Book of Jonah" in the Old Testament to find out. God commanded Jonah to go to Ninevites to repent from their "evil ways, and from the violence that is in their hands." (Jonah 3:8). But Jonah was loath to go as a warner unto the Ninevites, so he goes to Joppa instead of Nineveh, and takes a boat to run away from the Lord's command.

While at sea, there was a terrible tempest. According to the superstition of the mariners, a person fleeing from his Master's command creates such turmoil at sea. They began to inquire among themselves and said, "Come, let us cast lots, (like tossing of a coin, "head" or "tail") That we may know for whose cause this evil is upon us. So they cast lots, and the lot fell upon Jonah." (Jonah 1:7). Though there was a temporary lapse on the part of Jonah in fulfilling his mission, he manfully and most courageously volunteers: "And he said unto them take me up, and cast forth into the sea; so shall these be calm unto you: for I know that for my sake this great tempest is upon you (Jonah, 1:12).

Dead or Alive

Since Jonah was selflessly offering himself as a "vicarious" sacrifice there was no need for strangling him before throwing him into the sea, no need to spear him or break his arm or limb. In his own words: "Take me up and cast me forth. The question now arises, that when the shipmaster and the crew threw him overboard, was Jonah dead or alive? Any Christian child who attended Sunday school will give an immediate reply: 'Alive!' The storm subsides. Was this perhaps a coincidence? A fish swallows Jonah. Was he dead or alive when swallowed? The answer again is 'Alive!' Was he dead or Alive when "Jonah prayed unto the Lord. His God took him out of fish's belly"? (Jonah2:1)

Surely dead men don't cry and don't pray! The answer again is 'Alive'. For three days and three nights the fish takes him around the ocean: dead or alive? 'Alive!' is the answer. On the third day it vomits him on the seashore: dead or alive? A-L-I-V-E, of course! What had Jesus prophesied about himself? He said: "As Jonah was... so shall the son of man be" "soos Jonah" -- "jenga Jonah" -- LIKE JONAH. And how was Jonah? Was he dead or alive for three days and nights? Alive! Alive! Alive! Is the unanimous answer from the Jews, the Christians and the Muslims!

Unlike Jonah

If Jonah was alive for three days and three nights, then Jesus also ought to have been alive in the tomb, as he himself had foretold! But Christianity hangs on the flimsy thread of the "death" of Jesus for its salvation. So it has to answer that Jesus was dead for three days and three nights. The contradiction between his utterance and its fulfillment is obvious. Jonah Alive, Jesus Dead! Very unlike Jonah! Jesus had said 'Like Jonah' not 'Unlike Jonah'. If this is true then according to his own test Jesus is not the True Messiah of the Jews. If the Gospel record is genuine then how can we blame the Jews for rejecting 'Christ'?

The Doctor of Divinity and the Professor of Theology replies that in Matthew 12:40 under discussion, the emphasis is on the Time factor -- "as Jonah was three days and three nights in the belly of the whale, so shall the son of man be three days and three nights in the heart of the earth." "Please note", says the learned theologian, "that the word "Three" is repeated F-O-U-R times in this verse to prove that Jesus was going to fulfill the prophecy as regards the length of time he was going to remain in the tomb, and Not 'As Jonah was' in relation to his being alive or dead. If it is the time factor that Jesus was stressing then let us ask whether he fulfilled that aspect of his promise to the Jews as well. The Christian dogmatist answers "OFCOURSE!"

The question arises: when was Christ crucified? The whole Christian world answers: "FRIDAY!" Is this the reason they celebrate" Good Friday"?

There are numerous differences between the various sects and denominations of Christianity, but on the above they are unanimous. Jesus is supposed to be in the tomb on the night of Friday. He is still supposed to be in the tomb on the day of Saturday. He is still supposed to be in the tomb on the night of Saturday. Christians agree whole-heartedly with this. Gospels are silent as to when exactly Jesus came out of the tomb. His "secret disciples" could have taken him away on Friday night to a more congenial and restful place, but I have no right to assume about what the Gospel writers are silent.

In the final analysis, let us see whether Jesus was three days and three nights in the tomb:

It is One day and two nights, and not three days and three nights. According to the Christian Scriptures Jesus had failed a Second time. FIRST he was unlike Jonah, who was alive in the belly of the fish, which is exact opposite of what the Christians claim had happened to their master Jesus, who was dead for the same period of time.

Jonah was--alive.

SECONDLY, we discover that he also failed to fulfill the time factor as well. We must not forget that the Gospels are explicit in telling us that it was 'before sunrise' on Sunday morning (the First day of the week), that Mary Magdalene went to the tomb of Jesus and found it empty.

Mr. Robert Fahey of the 'Plain Truth' magazine delivered a lecture recently at the Holiday Inn, Durban. Orthodox Christianity supposes Mr. Fahey attempted to prove to his Christian audience that Jesus Christ was crucified on Wednesday and not on Friday, as for the past two thousand years. According to him if one counts backwards from Sunday morning deducting 3 days and 3 nights, one ought to get WEDNESDAY as the answer. The question arises, who deceived the millions of Christians for the past TWO THOUSAND years, GOD or the DEVIL? Mr. Fahey categorically answered: "THE DEVIL!" If this is the belief of the trend-setters of the Christian Faith in the world today, may we not then ask: is this not the mightiest hoax in history?

Let us now give a few examples how the Bible has blackened the characters of the Prophets of Allah (swt):

Noah [Nuh (as)] drank of the wine, and became drunk, and lay uncovered in his tent and Ham [his son] saw the nakedness of his father. (Gen 9:21)

David [Dawood (as)] dances naked before the people and before the Lord. (2 Sam. 6:20)

And so his sister Mariam the Prophetess dances, she took a tremble and dances with the women. (Exo.15:20)

Lot [Lut (as)] went up out of Zo'ar and dwelt in the hills with his two daughters. And the first-born said to the younger, "Our father is old, and there is not a man on earth to come to us after the manner of all the earth. Come let us make our father drink wine and we will lie with him, that we may preserve offspring through our father. So they made their father drink wine that night; and the first born went in and lay with her father; He did not know when she lay down or when she arose. And on the next day, the first-born said to the younger "Behold, I lay last night with my father, let us make him drink wine tonight also; then you go in and lie with him that we may preserve offspring through our father. So they made their father drink wine that night also, and the younger arose, and lay with him; and he did not know when she lay down or when she arose. Thus both the daughters of Lot were with child by their father (Gen.19:30).

Judah [Musa (as)] fornicates with his daughter-in-law: Ta'-mar When he saw her, he thought her to be a harlot, for she had covered her face. He went over to her at the roadside and said, "Come, Let me come into you" for he did not know that she was his daughter-in-law. She said, "What you will give me that you may come into me?" He answered, "I will send you a kid from the flock." And she said "Will you send me a pledge till you send it?" He said, "What pledge shall I give you?" She replied "Your signal and your cord and your staff that is in your hand." So he gave them to her, and went into her, and she conceived by him. About three months later, Judah was told, "Ta'-mar your daughter-in- law has played the harlot, and moreover she is with child by Harlotry. (Gen. 38:15)

David (Dawood as) arose from his couch and was walking upon the roof that he saw from the roof a woman bathing; and the woman was very beautiful, and David sent and enquired about the woman. And one said, "Is not that Bathshe'ba, the daughter of Eli'am, the wife of Uri'ah the Hittite?" So David send messengers and took her, and she came to him and he lay with her. Then she returned to her house; and she sent and told David, I am with child. David called her husband, and invited him, and ate in his presence and drank, so that he made him drunk. In the morning David wrote to Jo'cab, "Set Uri'ah in the forefront of the hardest fighting, and then draw back from him, that he may be struck down and die. When he died David sent and brought Uri'ah's wife to his house, and she became his wife. (2. Sam.11:1)

The Lord said to David, "Because you despised me, and have taken the wife of Uri'ah the Hittite to be your wife. Thus say the Lord, "Behold, I will take your wives (He punished David through his daughter and son not his wife as you will see) before your eyes, and give them to your neighbor and he shall lie with your wives in the sight of this sun." (2.Sam.12:10)

Amnon [the son of David] fell in love with his sister Ta'-mar. "Amnon was so tormented that he made himself ill because of his sister Ta'-mar; for she was a virgin, and it seemed impossible to Amnon to do anything to her. Amnon had a friend who said to him, "Lie down on your bed and pretend to be ill, and when [your father] the king comes to see you, you say to him: let my sister Ta'-mar come and give bread to eat from her hand. David sent Ta'-mar to her brother and ordered her to feed her brother by her hand. Ta'-mar took the cakes she had made, and brought them into the chamber to Amnon, but when she brought them near him to eat, he took hold of her, and said to her, "Come, lie with me, my sister", she said, "No my brother, do not force me." But he would not listen to her; and being stronger than she, he forced her, and lay with her."(2.Sam.13:1)

Solomon [solaiman (as)] had seven hundred wives, princesses and three hundred concubines; and his wives turned his heart after other Gods.... the Goddess of the Sido'nians. (1King11:3)

Aaron said to people of Israel, "take off the rings of Gold which are in the ears of your wives, your sons and your daughters. So they took off the rings of gold, and brought them to Aaron. And he received the Golf at their hand and fashioned it with a graving tool and made a molten calf and they said, "These are your Gods, O Israel, who brought you up out of the land of Egypt."(Exo.32:2)

How sex has been described in the Bible?

I have seen among the simple, I have perceived among the youth, a young man without sense, passing along the street near her corner taking the road to her house in the twilight, in the evening at the time of the night and darkness. And lo, a woman meets him, dressed as a harlot, wily of heart. She is loud and wayward. Now in the street, now in the market and at every corner she lies in wait. She seizes him and kisses him, and with impudent face she says to him: I have come to meet you, to seek you eagerly, and I have found you. I have perfumed my bed with myrrh, aloes, and cinnamon. Come, let us take our fill of love till the morning, and Let us delight ourselves with love. For my husband is not at home, he has gone on a long journey. With much seductive speech she persuades him; with her smooth talk she compels him. All at once he follows her, as an ox goes to the slaughter. (Prov.7:7)

Woman's Breast in the Bible!

My beloved is to me a bag of myrrh that lies between my breasts. Behold, you are beautiful, my beloved, truly lovely. Our bed is green. (In R.S.V. our couch) (Songs.1:13)

Upon my bed night I sought him whom my soul loves but not found him." When I found him whom my soul loves, I held him, and would not let him go until I had brought him into my mother's house, and into the chamber of her that conceived me. I adjure you, o daughters of Jerusalem, by the gazelles or the hinds of the field, that you steer not up nor awaken love until it pleases. (Song.3:1)

We have a little sister, and she the word bastard in the Bible!! (Song. 8:8)

A BASTARD should not enter into the congregation of the Lord. (Deut. 23:2) Then you are Bastards, and not sons. (K.J.V) (Hebrew 12:8) It means you are not real sons, but bastards. (G.N.B) (Hebrew 12:8)

Menses in the Bible!

"When a woman has a discharge of blood which in her regular discharge from her body, she shall be apart seven days. And whosoever touches her shall be unclean until the evening. And everything that she lies upon in her separation shall be unclean. Every thing also that she sits upon shall be unclean. And whosoever touches her bed shall wash his clothes and bathe him in water, and be unclean until the evening. And whosoever touches anything that she sat upon shall wash his clothes, and bathe him in water, and be unclean until the evening" (Levi.15:19).

God said to Eve when she tempted Adam, "I will greatly multiply your pain in childbearing, in pain you shall bring forth children, yet your desire shall be for your husband and he shall rule over you." (Gen 3:16)

Postpartum in the Bible!

"If a woman conceives, and bears a male child, then she shall be unclean seven days. But if she bears a female child then she shall be unclean two weeks." (Levi.12:2)

"But any woman who prays and prophecies with her head unveiled dishonors her head - it is the same as if her head were shaven, for if a woman will not veil herself then she should cut off her hair. But if it is disgraceful for a woman to be shorn or shaven, let her wear a veil. Judge for yourselves; is it proper for a woman to pray to God with her head uncovered?" (1Corin.11:5)

It seems that Christians are unaware of the obligation of the veil in the Bible, which made me put their verses in this book, and for those who attack the veil in Islam should notice these verses of their own Bible, and notice also this verse "Judge not, that you be not judged. For with the judgment you pronounce you will be judged, and the measure you give will be the measure you get.

Racism in the Bible

There is no God in all the Earth, but in Israel. (2 King 5:15)

Paul said, "We ourselves, who are Jews by birth and not Gentile sinners." (Gal.2:15)

Kill Women, Children, Animals!! (Gal.4:22)

And the Lord said, "Go through the city, and smite: let not your eye spare, neither have you pity. Slay utterly old and young, both maids and little children, and women, sword and fire in NEW TESTAMENT." (Ezek. 9:5)

"Do not think that I have come to make peace on earth? I have not come to bring peace, but a sword". "For I have come to set a man against his father and a daughter against her mother": (Said Jesus!) (Math. 10:34)

He said to Mary, "Woman, what have I to do with you." (John. 2:4) Then one said unto Jesus, "Behold, your mother and brethren stand without, desiring to talk to you" but he answered and said, "Who is my mother? And who are my brethren?" (Math. 12:47) (We only quote here what we believe not because we believe that Jesus one of the great prophets of God was more polite and kind to his mother than what the Bible shows.)

Hypocrisy in the Bible!

With the pure you show yourself pure, and with the crooked you show yourself perverse. (2Sam.22:27)

The genealogy of "Jesus" contains 28 names of his fathers. (Math. 1:18)

The genealogy of "Jesus" contains 42 different names of the fathers of Jesus than we find in Mathew. (If the Christians attempt to excuse that error by saying that the other descendants belong to Jesus threw his mother, while we find that his genealogy belongs to Joseph the carpenter, but we can analyze the contradiction clearly when we find two different fathers for Joseph the carpenter. His father in Mathew is Jacob while his father according to Luke is Heli.) Luke3:23)

Mathew gives the names of the disciples of Jesus. (Math. 10:2)

But Luke gives contradictory names of the disciples of Jesus to Mathew. (Luke 6:13)

Mathew and Mark add: Labaous and Simon the Cananean, and omit: Simon the jealous and Judah the brother of James. While Luke adds: Simon the jealous and Judah the brother of James. He omits: Labaoues and Simon the Cananean.)

Dear readers, as Muslims we must have faith on all the Prophets sent by Allah (swt) and the Sacred Books sent to them for the guidance of Mankind. And we as Muslims also believe that the purpose of sending Prophets were to preach that there is none but Allah (God) who is worthy of being worshipped. And we as Muslims are taught not to distinguish between the Prophets and also that the Prophets are brothers.

Now dear readers, can one Prophet of Allah (swt) blacken the character of another Prophet? NO? Does Allah (swt) teach Racism, Vulgarism, and Hypocrisy, chaos on the Earth? The emphatic answer is NO? NEVER? Now it is up to you the reader to decide whether the so-called 'Bible' can be the word of GOD?

Let us now compare some of the teachings from Bible and the Quran:

Bible: How long will you forget me, O Lord? (Psalm13:1)

Quran: My Lord never errs nor forgets. (20:52)

Bible: Awake, why do You sleep my Lord? Then the Lord awaked as one out of sleep, and like a mighty man that shouts by reason of wine. (Psalm 4:23)

Quran: Allah! There is no God but He, the living, the Self-subsisting Supporter of all. No slumber seizes Him or Sleep (Hab. 1:2).

Quran: Truly my Lord is he, the Hearer of prayer. (14:39) If you pronounce the word aloud, (it is no matter) for verily He knows what is secret and what is yet more hidden. (20:7)

Bible: The Lord said, "I will break my covenant with them." [Levi. 26:44] You said: O Lord! My covenants will I not break? But you cast off and abhorred, you have been wroth with your anointed. You have made void the covenant of your servant (Levi 26:38) You have made all his enemies to rejoice, you have also turned the edge of his sword, and have made him to stand in the battle. (Levi 26:43)

Quran: It is the promise of Allah. Never does Allah fail from His promise but most men know not (30:6).

Bible: God said to Jesus, "You are my son today I have begotten you" (Heb.5:5) God said to David, "You are my son today I have begotten you"(Psalm2:7)

Quran: Say: He is Allah, The One; Allah, The Eternal Absolute; He does not beget, nor is He begotten, and there is none like unto Him (112:1).

Bible: Resist not evil: But whosoever shall smite you on your right cheek, turn to him the other also. And if any man will sue you at the law, and take away your coat, let him have your cloak also. (Math. 5:38)

Quran: The recompense for an injury is an injury equal thereto (In degree): but if a person forgives and make reconciliation his reward is due from Allah: For (Allah) loves not those who do wrong. (42:40) let them forgive and overlook, do you not wish that Allah should forgive you? For Allah is Oft-Forgiving, most Merciful (24:22).

Bible: O Lord, bow down your ear: open your eyes and see. (2King. 19:16)

Quran: Allah! There is no God but He, the living, the Self-subsisting Supporter of all. No slumber seizes Him or Sleep. (2:255)

Bible: With the pure you show yourself pure, and with the crooked you show yourself perverse. (2 Sam. 22:27)

Quran: Verily, Allah knows the unseen of the heavens and the earth: and Allah Sees well all that you do (49:18).

Bible: God said to Jesus, "You are my son today I have begotten you" (Heb.5: 5) God said to David, "You are my son today I have begotten you"(Psalm: 2:7).

Quran: O you who believe stand out firmly for justice as witnesses to Allah even as against yourselves or your parents or your kin.(4:135)

Bible: I am the Lord, visiting the iniquity of the fathers upon the children unto the third and fourth generations. [Deut. 5:7] Prepare slaughter for his children for the iniquity of their fathers. (Isaiah 14:21)

Quran: Say: He is Allah, The One; Allah, The Eternal Absolute; He does not beget, nor is He begotten, and there is none like unto Him (112:1).

Bible: Resist not evil: But whosoever shall smite you on your right cheek, turn to him the other also. And if any man will sue you at the law, and take away your coat, let him have your cloak also. (Math. 5:38)

Quran: Every soul draws the mead of its acts on none but itself: no bearer of burdens can bear the burden of another (6:164).

Dr. W. Graham Scroggie of the MOODY BIBLE INSTITUTE, Chicago, one of the most prestigious Christian Evangelical Mission in the world, answering the question — "Is the Bible the Word of God?" (Also the title of his book), under the heading: It is human, yet divine. He says on page 17: "Yes, the Bible is human, though some, out of zeal which is not according to knowledge, have denied this. Those books have passed through the minds of men, are written in the language of men, were penned by the hands of men, and bear in their style the characteristics of men." Another erudite Christian scholar, Kenneth Cragg, the Anglican Bishop of Jerusalem, says on page 277 of his book, "The Call of the Minaret": "Not so the New Testament . . . There is condensation and editing; there is choice, reproduction and witness. The Gospels have come through the mind of the Church behind the authors. They represent experience and history."

We Muslims have no hesitation in acknowledging that in the Bible, there are three different kinds of witnessing recognizable without any need of specialized training. These are:

1. You will be able to recognize in the Bible what may be described as "The Word of God."

2. You will also be able to discern what can be described as the "Words of a Prophet of God."

3. And you will most readily observe that the bulk of the Bible is the record of eyewitnesses or ear witnesses, or people writing from hearsay. As such they are the "Words of a Historian"

You do not have to hunt for examples of these different types of evidences in the Bible. The following quotations will make the position crystal clear:

The First Type:

(a) I will raise them up a prophet . . . and I will put my words in ... and he shall speak unto them all that I shall command him." (Deuteronomy18:18)

(b) I even, I am the Lord, and beside me there is no savior." (Isaiah 43:11)

(c) "Look unto me, and be ye saved, all the end of the earth: for I am God, and there is none else."(Isaiah45:22)

Note the first person pronoun singular in the above references, and without any difficulty you will agree that the statements seem to have the sound of being GOD'S WORD.

The SECOND Type:

(a) "Jesus cried with a loud voice, saying Eli, Eli, lama sabachtani? . . ." (Mathew27:46)

(b) "And Jesus answered him, the first of all the commandments is, Hear, O Israel; the Lord our God is one Lord:" (Mark   12:29)

(c) "And Jesus said unto him, Why callest thou me good? There is none good but one, that is God." (Mark 10:18).
Even a child will be able to affirm that: Jesus "cried" Jesus "answered" and Jesus "said" are the words of the one to whom they are attributed, i.e. the WORDS OF A PROPHET OF GOD.

The THIRDT ype:

"And seeing a fig tree afar off having leaves, he (JESUS) came, if haply he (JESUS) might find anything thereon: and when he (JESUS) came to it, (Jesus) found nothing but leaves . . ." (Mark 11:13).

The bulk of the Bible is a witnessing of this THIRD kind. These are the words of a third person. Note the highlighted pronouns. They are not the Words of God or of His prophet, but the WORDS OF A HISTORIAN.

Thus the 'Bibles' that are available today contain 'Words of God', 'Words of the Prophet', and 'Records of the eye-witness' and thus should not be claimed as the"Words of God"

For the Muslim it is quite easy to distinguish the above types of evidence, because he also has them in his own faith. But of the followers of the different religions, he is the most fortunate in this that his various records are contained in separate Books!

ONE: The first kind — THE WORD OF Allah— is found in a Book called The Holy Qur'an.

TWO: The second kind — THE WORDS OF THE PROPHET OF GOD (Muhammad sas) are recorded in the Books of Tradition called the Hadith.

THREE: Evidence of the third kind abounds in different volume of Islamic history, written by some of high integrity and learning, and others of lesser trustworthiness, but the Muslim advisedly keeps these Books in separate volumes!

Muslims keep the above three types of evidence jealously apart, in their proper gradations of authority. He never equates them. On the other hand, the "Holy Bible" contains a motley type of literature, which composes the embarrassing kind, the sordid, and the obscene — all under the same cover — A Christian is forced to concede equal spiritual import and authority to all, and is thus unfortunate in this regard. The Quran written hundreds of years ago, and available in the world's leading museums is the same Quran that is available in the book stores even today. Anybody can check and verify the authenticity of the Holy Book 'Quran'. I am sure; the enemies of Islam have verified this truth and could not find a single letter not to speak of a word or a sentence different in this Holy Book of Allah (swt).

The Taurah we Muslims believe in is not the "Torah" of the Jews and the Christians, though the words — one Arabic, the other Hebrew — are the same. We believe that whatever the Holy Prophet Moses Musa (as) preached to his people, was the revelation from God Almighty, but that Moses was not the author of those "books" attributed to him by the Jews and the Christians.

Likewise, we believe that the Zabur was the revelation of God granted to Prophet Dawood (as) David but that the present Psalms associated with his name are not that revelation. The Christians themselves do not insist that David is the sole author of "his" Psalms.3

What about the Injil? INJIL means the "Gospel" or "good news" which Jesus Christ preached during his short ministry. The "Gospel" writers often mention that Jesus going about and preaching the Gospel (the Injil):
1. "And Jesus went . . . preaching the gospel . . . and healing every disease among the people." (Matthew9:35)

2. "... but whosoever shall lose his fife for my sake and the gospel's, the same shall save it." (Mark8:35)

3."...Preached the gospel..." (Luke20:1)

May Allah (swt) give us necessary and proper guidance to distinguish the 'Truth' from 'Falsehood,' and save us from the torment of punishment on the day of 'Final Judgment'? **Amin!**

*Michael H. Hart (1992), "The 100: A Ranking of the Most Influential Persons in History", Cidal Press, New York, USA.

**Bold added in the quotes.

Which Path is the Straight Path?

Allah [swt] made it obligatory to recite Surah Al-Fatiha in all rakats of any prayer. In ayahs 6-7, we recite from **Surah al- Fatihah:**

اِهْدِنَا الصِّرَاطَ الْمُسْتَقِيمَ ۙ صِرَاطَ الَّذِينَ أَنْعَمْتَ عَلَيْهِمْ غَيْرِ الْمَغْضُوبِ عَلَيْهِمْ وَلَا الضَّآلِّينَ

Guide us to the straight path - the path of those on whom You have bestowed favor, not (the way) of those who evoked [Your] anger, or of those who are astray.

Allah says, "This is for My servant, and My servant shall acquire what he asked for."

We ask Allah [swt] to guide us to the straight path. Now the question is which path is the straight path. Is there any guidance from Allah [swt] about the straight path? The answer is in the affirmative. In **Surah Maryam (19:36),** Allah [swt] says,

وَإِنَّ اللَّهَ رَبِّي وَرَبُّكُمْ فَاعْبُدُوهُ ۚ هَٰذَا صِرَاطٌ مُّسْتَقِيمٌ

[`Isa said], "And indeed, Allah is my Lord and your Lord, so worship Him. That is the straight path."

So, recognizing Allah [swt] as our creator and sustainer, and worshiping Him is the straight path. We have to believe in our heart and mind that Allah [swt] is the only one to be worshiped.

And also in **Surah an-Nisa' (4:175),** Allah [swt] asserts,

فَأَمَّا الَّذِينَ ءَامَنُوا بِاللَّهِ وَاعْتَصَمُوا بِهِ فَسَيُدْخِلُهُمْ فِي رَحْمَةٍ مِّنْهُ وَفَضْلٍ وَيَهْدِيهِمْ إِلَيْهِ صِرَاطًا مُّسْتَقِيمًا

So those who believe in Allah and hold fast to [depend on] Him - He will admit them to mercy from Himself and bounty and guide them to Himself by on a straight path.

The only way that Allah [swt] will guide us to the straight path as we ask Him in our prayers every time is to believe in Allah [swt] and remain steadfast at all cost.

This subject is also mentioned in **Surah an- Nisa' (4:116),** for Allah [swt] said,

إِنَّ اللَّهَ لَا يَغْفِرُ أَن يُشْرَكَ بِهِ وَيَغْفِرُ مَا دُونَ ذَٰلِكَ لِمَن يَشَآءُ

Indeed, Allah does not forgive association with Him, but He forgives what is less than that for whom He wills.

Imam Ahmad, Ibn Majah, in the Book of the Sunnah in his Sunan, and Al-Bazzar collected this Hadith. Ibn Jarir recorded that a man asked Ibn Mas`ud, "What is As-Sirat Al-Mustaqim [the straight path]." Ibn Mas`ud replied, "Muhammad left us at its lower end and its other end is in Paradise. To the right of this Path are other paths, and to the left of it are other paths, and there are men [on these paths] calling those who pass by them. Whoever goes on the other paths will end up in the Fire".

Allah's statement,

$$\text{فَٱتَّبِعُوهُ وَلَا تَتَّبِعُوا ٱلسُّبُلَ}$$

So follow it, and follow not [other] paths describes Allah's path in the singular sense, because truth is one. Allah describes the other paths in the plural, because they are many and are divided (Tafir-Ibn-Kathir).

Allah [swt] states in **Surah al-An`am (6:151-3):**

$$\text{قُل تَعَالَوْا أَتْلُ مَا حَرَّمَ رَبُّكُمْ عَلَيْكُمْ أَلَّا تُشْرِكُوا بِهِ شَيْئًا وَبِالْوَالِدَيْنِ إِحْسَانًا وَلَا تَقْتُلُوا أَوْلَادَكُم مِّنْ إِمْلَاقٍ نَّحْنُ نَرْزُقُكُمْ}$$

$$\text{وَإِيَّاهُمْ وَلَا تَقْرَبُوا الْفَوَاحِشَ مَا ظَهَرَ مِنْهَا وَمَا بَطَنَ وَلَا تَقْتُلُوا النَّفْسَ الَّتِي حَرَّمَ اللَّهُ إِلَّا بِالْحَقِّ ذَلِكُمْ وَصَّاكُم بِهِ لَعَلَّكُمْ}$$

$$\text{تَعْقِلُونَ وَلَا تَقْرَبُوا مَالَ الْيَتِيمِ إِلَّا بِالَّتِي هِيَ أَحْسَنُ حَتَّى يَبْلُغَ أَشُدَّهُ وَأَوْفُوا الْكَيْلَ وَالْمِيزَانَ بِالْقِسْطِ لَا نُكَلِّفُ نَفْسًا إِلَّا}$$

$$\text{وُسْعَهَا وَإِذَا قُلْتُمْ فَاعْدِلُوا وَلَوْ كَانَ ذَا قُرْبَى وَبِعَهْدِ اللَّهِ أَوْفُوا ذَلِكُمْ وَصَّاكُم بِهِ لَعَلَّكُمْ تَذَكَّرُونَ وَأَنَّ هَذَا صِرَاطِي}$$

$$\text{مُسْتَقِيمًا فَاتَّبِعُوهُ وَلَا تَتَّبِعُوا السُّبُلَ فَتَفَرَّقَ بِكُمْ عَن سَبِيلِهِ ذَلِكُمْ وَصَّاكُم بِهِ لَعَلَّكُمْ تَتَّقُونَ}$$

Say, "Come, I will recite what your Lord has prohibited to you. [He commands] that you not associate anything with Him, are kind and dutiful to your parents, and do not kill children out of poverty; We will provide for you and for them. And do not approach immoralities - what is apparent of them and what is concealed. And kill the soul which Allah has forbidden [to be killed] except for legal right. This has He instructed you that you may use reason. And do not approach the orphan's property except that in a way that is best [intending improvement] until he (or she) attains maturity. And give full measure and weight with justice. We do not charge any soul except [with that within] its capacity. And when you speak [testify], be just, even if [it concerns] a near relative. And fulfill the covenant of Allah. This has He instructed you that you may remember." And, [moreover], this is My path, which is straight, so follow it, and do not follow [other] ways, for you will be separated from His way. This has He instructed you that you may become righteous.

In these verses, Allah [swt] has Ten Commandments in which we are forbidden [made haram for us] doing ten things. The first and foremost one is not to worship any other person or thing accept Allah [swt]. This relates directly to Allah [swt]. The remaining nine are related to our worldly life. Fulfillment of these commandments is the basis of getting Allah's [swt] guidance to the straight path. In other words, those of us who lead our lives in this world abiding truthfully the commandments are surely being on the right path.

Allah [swt] reaffirms in **Surah al-Hijr (15:39-41):**

قَالَ رَبِّ بِمَآ أَغْوَيْتَنِى لَأُزَيِّنَنَّ لَهُمْ فِي الْأَرْضِ وَلَأُغْوِيَنَّهُمْ أَجْمَعِينَ ـ إِلَّا عِبَادَكَ مِنْهُمُ الْمُخْلَصِينَ ـ قَالَ هَذَا صِرَاطٌ عَلَيَّ مُسْتَقِيمٌ

[Iblis] said, "My Lord, because You have put me in eror, I will surely make [disobedience] attractive to them [mankind] on earth, and I will mislead them all except, among them, Your chosen servants." [Allah] said, "This is a path [of return] to Me [that is] straight."

Allah has assured that those who will be guided in the straight path; *Iblis* will fail to mislead them and will not be able to distract them from the path of Allah [swt].

Allah (swt) puts a question to the human beings in **Surah al-`Imrarn (3:101):**

وَكَيْفَ تَكْفُرُونَ وَأَنْتُمْ تُتْلَى عَلَيْكُمْ ءَايَتُ اللهِ وَفِيكُمْ رَسُولُهُ وَمَن يَعْتَصِم بِاللهِ فَقَدْ هُدِيَ إِلَى صِرَاطٍ مُّسْتَقِيمٍ

And how could you disbelieve while to you are being recited the verses of Allah and among you is His Messenger? And whoever holds firmly to Allah has [indeed] been guided to a straight path.

Trusting and relying on Allah [swt] are the basis of achieving the right guidance and staying away from the path of wickedness. They also represent the tool to acquiring guidance and truth and achieving the righteous aims.

May Allah [swt] bestow His mercy and help so that we can try our utmost to follow His Commandments in order to be on the right path? **Amin!**

Zakat: Share of the Disadvantaged on Our Wealth

Zakat is one of the major 5 duties required by Allah [swt] from the Muslims, the others being the Sahada [declaration of faith], Salat [contact prayers], and Fasting the month of Ramadhan and Hajj [Pilgrimage to Mecca]. Allah [swt] says in **Surah al-A'raf (7:156):**

فَسَأَكْتُبُهَا لِلَّذِينَ يَتَّقُونَ وَيُؤْتُونَ الزَّكَوةَ وَالَّذِينَ هُم بِآيَتِنَا يُؤْمِنُونَ

So I will decree it [especially] for those who fear Me and give zakat and those who believe in Our verses.

Allah has bestowed upon us the bounty of wealth and guided us to gain it through lawful means and prescribed the lawful means in which it should be spent. O Muslims! Continue thanking Him and observe what He has prescribed upon us to purify our wealth as pointed out in **Surah at-Tawbah (9:103):**

خُذْ مِنْ أَمْوَلِهِمْ صَدَقَةً تُطَهِّرُهُمْ وَتُزَكِّيهِم بِهَا وَصَلِّ عَلَيْهِمْ إِنَّ صَلَوتَكَ سَكَنٌ لَّهُمْ وَاللهُ سَمِيعٌ عَلِيمٌ

Take, [O Muhammad], from their wealth a charity by which you purify them and cause them increase, and invoke [Allah's blessings] upon them and Allah is Hearing and Knowing.

Zakat which is one of the Islamic pillars is not merely a tax that is collected from those who can afford it. It is designed and intended for a noble purpose also. Its foremost purpose is to sow the seeds of kindness, sympathy and benevolence, and to provide a chance to introduce among the various sections of the society the relationship of love and friendliness.

And avoid withholding what Allah has prescribed, because withholding leads to destruction and makes our property void of blessings. Allah [swt] is the original owner of all wealth and we are nothing but the temporary custodian. Think deeply. As soon as we die, all the worldly wealth [big houses, cars, and other amenities] that we claimed to be ours when alive is no longer ours. It becomes the wealth of others: wife, children etc. The best commandment of Allah is Zakat, the third pillar of Islam; it is closely related to Prayer. Both are usually mentioned together in the Holy Qur'an.

It is described in the Qur'an as a known and obligatory portion of the income. Allah [swt] will not call it known if it was not. We learn that it is a known percentage in **Surah al-Ma'arij (70:24-25):**

وَالَّذِينَ فِي أَمْوَلِهِمْ حَقٌّ مَّعْلُومٌ ۝ لِّلسَّآئِلِ وَالْمَحْرُومِ

And those within whose wealth is a recognized right [specified share i.e. zakat] for the one who asks and deprived.

This is to be paid out on the same day of the harvest [on agricultural products] we receive as described in **Surah al-An'am (6:141):**

وَهُوَ الَّذِى أَنشَأَ جَنَّتٍ مَّعْرُوشَتٍ وَغَيْرَ مَعْرُوشَتٍ وَالنَّخْلَ وَالزَّرْعَ مُخْتَلِفًا أُكُلُهُ وَالزَّيْتُونَ وَالرُّمَّانَ مُتَشَبِهًا وَغَيْرَ مُتَشَبِهٍ

كُلُوا مِن ثَمَرِهِ إِذَآ أَثْمَرَ وَءَاتُوا حَقَّهُ يَوْمَ حَصَادِهِ وَلَا تُسْرِفُوا إِنَّهُ لَا يُحِبُّ الْمُسْرِفِينَ

And it is He who causes gardens to grow, [both] trelised and untrelised, and palm trees and crops of different [kinds of] food and olives and pomegranates, similar (in kind) but different (in variety). Eat of [each of] its fruit when it yields and give its due [zakat] on the day of its harvest. And be not excessive [in eating] as well as in all things generally. Indeed, He does not love those who commit excess.

Zakat must be carefully calculated and given away on a regular basis. Zakat is due on gold and silver only when they reach the minimum amount (Nisab), which is equal to the amount due on gold and silver, it is 2.5%. Zakat is due also on cash provided that it reaches the minimum amount. The amount of Zakat due on it is 2.5%.

Zakat is due also on debts if they are gold, silver or cash if they reach the minimum amount [*Nisab*], whether this amount is reached by debts only or after adding them to the rest of his wealth, which he has by any other way of the same kind. If these debts are due on solvent, the owner is free to pay Zakat every year or after he gets his debts back. But if the borrower is poor, Zakat isn't due until the lender gets back his debts then he should pay Zakat due for one year because wealth in such case is regarded as wasted money.

Zakat is due on merchandise if it reaches the minimum amount [*Nisab*] whether by itself or after adding it to other kinds of wealth like money. The amount of Zakat due in this case is also 2.5%, provided that it remains in possession for a full Hijri year.

Allah's Apostle said, "There is no Zakat on less than five camels and also there is no Zakat on less than five Awaq [of silver]. And there is no Zakat on less than five Awsuq [a special measure of food-grains], [For gold 20, Dinars i.e. equal to 12 Guinea English]. No Zakat for less than 12 Guinea [English] of gold or for silver less than 22 [Fransa Riyals of Yemen.) (Bukhari, book #24, hadith #526)

The Prophet [sas] explained to his nation what should be paid on agricultural products [including fruits]. He stated that if plants are irrigated by rain, the sum of Zakat due on it is a tenth; however, if they are irrigated by machine, the amount of Zakat to be paid is a twentieth. This amount is set clear beyond any doubt and controversy. (Bukhari, book #24, hadith #560)

O servants of Allah! Souls are created with miserliness as an innate nature. The one who can transcend this innate nature is the successful one. Satan desires that we withhold Zakat. He is always making promises, but Satan's promises are nothing but deception. O Muslims! Evaluate our deeds and pay the particular amount assigned by Allah and His Messenger. Bear in mind that Zakat is enjoined, in the first place, to complete our other acts of worship and as a purification of our wealth, so do not neglect paying it. O Muslims! Know for certain that Zakat is not valid unless it is distributed in the ways in which Allah has assigned, like giving it to needy persons, the poor and the indebted people who are not able to pay back their debts. It is lawful to pay it to the needy among our relatives provided that we are not responsible for their expenses.

The specific recipients of the obligatory charity, Zakat, are clearly mentioned in **Surah at-Tawbah (9:60):**

إِنَّمَا الصَّدَقَاتُ لِلْفُقَرَآءِ وَالْمَسَاكِينِ وَالْعَامِلِينَ عَلَيْهَا وَالْمُؤَلَّفَةِ قُلُوبُهُمْ وَفِي الرِّقَابِ وَالْغَارِمِينَ وَفِي سَبِيلِ اللَّهِ وَابْنِ السَّبِيلِ

فَرِيضَةً مِّنَ اللَّهِ وَاللَّهُ عَلِيمٌ حَكِيمٌ

Zakat expenditures are only for the poor and for the needy and for those employed to collect (the funds) and for bringing hearts together [for Islam] and for freeing captives and for those in debt and for the cause of Allah and for the [stranded] traveler – an obligation [imposed] by Allah. And Allah is Knowing and Wise.

Allah [swt] describes the punishment of those on the Day of Judgment who will not pay due Zakat on their wealth in **Surah at-Tawbah (9:34-35)** as:

يَا أَيُّهَا الَّذِينَ ءَامَنُوا إِنَّ كَثِيرًا مِّنَ الأَحْبَارِ وَالرُّهْبَانِ لَيَأْكُلُونَ أَمْوَالَ النَّاسِ بِالْبَاطِلِ وَيَصُدُّونَ عَن سَبِيلِ اللَّهِ وَالَّذِينَ يَكْنِزُونَ

الذَّهَبَ وَالْفِضَّةَ وَلاَ يُنفِقُونَهَا فِي سَبِيلِ اللَّهِ فَبَشِّرْهُم بِعَذَابٍ أَلِيمٍ - يَوْمَ يُحْمَى عَلَيْهَا فِي نَارِ جَهَنَّمَ فَتُكْوَى بِهَا جِبَاهُهُمْ وَجُنُوبُهُمْ

وَظُهُورُهُمْ هَذَا مَا كَنَزْتُمْ لِأَنفُسِكُمْ فَذُوقُوا مَا كُنتُمْ تَكْنِزُونَ -

O you who have believed, indeed many of the scholars and the monks devour the wealth of people unjustly [through false pretense] and avert them from the way of Allah. And those who hoard gold and silver and spend it not in the way of Allah – give them tidings of a painful punishment. The Day when it [whose zakat was not paid] will be heated in the fire of Hell and seared therewith will be their foreheads, their flanks, and their backs, [it will be said], "This is what you hoarded for yourselves, so taste what you used to hoard."

Commenting on this verse, Allah's Apostle said, "Whoever is made wealthy by Allah and does not pay the Zakat of his wealth, then on the Day of Resurrection his wealth will be made like a bald-headed poisonous male snake with two black spots over the eyes". The snake will encircle his neck and bite his cheeks and say, "I am your wealth, I am your treasure." Then the Prophet recited the holy verses of **Surah al-'Imran (3:180):**

وَلاَ يَحْسَبَنَّ الَّذِينَ يَبْخَلُونَ بِمَا ءَاتَاهُمُ اللَّهُ مِن فَضْلِهِ هُوَ خَيْرًا لَّهُم بَلْ هُوَ شَرٌّ لَّهُمْ سَيُطَوَّقُونَ مَا بَخِلُوا بِهِ يَوْمَ الْقِيَامَةِ وَلِلَّهِ مِيرَاثُ

السَّمَوَاتِ وَالأَرْضِ وَاللَّهُ بِمَا تَعْمَلُونَ خَبِيرٌ

And let not those who [greedily] withhold what Allah has bestowed on them of His bounty ever think that it is better for them. Rather, it is worse for them. Their necks will be encircled by what they withheld on the Day of Resurrection. And to Allah belongs the heritage of the heavens and the earth. And Allah, with what you do, is [fully] acquainted. (Bukhari, book #24, hadith #486)

Narrated Al-Ahnaf bin Qais: While I was sitting with some people from Quraish, a man with very rough hair, clothes, and appearance came and stood in front of us, greeted us and said, "Inform those who hoard wealth, that a stone will be heated in the Hell-fire and will be put on the nipples of their breasts till it comes out from the bones of their shoulders and then put on the bones of their shoulders till it comes through the nipples of their breasts the stone will be moving and hitting." After saying that, the person retreated and sat by the side of the pillar, I followed him and sat beside him, and I did not know who he was. I said to him, "I think the people disliked what you had said." He said, "These people do not understand anything, although my friend told me." I asked, "Who is your friend?" He said, "The Prophet said [to me], 'O Abu Dhar! Do you see the mountain of Uhud?' And on that I [Abu Dhar] started looking towards the sun to judge how much remained of the day as I thought that Allah's Apostle wanted to send me to do something for him and I said, 'Yes!' He said, "I do not love to have gold equal to the mountain of Uhud unless I spend it all [in Allah's cause] except three Dinars [pounds]. These people do not understand and collect worldly wealth. No, by Allah, neither I ask them for worldly benefits nor am I in need of their religious advice till I meet Allah, The Honorable, The Majestic." (Bukhari, book #24, hadith #489)

Zakat is neither a gift nor a charity but the right of the disadvantaged upon the wealthy. Gold and silver are not to be heated in a fire like that of our worldly life, rather in a fire whose heat is ninety-nine times hotter than ours. After being heated it will be a grievous chastisement not for a single part of the body; rather, it will touch every part and side of the body, from the top to the bottom, from the front to the back O Muslims! After branding every part of the body by the heated gold and silver, they will not be allowed to lose their heat; rather, they will be heated again and again.

O servants of Allah! O you who believe in Allah and His Messenger! O you who believe in the holy Qur'an and Sunnah! What is the benefit of wealth if not purified by Zakat? Surely, it will be a chastisement inflicted upon us and the benefit goes to others whom Allah wills. We cannot tolerate the flame of this worldly fire, so how could we tolerate the Hellfire? O servants of Allah! Fear Allah by paying Zakat willingly. O Muslims! Zakat is due upon gold and silver, be they coins, ingots or jewelry and whether they are used for wearing or selling or renting because there are explicit texts in the holy Qur'an and Sunnah that enjoin Zakat on gold and silver, especially in the case of using them as jewelry.

Pay the due Zakat, which Allah has enjoined on us to receive the recompense in this worldly life and the great reward and gifts in the Hereafter. Do not think that by paying Zakat, our wealth will decrease. As Allah [swt] says in **Surah Saba'(34:39):**

قُلْ إِنَّ رَبِّى يَبْسُطُ الرِّزْقَ لِمَن يَشَآءُ مِنْ عِبَادِهِ وَيَقْدِرُ لَهُ وَمَآ أَنفَقْتُم مِّن شَىْءٍ فَهُوَ يُخْلِفُهُ وَهُوَ خَيْرُ الرَّازِقِينَ ٠

Say, "Indeed, my Lord extends provision for whom He wills of His servants and restricts [it] for him. But whatever thing you spend [in His cause] - He will compensate it; and He is the Best of Providers."

O servants of Allah! Do we think that the sum of Zakat that we pay is lost and we have nothing in return? No, by Him Who has created the grain, and initiated the air; all that we pay [as Zakat] is, really, the permanent and preserved money for us. As Allah [swt] says in **Surah al-Muzzammil (73:20):**

إِنَّ رَبَّكَ يَعْلَمُ أَنَّكَ تَقُومُ أَدْنَى مِن ثُلُثَىِ الَّيْلِ وَنِصْفَهُ وَثُلُثَهُ وَطَآئِفَةٌ مِّنَ الَّذِينَ مَعَكَ وَاللَّهُ يُقَدِّرُ الَّيْلَ وَالنَّهَارَ عَلِمَ أَن لَّن تُحْصُوهُ فَتَابَ

عَلَيْكُمْ فَاقْرَءُوا مَا تَيَسَّرَ مِنَ الْقُرْءَانِ عَلِمَ أَن سَيَكُونُ مِنكُم مَّرْضَى وَءَاخَرُونَ يَضْرِبُونَ فِي الْأَرْضِ يَبْتَغُونَ مِن فَضْلِ اللَّهِ

وَءَاخَرُونَ يُقَاتِلُونَ فِي سَبِيلِ اللَّهِ فَاقْرَءُوا مَا تَيَسَّرَ مِنْهُ وَأَقِيمُوا الصَّلَوةَ وَءَاتُوا الزَّكَوةَ وَأَقْرِضُوا اللَّهَ قَرْضًا حَسَنًا وَمَا تُقَدِّمُوا

لِأَنفُسِكُم مِّنْ خَيْرٍ تَجِدُوهُ عِندَ اللَّهِ هُوَ خَيْرًا وَأَعْظَمَ أَجْرًا وَاسْتَغْفِرُوا اللَّهَ إِنَّ اللَّهَ غَفُورٌ رَّحِيمٌ

Indeed, your Lord knows [O Muhammad], that you stand [in prayer] almost two-thirds of the night, or half of it, or a third of it, and [so do] a group of those with you. And Allah determines [the extent of] the night and the day. He knows that you [Muslims] will not be able to do it and has turned to you in forgiveness, so recite what is easy [for you] of the Qur'an. He knows that there will be among those who are sick and others traveling throughout the land seeking of Allah's bounty and others fighting for the cause of Allah. So recite what is easy from it and establish prayer and give zakat and loan Allah a goodly loan. And whatever good you put forward for yourselves – you will find it with Allah. It is better and greater in reward. And seek forgiveness of Allah. Indeed, Allah is Forgiving and Merciful.

On the other hand, the wasted and lost money is that which is stored with us in this world; either it will be eaten in this world or left to our heirs who will take the advantage of our wealth. This is the reality of the wealth we leave behind in this world and the reality of the wealth we store with the All-Knowing King.

Allah [swt] warns us to be careful in giving charity in **Surah al-Baqarah (2: 263-264)** when He says:

قَوْلٌ مَّعْرُوفٌ وَمَغْفِرَةٌ خَيْرٌ مِّن صَدَقَةٍ يَتْبَعُهَآ أَذًى وَاللَّهُ غَنِيٌّ حَلِيمٌ يَأَيُّهَا الَّذِينَ ءَامَنُوا لَا تُبْطِلُوا صَدَقَتِكُم بِالْمَنِّ وَالْأَذَى كَالَّذِي

يُنفِقُ مَالَهُ رِئَآءَ النَّاسِ وَلَا يُؤْمِنُ بِاللَّهِ وَالْيَوْمِ الْأَخِرِ فَمَثَلُهُ كَمَثَلِ صَفْوَانٍ عَلَيْهِ تُرَابٌ فَأَصَابَهُ وَابِلٌ فَتَرَكَهُ صَلْدًا لَّا يَقْدِرُونَ عَلَى شَيْءٍ

مِّمَّا كَسَبُوا وَاللَّهُ لَا يَهْدِي الْقَوْمَ الْكَفِرِينَ-

Kind words and forgiveness are better than sadaqah [charity] followed by injury. And Allah is rich [free of all needs] and Forbearing. O you who have believed, do not invalidate your sadaqah [charities] with reminders [of it] or injury as does one who spends his wealth [only] to be seen by the people and he does not believe in Allah and the Last Day. His example is like that of a [large] smooth stone upon which is dust and is hit by a downpour that leaves it bare. They are unable [to keep] anything of what they have earned. And Allah does not guide the disbelieving people.

We seek Allah's refuge from the accursed Satan, Allah says in **Surah al-A`la (87:14-15):**

$$قَدۡأَفۡلَحَ مَن تَزَكَّىٰ ۔ وَذَكَرَ اسۡمَ رَبِّهِ فَصَلَّىٰ$$

He has certainly succeeded who purifies himself. And mentions the name of his Rabb and [lift his heart] in Prayer.

May Allah guide us to observe what we are enjoined to observe with regard to rights due on wealth and other obligatory deeds in the way that might meet Allah's pleasure, willingly and in full observance? We pray to Allah to grant us more of His blessings that help us to become nearer to Him and lift us to higher levels, surely. **Amin!**

Zikrullah: The Rememberance of Allah

Allah [swt] says in **Surah ar-Ra'd (13:28):**

$$\text{الَّذِينَ ءَامَنُوا۟ وَتَطْمَئِنُّ قُلُوبُهُم بِذِكْرِ ٱللَّهِ ۗ أَلَا بِذِكْرِ ٱللَّهِ تَطْمَئِنُّ ٱلْقُلُوبُ}$$

Those who have believed and whose hearts are assured by the remembrance of Allah. Unquestionably, by the remembrance of Allah hearts are assured.

It is clear from this ayah that wealth, children, power can never bring satisfaction in the hearts of the believers. The satisfaction of hearts can only be attained through the remembrance of Allah [swt]. *Subhan Allah!*

There are over 150 references in the Qur'an to words from the root dh-k-r [to remember, to mention, and to invoke]. Our focus here is specifically on Zikr [whether *qalbi, 'aqli, lisani, 'amali,* whether singularly or in congregation] as it pertains to ways in which Allah is remembered [by name or in essence] as the Supreme.

To pronounce words reflecting the attributes or glory of Allah is Zikr by tongue. To understand and reflect on Allah's Majesty is Zikr by heart. These desirable modes of remembrance reinforce each other; so conscious oral repetition engraves the words in the heart while understanding and reflection gives meaning and life to the spoken word.

Zikr is the companion and spirit of actions. See how Allah has paired it with salah that is the best of all acts of worship, and made Zikr the very reason for it, when He says in **Surah Ta-Ha (20:14):**

$$\text{إِنَّنِى أَنَا ٱللَّهُ لَا إِلَٰهَ إِلَّا أَنَا۠ فَٱعْبُدْنِى وَأَقِمِ ٱلصَّلَوٰةَ لِذِكْرِىٓ}$$

Indeed, I am Allah. There is no deity except Me, so worship Me and establish prayer for My remembrance.

Allah [swt] also says in **Surah al-Ahzab (33:41):**

$$\text{يَٰٓأَيُّهَا ٱلَّذِينَ ءَامَنُوا۟ ٱذْكُرُوا۟ ٱللَّهَ ذِكْرًا كَثِيرًا}$$

O, you who have believed, remember Allah with much remembrance.

Zikr is a reciprocal relationship between Creator and creation. Allah [swt] says in **Surah al-Baqarah (2:152):**

$$\text{فَٱذْكُرُونِىٓ أَذْكُرْكُمْ وَٱشْكُرُوا۟ لِى وَلَا تَكْفُرُونِ}$$

So remember Me [by praying, glorifying]; I will remember you. And be grateful to Me [for My countless favors on you] and do not deny Me.

And in **Surah al-'Ankabut (29:45)** Allah [swt] says:

وَلَذِكْرُ اللهِ أَكْبَرُ

And the remembrance (praising) of Allah is greater.

Remembrance of Alláh is the greatest thing in life. It's a short, simple statement. And it carries such power and beauty, because it's absolutely true. This gem of wisdom should be kept uppermost in our minds at all times. To put it another way, the greatest thing in life is to remember The One Who gave us life, to remember the purpose of our life and to work hard to complete that purpose.

The meaning of remembrance of Allah is to Praise Him with His names and perfect attributes, to supplicate to Him and to deem Him free from all that does not benefit His greatness. Remembrance of Allah can be through physical acts of worship, or it can be with the tongue or in the heart. The best Zikr [remembrance of Allah] is the one done with the body, tongue and heart; like prayer, hajj and Jihad [fighting in the cause of Allah] followed by the one done with the tongue and heart alone. The best oral act of remembrance is recitation of the Glorious Qur'an, for the Qur'an is the life of the hearts and minds and the guide to Allah's pleasure and the blissful Paradise.

It is especially important these days, when life has become so frenetic, so full of countless distractions. We're all caught up in the daily rush to get to work, to get to school or to lectures, the rush to get home, to fetch children, to watch football or to be in time for some appointment. Everything is a rush, and it seems we don't have enough time to do all the things we need or want to do.

Yet somehow, life can be manageable, we can cope, if we get our priorities right. That is why Salah and Zhikr are so important. No matter how busy we are, we must make time for regular, conscious remembrance of our creator, for contemplating our relationship with Allah. If we neglect this or forget, we will be lost in perpetual distraction, spending endless hours on what we think is important. But we must get back to basics. Where have we come from? And where are we going? The Holy Qur'an answers these important questions in one short statement of **Surah al-Baqarah (2:156):**

إِنَّا لِلهِ وَإِنَّا إِلَيْهِ رَاجِعون-

Indeed we belong to Allah, and indeed to Him we will return.

When we remember that our beginning and ending is with Alláh, it stands to reason that everything in the middle has to be dedicated to Him as well. Our whole life, from childhood to youth and through maturity to old age, has a clear purpose, and whatever we do we must be in continuous awareness, consciousness, of Allah. We must serve

Alláh and be mindful of what pleases him and what displeases him. That is why our prayer times have been so strategically placed throughout the day. It is to keep us constantly aware of our duty to our Creator.

True Believers those who spend every waking moment in conscious awareness of Alláh, they transform even the most mundane human activities into acts of worship. Therefore, when others are fretting and filled with anxiety whilst waiting for a bus or a train, or stuck in a traffic jam, the true believer finds an opportunity to recite his praises to his Rabb; his heart is filled with serenity and beauty, while other hearts are full of stress and distress.

Allah [swt] says in **Surah al-A'raf (7:205)**:

وَاذْكُر رَّبَّكَ فِي نَفْسِكَ تَضَرُّعًا وَخِيفَةً وَدُونَ الْجَهْرِ مِنَ الْقَوْلِ بِالْغُدُوِّ وَالْآصَالِ وَلَا تَكُنْ مِنَ الْغَافِلِينَ-

And remember your Rabb within yourself in humility and fear without being apparent in speech – in the mornings and early evenings. And do not be among the heedless.

The Qur'an itself is referred to as al-Zikr [the Remembrance] in **Surah al-Hijr (15:9)**:

إِنَّا نَحْنُ نَزَّلْنَا الذِّكْرَ وَإِنَّا لَهُ لَحَافِظُونَ-

Indeed, it is We who sent down the message [the Qur'an], and indeed, We will guard it [from corruption].

Allah furthermore states in **Surah al-Qamar (54:17)**:

وَلَقَدْ يَسَّرْنَا الْقُرْءَانَ لِلذِّكْرِ فَهَلْ مِن مُّدَّكِر-

And We have certainly made the Qur'an easy for remembrance, so is there any who will remember?

Together they assist us in focusing on our destination while journeying through life in this world. All forms of Zikr help us develop and reinforce our relationship with Allah [swt]. Allah [swt] directs us in **Surah al-Muzzammil (73:8)**:

وَاذْكُرِ اسْمَ رَبِّكَ وَتَبَتَّلْ إِلَيْهِ تَبْتِيلًا-

And remember the name of your Rabb and devote yourself to Him with complete devotion.

The Prophet said: Allah says: "I am just as My slave thinks I am [i.e. I am able to do for him what he thinks I can do for him] and I am with him if He remembers me. If he remembers me in himself, I too, remember him in Myself; and if he remembers me in a group of people, I remember him in a group that is better than they; and if he comes one span nearer to Me, I go one cubit nearer to him; and if he comes one cubit nearer to Me, I go a distance of two outstretched arms nearer to him; and if he comes to Me walking, I go to him running." (Bukhari, book #93, hadith #502)

If we are obedient to Allah [swt] and His Messenger, we have Allah on our side, and we need nothing else. Do we think that if we do something for Allah, Allah will let us down? A good business transaction yields large profits, but people may cheat us or not pay us on time. We will always profit from a good relationship with Allah; Put our trust in Allah, and Allah will guide us out of our dilemma and provide us with blessings. We must have Allah as a priority in our life. The Prophet said, "[There are] two words which are dear to the beneficent [Allah] and very light [easy] for the tongue [to say], but very heavy in weight in the balance. They are: 'Subhan Allah wa-bi hamdihi' and 'Subhan Allah Al-'Azim." (Bukhari, book #93, hadith #652)

Allah [swt] says in **Surah at-Tawbah (9:24)**:

قُلْ إِن كَانَ ءَابَآؤُكُمْ وَأَبْنَآؤُكُمْ وَإِخْوَٰنُكُمْ وَأَزْوَٰجُكُمْ وَعَشِيرَتُكُمْ وَأَمْوَٰلٌ اقْتَرَفْتُمُوهَا وَتِجَٰرَةٌ تَخْشَوْنَ كَسَادَهَا

وَمَسَٰكِنُ تَرْضَوْنَهَآ أَحَبَّ إِلَيْكُم مِّنَ اللَّهِ وَرَسُولِهِ وَجِهَادٍ فِى سَبِيلِهِ فَتَرَبَّصُوا حَتَّىٰ يَأْتِىَ اللَّهُ بِأَمْرِهِ وَاللَّهُ لَا يَهْدِى الْقَوْمَ الْفَٰسِقِينَ

Say, [O Muhammad], "If it be that your fathers, your sons, your brothers, your wives, or your relatives, wealth which you have gained; commerce in which you fear decline, and dwellings with which you are pleased are more beloved to you than Allah and His Messenger and jihad [striving] in His cause, then wait until Allah executes His command. And Allah does not guide the defiantly disobedient people."

Allah [swt] says in **Surah al-Ahzaab (33:35)**:

إِنَّ الْمُسْلِمِينَ وَالْمُسْلِمَٰتِ وَالْمُؤْمِنِينَ وَالْمُؤْمِنَٰتِ وَالْقَٰنِتِينَ وَالْقَٰنِتَٰتِ وَالصَّٰدِقِينَ وَالصَّٰدِقَٰتِ وَالصَّٰبِرِينَ وَالصَّٰبِرَٰتِ

وَالْخَٰشِعِينَ وَالْخَٰشِعَٰتِ وَالْمُتَصَدِّقِينَ وَالْمُتَصَدِّقَٰتِ وَالصَّٰئِمِينَ وَالصَّٰئِمَٰتِ وَالْحَٰفِظِينَ فُرُوجَهُمْ وَالْحَٰفِظَٰتِ وَالذَّٰكِرِينَ اللَّهَ

كَثِيرًا وَالذَّٰكِرَٰتِ أَعَدَّ اللَّهُ لَهُم مَّغْفِرَةً وَأَجْرًا عَظِيمًا-

Indeed, the Muslim men and women, the believers men and women, the obedient men and the women, the truthful men and women, the patient men and women, the humble men and women, the charitable men and women, the fasting men and women, the men and the women who guard their chastity and the men and women who remember Allah often with their hearts and tongues – for them Allah has prepared forgiveness and a great reward. It is also part of the rewards of remembrance of Allah that it erases one's sins and removes distress.

The best Zikr is the recitation of the Holy Quran, as Allah [swt] has decreed in **Surah al-Anbiya (21:50)** as,

وَهَـٰذَا ذِكْرٌ مُّبَارَكٌ أَنزَلْنَـٰهُ ۚ أَفَأَنتُمْ لَهُ مُنكِرُونَ

And this [Quran] is a blessed message which We have sent down. Then are you with it unacquainted?

The Apostle of Allah [sas] went out from Juwayriyyah [wife of the Prophet]. Earlier her name was Barrah, and he changed it. When he went out she was in her place of worship, and when he returned she was in her place of worship. He asked: Have you been in your place of worship continuously? She said: Yes. He then said: Since leaving you I have said three times four phrases which, if weighed against all that you have said [during this period], would prove to be heavier. They are, *"Subhan Allah Wa BiHamdihi, 'Adada Khalqihi, Waridwa Nafsihi, Wa Zinata 'Arshihi, Wa Midada Kalimatihi."* meaning "glory be to Allah, and thanks as great as the number of His creations, the extent of His satisfaction, the weight of His throne and the ink [extent] needed to write down His countless words." (Abu Dawud, book #8, hadith #1498)

Brothers and sisters in Islam! Allah's remembrance can be done at any time anywhere. If we are waiting in a hospital or clinic, waiting in a line in a shopping center, driving a car, waiting for a bus etc. we can perform Zikrullah by simply saying *"Subhan-Allahi –o-bihamdihi, Subhan-Allah-il Azhim"*, or *"Subhan- Allah, Ol-Hamidulillah"*.

Brothers and sisters in Islam, We should remember the Almighty with every breath we take. Allah's [swt] remembrance [zikr] can be done by *Qalb* [heart] i.e. in silence mode; and by tongue [with sound]; and also by words and deeds i.e. by following the directions put forward in the Holy Qura'n and the hadiths of prophet [sas]. Zikr polishes the heart; brings peace of mind & removes difficulties in this world & uplifts the punishment in the grave. May Allah [swt] help us in remembering Him in all our words and deeds?

Let us pray to Alláh to help us all to increase our awareness and consciousness of Him at all times. O Alláh, help us to filter out the many distractions that creep into our lives. Help us to keep our hearts and minds, focused on what pleases You. Help us to be mindful of our priorities, and to keep us away from anything that might lead us to shame and humiliation or that may invite your displeasure. O Alláh, help us to live and die as Muslims. And let us build strong foundations for our children and for the generations to come. May Allah [swt] guide us to be of those who rely on Him alone for everything? **Amin!**